THE VALUE-PHILOSOPHY OF ALFRED EDWARD TAYLOR:

A Study in Theistic Implication

Charles W. Mason
University of Delaware

University Press of America™

Library of Congress Catalog Card Number: 79-52512

ACKNOWLEDGMENTS AND CREDITS

To the following publishers, authors, or executors, whose words in books or journal articles have been used by permission, I acknowledge my thanks and appreciation. Detailed recognition will be found in footnotes and in the bibliography.

Columbia University Press, New York
  Review of A. E. Taylor's THE FAITH OF A MORALIST by
  Brand Blanshard in THE JOURNAL OF PHILOSOPHY, Volume
  29 (March 3) 1932.
Cooper Square Publishers, Incorporated, New York
  PLATONISM AND ITS INFLUENCE by A. E. Taylor, 1963.
Wm. B. Eerdmans Publishing Company, Grand Rapids,
Michigan
  THE CHRISTIAN VIEW OF GOD AND THE WORLD by James Orr,
  1948.
Longman Group Limited, Essex, England
  "On the Radical Evil of Human Nature," by Immanuel
  Kant in KANT'S CRITIQUE OF PRACTICAL REASON AND
  OTHER WORKS ON THE THEORY OF ETHICS (Translated by
  T. K. Abbott), 1923.
Associated Book Publishers Limited, London, England
  ELEMENTS OF METAPHYSICS by A. E. Taylor, 1903.
The Newman Press and the Paulist Press, New York
  CONTEMPORARY PHILOSOPHY by Frederick Copleston, 1956.
Prentice-Hall, Incorporated, Englewood Cliffs, New
Jersey
  ETHICS by William K. Frankena, Copyright 1963.
University of Chicago Press, Chicago
  "Morality and Religion," by Sterling Lamprecht in
  INTERNATIONAL JOURNAL OF ETHICS, XLI (July 1931).

Oxford University Press, Oxford, England
  "Metaphysics," by Aristotle in THE OXFORD TRANSLATION
  OF ARISTOTLE (Translated and edited by W. D. Ross),
  Volume 8, 1928.
  TREATISE OF HUMAN NATURE by David Hume (Edited by
  L. A. Selby-Bigge), 1888.
The Sage School of Philosophy, Cornell University,
Ithaca, New York and Professor John R. Searle
  "How to Derive 'Ought' from 'Is,'" by John R. Searle
  in THE PHILOSOPHICAL REVIEW, LXXIII (January 1964).
Ernest Benn Limited, London, England
  THE PROBLEM OF EVIL by A. E. Taylor, 1929.
Macmillan Administration (Basingstoke) Limited, London,
England
  "The Belief in Immortality," by A. E. Taylor in THE
  FAITH AND THE WAR (Edited by P. J. Foakes-Jackson),
  1915.
  DOES GOD EXIST? by A. E. Taylor, 1945.
The British Academy, London, England
  "Descriptivism," by R. M. Hare in PROCEEDINGS OF THE
  BRITISH ACADEMY, XLIX (1963).
  "Alfred Edward Taylor 1869-1945," by W. D. Ross in
  PROCEEDINGS OF THE BRITISH ACADEMY, XXXI (1945).
Charles Scribner's Sons, New York
  "Identity," by A. E. Taylor in ENCYCLOPAEDIA OF
  RELIGION AND ETHICS (Edited by James Hastings),
  Volume 7 (1912).
  "Theism," by A. E. Taylor in ENCYCLOPAEDIA OF RELI-
  GION AND ETHICS (Edited by James Hastings), Volume 12
  (1912).
Simon & Schuster, New York
  A HISTORY OF WESTERN PHILOSOPHY by Bertrand Russell,
  1945.
Blanche B. Stace (Executrix), Laguna Beach, California
  A CRITICAL HISTORY OF GREEK PHILOSOPHY by Walter
  Terence Stace, 1962.
Macmillan Publishing Company, Incorporated, New York
  SCIENCE AND THE MODERN WORLD by Alfred North
  Whitehead, 1925.
  MILL'S ETHICAL WRITINGS by John Stuart Mill (Edited
  by J. B. Schneewind), 1965.
  "Value and Valuation," by William K. Frankena in
  ENCYCLOPEDIA OF PHILOSOPHY (Edited by Paul Edwards),
  Volume 8, 1967.
St. Martin's Press, New York
  CRITIQUE OF PURE REASON by Immanuel Kant (Translated
  by Norman Kemp Smith), 1965.

George Allen & Unwin Limited, London, England
  "Biographical" by A. E. Taylor in CONTEMPORARY
  BRITISH PHILOSOPHY, Second Series (Edited by J. H.
  Muirhead), 1925.
  "The Freedom of Man," by A. E. Taylor in CONTEMPORARY
  BRITISH PHILOSOPHY, Second Series (Edited by J. H.
  Muirhead), 1925.
Cambridge University Press, American Branch, New York
  "Freedom and Personality," by A. E. Taylor in
  PHILOSOPHY, XIV (1939).
  "Freedom and Personality Again," by A. E. Taylor in
  PHILOSOPHY, XVII (1942).
  "Some Features of Butler's Ethics," PHILOSOPHICAL
  STUDIES, 1934.
  "Science and Morality," by A. E. Taylor in PHILOSO-
  PHY, XIV (1939).
  "Back to Descartes," by A. E. Taylor in PHILOSOPHY,
  XVI (1941).
  "On Morality's Having a Point," by D. Z. Phillips
  and H. O. Mounce in PHILOSOPHY, XL (1931).
Dover Publications, Incorporated, New York
  LANGUAGE, TRUTH AND LOGIC by Alfred Jules Ayer,
  Second Edition, 1946.
Paulist Press, New York
  A HISTORY OF PHILOSOPHY, Volume II, Mediaeval Philo-
  sophy, Augustine to Scotus, by Frederick Copleston,
  S.J., Copyright 1950 by The Newman Press. Reprinted
  by permission of the Paulist Press.
Hibbert Trust, London, England
  Review of A. E. Taylor's THE FAITH OF A MORALIST by
  J. H. Muirhead in the HIBBERT JOURNAL, XXIX (1931).
The Bobbs-Merrill Company, Incorporated, Indianapolis,
Indiana
  DIALOGUES CONCERNING NATURAL RELIGION by David Hume
  (Edited by Norman Kemp Smith), 1947.
  FOUNDATIONS OF METAPHYSICS OF MORALS by Immanuel
  Kant (Translated with an Introduction by Lewis White
  Beck), 1959.
  THE WAY OF PHILOSOPHY by Philip Wheelwright (Revised
  Edition), 1954.
Basil Blackwell Publisher Limited, Oxford, England
  Review of A. E. Taylor's THE FAITH OF A MORALIST by
  C. D. Broad in MIND, XL (1931).
  "The 'Is-Ought': An Unnecessary Dualism," by M.
  Zimmerman in MIND, LXXI (January 1962).
  "Zimmerman's 'Is-Is': A Schizophrenic Monism," by
  Kenneth Hanley in MIND, LXXIII (July 1964).

"Conception of Immortality in Spinoza's Ethics," by
A. E. Taylor in MIND, V (April 1896).

RETREAT FROM TRUTH by G. R. G. Mure, 1958.
Philosophical Library, Publishers, New York

"Logical Empiricism," by Herbert Feigl in TWENTIETH
CENTURY PHILOSOPHY (Edited by Dagobert D. Runes),
1943.

INTRODUCTION

If for no other reason, the eminence of A. E. Taylor has been secured by his work in early Greek philosophy. Translations, critical reviews and essays, numerous journal articles, books, and, perhaps most of all, his justly famous commentary, PLATO: THE MAN AND HIS WORK, have combined to give his name lasting importance.

But, as John Laird remarked in the Academy Memoir, "Taylor was much more than a Grecian with a darting eye for all the Atticisms of the modern world. He refreshed himself continually from many other wells in the philosophical and cultural tradition." If from these 'other wells' Taylor drew substance for challenge and reflection, to them in turn he delivered bounties in sustained analyses in science, logic, ethics, metaphysics, psychology, history, and the meaning of God for human experience.

With an emphasis more aligned to the jenseitigkeit Philosophie of the Continent than to the diesseitigkeit Philosophie that has become known as British Empiricism, Taylor defends a theistic world-view believed supportive of the essential concerns of man. Even as Taylor evidenced a progressive willingness to explore sympathetically the essential commitments to which Judeo-Christian theism invites attention, he did so by undergirding these defenses with an uncompromising adherence to rationality--itself considered the ultimate epistemological category--without which there could be neither truth nor validity for any position.

Throughout, Taylor directs attention away from the contemporary preoccupation with narrowed epistemological concerns that frequently identify with logical positivism, linguistic analysis, symbolic logic, etc., to a return to "the vital interests of humanity." "I am content," writes Taylor, "with Plato and Kant, to be so much of a 'common fellow' as to feel that the serious questions for each of us are 'What ought I to do?', 'What may I hope for?' and that it is the duty of philosophy to find answers to them, if she can. If none can be found, so much the worse for philosophy, but her incompetence is not to be assumed lightly."

For Taylor, philosophical effort is thought to enter unwittingly into an unnatural bondage in refusing to recognize those value-assumptions that are the backdrop of our thought and action. Is it not true that the forms of the esthetic, the moral, the rational, are deeply constitutive of human nature? Does not a virtually undeviating exhibition of this characteristic of man punctuate the totality of human history? More pertinently still, does not this ubiquitous assumption of unifying bond afford an important clue to the existence of that wider dimension of reality to which man relates in (generally) unconscious dependence?

It is precisely this transcendent realm of normative assumptions, for Taylor, that constitutes the unifying bond of the human family when engaged in attempts at philosophical orientation. It is this (often unconsciously-held) quiet assumption of overarching universals that preserves such meaning for discourse as is required for science or any other knowledge-claim. But a fruitful and responsible philosophical effort, Taylor believes, ought not be satisfied with mere descriptive endeavor and unacknowledged dependence upon these assumed foundations; it ought, rather, to declare openly its dependence upon this transcendent dimension of reality and thereby avoid that false abstraction that views both man and his environment as radically lacking in any principle of internal continuity and divorced thereby from claiming any pattern of wholeness. When this charge of a false abstraction is heard, it will be understood why Taylor has made an effort to achieve serious reconsideration of such perennial concerns of man as purpose, freedom, duty, immortality, God.

Taylor's contribution, therefore, is not that of defending the narrower doctrinal concerns of Judeo-Christian theism, but rather that of articulating a broad base in theistic presupposition, a necessary condition for the defense of narrower concerns and for retaining a due sense of normative value.

We have been asked by the value-relativist to regard the near-universal assumption of objective and governing norms of valuation as totally unsupported by any objective fact of such norms' real existence and authority. In contrast to this sweeping denial of the real existence and authority of normative value, it is Taylor's eminently sensible thesis that, rather than attempt to build a picture of coherence upon the assumption of the total falsity of this objectification, it is wiser and better to attempt a picture of coherence upon the assumption of its truth. It is Taylor's further conviction that this locus of normative value—without which meaning is lost to every human enterprise—ought to be regarded as a proper explication of what is meant by the existence of God and his necessary relation to philosophical effort.

A N A L Y T I C A L   O U T L I N E

CHAPTER I--A. E. TAYLOR: THE MAN AND HIS WORK

CHAPTER II--CLASSICAL VIEWS OF MORAL VALUE

b. Even the teleological ethic tries for
universalization.
c. The supreme principle of morality must
ground in rationality--"otherwise the conformity
is merely contingent and spurious."
d. But even a true moral philosophy can
have an empirical application--even as there is
an applied mathematics.
e. The imperative(s):
hypothetical
categorical
f. The validity of the categorical imperative is demonstrably independent of results,
ends, goals.
g. Conclusion: Kant has demonstrated that
formalism contributes a necessary condition to
the question of obligation.

TAYLOR'S COMMENTS   39

a. Two questions: (1) Does Kant's system
provide a sufficient condition as well as a
necessary condition, and (2) Are positive duties
deducible from the categorical imperative?
(Taylor returns a negative answer to both).
b. Acceptable is a variant of "rule-
deontology": the specific positive duty differs
with circumstance even while the formal aspect
of duty remains constant.
c. But the law to which we give assent,
which rightly commands us, "is only communicated
to us in part and gradually," and, as embodied in
God, passes from mere respect into unqualified
reverence.

ETHICS AS "EMOTIVE"   47

a. The meaning of "meaning"--and principle
of verifiability.
b. Reduction of ethical terms to non-
ethical terms.
c. Absolutistic and intuitionistic ethics
make statements of value unverifiable;
d. Therefore, disqualification of ethics
as a normative science.

    a.   Requirements for a moral science.
        1.   The assertions which compose it
           must be true.
        2.   They must be systematically inter-
           connected by logical interrela-
           tions. (It is recognized that
           Ayer would deny both.)

    b. But, it is conceded that ethical predicates can arouse feeling and stimulate action. Taylor infers from this that this is true only because the listeners assume the ethical predicates to have a meaning and are truly applicable to the conduct to which they are being applied. Purely meaningless language, recognized as such, would have no effect upon the hearer.

    c. It is noted that there are no necessary (and rarely if ever any actual) disjunctions between objectively verifiable statements of whatever kind and attending emotional overtones. Therefore, the mere presence of emotion does not undermine the objectivity of the situation.

    e. The contrasting principles:
        1. the scientific law is a "universal" strictly immanent in the particular instances and in each of them;
        2. the moral principle is a priori, separate and transcendent.

    f. Conclusion: Either a priorism may legitimately be admitted into the language of ethical discourse, or we must be satisfied to have morality reduced to mere description of human behavior. But, to the latter none appears to yield in practice. Therefore, for Taylor, a priorism may legitimately be admitted into the language and meaning of ethical discourse--an admittance that is a fulfilling condition of the presupposition of ethics as a normative science.

CHAPTER III -- MORAL VALUE AND EXISTENCE

e. The wide-spread disputes in value-
predication strongly suggest their subjectivity.

THE CASE FOR CONJUNCTION   62

     a. It has been the universal experience
of mankind to invest existential situations with
value-predicates--suggestive of the fact that
in some sense values are deeply constitutive of
reality and not accidental in every sense.
     b. The relation of fact to value demands a
point of view broader than that espoused by the
Analyst who can never find value as a sensory
impression.
     c. Though virtue, art, science, health may
be considered in their concreteness or abstraction,
as abstractions, they are never objects of value-
predication. This implies that if value-predication
is to be indulged at all, the conjunction of the
value involved and actuality is guaranteed.
     d. At this stage in the argument, values and
actuality do not constitute a co-extensive relation.
Values imply actuality, but actuality does not (yet)
imply value. But the existent is a necessary condition for value-predication.
     e. Other necessary conditions for value-
recognition:
          1. Knowledge. Not only must there be
     the existent for there to be value, but there
     must be knowledge of the existent.
          2. Minds. Because knowledge implies
     minds, and because knowledge has been named
     as a necessary condition for value-predication,
     it follows that minds are a necessary condition
     for value-predication.
     f. If an abstract value-universal is to have
any value--other, that is, than that of a clear and
distinct idea--it must be that of a universal "embodied in rebus" and not that of the nominalist
logicians. This stipulation again returns one to
the conjunction of value and existents.
     g. The alleged "accidental" character of value
is denied. When it is of the very nature of intelligence and appetition to pass on those values that are
their normal concerns, it can no longer be affirmed
that values are accidental. There is no other function

                         xvi

of the rational, the ethical, the esthetic faculties,
than that of discriminatory appraisals among value-
situations representing these universes of discourse.
And this holds even though the pronouncements may
actually be in error.

      h. A further implication for the conjunction
of value and actuality derives from the knowledge of
value. Every proposition, directly or indirectly,
must be an assertion about being. This is true in
spite of all of the remaining disharmonies and confu-
sions in our thinking. /Indeed, as Taylor argues in
Chapter VIII, this one-for-one relation between
thought and thing is what eventually secures the
validity of the ontological argument. But, the residue of disharmony and confusion must, in principle,
be eliminated./ Because, then, all knowledge is
about being, and because it is of the essential nature
of mind to evaluate and to invest being with value,
it follows that the mind intends the conjunction of
value and being as its natural function.

      i. Logic confirms as natural the allegation
that all propositions are about being:

          1. Singular propositions clearly assume
it.

          2. Particular propositions are equivalent
to groups of singular propositions.

          3. Universal propositions are "something
less than an actual proposition," actually a
"formal implication" between propositional
functions.

          4. And confirmation of the thesis that
only of an existential situation can truth-
value be predicated is found in the null-class
wherein all assertions are equally true.

      j. Any severance of value from actuality falsi-
fies the facts of real life. Existence and value
are always distinguishable, but never disjoined.
The logical separation (for purposes of analysis)
should not encourage the suspicion that they are
actually disjoined.

CHAPTER IV -- MORAL VALUE AND TIME

"...time is the characteristic form of the life
of moral endeavour."

MANY FRUITFUL CATEGORIES FOR TIME'S ANALYSIS-- AND THE "CONATIVE" FUNCTION

As over against perceptual and conceptual
aspects of time; questions of time's infinity,
divisibility, continuity and relativity; problems
related to paradoxes and antinomies; empirical
and metaphysical approaches--Taylor introduces
his "conative" function of time with its emphasis
on effort, endeavoring, striving, volition, and
this with emphasized teleological consideration.

TO KNOW TEMPORALITY MEANINGFULLY IS TO TRANSCEND IT

a.   In general, to know a fact meaningfully
is to transcend it.
b.   Particularized, to know a moral fact
meaningfully is to transcend it.
c.   Temporality, as particularity, yields
to eternity by this dialectic.
d.   But because we are engaged with the
conjunction of a person-in-temporality, the universal to which dialectically we are pointed is
also personal--and God enters Taylor's system.

"We have so far tried to find the inmost
meaning of the moral life of man by regarding it
as an endeavour towards an eternal good made by a
creature who, in so far as he achieves the end of
his endeavour, achieves also a derivative, or
communicated eternity."

a. "...he who would make us gods to begin
with and hence render of negligible consequence
what kind of effort one makes..." and
b. "...he who would espouse a thoroughgoing
naturalism and hence know no higher goal than 'a
roaming in a wilderness where he is destined to
lay his bones'..."

"In plain language, we break with the presuppositions of the moral life equally whether
we eliminate the natural or the supernatural from
our conception of things."

A DIALECTIC OF VALUE   98

a. We begin by valuing, by evincing an
interest.
b. Next, we ask about the nature of the
value(s) espoused, whether, that is, there is
husk and kernel, accidental and essential feature, involved.
c. This leads to a probing to what is our
genuine concern. It is a stabbing with ever
greater awareness at what is the true object of
our value-concern.

"This movement begins with a desire for a
little greater freedom and ends with the discovery that 'nothing less than complete freedom
would satisfy the impulse which led us to break
the first link.'" This complete freedom lies
beyond temporality.

THE NATURE OF ETERNITY AND SUPERNATURE   100

a. They constitute logically discernible
aspects of the same reality.
b. Neither is to be viewed as out of all
relation to man, but rather they combine to
provide not only a proper goal but in an important sense they may be regarded as the continuation of those qualities essential to man's
nature.

a. The rational will is realized in the course of events--a fact that in itself is supportive of objectivity, necessity and universality.

b. Such a will cannot be the will of any finite creature but is supreme over the whole temporal order.

c. This will, though legislative in the moral world, is not sovereign: God is the constitutional monarch.

It would appear that Kant's possible intentions were at least close to those of Taylor--that in morality becoming aware of its own tendencies, it reveals a disposition toward an eternal good that is simultaneously both the object of moral aspiration and its commanding principle.

ETHICS WITHOUT RELIGION?   102

Not really. That is to say, the religious ground may be obscured to many while being available to the insight steered by the value-dialectic and believed, by Taylor, to be the hypothesis best calculated to render coherent the deeper awareness of our value-commitments.

A UNIVERSE OF INTELLIGIBILITY AND MORAL PURPOSE   103

a. The argument: if the universe is in fact the kind that reason and conscience can approve, then there must be a pervading evidence of intelligibility and moral purpose. Such characteristics are evident. Therefore a presumption is established that the universe is in fact the kind that reason and conscience can approve.

b. And so committed are we to the fact of a universe that supports both intelligibility and moral purpose that through total recorded history man has everywhere assumed that both characteristics hold and demonstrates his complete confidence in that fact by suiting action to belief in (1) scientific investigation and (2) by keeping alive the ethical imperative as a goad and corrective of the moral enterprise.

     c. Neither can one disjoin moral purpose and intelligibility: moral purpose must be intelligible, must commend itself to analysis, to evaluation, to comparison with such standards as it may claim, must honor consistency and coherence, and must respect the need for universality and necessity.

     d. Such considerations lead naturally, for Taylor, to a claim for Theism as the presupposition of a thoroughly rationalized ethics. The argument, as a corollary, carries the prediction that an ethics systematically and consistently attempted on a basis of secularism and humanism must fail.

CLASSICAL DIVISIONS   107

    a. Moral evil.
    b. Natural evil.

    For Taylor, "...for the purely ethical atti-
tude of mind the world has to be thought of as...
essentially out of accord with what it ought to
be...that the world...contains imperfections and
evil which must be done away with: ...a practical
presupposition without which morality itself would
have no raison d'etre." Further, such an assumption about the world is valid only under the further assumption that the norm that brings about
the sense of this deep opposition is ultimately
the person of God.

THE FINITE GOD HYPOTHESIS   108

    a. A dilemma is seemingly suggested in
the identification of the Absolute with God--
the thought being that evil is some manifestation
of his nature.
    b. To deny the identity of the Absolute
and God leaves a possibility to account for
evil within the finitude of God.
    c. Even Absolutism--it is alleged--seems
to admit limitations as true of God, viz., that
he has no option but to exist and that he must
bow before the law of contradiction.
    d. Human persons well know how error (and
evil) crowds in as a result of finitude. May it
not be therefore that, analogously, the virtually
universal presence of evil suggests a finite god
unable to guard against defect of finitude?

     a. The hypothesis only makes evil appear
in a double form: it exists both <u>outside</u> God as
a hostile factor limiting his power of shaping
the world to his purpose, and as "<u>inside</u>" God
because every case of finitude is a case of defect
in some sense. Evil remains a problem to be
explained.
     b. The finite god hypothesis has no greater
merit than that of postulating another person in
the world and leaves the problem of evil's strange-
ness where it was.

<u>BUT</u> <u>CAN</u> <u>WE</u> <u>WORSHIP</u> <u>THE</u> <u>ABSOLUTE</u>?   111

     Taylor's answer is "Yes." The Absolute is
that "concrete individual reality in which our
ideals have actual existence." The Absolute is
the ultimate ground of the being of all particularity. We, therefore, as particular beings not
only may but must look to the ground of our being
as that on which we are dependent. This is a
first and necessary condition for worship. And
it is valid.

<u>IS</u> <u>THE</u> <u>ABSOLUTE</u> "<u>GOOD</u>"?   115

     Taylor's answer is "Yes." It is the embodi-
ment of all our ideals, or, more accurately, all
that our ideals should be. There is no fuller
meaning for <u>good</u> than this meaning.

<u>IS</u> <u>THE</u> <u>ABSOLUTE</u> "<u>ETHICALLY</u> <u>GOOD</u>"?   115

     Taylor's answer is "No"--with qualifications.
If "ethical goodness" is understood as the goodness of "gradual assertion of the ideal against
apparent evil," then the Absolute may not be con-
sidered <u>ethically</u> <u>good</u> or <u>moral</u>--it being itself
the norm by which significant approximation and
defect are measured.

d. Its polluting quality: an implicit
protest is seen to a naturalism which if successful would have eliminated the "dirtiness" of
"dirt" at both physical and moral levels. Man's
felt involvement with moral pollution is a fulfilling condition of this uniquely differentiating
quality.
	e. The subject defiled by moral evil is
"the _true_ self, or, _the ideal self_." For Taylor,
it is this contest between the real and the ideal
self that enables us to become acutely aware of
the character possessed by each.
	f. A further uniquely differentiating prin-
ciple of moral evil, Taylor believes, is (as Plato,
Kant, and Christianity are believed to teach) that
moral evil "absolutely ought not to be,"--a further
reason, if true, that separates evil from all
naturalistic interpretation.

	/Our allegiance to ideal selfhood now expands
until we see that there is no stopping-point short
of allegiance to an ideal Person--even God. A
further hint of this tendency is seen in personify-
ing causes and principles./

THE NOTION OF A FREE AGENT   134

	a. Supportive of our deepest sense of
moral awareness.
	b. To seek a cause behind the choice of
the free agent is to stultify the hypothesis of
free agent. The only remaining question is whether the idea of a "free agent" as originating
cause is forbidden by any rational consideration.
	c. One eventually reaches freedom in any
case--for example, in whatever conception we hold
of ultimate reality: such must be free of any
prior cause or limitation by its very meaning.

RE: BRADLEY'S ALLEGED "ANTINOMY" OF MORALITY,
VIZ., THAT MORALITY'S ONLY REASON FOR BEING IS
TO DESTROY ITSELF   136

	Taylor's reply: There is a positive side
to morality. This positive side is as independent
of the war against evil as science's positive side

is independent of the war against error. "...there is nothing irrational in anticipating a state in which the process of forming character is over, while the activity issuing from character remains."

EVIL--AND PRIVATION   137

Evil (like error) is no substantive reality. It is a privation of good (even as error is a privation of truth). The non-coordinate aspect, therefore, in principle, instructs that the "solution" of the problem of evil must ever look to a concept of good without which evil can have no meaning at all.

CHAPTER VI -- MORAL VALUE AND FREEDOM

Note taken of the fact of an abiding confusion between these two aspects of freedom--
especially since the affirmation of freedom at
the empirical level may coincide with a denial
of freedom at the metaphysical.

a. Not the free-fall of a body in accordance with gravity's law.
b. Not the "mere capacity of spontaneous
or internally initiated movement."
c. Not the illusory freedom of Spinoza's
stone in flight.
d. Not a sufficient condition of the
morally good life.
e. Not the mere equivalent of animal
instinct.

Moral freedom is (a) a choice or decision
of some end for action, (b) in terms of norms
believed relevant, and (c) by rational means of
discrimination. It is believed stultifying to
Taylor's position to say more precisely and
definitively what moral freedom is. This is
precisely because the norm by which moral value
is highlighted and justified is that universal
that while illuminating particular moralities
is not caught in the direct illumination of its
own light. This is Taylor's "presuppositionalism."

    a. Duly to apprehend what rationality is,
to understand what it is that preserves validity
for a conclusion, is, at the same time and for
the same reason, to understand that an essential
attribute of rationality is its freedom.
    b. It is freedom in this rational sense
that tempts the will to action and it is this
same sense that preserves whatever meaning is
present in a doctrine of libertas arbitrii.

RE: DETERMINISM   146

    a. Grounding moral choice and consequent
action in rationality for Taylor is to render
such choice and action incompatible with "scientific determinism."
    b. All moral choice must depend upon "the
worth of the evidence" and, implicitly or explicitly, the rational factor must be present.
    c. A motive is not an impelling cause in
the sense of mechanics; rather, to act with a
motive is to regard one's act as justified by
certain considerations. A motive is always
something which, at the time of acting, the
agent regards as a reasonable incentive.
    d. "What morality demands is that the pre-
sent perception of an act as good and obligatory
should be a sufficient condition of its execution."
    e. The determinist is believed to be in
practical self-contradiction in that he finds it
necessary to assume that his conclusions are free
of non-rational causation.

INDETERMINATION   151

    a. The phrases, "I will," "I determine,"
"I act," for Taylor, require the absence of any
idea of the one so acting being merely the
transmitting medium of the thrust of non-rational
antecedent events.
    b. What precisely is denied in "indetermi-
nation" is not that no cause is involved--the one
determining is the cause; what is denied is that

every event "is a one-valued function of earlier events, and nothing but earlier events."

    c. Taylor's defense of "indetermination" in a word: between the decision to do a thing and the doing of it there is an interval across which it is impossible to trace that causal bond necessary for the determinist to make his point; and, second, there is in the very nature of a rational decision that which forbids the determinist's non-rational account of the act.

    d. In short, we move from free thought to free will.

    e. In the course of this discussion, man's rationality is being rediscovered--as revelatory of man's personality, meaning, and essential character. "That intelligence, or rationality, is a principle of indetermination within us is, in fact, only another way of saying that it is the universal in us, in virtue of which each of us transcends his own particularity."

CONTINGENCY   157

After Hume, the radical contingency that empiricism thus reveals can only challenge the determinist's faith in the alleged total interlock of events. As Taylor puts it, "...contingency is found to be a universal character of whatever is temporal and mutable." Accepting this, Taylor believes that a number of narrower phenomena are explained:

    a. the recoverability of the past and the anticipation of the future appear to be impossible;

    b. that there is no cyclical movement or periodic rhythm to "the whole movement of things";

    c. that "explanation" of particular phenomena leads to higher generalizations that, in turn, require explanation;

    d. that a species of the "irrational" is introduced in such sweeping revisions as that occasioned by the desertion of the old Euclidean conception of space with its dependable uniformities in favor of a space-time of the new physics that is "variegated and non-uniform."

Taylor's theistic system works from both
ends to emphasize the aspect of contingency
that he teaches.

a.   From the starting-point of experience
(the Hume analysis), no necessary connection can
be found between and among the discrete impressions.
b.   From the side of the hypothesis that God
stands to the world in the relation of creator and
sustainer, the very fact that full causal power is
exerted downward vertically (to use a metaphor) would
indicate why it might be predicted that one would not
find the same causal connection exerted laterally.
This is probably almost exactly what Berkeley must
have meant by his assertion that ideas were purely
passive.
c.   Contingency, therefore, in Taylor's system
belongs strictly to a world of the temporal and
mutable. He secures his hope of uniformity and
dependability by pleading an extra-natural or theistic reference.
d.   Supporting this notion to some extent,
Russell, in writing of the principle of induction,
says, "The principle itself cannot without circularity, be inferred from observed uniformities, since it
is required to justify any such inference. It must
therefore be, or be deduced from, an independent
principle not based upon experience."

xxx

CHAPTER VII -- MORAL VALUE AND IMMORTALITY

"If the order of the Universe is to be pronounced truly reasonable, it must not be at hopeless variance with the foundations of the moral
order."   168

AN ARGUMENT FOR IMMORTALITY   169

a. Not from the premise of the soul's
simplicity;
b. Not from the alleged evidence of
spiritualism or necromancy;
c. But from the nature of moral obligation. "A genuine moral argument for immortality," declares Taylor, "must be one to the effect
that the destruction of human personalities
would make the moral end unattainable. If this
can be proved, the proof will be sufficient for
those who believe in the absolute objectivity
of moral obligation, though for no others."

MAN'S ESSENTIAL STRUCTURING   170

a. The intellectual character.
b. The moral character.

It is the moral and intellectual character
that has been long in building and it is precisely this characteristic of man that gives him
his unique meaning and his sense of worth and
his hope for commensurate goals along the line
of the same advance. It is not mere immortality
as such but an immortality that is structured
with the essential moral thrust of its earlier
beginnings to which will now be added the promise
of continuance in that very value-participation
that has given man essential meaning.

"We may fairly argue from the reality of
a function to the reality of an environment in
which it finds its use." Taylor believes that
one cannot reasonably doubt the validity of
this formula nor the procedure to which it directs us. "The real problem to be faced is not
whether reasoning of this kind from the reality
of function to the reality of the environment in
which it can function is valid. To raise doubts
on that point would be fatal to the admission of
enough rationality into the cause of things to
make science itself possible. The real question
is rather whether in fact examination of the moral
life reveals the reality of any such functions."

THE ALLEGED REALITY OF THE FUNCTIONS (Intimations
of immortality)   173

     a. The feeling of an imperative that we
ought to practice virtue. Here is the recognition of a categorical imperative that cannot be
confused with mere efficiency or wide distribu-
tion of benefits or pleasure under pain of committing a variant of the "naturalistic fallacy."
The principle that approves or condemns any or all
of these particular attainments cannot itself be
one of them.
     b. Sacrificial living and giving. There are
sacrifices that are felt justified--even commanded--
just because they are right--a declaration that
must sound perfectly vacuous were it not for the
combined considerations that experience cannot quite
justify them and yet there is the conviction that
they are not only right but many times a matter of
felt duty.
     c. Instinctively nationalism hesitates before
it boldly announces "My country, right or wrong!"
The hesitancy, Taylor urges, derives from the unconsciously held presupposition of a norm of right that
transcends time and place. To recognize what one's
country is doing is one thing; to declare that that
same "doing" is right or wrong is quite another thing
and opens a totally new dimension of involvement.

    d. The intrinsic meaning of virtue dialec-
tically points to the fact that it derives its
justification from some principle other than the
specific acts that we call virtuous. For Taylor,
the validating universal cannot be found in the
secular-temporal dimension.
    e. The function of conscience. The appeal
to conscience, for Taylor, is a case of finding
authority that is not formal infallibility; "...not
infallible: yet its authority constitutes a strict
obligation." This "form" that conscience believes
in contrasts with the "matter" of specific applica-
tion--and the distinction is not only in the common
practice of mankind but is recognized by many ethical analysts.

WHAT IS DEATH?   180

    a. "...it is a familiar fact that death
is constantly coming as a violent and irrational
interrupter of unrealized plans and inchoate work.
The self seems to disappear not because it has
played its part and finished its work, but as the
victim of external accident."
    b. Man never builds on a total assumption of
irrationality; if the irrational is recognized, it
is always against the backdrop of the rational which
alone can interpret irrationality for the privation
that it is. And so Taylor asks, "Now, what is the
logical value of this feeling /the feeling that death
is an irrational interrupter/ as a basis for argument?"
And the answer: "We may fairly say...that it rests on
a sound principle. For it embodies the conviction,
of which all Philosophy is the elaboration, that the
real world is a harmonious system in which irrational
accident plays no part, and that, if we could only
see the whole truth, we should realize that there is
no final and irremediable defeat for any of our aspirations, but all are somehow made good."
    c. Further, there is no a priori need to admit
the dissolution of the self. There is nothing in
the very meaning of the self that demands its termi-
nation. (This is reminiscent of the arguments of
Butler.)
    d. Further still (and again as Butler argued)
all the empirical evidence does is remove observable

effects of life from further inspection: we are
never permitted to see existence passing into
non-existence.

THE MIND-BODY PROBLEM   182

      a. No reductionism is to be preferred to
some variant of a dualistic (even interactionis-
tic) account of mind-body. "...a defense and a
modified restatement of the old doctrine of Interaction.../is/ at present, the most satisfactory
theory of the connexion between body and mind."
In support, it is noted that even discussions that
have no thought of capitulating to dualism, in their
very retention of the terms, give some thought of
recognition to the apparent permanence of the difference.
      b. Even as it was necessary, for Taylor, to
free the rational faculty from the grip of an irrational determinism under pain to losing all critical distinction between valid and invalid argument,
so the attempted identification of mind and body--
and the current tendency is in favor of a reduction
in favor of body--again threatens the preservation
of rational discrimination.
      c. The dualism that emerges in Taylor's argu-
ment preserves the common-sense attitude that virtually every man takes toward mind and body.
      d. Taylor declares that "Descartes was funda-
mentally in the right in opposing the 'physical'
and the 'subjective' to one another as ultimately
irreducible modes of being. Nothing that is physical is 'subjective' and nothing that is 'subjective'
is physical."
      e. Thus the tentative establishing of dualism
is to provide one of the fulfilling conditions for
a further defense of immortality.

THE QUESTION OF PERSONAL IDENTITY   184

      a. Personal immortality depends upon a
clear separation of the psychical from the
physical--"as ultimately irreducible modes of
being."
      b. Personal identity seems to be essen-
tially psychical.

c. Personal identity is "formal," not some
sort of substratum. That is to say, the formal
is neither an identity of content nor an identity
of matter. Rather, "What is required is that the
succession of changes in mental and moral character
should be linked together as a continuous development according to a law of growth which in its concrete fullness is characteristic of the person and
of no other being in the universe."

d. There is thus introduced a sort of Aristotelian "entelechy" or built-in blueprint that the
"law of growth" follows in the development of the
living form. It is thus a dynamic view and contrasts
with the inert view that is implied in the "substratum" theory that he rejects.

e. Memory is appealed to as a necessary (though
not sufficient) condition of identity. The Taylor-
Aristotelian entelechy provides the linkage that
memory can benefit from--in contrast to Hume who
began with memory and ended (inevitably) with the
announcement that personal identity was an illusion.

CHAPTER VIII -- MORAL VALUE AND GOD

This chapter begins with a brief recapitulation
of the preceding chapters emphasizing the point that
"It is recognized that the gradual emergence of God
as the ultimate presupposition of thought has been the
eventual point to which each of the preceding chapters
has come."   197

THE COMMON GROUND OF THEIST AND ATHEIST   199

This "common ground" is the fact of their
dependence upon such forces as have given them
their individual existences.

THE PARTING OF THE WAYS   199

a. The theist will endeavor to maintain
that there is a continuum between the intelligence of man and that of the forces that have
created and do preserve him.
b. The atheist must deny this continuum--
for if he were to affirm intelligence of the
forces that produce and preserve, the situation
would be to all intents and purposes a theism.

THEISM DEFINED (tentatively)   200

"...the doctrine that the ultimate ground
of things is a single supreme reality which is
the source of everything other than itself and
has the characters of being (a) intrinsically
complete or perfect and (b), as a consequence,
an adequate object of unqualified adoration or
worship."

a. Strong tendencies toward a theism in
Plato (The LAWS).
b. Greek philosophy succeeds in being
fully theistic only in Neo-Platonism.
c. The modern period of philosophy carries much of the medieval emphasis in such
thinkers as Descartes, Leibniz, Locke, Berkeley,
Kant. (Kant's Second Critique)

WHAT HAS DISPUTED THIS REIGN OF THEISTIC PHILOSO-PHY?   201

In general, the challenging restriction has
been that associated with the alleged limitations
of reason when reason is said to go beyond experience. Particularly true in the type of philosophy
represented by the radical empiricism of Hume and
the attack on speculative theology (by Kant's
first critique).

EXPERIENCE--A CURIOUSLY COMPOUNDED AFFAIR   202

a. Rejection of the Hume reduction of
experience to impressions. Basically, the
complaint about this reduction is the old one
that such a reduction, in itself, fails to
supply a conception of unity.
b. Unity itself is only a genus term for
the many relations that may be comprehended
within and beneath it. Such relations are in
their turn pleaded as protests to the allegedly
barren notion of "pure" experience.

A RESTATEMENT AND DEFENSE OF THE ONTOLOGICAL ARGUMENT   203

In keeping with the analysis of experience,
Taylor looks to the ontological argument with
somewhat less distrust than that usually generated
by the Kantian criticism. That is to say, experience is saturated with its own transcendent ground
and the genuine kernel of the ontological argument
is seen as a forced concession to a transcendent real.

a. Brief statement of Kant's criticism.
b. Brief statement of Hume's position.
c. Taylor's restatement. The ontological
argument, it is conceded, cannot validly be
claimed to prove the existence of space-time particulars. But the principle of the ontological
argument is not necessarily condemned by its failure to be universally applicable. But there is no
idea so poor and untrue as not to have some meaning
and objective reference beyond its own present existence. The ontological argument, for Taylor, "in
its most general form," is simply a statement that
reality and meaning for a subject mutually imply
one another. If then one could eliminate the disharmony and confusion from his thought, the remainder, even a remainder of an infinitely perfect being,
would validly indicate the real existence of such a
being.
d. Confirmation of this epistemological
assumption, for Taylor, is found "in the interpretation and reconstruction of historical facts
/where/ the internal coherence of a systematic and
comprehensive interpretation is taken as itself
the evidence of its truth."
e. Further solidifying of this position is
attempted through noting its relation to a general
idealistic position and to the conception of truth
as best preserved under a coherence theory.

SCIENCE--AND THE QUESTION OF GOD'S EXISTENCE   208

a. The business of science has nothing to
say one way or another about God's existence.
b. Natural science's exclusive concern is
with "the detection of 'laws of nature' and uniformities of sequence in the course of events."
c. Exact science and knowledge are not co-
extensive: science is the smaller word. This
permits Taylor's "presuppositionalism" in that
the science in its dependencies indicates the
larger dimension from whence it draws its fuller
meaning. Such is the above noted function of
unity with its particular aspects in relations.
d. Explicit "dependencies" of science include
     1) Realism. There is a domain external
to the investigator that is everywhere assumed

to justify the investigation and to validate
the assumption of such existence in the investigation. The denial of this staggers under
the virtually infinite improbability of any
unified language of communication being possible.

2) The knowing-act. This is basically
the old observation of Kant that the act of
knowing a series of impressions as a succession implies that there is a unity of consciousness that precedes the recognition of the data
of intuitions.

3) The witness of language. Taylor notes
Hume's use of such words as "perceptions,"
"impressions," "ideas," and remarks, "We are
really left with a 'heap' of states which are
not states of anything and convey no knowledge
of anything. The determination to recognize
no knowledge but 'scientific' knowledge has
destroyed knowledge itself."

A VARIANT OF THE TELEOLOGICAL ARGUMENT   215

a. Brute fact is a mute fact and requires
an enlargement of reference into some way of
recognizing the relevance and necessity of universals.

b. It is assumed as a working hypothesis
that reality is totally interconnected and, as
a result, no isolated aspect of that reality could
be autonomously interpreted or evaluated.

c. Next, concerning this interconnected
manifold, Taylor asks, "Do the facts of the world-
order, so far as the sciences take them into account, disclose, or even suggest, the presence of
a directing purpose...?" "Does nature exhibit
recognizable traces of what Paley called 'prospective contrivance'?" Taylor thinks he finds such
traces.

1) The inorganic world interconnects
with the organic world at (practically speaking) an infinite number of points. And it
is within the organic world, particularly,
that Taylor finds evidence for his teleological interpretation. The interconnection,
however, will eventually unite both worlds

under the interpretation that is most conspicuously teleologically evidenced at the
organic level.

    2) The offer of emergent evolution to
include mind is resisted. However, mind, as
a prime exhibit of teleology, can occupy the
forefront of analysis and speculation without
doing violence to anything that may be claimed
for emergent evolution at lower levels.

    3) The attempted pairing of non-intellectual
causes with intellectual causes by Hume is declared to be a case of question-begging--for it
omits to consider the latent teleology in those
causes denominated non-intelligent.

    4) It is noted that in no case can "pur-
pose," even if operating in nature, be detected
by strictly descriptive and empirical means.
This casts radical empiricism into deeper doubt
as to its adequacy to address itself to the full
range of human experience. Even if Aristotle's
"entelechy" be a fact, it could never be recognized by radically empirical observation.

    5) Purposive behavior works in conformity
to the laws of physics and chemistry but, in so
doing, exhibits a contrast to anything that the
laws of physics and chemistry may demand. In
any case of purposive behavior, as Whitehead has
said, there are countless ways in which the electrons might run--all of them in accord with the
known laws of physics--but the actual way in
which they do tend to run is always one which
is "prospectively" adapted to the narrow and
specific end which is the purposed end. With
all controls removed, there is a virtually infinite improbability of the precise end normally
associated with the purposed end being realized
in the organic realm.

    d. The introspective evidence. "The one case,"
Taylor says, "in which the existence of mind as a
fact is directly and immediately disclosed to us is
our own, and nothing is clearer than that, in our
own case, the distinctive character of mind is that,
by its very nature, it is forward-reaching and shows
its presence by the devising of adaptations to situations not yet present, but anticipated."

e. Mind, thus, emerges in Taylor's treatment of the whole teleological question as fundamental in importance. Whether it is the mind of man or the larger analogue of mind that is reflected in nature, mind is led up to as modally distinct among the many facets of reality.

f. The unique modality which is mind finds a natural affinity with nature. That is to say, it is everywhere both the "faith" of the scientist and the result of scientific effort that the thesis becomes commanding that nature is everywhere open to the penetration of mind. It conforms to the idealistic position that whatever reality is it appears to be close to what mind is. It would appear that the mind nowhere encounters the utterly opaque. Blocks to the mind's penetration and ordering of nature are always mere difficulties of the moment. It would appear that the mind of man is so much "at home" in the world and so little has to yield to the suggestion that there is the utterly non-rational to contest its powers of penetration and analysis, that the grander conclusion seems to be the sole remaining alternative, viz., that there is nothing encountered nor encounterable save that of a cosmos that not only is thoroughly saturated by mind but is mind. This is but to say that God it is that identifies with the nature of ultimate reality.

CHAPTER IX -- "THE MAJOR DISPUTED ASSUMPTIONS"

meaningful discourse either to propositions whose
subjects already contain their predicates--Kant's
analytic judgment--or to existential propositions
whose truth can be confirmed by some technique of
empirical verifiability.

b. Transcendence may be defended by broadening epistemology's genuine concerns and dependencies to show that even the most radically conceived empiricism is saturated with a meaning-
complex that transcends sensuous experience.   238

EMPIRICAL PARTICULARITY   239

Such particularity can never be carried to
an ultimate reduction without remaining partially
informed or simply passing beyond the last possibility of formation into nothing at all. There
is a resident formation, conceptually apprehended,
that transcends sensuous experience.

THE TRANSCENDENTAL DIMENSION INTRODUCED THROUGH
A PARADIGM EXAMPLE OF CHANGE   240

In keeping with Aristotle's compromise
between the extremes of Parmenides and Heraclitus,
being is introduced as a conceptually apprehended
constant without which becoming loses its meaning.
Unchanging being is never grasped empirically, yet
cannot be denied. It therefore qualifies as a
transcendental aspect of reality. This leads us
to affirm:

NO EPISTEMOLOGY WITHOUT ONTOLOGY   241

The very reality that gives substance to
epistemology at surface levels is not less real
at the conceptual level to which the mind is
driven in order to preserve the meaningfulness
of change.

THE INSTABILITY OF PLURALISM   242

Pluralism is believed helpless before the
question, What is the relation of the parts to

each other? Since the question cannot be dismissed, any attempted answer elevates whatever
the relationship is into a dialectically enforced unity.

THE MEANING OF BEING   243

     Epistemologically, being is the absolutely
ultimate category. To use Weedon's phrase--
actually employed of Spinoza--being is "that
which 'is', preeminently and without qualifica-
tion--the source and ultimate subject of all
distinctions." Its meaning is as certain as
the fact that there is a difference between
something and nothing.

"SEDUCTIVE FALLACIES OF METAPHYSICS" (Herbert
Feigl)   244

     a. Feigl believes it an impossible demand
to justify the very principles of all justification and (particularly with respect to the Principle of Induction) recommends a pragmatic rule
of procedure and an empirical reduction of epistemology to "What is What."
     b. Bertrand Russell is noted as declaring
that induction rests upon "an independent logical principle" that cannot be deduced from formal
logic nor, without circularity, inferred from
experience, and this in turn is claimed to be
adjustable to the thesis of this paper in that
the meaningful use or interpretation of experience
reveals its dependence upon an extra-experiential
factor.

THE CONCEPTUAL BOND OF EXPERIENCE   246

     a. Being, we have seen, is such a bond.
     b. Relations, also, serve to unite par-
ticulars of sensuous experience in such a way
as not themselves to fall with the narrower
domain of sensuous experience. The causal bond
is one such relation.

c. Epistemological successes cannot be
squared with subjective idealism. In a pure
case of subjective idealism there would be no
reason to anticipate nor possibility of sharing
in the de facto experience of agreement. The
objectivity that the realization of agreement
ushers in is at the same time evidence of a
situation transcendent to pure human subjectivity.

d. By the same token, philosophic effort
must go beyond linguistic analysis; it must reintroduce the hope of arriving at the "true" meaning of a word. The "something" that language is
about must exceed the language itself.

e. We can argue and do argue concerning
the rightness and wrongness of actions and this
fact is a declared reflection of a conceptual
bond of experience (an ethical norm) that transcends experience itself.

f. There is a subject-object relation in
the knowing act. The objects of knowledge do
not interpret themselves. Interpretation comes
from the subject-side. Thus, norms are introduced
that transcend experience.

AND SO--PHILOSOPHIC EFFORT IS ABANDONED UNLESS
ONE GOES BEYOND "RULES OF PROCEDURE" AS PRAGMATIC
(FEIGL) TO "RULES OF PROCEDURE" AS DERIVATIVE   251

It would appear that Feigl intends his
"rule of procedure" to be a critically forged
substitute for what he regards as the "impossible demand to justify the very principles of
all justification." This is called an "impossible demand" because it cannot be deduced from
formal logic nor, without circularity, from
experience. The "rule" then is indeed a rule
and not merely procedure. It quietly prepares
for the future in the spirit of a dependence
that is never really weakened or embarrassed
by its professed recognition of radical contingency and disconnectedness. This is active
dependence upon an extra-experiential principle
without which science is impossible.

THE DIALECTIC OF MORAL VALUE   252

a. In principle, the same dialectic
that appeared in Part I lifts the mind above
feeling to a norm or standard that is presupposed. This may be claimed as the unconscious
assumption of man and is reverted to in such a
natural way as to create the presumption that
man is in unconscious dependence upon a transcendent norm of moral value.

b. Conversely, the denial of this approach
is so unnatural that language will scarcely bear
the burden of the denial while the natural tendency of man asserts itself by slipping back into the
attitude of dependence upon ethical standards.

MORAL PURPOSIVENESS   254

a. Purpose is a forward-looking, forward-
reaching condition and the object or goal of
that forward effect is always some value.

b. Time is necessarily involved and is
defended as the "form" of the moral life. This
intimately-related sense of temporality is revealed as essential to the "conative" disposition
of the human being with effort, endeavoring,
striving, volition, providing an emphasis of
teleological consideration.

c. Purposive living is so fundamental that
it may be said to point along the line of the
mind's genuine and immediate concerns to that ultimate presupposition of value which, denied, renders
impossible the validating of the least of claimed
purposive actions.

d. Temporality, along the line of human advance, is more than mere 'succession,' and provides
that continuum that marks man's past, present, and
future with a distinctly human meaning.

e. Even allegations of pessimism, recognitions
of disvalue, and claims of absurdity and meaninglessness of existence call attention in their very negations to the norm of ideal value without which these
privations would have no meaning.

a. To know temporality meaningfully is to
transcend it. This is the implied dialectic of
finitude. The presupposition of all limitation
whatever is infinity and, within the universe of
discourse to which temporality belongs, <u>eternity</u>
appears to be the proper presupposition to confer
appropriate meaning to the time-limitation.
b. If the implication of an infinite dimension, derived from the conception of finitude is
valid, then we may claim that in the sense of
temporality, eternity may be said to have already
been entered upon--the reality of the one implying
the equal reality of the other.
c. The above will indicate the deliberate
purpose of securing an identification of true
thought with right action.
d. Further, the striving person, seeking a
goal commensurate with all that his personality
requires for its fulfillment and aspiration, finds
that the ultimate locus of true value can be not
other than itself Personal. God enters the value-
system.

<u>A</u> <u>VARIANT</u> <u>OF</u> <u>THE</u> "<u>NATURALISTIC</u> <u>FALLACY</u>"   258

The loose identification of the good with
'utility,' 'pleasure,' 'health,' 'knowledge,'
etc. is meaningful only in that sense of class-
inclusion that permits 'the good' to exceed these
terms. But that also permits the transcendental
character of <u>the</u> <u>good</u>. If an absolute identity
is intended, then the charge may be leveled that
we have unnecessarily complicated the issue by
adding the word 'good' to what otherwise is perfectly clear and understandable without it. And
this is a variant of the "naturalistic fallacy."

<u>THE</u> <u>IS-OUGH</u><u>T</u> <u>CONTROVERSY</u>   259

a. Conveniently introduced by reference to
the famous passage in David Hume's TREATISE.
b. Some attempts to derive <u>Ought</u> from <u>Is</u>.

1. George I. Mavrodes. Thinks that if _ought_ implies _can_ (Kant), the contra-position shows an _ought_ derived from an _is_. Reply.
2. Max Black. Claims that valid _arguments_ need not obey the rule of valid _syllogisms_ and that conclusions may _legitimately_ include terms that do not appear in the premises. Reply.

   Admits that he cannot claim entailment for his "should-conclusions," but characterizes them as possessing "latent" or "virtual" necessity. Reply.
3. John R. Searle. Claims to be able to derive an _ought_ from an _is_ by dis-tinguishing between "statements of brute fact and statements of institu-tional fact," the latter being "systems of constitutive rules or conventions." Reply.
4. M. Zimmerman. Advocates a solution along the lines of simple abandonment of an ought-language in favor of a thorough "is-supportable" language. Reply.

  c. The above attempts to derive an _ought_ from an _is_ are believed to have lowered the quality of the issues suggested by the larger view of the ethi-cal dimension.

  d. Remarks on the difficulties of derivation of _ought_ from _is_ from R. M. Hare, D. Z. Phillips, and H. O. Mounce.

VALUE-RELATIVISM   270

The idea is commonly circulated that there is no virtue anywhere but what has been consid-ered a vice somewhere, that in matters of ethical standards man is the measure. The cumulative evi-dence for a naturalistic view of human nature is presumed overwhelming and the non-naturalistic view gradually lost in the cultural evolution.

     a.   There is an important sense in which
'naturalistic' considerations can never upset
the claims of moral value. Moral value may
arise upon the occasion of specific behavior,
but it does not reduce to that behavior. Between
the moral dimension and the behavior of men is
the whole distance of the 'ought' from the 'is,'
the difference between the imperative and the
indicative.
     b.   It is frequently the case that instead
of recognizing the rule of universals in ethical-
value controversy, it is particular cases of application that are seen to the exclusion of the higher
norms that regulate them.
     c.   The above leads to the recognition that
in disputes of ethical standards it is not the
predicates of the propositions that are seriously
disputed, but the real issue is whether the subject
does or does not participate in the class of things
called 'right.' If this were not the case, there
could be no dispute.

THE USE OF PRESUPPOSITIONS   275

     a.   Presuppositions are assumptions on which
we are in perpetual dependence. They appear to
enter into the essentiality of our being. Function-
ally, they are guides and correctives normally identified with the norms and yardsticks of human
thought and behavior. They may be thought as particularized within the broad categories of the
rational, the esthetic, and the moral.
     b.   These 'presuppositions,' as thus identified,
seemingly may not be successfully disputed, if,
that is to say, it is uncovered that they are covertly
being employed even in the attempt to dismiss them.
Such would be the case of a logical argument designed
to overthrow the claim of rationality.

THE WITNESS OF EVIL TO TRANSCENDENCE   277

     a.   There is something virtually unique in
a situation that can be called 'evil.' We are

simultaneously compelled to recognize the dislocating force of evil in our midst while we are totally unable to pinpoint it as an isolatable factor in experience.

b. Descriptivism cannot pinpoint either good or evil. Because evil cannot be isolated as one can presumably isolate a microscopic organism and yet cannot be denied, it would appear to follow that evil signals some transcendent norm by the aid of which evil--as a privation from good--is identified with respect to its true character.

IN SUMMATION: MORAL VALUE MAY BE SAID TO TRANSCEND EXPERIENCE
280

a. Only thus can it preserve its normative function. Experience is never its own norm. Experience cannot approve, correct, measure, interpret, itself.

b. As such, transcendent moral value qualifies as an ideal. And the ideal is participant in the reality that is vouchsafed to universals. Ideals, too, are universals.

c. Moral value is thus 'abstract,' but only in the sense that it lifts the conceptually apprehended essence of moral acts from their several differences and, in the manner of all universals, clarifies the principle by which the many relate to their one.

d. The real status of the transcendent moral-value universal is guaranteed in the same way that all universals are guaranteed, viz., by noting that they begin with undisputed reals and in abstracting from the plurality the essential character of each preserves thereby their own true (real) nature. That moral discourse is indeed involved with 'undisputed reals' is what is believed shown by the assumption of univocity in the moral predicates of ethical discourse.

HYPOSTATIZATION OF THE LOCUS OF IDEAL MORAL VALUE 283

Such a 'locus' is more than a focal point for the consciousness of aspiring man; it is the locus of moral mandate. The moral obedience of persons can only be commanded by personality. Only by the resolute denial of all meaning to ethical impera- tives can the dialectical itinerary of the mind be stopped short of the further postulation of God.

In view of the interpretative and evaluative effort that accompanied this discussion of the immanent <u>transcendental</u> in moral and general epis- temology, some attention should now be given to rationality itself which has been throughout pre- supposed. It would appear, further, that attention should be paid to the relation that rationality sus- tains to moral value, the relation of both in the hierarchy of being, and the nature of that apex of the hierarchy that is disclosed by virtue of the dual relation of moral value and rationality in the total structure.

<u>RATIONALITY CANNOT BE "NATURALIZED"</u>   283

Rationality, like the norms of the ethical dimension, protests reduction to the base ingre- dients of experience that it is by its very nature called upon to judge. It cannot be "naturalized" for what are fundamentally the same reasons that hold for all norms whatever, <u>viz.</u>, the loss of critical function. Rationality must be regarded as <u>above</u> the experience that it is called upon to interpret. This elevation of rationality is at the same time to recognize its transcendence.

<u>THE HIERARCHY--IN BEING AND IN EPISTEMOLOGY</u>   285

a. In the order of approach to the apex of the hierarchy of being, we may mention moral value, rationality, and, lastly, <u>being</u> itself.
b. <u>Being</u> is not only a meaningful category, it is the most ultimate category. Behind <u>being</u> one cannot go; as far as <u>being</u> one must go.

c. Below _being_ in the order of our logical
descent is rationality. One may think of _being_
as non-rational without outside information.
That is to say, the concept of _being_, _per se_,
does not carry the category of rationality within
it. But, one cannot think of rationality without
some ground. Rationality must _belong_ somewhere.
It does not carry its _being_ in the concept of
rationality itself.
d. Moral value would be in the third logical
descent from _being_. To articulate the claims of
moral value requires dependency upon rationality
which, in turn, must ground in _being_. The ground
of moral value--like the ground of rationality--
is not given in the concept of moral value. Neither
is the concept of moral value found in the rationality above--although the rational category must be
depended upon to evaluate the truth-claims and the
validity-claims that may arise within ethical discourse.
e. In these recognitions of distinctions
within the hierarchy, it must be remembered that
they are always _logical_ ways of viewing the attributes of what otherwise is a non-fragmented category
of being not suffering from real divisions.

_A_ WELTANSCHAUUNG   287

a. In this Chapter, as in the Chapters preceding, there is a wide-ranging appeal that moves
frequently far beyond the narrower concerns of
moral value to embrace the entire range of cosmological, teleological, axiological, and ontological
concepts. This appears inevitable in the sense
that the apex of the argument from moral value is
at the same time the apex of the arguments from
the other considerations as well. It is claimed
therefore that the wider range of appeal gives
support to the narrower concern of moral value in
the sense that the apex of the argument is not
isolated from that fuller world-view that knows
no alternative to a harmony in principle of the
multivaried aspects of reality.
b. As we have seen with pluralism, there is
frustration encountered when the parts are refused
subsumption under any order of higher relation, so

it with the attempts to keep arguments that begin
with that single aspect of real experience--moral
value--separated ultimately and utterly from considerations of the rational, esthetic, empirical,
and ontological.

THE UNIQUE WITNESS OF RATIONALITY   290

a. The high priority of rationality seems
guaranteed. The honoring of consistency and coherence and obedience to the law of contradiction
are always presupposed--in ideal if not in practice. The penalty paid for repudiation of rational procedure would be the total absence of evaluation in any and every field. In such an extreme
position, the repudiation itself could not be
evaluated and could not be defended. Though one
could fight, one could not evaluate the moral
worth of the cause nor defend any reason for
either continuing the fight or abandoning it.
b. Rationality, though given high priority
in Plato's doctrine of the Ideas, is given even
higher eminence in Augustine. Augustine, while
not denying to the Ideas the supreme principle of
intelligibility, by identifying them with the personality of God, permitted Intelligence as well
as intelligibility. In Augustine, therefore, one
might say that the universals know the world. The
idea of a reciprocal rationality is introduced into
the world-view.
c. With the apex of the hierarchy now identified with rationality, a further possibility occurs,
viz., that the totality of reality wherever encountered is either itself rational or is at least penetrable by the advance of rational techniques and
analyses. A prediction is possible: rational man
in his approach to reality in any of her forms would
be unconsciously committed to the optimism that
reality will never turn an opaque side to his approaches. This is what we might call the faith of
the scientific investigator. Such 'faith' evidently
exists.
d. The concept of rationality sustains an
intimate relation to words like 'reason,' 'judgment,'
'intelligence,'--even 'wisdom.' This near-synonymity,
taken together with the universality of rationality,

now reveals with even greater plausibility the
fact of a theistically-oriented universe.

'WISDOM'--AS A LINK BETWEEN RATIONALITY AND VALUE

Wisdom is more than knowledge; it is more
than intelligence; it is different in some sense
from rationality. In another sense, it belongs
to all three. Widsom contains value-overtones.
Wisdom is not to be considered dispossessed of
rational insight, but the value-factor is revealed
in that it performs a guidance-function, a selection-
operation, a discrimination among possible ends.
Wisdom, therefore, carries a special importance for
a thesis that has everywhere maintained that ethical
and rational norms cannot be forever separated.

THE ANALOGY OF LANGUAGE FOLLOWS THE ANALOGY OF BEING

a. But the utility of this device is disputed on much the same grounds that logical
positivism disputes the possibility of valid
knowledge of metaphysics, theology, or normative
ethics.

b. It is observed, however, that the linguistic point of view has reintroduced a consideration of problems that in turn should encourage
a thorough investigation of analogical language.

c. Language has need to prepare itself to
move across the line set by any of the narrower
aspects of experience to that other reality on
which experience depends for its meaning.

d. It is believed that neither sameness
nor difference can be denied between and among
the plural aspects of the world and the word
uniquely capable of designating that condition
is the word 'analogy.'

e. So it is necessary to distinguish between
an illegitimate anthropomorphism and a legitimate
use of analogical language.

f. Analogy, it is concluded, has a legitimate
province when applied to the horizontal level of
perceptions or to the vertical level of conceptions.

g. An analogical understanding of reality is
a safeguard against being forced to regard meaning
as univocal and the existents of the world as
qualitatively one.

THE CONJUNCTION OF VALUE AND EXISTENCE   300

a. In the everyday use of value-predicates
we assert the conjunction of the value with some
existent. It hints of a natural affinity that
value and existence bears.
b. This prepares us to accept the ultimate
identification of the apex of value and God.
c. But the relation of value and existence
is not strictly speaking an identity; it is rather
a conjunction. This relation explains why one
cannot find value by deliberate analysis; the sense
and awareness of the conjunction of value with existence is upon the occasion of experience but not
reducible to experience.
d. Ordinarily, one does not find value entailed in existence; one does, however, find existence entailed in value. But at a different
level of understanding--that of divine purpose--
even existence itself in its every particularity
may be said to have the value associated with the
divine purpose.

THE ULTIMATE CONJUNCTION   302

God becomes the presupposed repository of
normative value which, we have seen, must ground
in being. And if such is the case at the ultimate level, the conjunction of value with existence
at the human level are reflections of the higher
reality.

CONTENTS

CHAPTER I

A. E. TAYLOR: THE MAN AND HIS WORK

Alfred Edward Taylor was the son of Wesleyan
Methodist parents who had been at one time mission-
aries to the Gold Coast (now the independent Republic
of Ghana) and was born in the small English town of
Oundle on the 22nd of December in the year of 1869.
His mother died early and Taylor with a brother and a
sister was reared by his father.   Even as a boy he was
an insatiable reader and a writer of long stories
which he would tell to his brother and sister.   Taylor's SOCRATES, (first published in 1933 in England)
and dedicated "To the Boys and Masters of Kingswood
School, Bath," pays a partial debt of gratitude and
affection to the source of his earlier education.
Taylor completed his formal education at New College,
Oxford, and in 1891 was elected a Fellow of Merton
which Fellowship he held until 1898.   He was re-
elected in 1901.   In 1896, Professor Samuel Alexander,
then of Victoria University, Manchester, secured Taylor as Lecturer in Greek and Philosophy at Owens College, Manchester, in which post he remained until
1903.   In 1899 he competed for the Green Moral Philosophy Prize offered at Oxford and won.   Taylor married in 1900 and in 1903 went to Montreal where for
five years he was Professor of Philosophy at McGill
University.

In 1908 Professor Bernard Bosanquet left his post
at the University of St. Andrews which position as
Professor of Moral Philosophy Taylor secured and held
until 1924.   During this interim at St. Andrews Professor John Laird was Taylor's assistant and after
Taylor's death began to write the Academy memoir of
him.   But he did not live to finish the task begun.
Instead, W. D. Ross has given us the most complete
sketch of Taylor's many academic activities, and from
Laird's notes quotes "a characteristically lively
sketch of Taylor which he /Laird/ wrote during his own

1

last illness."[1]

When I was his assistant, Taylor had abandoned
his excursions into general philosophy, where his
ELEMENTS OF METAPHYSICS--a sort of Bradley-for-
the-Million combined with much informative viva-
city about contemporary scientific philosophy--
had earned its unusual success. He had turned to
the main interest of his irrepressible literary
career, the re-discovery (as he thought) of the
historical Plato and of the historical Socrates,
of the Platonic tradition, and of the unconscious
Platonism of the modern world. Here he out-
Burneted Burnet, but without very much active discussion with Burnet.

More suo, he imposed a certain strain upon his
interlocutors, who were expected to make intelligent remarks about Greek dowries, or any other
sweeping from the Platonic epistles. But even if
one couldn't help, one could admire and be exci-
ted. I had never met, or at any rate had never
known, a philosopher to whom the Greek or any
other past philosophy had been the burning heart
of present existence, fresher than the morning's
news. A traditionalism of that kind, especially
when combined with such a range and versatility
of application, would stir the intellectual pul-
ses of the humblest.

Besides, Taylor was much more than a Grecian with
a darting eye for all the Atticisms of the modern
world. He refreshed himself continually from
many other wells in the philosophical and cultural
tradition, and, at the time I am recording, had
become engrossed in another of his major interests, St. Thomas Aquinas. There we did not try,
or pretend to try, to follow him; but he seemed
to assume, quite undaunted, that we were respec-
table mediaevalists as well as passable Grecians.
He always spoke as if his own enthusiasms extended over all the literate earth. We, for our
parts, thought that Taylor's excitement about St.
Thomas was just an aspect of his attitude towards

1. W. D. Ross, "Alfred Edward Taylor 1869-1945,"
    PROCEEDINGS OF THE BRITISH ACADEMY, XXXI (1945),
    p. 408.

Christian theology and the Christian religion. .
. .He had become a High-Church Episcopalian, a
member of the Church Catholic though never a Roman Catholic. In our eyes that was an eccentricity. I dare say that our eyes were holden. We
were not greatly moved by Taylor's new scholasticism.

I shall never forget those days of my assistant-
ship. On any given afternoon, and there were very
few afternoons when Taylor did not walk and talk
with his assistant as a matter of kindly course,
the odds were that one discussed Greek medicine,
Dante's genius, the character of Bishop Bonner,
and the delight that was Max Beerbohm. Mrs. Taylor would join us at tea-time and conduct a cross-
conversation about Dickens and Anthony Trollope.
Some quick thinking was necessary to keep both
streams of conversation going, and I fear I did
not always mix my "Yes's" and "No's" quite accurately. In that case there was a lull, sometimes
a surprised lull, but not for long. For self-
protection I read rather widely at that time.[2]

Taylor left St. Andrews in 1924 to accept the
chair of Moral Philosophy at Edinburgh. There he remained until his retirement in 1941. Three years before retirement, Ross writes,

Taylor suffered the greatest sorrow of his life,
by the death of Mrs. Taylor. His son had already
been many years in India; after his wife's death
he was a lonely man, and his vitality never re-
covered from the blow. He died in his sleep, in
his house in Edinburgh, on 31 October 1945.[3]

Ross continues by remarking,

He had received many honours, but no more than
his due; he was a Doctor of Literature of St.
Andrews and of Manchester, an LL. D. of Aberdeen
and of St. Andrews, an Honorary Fellow of New
College, a Foreign Member of the Accademia dei
Lincei, a Corresponding Member of the Prussian

---

2.   Ibid., pp. 408-409.

3.   Ibid., p. 409.

Academy of Sciences, and had been Gifford Lecturer at St. Andrews.[4]

And Taylor's students, Ross continues,

recognized, as they were bound to do, that they were being taught by one of the greatest scholars in the country, and many caught the infection of his enthusiasm for philosophy and for literature.[5]

In a short autobiographical sketch which prefaced "The Freedom of Man,"[6] Taylor has given us his own recollection of his philosophical development from its earliest remembered beginnings until (significantly for the thesis of this paper) the year before the Gifford Lectures were delivered at St. Andrews. In the account of this development it is safe to say that the gradual emergence of the heightened sense of value's relevance to the formation of a living philosophy can unmistakably be traced. As a child Taylor confesses to have been puzzled by the solipsistic doubt whether he alone was real and the world including his parents was but fancy. And but a little later he was already struggling with doubts connected with the alleged subjectivity of values. When Taylor went up to Oxford in 1887 he already had read something of Berkeley, had learned the fascination for Plato that never deserted him, and had had an introduction to Kant by way of De Quincy. Having been brought up in an atmosphere of respect for the relevance of biblical revelation, he was distressed by the counter-claims stemming from biological evolution and biblical criticism. And Taylor wrote, "What I looked for in philosophy was some sane defence of convictions which I felt were essential for the conduct of life against what seemed to be the disintegrating influences of scholarship and biological science."[7]

---

4. Ibid.

5. Ibid., p. 410.

6. Alfred Edward Taylor, "Biographical," CONTEMPORARY BRITISH PHILOSOPHY. Second Series. Edited by J. H. Muirhead. (London: George Allen & Unwin Ltd., 1925), pp. 270-272.

7. Ibid., p. 270.

Idealism was the dominant philosophy at Oxford when Taylor "began to read philosophy seriously in 1889." Thus he came to philosophy by way of the still predominant influence of Green, by way of Bradley whose close friendship he was able to know for much of his stay at Oxford, by way of Kant as interpreted by Green and Caird, together with further study in Plato and Aristotle. Taylor's friendship with Bradley together with the obvious influence that idealism in general exerted on his life and writings could easily obscure the influence that realistic and historical emphases had made in quite another direction. Taylor was early impressed with "an insoluble puzzle" found "in what seemed to be T. H. Green's conception of a world composed of relations between terms of which we could say nothing, except that they were the terms of the relation."[8] And from Bradley himself, Taylor confesses, came the suggestion

> to study Herbart as a wholesome corrective of undue absorption in Hegelian ways of thinking, and his repeated exhortations to take empirical psychology in earnest. These studies in the end led to a natural reaction against what now seemed to me the unhistorical character of the philosophy on which I had been feeding myself.[9]

And Taylor remarks that "at this time of my life I was not far from developing into a kind of 'Positivist.'"[10]

> The reaction towards the empirical and given continued, along with a new interest in the principles of physical science, provoked by the writings of E. Mach and others, during the years in which I was associated at Manchester with Professor Alexander (1896-1903), a period also fruitful for me in leading to a serious study of the great seventeenth-century thinkers, Galileo, Descartes, Leibniz. The "pan-mathematism" of Leibniz, like that of Plato, fascinated me deeply; even now that I am convinced that pan-mathematism, like absolute Idealism, is incompatible with a full

8. Ibid., p. 271.

9. Ibid.

10. Ibid.

sense of the "historical," I am keenly conscious
of the attraction and cannot avoid thinking it
the right and proper goal of the sciences of
physical nature.[11]

To James Ward Taylor pays an added acknowledgment of having taught him to appreciate the meaning of
"history" and from whom he learned "the impossibility
of eliminating contingency from Nature."[12]

For twelve years--seven years at Manchester, and
five years at McGill University in Montreal--Taylor
had been coming slowly to a re-evaluation of the role
that metaphysics ought to play in an overall philosophy. Even toward the end of his Manchester years he
found the tendencies towards empiricism and positivism
"passing away without any loss of the interest I had
acquired in the empirical and the ideas and methods of
the sciences."[13] It is clear that the claim that the
empirical, as such, had made in those formative years
was not abandoned in those later years in favor of a
return to the idealism of his earliest years at Oxford.
It is also clear that Taylor does not emerge an empiricist or positivist. The empirical emphasis is found
in the conviction that "the business of metaphysical
philosophy is, in a way, a modest one."[14]

> It has to be content to recognize that in the
> sciences, in history, in morality and religion
> it is dealing with a reality which is in the end
> simply "given" and not to be explained away.
> Its concern is with the various intellectual in-
> terpretations of the 'given,' and its supreme
> task is not, as I once used to suppose, the
> 'unification of the sciences,' but the neces-
> sarily imperfect and tentative reconciliation of
> the exigencies of scientific thinking with the
> imperative moral and religious demands of life.
> It has not to invent an improved substitute for
> historically real religion and morality, but to

---

11. Ibid.

12. Ibid.

13. Ibid., p. 272.

14. Ibid.

fathom as much as it can of their significance. There is no special infallibility about metaphysics and its methods are necessarily 'dialectical' in the Aristotelian sense.[15]

Taylor, therefore, ended his life's quest, not by succumbing to a Hegelian metaphysics--"a great danger"--which "dissevers the 'eternal verities' from all contact with 'historical' actuality,"[16] but, in spite of this, and perhaps, even because of it, he did find firm ground. "I seemed to have found what I was in search of, a view of things which would protect the realities of religion and ethics against all danger from 'naturalistic' attacks."[17]

Here then is indicated the approach that Taylor will honor in the examination of values--whether religious, moral, or other. He will on one hand widen his list of what is the given (the empirical recognition) but he will employ a telic approach to this mass of the given. Completeness, however, cannot be attained by mere perceptual enumeration. It cannot be attained by statistical description. These approaches are necessary but they are not enough to give a philosophy of completeness. The "dialectic" of the Aristotelian sense will appear in Taylor's analysis of value as spotlighting the idea of function. And it will mean that implicit within our values is the tendency towards their fulfillment, their proper goal.

A slowly dawning consciousness of the ultimate ground of ethics can be traced in Taylor's writings. THE PROBLEM OF CONDUCT (1901) continued the general theme of his essay that had won the Green Prize at Oxford in 1899 ("On the Reciprocal Relations Between Ethics and Metaphysics"). Ethics is not to be grounded in metaphysics whether metaphysics is conceived as a generalized study of nature or of experience; rather it is to be identified in its truest character when studied in that revelation vouchsafed by the testimony of moral consciousness. In this, Taylor already manifests an allegiance to a principle of argument

---

15.   Ibid.

16.   Ibid., p. 271.

17.   Ibid.

reminiscent of Kant. Taylor senses something of a
true ethic when it is identified with devotion to the
good. Even devotion to what is objectively bad but
which is thought of as good qualifies under a truly
ethical attitude. Slowly, however, the implication of
devotion, concern, or commitment, changed, or, perhaps
I should say, deepened, to that of a frankly acknowledged theism, and, still later, to a more articulate
Christian theism. Taylor's "The Belief in Immortality," in THE FAITH AND THE WAR (1915) clearly identifies "a right rule for the ordering of our walk and
conduct in life" with a right concern "in deciding for
or against the Christian faith in immortality." Still
later, in the Gifford Lectures (1926-1928) in the spirit of greater philosophical depth, Taylor announces
that "To think of the moral life adequately we must
think of it as an adventure which begins at one end
with nature, and ends at the other end with <u>superna-
ture</u>." This conclusion is developed by Taylor by
means of his use of "function"--conceived to be a major
part of the "dialectic" taught by Aristotle. In this
sense, the <u>final cause</u> of morality lies beyond all approximations that man knows in his earthly pilgrimage
and is embodied in that living presupposition of meaningful moral concern: God. Still later, in DOES GOD
EXIST? (1945) Taylor declares, "...we cannot escape
facing the question whether God can be eliminated from
either the natural or the moral world without convert-
ing both into an incoherent nightmare."

The close relation of what is ostensibly a philosophical enterprise with its summation borrowing un-
disguisedly from the traditional teachings of the
Christian religion would naturally enough raise the
question (as does Professor Brand Blanshard) "whether
Professor Taylor's great speculative gifts are longer
free, or whether they have not, in the true Catholic
manner, entered a voluntary servitude to faith."[18]

The only possible answer to this fear is the examination of the argument itself. If the argument is
valid, it can matter little from whence the clue to its
formulation came. And, as a fact, this is Taylor's attitude. There is no necessary undermining of the

---

18. Brand Blanshard, THE FAITH OF A MORALIST. By A.
     E. Taylor. (New York: Macmillan Co., 1930.)
     Review. THE JOURNAL OF PHILOSOPHY, XXIX (March 3,
     1932), p. 130.

general value of an argument by the discovery that its controlling postulates are identical with the postulates of revelation--nor, indeed, even if those controlling postulates are deliberately taken from revelation. The test--and there is no other--is whether tnese postulates are consistent within themselves and whether in being pressed into the service of explanation they can prove their worth by demonstrating their ability to promote the widest possible coherence in the total manifold of experience. Blanshard himself forgets his fears when Taylor's argument turns up a conclusion with which Blanshard is already in agreement. Agreeing with Taylor in the matter of finding duties impossible by empirical reduction, Blanshard says,

> That there is no way of accounting for either the fact or the content of duty on naturalistic grounds, i.e., by the sort of causes that are studied in psychology, he succeeds in making clear.
> ...Professor Taylor is here driving an extra but effective nail into the coffin of a naturalism that is, or ought to be, dead.[19]

So Taylor makes a point--and his religious postulates do not destroy the validity of his argument. This, or something like it, can become a paradigm example of how any argument may be evaluated. To repeat: where the controlling postulates or proffered hypotheses come from is totally irrelevent. The severer task of demonstrating the larger coherence is still before us.

Taylor's fundamental principle: Theistic Presuppositionalism. Taylor asks,

> Does morality, if its claims are to be justified to the critical intelligence, involve any presuppositions which point beyond itself? Does it supply its own raison d'etre? If not, does it receive its missing completion in the activities, however we define them, which are commonly called

---

19. Ibid., p. 134.

9

religious?[20]

From the unconsciously held presuppositions that
determine men's actions and values, Taylor erects an
apologetic for his particular value-philosophy that
has for its frankly stated goal a Theism that in principle has had long historical endorsement. Taylor
sees in this unconscious assumption much of the bul-
wark of moral society. In its conscious and deliberate espousal he sees the hope of a significant philosophy; in its consistently applied denial he predicts
disintegration and chaos.

The most inclusive word descriptive of the postulational field from which Taylor draws the interpretation for the narrower specifications of his system is
theistic. Philosophical systems that draw their
structural uniqueness from such a starting point, Taylor recognizes, begin at least with Plato, are sharp-
ened under Neoplatonism, and constitute one of the
main emphases of Western philosophic thought to the
present day. The particular set of characteristics
that Taylor's theistic postulate bears is revealed
best by considering their ontological and epistemological implications. (1) Taylor's postulate must be
called transcendent. This, for Taylor, calls attention to the alleged insufficiency of experience to
provide an account of itself. The brute factuality of
experience can contribute no meaning to its own factuality. Meaning begins for experience when generalization is appealed to, and the highest generalization
possible, in principle, becomes one of the defining
characteristics of transcendence. (2) Generalization
thus becomes hierarchical and that generalization at
the apex is for Taylor's system a concrete universal.
The "concrete" aspect calls attention to the fact
that this highest universal is not empty but is rather
the fullest concretization of meaning. It is the
mind's implicitly ultimate reference in giving full
account of reality. (3) Another characteristic of this
postulate is that it is infinite. This affirms that
no limitations can be imposed from without; indeed,
the fact that all limitation, all finitude, is recognized and identified as such introduces the norm by

---

20. Alfred Edward Taylor, THE FAITH OF A MORALIST,
     The Gifford Lectures, 1926 to 1928. Series I:
     The Theological Implications of Morality (London:
     Macmillan & Co., 1930), p. 24.

which finitude is discovered and recognized. In a manner reminiscent of Descartes, our conception of the infinite is <u>logically</u> <u>prior</u> to our identification of the finite. (4) The postulate is <u>one</u>. It is both unity and the principle of unity. The singling out of a plurality of characteristics of this unified postulate is merely an abstraction convenient for the purposes of analysis and does not constitute a claim against the essential unity of this ultimate principle. Taylor believes that pluralism stands helpless before the question of the relation of the parts to each other--such a question being unavoidable and implying that whatever the relation, it tends to return to a unity of some sort. (5) This ultimate postulate is <u>being</u>, <u>existence</u>, <u>reality</u>. That is to say, the postulate is not merely formal--though it subserves all of the demands of formal principle. The concrete reality of experience, in pointing to this supreme universal as its ground of final interpretation, cannot find its own "concreteness" explained by mere formal principle but looks to a formal principle that grounds in being and existence. (6) This leads to say that in this ontological nature we find the <u>principle</u> <u>of</u> <u>ultimate</u> <u>intelligibility</u>. Again, in a manner that is at the same time reminiscent of both Plato and Augustine, we find Taylor affirming the Platonic position that only in the <u>Ideas</u> (i.e., <u>universals</u>) can one find the principle of intelligibility, but, going beyond Plato, Taylor affirms with Augustine that these Ideas are the mind of God. This permits the Platonic principle of ultimate intelligibility to identify with intelligence. Not only may man know the Ideas in a reflected light, but the Ideas may be said to know man in a direct way. (7) This leads to the last word: Taylor's theistic postulate may be said to be <u>personal</u>--carrying with it the ideas of intelligence and will.

The epistemology of Taylor, both in fact and in principle, grounds in his ontological presupposition. The characteristics, therefore, that more narrowly identify Taylor's epistemology inevitably overlap and identify with the ontological aspect of his theistic postulate. This postulate, being the locus of rational, ethical, and esthetic norms, is apprehended conceptually and is an <u>a priori</u> part of any knowledge. <u>In short, for Taylor, without ontology, there is no epistemology.</u> Experience may be said to trigger our awareness of this locus of norms, but knowledge of this postulational field arises only <u>upon the occasion</u> of

experience and is never reducible to experience. Mind-
ful of the dictum of Kant that concepts without percepts are empty and percepts without concepts are
blind, Taylor looks always to the formalism of his
theistic postulate for the principles of interpretation of experience while looking to experience for
the proper subject-matter to be thus interpreted. In
the manner of Augustine (again), Taylor argues that
the principle that interprets the particulars of experience cannot itself be one of the particulars, that
the light by which particular truths are illuminated
does not wholly and in the same manner illuminate itself, and that those rational and ethical norms on
which man is in constant dependence cannot become
"naturalized" under pain of losing their critical
function. Lastly, there is an "efficient causality"
about Taylor's theistic postulate by virtue of which
there is instilled in man an awareness of rational,
ethical, and esthetic norms of perpetual validity
even as this same postulate becomes the directive impulse and the goal of moral endeavor.

Moral Value--and the difficulties of standardization. At the outset, it may be recognized that there
are two factors that compete with any attempt to stan-
dardize value-claims: the subjective factor and the
normative aspect. Acknowledgment of these difficulties is proper in the light of what Taylor's task
must be in overcoming subjectivism and defending a
norm that guarantees universality and necessity.

The subjective factor. In the nature of the case,
it is people who make valuations. That is to say,
they declare worth to exist and it is manifest that
they mean that the worth exists for them or for some-
body. Now, while there appears to be an objective
element present in this observation, the declared
value is always screened through the one making the
valuation. Thus, the subjective factor becomes prominent. The subjective factor becomes increasingly
emphasized when it is observed that the same valuations are not made by all persons with that sort of
consistency of agreement with which descriptions of
space-time objects are made. That is to say, one
does not write off as a personal preference a disagreement about price, distance, weight, size, number. Disagreements there are, to be sure in these areas, but
they can be settled by the appropriate application of
tests and measurements. And it may well be a case of
question-begging to say that there are real

12

disagreements in the area of differences in moral eval-
uations--the question of their objective status not
yet being certainly determined. Indeed, the subjective aspect of valuations is noticeably increased by
the proportionate lack of the usual criteria--or, perhaps, any criteria--for the resolution of differences
in moral valuations. It has been this feature that
has so markedly supported the non-cognitive theories
of ethics.

The intimacy, however, of the subjective factor
in the making of moral valuations does not imply an
identity. That is to say, it still may be true that
there is an objective aspect to the moral valuation in
a way comparable to the objective aspect that is virtually undeniable in the cases of judgments about
price, distance, weight, size, and number; for in
these cases, too, there is the person as subject making the decision. Indeed, to recognize the necessary
role that a person as subject must play in any judgment is to discover, perhaps, the element of truth
that the "subjectivity" of valuations plays.

The normative aspect. If the subjective factor
has proved difficult because of the feeling that personal preferences were taking the place of objective
reference, the normative aspect offers a difficulty in
the opposite direction, viz., that a too-decided claim
on objectivity is made--and a claim, moreover, that so
by-passes the usual criteria of verifiability as to
prepare a near-perfect triumph for the noncognitivists.

What does one do with the notion of "ought" when
its only justification is to be found within the descriptive world or not at all? It is particularly when
the "ought" manifests itself in a corrective way that
the conflict is felt between its pronouncement and that
of the descriptive order of things. In what meaningful
sense can it be said that the descriptive order of
things "ought" to be other than it is? This is not
language appropriate to science that investigates and
pronounces upon the physical world. But man is in
some sense a part of this physical world. How then
may it be said meaningfully that his acts, thoughts,
and states of being "ought" to be other than they are?
If, however, "ought" does not manifest itself as a corrective word, even the physical world can admit of its
application in the sense of probability or natural consequence. Given the accuracy of our generalized laws
of nature in their descriptive sense and add to them

13

assumptions of uniformity, the observation that events "ought" to turn out the way they do appears to be conformable to common usage and violates none of the natural meanings that we associate with the word.

It is, rather, when ideas of duty and moral rightness are employed that the genuinely moral sense of "ought" confronts us and is demanding of some form of justification. At this point, we are in the realm of normatively employed rules or principles wherein, in the case of a plurality of such rules or principles where conflict is either real or possible, some order of precedence is agreed upon. This is the realm of the normative in moral value, but it does not help or advance insight to appeal to what is as a matter of fact the accepted norms of a social group; the real demand is that of demonstrating through analysis and critical discrimination the various meanings that are implicit in our assumptions and what eventually is their justification. This goes beyond the merely normative aspect of moral value and becomes metaethics.

That there is an intimate relation between normative ethics and metaethics would seem to be clear. To call attention to this intimacy of relation is to warn against two tendencies: (1) to occupy oneself with appeal to actually practiced and believed-in norms--avoiding the analysis and justification of these norms as an enterprise too distant from the vital demands of the ethical life, and (2) to involve oneself in analysis of meanings and logical justifications of meaning without coming back to the fundamental obligation of applying the justified and clearly articulated meaning to human living. In the case of (1), there is a tendency towards brute, unanalyzed factuality; in the case of (2), there is the tendency of withdrawal to a merely conceptual preoccupation that appears to bid farewell to what in ethics has justified the phrase "practical reason."

In emphasizing the roles that normative ethics and metaethics play in relation to each other, it is proper to acknowledge in a section dedicated to comment on classical views of moral value one special difficulty that inclusion of the traditionally normative aspect of ethics brings in its wake. It is the problem that arises in the application of the norm--with two invidious tendencies attached: one tendency, that of articulating the norm so broadly as virtually to

14

deprive it of any practical application; the other, that of so sharply articulating its sphere of application as to fall prey to an excessive narrowness and arbitrariness. Eventually, it would appear, one must come to grips with this dilemma and attempt to supply a content to the norm that does not lack in practical specificity nor fail of proper generalization. To uncover the arbitrariness of specific norms is the triumph of one form of ethical skepticism; to exhibit an empty universal is the triumph of another.

The scope of the moral dimension. The impact of the problem of moral value has not arisen within any one epoch of human history nor in any one locality. It is a safe venture that of all of the characteristics that come close to qualifying as essential to man, the sense of an ethical responsibility must rank with the highest. This, of course, is not to say that this sense of ethical responsibility has always been honored in the personal deportments of those who have nurtured it as an unconscious presupposition; rather it is perpetuated as implied in all cases while rendered explicit in many. When St. Paul remarks, "When the Gentiles who have not the law do by nature what the law requires,...They show that what the law requires is written on their hearts, while their conscience also bears witness and their conflicting thoughts accuse or perhaps excuse them...,"[21] he is pointing to an analogous case of a partially implicit, partially explicit, testimony to an inheritance of a sense of moral value. It is this exhibition of virtual ubiquity that presents an effect that justifies that search and analysis that will identify its true cause. In summary, I have noted in these remarks on the general theme of moral value the following: (1) certain difficulties with which the understanding of moral value has been burdened, viz., subjectivism, and its lack of any account of the objective features of moral value, and the normative aspect, with its sometimes hasty and arbitrary willingness to establish those very objective references; (2) I have noted the role that metaethics plays, viz., that of analyzing and seeking justification for the varied proposals of the normativists; (3) I have thought it well that in the final adjudication the normative aspect of moral value and the metaethical aspect be not sundered but allow the normative to perform the role of supplying

---

21. Rom. 2:14-15 (RSV)

the principles for the analysis of the metaethecist; and (4) I have indicated briefly that the scope of the exhibition of the consciousness of moral value throughout human history together with the virtual mandate that has accompanied that consciousness to fulfill duty and moral rightness is a universal effect that demands a cause equally universal for its explanation.

Preview of the following chapters. In the sections to follow a development is pursued that is progressive and systematic. In Chapter II, because Taylor's concern in his discussion of moral value has constant reference to formalism on the one hand and to the ethics of consequences on the other, it was thought well to preface the subsequent chapters by a review of these two positions--particularly as they have been represented by Kant and by Mill. The sharp rejoinder to all forms of normative ethics had already made itself felt in the Oxford circles and Taylor took notice of it in his article "Science and Morality." Inclusion of "Emotivism," together with Taylor's observations, therefore, becomes a part of this review.

The chapter on the relation of moral value to existence insists on their conjunction. It is here basically that Taylor finds foundation for his attack on subjectivism. Value and existence are so intimately related, so interfused in the experience of man's history, that the strongest impulse is given to theory to follow action in the matter of recognizing that a rigorously imposed disjunction would destroy meaning at all levels of the esthetic, the ethical, and the rational.

The chapter on moral value and time allows Taylor to develop his thesis that time is the form of the moral life. Here, paralleling to some extent the divisions of McTaggart who distinguishes two different series in the time order, viz., the series of merely before and after, and the series of a past, present, and future, Taylor, building on the second of these series, sees their meaning contributing to the possibility of time's significant unity by the moral thread of conative exhibition that, in running through them, at the same time, unites them.

The discussion on moral value and evil reveals Taylor placing great significance upon the experienced confrontation with a moral ought. In the vast domain of literature on ethics, Taylor finds, only Plato and Kant ("though two of the greatest") have emphasized human sinfulness and wickedness as essential character- istics of evil--and in so doing have indicated most clearly a dependence upon an externally imposed moral mandate. The phenomenon of evil is encountered at personal and impersonal levels, but at no level can it properly be denominated "evil" without committing a sort of "naturalistic fallacy" unless a supernatural reference is implied. Taylor finds no promise of so- lution in theistic finitism--a suggestion that merely postpones the problem or repeats a naturalization of evil. Although the Absolute and God are identified for Taylor and although therein is discovered the ul- timate locus of moral value, this Absolute God is not to be considered ethical per se because "it is already all that ethical life consists in striving to become."

In Taylor's defense of freedom (libertas arbi- trii, indetermination, the doctrine of the "open mind"), Taylor moves from free thought to free will. The strategy of Taylor's exposition and defense of freedom lies in subsuming the freedom of moral choice under the freedom of rational choice. And because it is of the very nature of rationality to be free, the freedom of moral choice, in principle, is guaranteed. Motives are never sufficient causes, but at best reas- onable incentives. The determinist is placed in the position of practical contradiction in that while holding that his conclusions are the effects of a one- for-one relation to antecedent events, he is, never- theless, disposed to regard his conclusions as poss- essed of truth and validity--a conclusion, Taylor be- lieves, meaningless on the determinist's fundamental assumptions. The freedom thus claimed at the rational and ethical levels is supported when analysis of na- ture reveals a certain lateral or immanent support to Berkeley's and Hume's affirmation of the passivity of ideas. Nature reveals itself as radically disconnect- ed and contingent.

Immortality grounds primarily, for Taylor, in the nature of moral obligation--a doctrine reminiscent of Kant and, for Taylor, emphasizing both the moral and intellectual aspects of man that give to man

> his unique meaning and his sense of worth and his
> hope for commensurate goals along the line of the

same advance. It is not mere immortality as such
but an immortality that is structured with the
essential moral thrust of its earlier begin-
nings--to which will now be added the promise of
continuance in that very value-participation that
has given man essential meaning.[22]

A principle of argument guides Taylor that is reminiscent of Aristotle, viz., "We may fairly argue from the
reality of a function to the reality of an environment
in which it finds its use." The secular-temporal
scene reveals implications of dependence upon a larger
dimension of right, or, in other words, the manifest
evidence of a function is there for which the purely
secular-temporal scene is no proper environment. Supporting this argument is Taylor's dualism--even "inter-
actionism"--of the mind and body together with an exposition of "self-identity" along the lines of a
purely "formal" continuity.

Taylor's exposition on moral value ends with God.
Indeed, as remarked in the beginning of Chapter VIII,
"It is recognized that the gradual emergence of God as
the ultimate presupposition of thought has been the
eventual point to which each of the preceding chapters
has come." "The challenging restriction," that has
disputed the reign of theistic philosophy is identified by Taylor as a too narrow conception of experience. Kant, it is allowed, asked the right question,
viz., What kind of a world must exist in order to account for the knowledge we have? And the answer Kant
gives, it will be recalled, was such as to expand the
conception of experience beyond that radical disconnectedness, that ultimate pluralism of discrete impressions of Hume. Similarly, Taylor recognizes the
"compounded" nature of experience, and, in seeking out
its principle of unity, is forced to go beyond sensory
experience to knowledge of that ground of experience
that arises upon the occasion of experience, but is
not reducible to experience. To this end, both the ontological and the teleological arguments are brought
to bear upon the discussion--with their respective en-
dorsements of the unique modality which is Mind.

---

22. These words repeat in Chapter VII of this work and
    are here inserted to give emphasis not only to
    Taylor's commitment to immortality but to his oth-
    er emphasis (of Chapter IX) on the essentially
    "conative" disposition of the human person.

BRIEF CHRONOLOGY OF MAJOR EVENTS

1869   Born at Oundle in Northamptonshire,
              December 22.

1887   Entered Oxford University.

1891   Elected a Fellow of Merton.

1896-1903   Lecturer in Greek and Philosophy at
              Owens College, Manchester.

1899   Won the Green Moral Philosophy Prize at
              Oxford.

1900   Married Lydia Jutsum Passmore.

1901   Re-elected a Fellow of Merton.

_____   THE PROBLEM OF CONDUCT.

1903-1908   Professor of Philosophy at McGill
              University, Montreal.

1903   ELEMENTS OF METAPHYSICS.

1908-1924   Professor of Moral Philosophy at the
              University of St. Andrews.

1908   PLATO

_____   THOMAS HOBBES.

1911   EPICURUS.

_____   VARIA SOCRATICA.

1912   ARISTOTLE.

1924-1941   Professor of Moral Philosophy at the
              University of Edinburgh.

19

1924	HUMAN MIND AND WILL.
____	ST. THOMAS AQUINAS AS PHILOSOPHER.
1925	PLATONISM AND ITS INFLUENCE.
1926-1928	Delivered the Gifford Lectures at the University of St. Andrews.
1926	PLATO: THE MAN AND HIS WORK.
1927	DAVID HUME AND THE MIRACULOUS.
1928	A COMMENTARY ON PLATO'S TIMAEUS.
1929	THE PROBLEM OF EVIL.
1930	THE FAITH OF A MORALIST. (The Gifford Lectures)
1933	SOCRATES.
1934	PHILOSOPHICAL STUDIES.
1938	THE CHRISTIAN HOPE OF IMMORTALITY.
____	Death of Mrs. Taylor.
1941	Retired from the University of Edinburgh.
1945	DOES GOD EXIST?
____	Died in Edinburgh, October 31.

CHAPTER II - CLASSICAL VIEWS OF MORAL VALUE

The brief reviews of the following positions provide a backdrop of general recognition of certain influential philosophies. Two of them have attempted to defend the cognitive aspect of moral value (though dividing on the question whether such defense is to be discovered in experience or independent of experience) and a third has attempted to deny the meaningfulness of any such attempt. Added clarification of Taylor's own position is gained through the instrumentality of his comments on this broader range of value-interpretation. The range itself thus envisioned is promising, forcing as it does Taylor's comments on the ethics of consequences (teleological theories) as well as the ethics of formalism. In addition, Taylor's reply to the "Logical Analysts" serves to recognize the claim that in neither of the two systems of ethics mentioned can a coherent defense be managed, that, in both, meaning has strictly speaking been abandoned.

To each of these attitudes toward the claim of a normative science, Taylor concedes an element of truth. To the logical analysts who claim not to be able to find verification for the claims of a normative science in experience, Taylor grants their contention; however, not ethics alone, but rationality as well must be surrendered if radical experience is not in dependence upon universals that transcend it. To formalism that endeavors to identify the normative aspect of ethics with a principle of rationality that secures universality and necessity, Taylor grants such a need as a necessary condition for the normative needs of ethics, but contends that the specifics of ethical mandate cannot be deduced from such formal principle. To the more experientially-oriented ethical explanation that looks hopefully to experience to find the norms of ethical obligation, Taylor grants the propriety of involving oneself deeply and seriously in the affairs of human action, but in neither the ends

21

of human action nor in the pleasures or pains of attaining those ends does Taylor find the principle of
duty or obligation. Experience, for Taylor, does not
permit us to rise above the psychologically descriptive; the "ought" of obligation cannot be found in the
"is" of descriptive fact. One cannot deduce an imperative from an indicative sentence. Therefore, for Taylor, if the locus and direction of normative value in
the ethical dimension must be taken seriously and if
it cannot be found in either formalism or experience,
taken separately, then there is no other solution,
Taylor believes, than to recognize the existence of
the locus of normative value above experience yet ad-
dressing itself to experience in terms of a categorical imperative.

While the range of Taylor's considerations given
to writers who have dealt with the problem of moral
value is considerable, special attention is given to
Mill and Kant--as perhaps representing most forcibly
the claims of a teleological and formal ethics respectively. The consideration given to those writers
whom Taylor simply identifies as the "Logical Analysts" is done without naming their representatives.
Although the burden of Taylor's defense of his philosophy of moral value is a positive one and becomes explicit through the attention he gives to the subjects
of the succeeding chapters, his remarks on Mill and
Kant are valuable in that the weaknesses alleged to
hold in these positions allow opportunity for Taylor's
own position to appear. Following, therefore, are
brief statements on Mill and Kant together with Taylor's evaluations. Then, the position of Ayer follows with Taylor's reaction to a total disclaimer of
cognitive meaning in any claim of moral value as a
normative science.

Utilitarianism. There is one form that the
teleological ethic has taken that is foremost among
the systems of ethics that appeal to consequences as
the fundamental principle of its justification. John
Stuart Mill stands to the teleological ethic with much
the same strength that Kant stands to formalism. Because Taylor remarks adversely on the ethic of conse-
quence--and particularly singling out Utilitarianism--
it is proper to give a special consideration to Mill.

There can be no doubt that Mill understands the
ethical question a meaningful one noting that "From

22

the dawn of philosophy, the question concerning the
summum bonum or, what is the same thing, concerning
the foundation of morality, has been accounted the
main problem in speculative thought"[1] and moving
quickly and surely to emphasize the consequence-type
of ethic, declares, "All action is for the sake of
some end; and rules of action, it seems natural to
suppose, must take their whole character and color
from the end to which they are subservient."[2] The
constraint built around this "end" will be for Mill
the force of a general law, he remarking that with regard to the intuitive and the inductive schools of
ethics "both agree that the morality of an individual
action is not a question of direct perception, but of
the application of a law to an individual case."[3]
"Proof" of this "ultimate end" of ethics, for Mill,
"cannot be proof in the ordinary and popular meaning
of the term. Questions of ultimate ends," Mill goes
on to say, "are not amenable to direct proof."[4] It is
not health, nor pleasure, nor even utility, in themselves, that carry the sense of proof, but rather the
back-sweep of the special efficacy and causality of
these words as they are made to apply at the widest
possible human experience. It is in this sense of extending the applied beneficence to the widest possible
coverage that Mill's utilitarianism will ultimately be
dedicated.

The essence of this position is declared by Mill
to be as follows:

The creed which accepts as the foundation of morals Utility, or the Greatest-happiness Principle,
holds that actions are right in proportion as
they tend to promote happiness, wrong as they
tend to produce the reverse of happiness. By
happiness is intended pleasure and the absence of

---

1. John Stuart Mill, MILL'S ETHICAL WRITINGS, edited
    with an Introduction by J. B. Schneewind, (New
    York: Collier Books, 1965), p. 276.

2. Ibid., p. 277.

3. Ibid.

4. Ibid., p. 279.

pain, by unhappiness, pain and the privation of pleasure.[5]

Pleasure, however, is an ambiguous word and so those who endeavored to reduce pleasure to a system of quantification must have found. Mill, however, is not victimized by this reduction to quantification, but declares,

> It would be absurd that while, in estimating all other things, quality is considered as well as quantity, the estimation of pleasures should be supposed to depend on quantity alone.

And again,

> ...we are justified in ascribing to the preferred enjoyment a superiority in quality so far outweighing quantity as to render it, in comparison, of small account.[6]

So far, then, is this not "a doctrine worthy only of swine," "It is better to be a human being dissatisfied than a pig satisfied, better to be Socrates dissatisfied than a fool satisfied. And if," Mill adds, "the fool or the pig are of a different opinion, it is because they only know their own side of the question. The other party to the comparison knows both sides."[7]

The quality of pleasure being duly recognized, the scope of pleasure is greatly enlarged and humanized. Not only, as we have seen, does the utility creed promote happiness, but happiness means pleasure and the absence of pain. And when this fundamental position is declared to be "not the agent's own greatest happiness, but the greatest amount of happiness altogether," we discover that a basis has been laid for the summary declaration that "the end of human action" as thus portrayed "is necessarily also the standard of morality."[8]

---

5. Ibid., p. 281.

6. Ibid., p. 283.

7. Ibid., p. 284.

8. Ibid., p. 286.

These are important words and Mill is not unaware that the source of <u>obligation</u> of this "standard of morality" must be <u>identified.</u> Mill writes,

> The question is often asked, and properly so, in regard to any supposed moral standard, What is its sanction? what are the motives to obey it? or, more specifically, what is the source of its obligation? whence does it derive its binding force? It is a necessary part of moral philosophy to provide the answer to this question.[9]

The sanctions Mill finds in both external and internal considerations. Of the external sanctions of which Mill declares "it is not necessary to speak at any length"[10] there is meant

> ...the hope of favor and the fear of fellow creatures, or from the Ruler of the universe, along with whatever we may have of sympathy or affection for them or of love and awe of him, inclining us to do his will independently of selfish consequences.[11]

Because these considerations provide no reason for Mill "why all these motives for observance should not attach themselves to the utilitarian morality as completely and as powerfully as to any other,"[12] Mill turns to the internal sanction as the truly determinative source of consideration for the solution of the source of ethical obligation. Mill defines this area of sanction as follows:

> The internal sanction of duty, whatever our standard of duty may be, is one and the same--a feeling in our own mind, a pain, more or less intense, attendant on violation of duty, which, in properly cultivated moral natures, rises in the more serious cases into shrinking from it as an

---

9. <u>Ibid.</u>

10. <u>Ibid.</u>, p. 301.

11. <u>Ibid.</u>

12. <u>Ibid.</u>

impossibility.[13]

And again,

> The ultimate sanction, therefore, of all morality
> (external motives apart) being a subjective feel-
> ing in our own minds, I see nothing embarrassing,
> to those whose standard is utility, in the ques-
> tion, What is the sanction of that particular
> standard? We may answer, The same as of all
> other moral standards--the conscientious feelings
> of mankind.[14]

For Mill, were it not for the fact that the above delineated "essence of Conscience" were

> all incrusted over with collateral associations,
> derived from sympathy, from love, and still more
> from fear, from all the forms of religious feel-
> ing, from the recollections of childhood, and of
> all our past life, from self-esteem, desire of
> the esteem of others, and occasionally even self-
> abasement,[15]

the simpler and truer conclusion of a morality grounded
in utility and an obligation grounded in "a subjective
feeling in our own minds" would, Mill believes, be apparent to all. Quite independent of the question whether moral feelings are innate or acquired, Mill points
to the social feelings of mankind:

> ...there is, Mill declares, this basis of power-
> ful natural sentiment, and this it is, which,
> when once the general happiness is recognized as
> the ethical standard, will continue the strength
> of the utilitarian morality.[16]

Mill is thus seen to be in dependence upon what
he conceives to be a powerful sense of social unity
and one that "tend(s) to become stronger, even without

---

13. Ibid., p. 302.

14. Ibid., p. 303.

15. Ibid., p. 302.

16. Ibid., p. 305.

express inculcation from the influences of advancing civilization."[17]   It is only a sense of "savage independence" that militates against this more natural tendency toward a happy social unity.   One's personal philosophy is justified in keeping pace with this social tendency with the result that Mill's utilitarianism becomes the conceptual expression of society's normal goal.

UTILITARIANISM is an optimistic writing.   However retarded may be man's development into a realization of that state of "the greatest amount of happiness altogether," Mill never places in the way of that development any competing irrational factor that could militate against society's implicit optimism.   There is no competing <u>surd</u> in the universe that dualistically sets up an opposition that might overcome ethically striving man.   It is true that nature is sometimes castigated by Mill as no proper example for man to follow; but neither is it true that man must follow it.

> Any condition, therefore, which is essential to a state of society, becomes more and more an inseparable part of every person's conception of the state of things which he is born into, and which is the destiny of a human being.[18]

Because the utilitarian argument is most severely tested at the point of its account of obligation, it is worth-while to review what Mill regards as "psychologically true" of human nature in its account of what constitutes a proof of the principle of utility.   Mill writes:

> Questions about ends are, in other words, questions what things are desirable.   The utilitarian doctrine is that happiness is desirable, and the only thing desirable, as an end, all other things being only desirable as means to that end.   What ought to be required of this doctrine--what conditions is it requisite that the doctrine should fulfill--to make good its claim to be believed?[19]

---

17.   <u>Ibid</u>.

18.   <u>Ibid</u>.

19.   <u>Ibid</u>., p. 309.

To this question, Mill answers in a famous passage:

> The only proof capable of being given that an ob-
> ject is visible is that people actually see it,
> the only proof that a sound is audible is that
> people hear it, and so of the other sources of
> our experience. In like manner, I apprehend,
> the sole evidence it is possible to produce that
> anything is desirable is that people do actually
> desire it.[20]

For Mill, this ultimately desired end is not an
end without moral constituents; rather, even virtue,
for those who love it disinterestedly, "is desired and
cherished, not as a means to happiness, but as a part
of their happiness."[21] Indeed, virtue may even be
considered so patently a good in itself that in the experience of the individual it is nothing less than "a
psychological fact"[22] permitting one to hold "that the
mind is not in a right state, not in a state conformable to utility, not in the state most conducive to
the general happiness, unless it does love virtue in
this manner."[23] Thus is emphasized the fact that Mill
is counting heavily on the accuracy of psychological
description of human behavior to give the "proof" he
needs of his principle of utility together with the
involved notion of obligation.

Nor is the "psychological fact" abandoned when
the idea of justice is under analysis. For all tendencies to the contrary, tendencies that invest justice with "an inherent quality," "something absolute,"
and "generically distinct from every variety of the
Expedient,"[24] Mill's final word is a reduction:

> ...the sentiment of justice appears to me to be
> the animal desire to repel or retaliate a hurt or
> damage to one's self or to those with whom one

---

20. Ibid.

21. Ibid., p. 310.

22. Ibid.

23. Ibid.

24. Ibid., p. 315.

sympathizes, widened so as to include all persons, by the human capacity of enlarged sympathy, and the human conception of intelligent self-interest. From the latter elements, the feeling derives its morality; from the former, its peculiar impressiveness and energy of self-assertion.[25]

Taylor's comments on Mill's Position. Fundamentally, the discontent that Taylor feels with Mill's account is a reflection of Taylor's conviction that "one-level" theories of reality and morality are stifled by their immanent categories.[26] Even Mill's theistic finitism is never really pressed into the service of preserving those "external" norms without which we surrender the ability to indulge in critical discrimination. Truth and validity become unmanageable as they become identified with our personal psychology. Our deepest source of appeal or reference when the demand is to give an account of ethical obligation is, according to Mill, to point to the "internal sanction of duty, ...a feeling in our own mind, a pain, more or less intense."[27] And again, "The ultimate sanction...of all morality.../ is / a subjective feeling in our own mind.[28] And Taylor observes,

it is, or should be, the stalest of ethical commonplaces that emotions cannot be classified into the morally good and the morally evil, and that if "motive" is taken to mean what Mill took

---

25. Ibid., pp. 326-327.

26. "We have to note," writes Taylor, "that no pure 'immanence' philosophy can take morality with sufficient seriousness. Denial of divine 'transcendence' leads to Pelagianism in theory and self-righteousness in practice, denial of divine 'immanence' to antinomianism. In moral practice you cannot rise above your present level by 'lifting yourself by your own hair,' nor by the strength of an ideal which is only 'your own ideal.'" Taylor, THE FAITH OF A MORALIST, Series I, p. xiv.

27. Mill, ETHICAL WRITINGS, p. 301.

28. Ibid., p. 302.

it to mean, the "feeling" which "makes a man act" by breaking down a kind of mental and moral inertia, the view that the worth either of our acts or of our character is a function of our "motives" would be the ruin of coherent thinking about conduct.[29]

Taylor does not merely measure Mill (and secularism in general) against the standard of the Platonic and Christian view, but he pauses to remember that if the Platonic and Christian view is true, "it must follow 'as the night the day' that we dare not lose our hearts to any temporal good," and, if, on the other hand, the secularists are right (a concession that Taylor cannot possibly concede under pain of stultifying his account of what justifies "right"), "the moral business of man will be wholly to secure the temporal goods, the only goods there are, in the life of 'practice.'"[30]

So much of that life that is lived under a sense of obligation is a life of sacrificial living and giving that Taylor wonders at the moral tone of a secularism that can find no higher justification for sacrifice than that of a "subjective feeling."

> There will be plenty of room, /Taylor remarks/ for care and delicate discrimination in preferring the higher of these goods to the lower, but there will be no justification for any sacrifice of temporal good to "some better thing" which, on the theory, must be an illusion.[31]

Not that the secularist fails in the practice of sacrificial living, but by his calculation no sacrifice is justified that does not exchange one secular good for a secular better, or at least the probability of such an improved exchange.

Not wishing "to gain an easy victory over a 'man of straw' of our own manufacture," Taylor endeavors to

---

29. Taylor, THE FAITH OF A MORALIST, Series II, p. 99.

30. Taylor, THE FAITH OF A MORALIST, Series I, pp. 283-284.

31. Ibid., p. 284.

state the secularist position "in the form most favourable for the secularist":

> Under the head of secular good, then, I mean now to include everything which can be really attained and enjoyed in human life on the assumption that human life means no more than existence as a member of the human species, under the conditions imposed on us by place and time, as part of the "complex event we call nature." Thus I mean the phrase, in the present context to cover not only physical health, longevity, comfort, and fertility, but the minimizing of all the ills which attend disharmony with our physical environment and friction with other members of our social world, as well as the satisfaction of our interests in natural knowledge and sensible beauty. The ideal proposed for valuation shall be that of the progressive establishment of a human society on earth in which want, disease, physical pain and mental deficiency are, if not abolished, at least reduced to a minimum, offences against the social order obviated by a sound tradition of human good will and solidarity, and art and natural science made the delight and business of everyone. It may fairly be said that such a conception of a secularist ideal, if it sins at all, sins rather by generosity than by niggardliness.[32]

Having painted a picture of "our secularist's ideal thus to include everything which has been recognized as good by a high-minded Utilitarianism like that of Mill, or an aesthetic Utopianism like that of William Morris,"[33] Taylor is prepared to put what he considers the test question, a question, that is to say, that measures the highest of what the secularist ideal can provide against an insistent demand of man's nature.

> The question I wish to propound is this: ...is the perpetuation of such a social life of humanity through the largest vista of successive generation a wholly satisfactory final aim for moral

---

32. Ibid., p. 286.

33. Ibid.

aspiration? Or do we all feel that, if the Utopia became fact, we should not, after all, have attained the best, that there would be missing something elusive and impossible to define precisely, and that something _the_ thing without which everything else loses _its_ value? May it not be that all along, if we make humanitarianism, however generous, our supreme rule of life, we are living only for a second-best?[34]

"'There comes a time,' writes Aldous Huxley, 'when one asks even of Shakespeare, even of Beethoven, is this all?'"[35]

The position for which Taylor would plead is not that where assumed virtue asks its appropriate reward in "felicity beyond this life"; indeed, Taylor expresses a doubt whether such "has ever been the real inspiration of the hope of immortality in any mind of the first order," to which he charitably adds,

> Even those who speak most often of "reward" probably do their own thought an injustice by the language in which they express it. And I might remark in passing that, when this language is employed, it is most often not used by a man about himself. It is much more common to say of another that he has "passed to his reward" than it is to speak of myself as expecting my reward, and the fact should not be insignificant to a really acute psychologist.[36]

It must be emphasized that Taylor's concern in the above position against variants of secularism does not arise from the observation that many nurture a wish for some vague continuance of whatever values they may seem to honor at the moment and with which they hope to identify in some more permanent state. Actually, even this minimal appreciation of a true value-complex would not be for Taylor objectionable

---

34. _Ibid_.

35. Quoted by Huston Smith, THE RELIGIONS OF MAN, (New York: Harper & Row, Publishers, 1958), p. 23.

36. Taylor, THE FAITH OF A MORALIST, Series I, p. 287.

within the limits of its realization of the truth for
which he is arguing, but, to repeat, the weight of his
argument does not rest upon a foundation so fragile.
Rather, the above protest to secularism in general and
to Utilitarianism in particular stems from what is the
major contention of Taylor in his treatment of every
phase of the value-problem. This "major contention"
is that man is in actual dependence upon a host of
ideals, norms, presuppositions, and these enter into
the warp and woof of his thinking and his acting.
They are the ultimate rationales without which neither
logical values, esthetic values, nor ethical values,
have the slightest coercive cogency. The meaning of
fact is always within the universal (the eternally
valid insight of Plato) and it is for this reason,
fundamentally, that "all secular good" is declared
"defective."

When the validating principle of ethics is declared to be found in the consequence of an act or in
the consequence of a program of action, it really matters little whether it is the individual or society in
the large that receives the value. When the value of
the act or program terminates upon the individual or
society, it may be conceded that it is pleasant that
it did so. It is not equally clear that the individual was under any obligation to see that this value
terminated upon him or society. The touchstone of obligation becomes fundamental in this sort of inquiry.
The suspicion, however, that because obligation is not
discoverable within the simple fact of a value termi-
nating upon either an individual or society, that
therefore, there is no obligation attendant upon this
conjunction, is not justified. It does, indeed, appear
to be an established conviction that a matter of indifference concerning the welfare of the individual or
society is not an ethical position. What appears to
be the situation is that while one may not be indifferent to the welfare of the individual or society, the
emergence of a theory of ethical egoism or ethical
universalism may possibly not carry with it the saving
of obligation in the sense that this obligation is implicit or entailed in the consequences of the act or
program. Now, this indictment would not justify the
assertion that no obligation can be discovered upon
the occasion of acts of self-preservation or upon the
occasion of acts of societal benevolence. But, that
obligation is discoverable upon the occasion of variations of the teleological ethic does not entail the

33

conclusion that the obligation is to be identified with the particular consequence. If, therefore, indifference to the welfare of the individual or society is not proper, nor is it possible to find obligation in the consequence itself, may it not be that the principle of obligation is being covertly applied--having been borrowed from a source independent of the consequence? To answer this question affirmatively, is essentially Taylor's position--a position that borrows from the general Platonism that impregnates nearly all of his thought. Taylor would agree with the essential rightness of a person's honoring that selfhood that has been vouchsafed to him. He would similarly agree that there is a duty to the larger society. There are, furthermore, proper and ordinate values that both the individual and society may legitimately seek and which it may be everyman's duty to assist them to attain. But, that the obligation so to do can be discovered within the act itself Taylor denies.

It should follow from the above alleged inability to find obligation in a teleological ethic that no amount of permuting the possible characteristics of the consequences of the act or program can improve it. That is to say, the hedonistic complexion that many teleologists give to their ultimate goals--in terms of that too flexible word "pleasure"--only serves to narrow the argument to whatever specific meaning "pleasure" is made to bear. Pleasures of physical sensation, pleasures of spiritual exhaltation: however insistent these may be as identifying with those values that supremely count for any individual, their principle of obligation does not appear to be given in the pleasure itself; and if we have any genuine duty to provide such pleasures to ourselves or to our larger societal environment, it might be the case, as Taylor declares, that the sources and ground of the obligation must be discovered elsewhere.

Self-protection, it is frequently observed, is a compelling motive. Undoubtedly, this is true. Advantage has been taken of this fact to give to the egoistic form of the teleological ethic a psychological basis. Thus it is affirmed that self-choosing, self-preference, is a fundamental "law" of human behavior. This is then appealed to as justifying, not only the direct seeking of positive benefits for the individual, but an equally egoistic explanation of why benefits are sought for others. Thus every act is given an ultimately egoistic reference. I merely point out here the usual reply that however true as a <u>psychological</u> premise, it is wanting in terms of <u>obligation</u> (which is <u>an</u> <u>ethical</u> <u>concern</u>) and may justify the remark that we are no longer maintaining a discussion about an ethical category.[37] Psychological egoism may be a case of identifying one meaning of "ought" with the "ought" of probabilities and consequence, but, as we have recognized, this is not the "ought" of ethical concern, but of biology, or maybe physics.

A final remark on Utilitarianism (really a par- ticularization of Taylor's general position on any form of naturalism) is that once the Utilitarian rec- ognizes the real locus of values from which he is un- consciously drawing his fervent affirmations about duty and obligation he may return to his occupation of securing the "greatest amount of happiness altogeth- er." There is a generously provided place in Taylor's account of moral value--both personally and socially-- for the greatest possible exhibition of concern. But there is also a need to be able to answer questions about <u>the</u> <u>principle</u> of obligation in matters of ethi- cal value and it is of concern to Taylor that the Uti- litarian with his subjective basis of reference cannot offer an adequate reply. The Utilitarian is in the position of fulfilling the role of a moralist and not knowing why.

<u>Formal</u> <u>ethics</u>. By implication if not by direct declaration one of the first principles of a moral maxim is that it must be capable of universalization. However much a teleological ethic may have been jus- tifiably indicted for failure to support a genuine moral obligation, it must be agreed that it tried. The analyses of both ethical egoism and ethical uni- versalism endeavor to show that their best insights lay claim to no significant exceptions. It is

---

37.   William K. Frankena writes, "...it seems to me... that prudentialism or living by the principles of enlightened self-love just is not a kind of <u>mora-</u> <u>lity</u>. As Butler said, and as Kant would have agreed, prudentialism is 'by no means...the moral institution of life' even though it is 'a much better guide than passion.' This is not to say that it is immoral, though it may be that too, but that it is nonmoral." ETHICS, (Englewood Cliffs, New Jersey: Prentice-Hall, Inc., 1963), p. 18.

fundamentally because of their dependence upon what in
the last analysis is an empirical foundation that Taylor judges them to have failed. Investigations of
descriptive anthropology and psychology may give one
what as a matter of fact is happening, but it does not,
seem capable of showing at the same time and for the
same reasons that it ought not to have happened--
"ought", that is to say, in a moral sense. Such investigations Taylor insists, confuse the matter of experience with the form by which alone interpretation
may be accomplished and justified.

Despite the limitations that have been alleged as
true of the ethical system of Kant, it is virtually
beyond dispute that of those who have supported a formalism in ethics he is unique. Beyond and beneath the
vast spectacle of the sociology of moral behavior,
Kant aimed at discovering what he called in the Preface to his FOUNDATIONS OF THE METAPHYSICS OF MORALS
"the supreme principle of morality."[38] This must be a
standard good for the judging of all moral conduct
such that the claim to universalization can never be
in doubt. But as Hume demonstrated, and as Kant was
willing to accept, this principle in which universality was accompanied by necessity is not a principle
that one can discover in empiricism. If discovered at
all, it may be found upon the occasion of experience,
but never reducible to it. Nothing other than rationality fulfills this demand. "The supreme principle of
morality," therefore, in order to fulfill both universality and necessity, must rest upon rationality.
Right action must conform to rational action and although the will may be motivated by many causes to
act toward ends that may be adjudged objectively moral, the motivation itself is moral only if it is out
of deference to rational principle.

As I shall show in Chapter III, Taylor will make
a determined effort to show that value grounds in actuality. But here, too, Kant's moral value--though
fundamentally guided by no principle save that of ra-
tionalist--expresses the "inwardness of virtue" and
thus grounds in human personality expressing itself

---

38. Immanuel Kant, FOUNDATIONS OF THE METAPHYSICS OF
     MORALS, Translated with an Introduction by Lewis
     White Beck, (New York: The Liberal Arts Press,
     1959), p. 8.

according to rational form. With Kant also--as for
Taylor--not only does man's morality ground in what I
referred to as "inwardness of virtue," but the ultimate ideal of rational morality suggests a highest
good in terms of concrete actualization (and thereby
for Kant, a divine ground): "...whence do we have the
concept of God as the highest good?" Kant asks, and
answers, "Solely from the idea of moral perfection,"--
and adds, "which reason formulates a priori and which
it inseparably connects with the concept of a free
will."[39]

    Like Taylor, Kant appears to recognize in duty's
voice an imperative that he cannot escape. "That
there must be such a philosophy," Kant declares, "is
self-evident from the common idea of duty and moral
laws."[40] And again, "...unless we wish to deny all
truth to the concept of morality and renounce its application to any possible object, we cannot refuse to
admit that the law of this concept is of such broad
significance that it holds not merely for men but for
all rational beings as such."[41]

    Kant does not deny that moral philosophy can have
its empirical part. Indeed, there may be said to be
an applied morality in much the same way that there
can be claimed to be an applied mathematics. But,
"...the pure philosophy of morals (metaphysics) can be
distinguished from the applied (i.e., applied to human
nature), just as pure mathematics and pure logic are
distinguished from applied mathematics and applied logic."[42] However much applied morality may be conceded, what Kant calls "the supreme principle of morality" may never be disjoined from the principle of pure
rationality. "If," as William K. Frankena says, "one
takes a maxim as a moral principle, one must be ready
to universalize it."[43] Kant seeks to make good this
need for the preservation of the essence of moral

---

39. Ibid., p. 25.

40. Ibid., p. 5.

41. Ibid., p. 24.

42. Ibid., pp. 26-27.

43. Op. cit., p. 17.

37

principle by laying down the only basis on which such "universalization" may be grounded. "Everyone must admit," says Kant, "that a law, if it is to hold morally, i.e., as a ground of obligation, must imply absolute necessity." And this "ground of obligation... must not be sought in the nature of man or in the circumstances in which he is placed, but sought a priori solely in the concepts of pure reason."[44] Only here is "the guide and supreme norm," only here, "the supreme principle of morality."[45] And mere conformity to this law is never enough: the morally good act must be done for the sake of the law. "Otherwise the conformity is merely contingent and spurious."[46]

The imperative. Kant defines: "The conception of an objective principle, so far as it constrains a will, is a command (or reason), and the formula of this command is called an imperative."[47] Now imperatives, for Kant, command either hypothetically or categorically. In the case of a hypothetical imperative, some end is proposed to one's desire to the end that one would say, "If you desire to have this end, then you must do thus and so." But, there is no necessity that you possess this end. The nonpossession of this goal does not involve any contradiction. In the case of the categorical imperative, no end is contemplated as the justifying feature of the impulse to honor it. But, failure to honor the categorical imperative is to involve a contradiction in principle. As Kant states it,

> The hypothetical imperative...says only that the action is good to some purpose, possible or actual....The categorical imperative...declares the action to be of itself objectively necessary without making any reference to a purpose.[48]

---

44. Kant, FOUNDATIONS OF THE METAPHYSICS OF MORALS, p. 5.

45. Ibid., pp. 6 and 8.

46. Ibid., p. 6.

47. Ibid., p. 30.

48. Ibid., pp. 31-32.

It is this utterly rational aspect of the categorical
imperative that unifies its command and permits Kant
to declare,

> There is, therefore, only one categorical impera-
> tive. It is: Act only according to that maxim
> by which you can at the same time will that it
> should become a universal law.[49]

It is sometimes alleged that Kant veers from his
pure intention of maintaining a thoroughly formal ethic. The allegation points to the fact that Kant is
willing to show that the result of breaking faith with
the categorical mandate is a demonstrable breakdown of
the individual or society when the decision to part
from duty is universalized. I think that this is to
misinterpret Kant. The fact of the ultimate destruction is in the thorough irrationality of the present
proposal. The contradiction awaits consequences only
for him who cannot perceive the destruction in the premise. The point is closely related to Plato's "justice
writ large" in the REPUBLIC. Injustice was no less injustice when proposed for the individual, but, for
those who cannot see the certain collapse in the individual, there remains the fruit of that irrationality
that opens to inspection at the "results" level.
Again, as in geometrical demonstration, one may need
the result of an elaborate deduction to see that the
truth represented by the deduction is indeed demonstrable. But, it is no less true when concealed in the implicit form of the postulational field.

Kant is, therefore, the strongest at that point
where he recognizes that unless the moral dimension is
to be discarded utterly it must be defended at a level
that guarantees universality and necessity. And, because no form of the teleological ethic can underwrite
that guarantee, it follows that it must be sought elsewhere. The clearest and only alternative is that of
the principle of rationality itself. It would appear
that Kant has demonstrated that formalism as thus exhibited has contributed a necessary condition to the
question of obligation.

Taylor's comments on Kant's position. There are

---

49. Ibid., p. 39.

two questions that Taylor raises with regard to Kant's system: (1) Does Kant provide for the sufficient condition as well as the necessary condition for positive and specific duties? (2) Are positive duties deducible--even in principle--from the categorical imperative?

Taylor entertains a lively doubt regarding the presence of a sufficient condition in Kant's system, and remarks,

> Not to dwell on the point that there seems to be a great deal of very bad morality which would stand the Kantian test quite successfully, it is obvious that at the best the test will only secure you against "flagrant sin." It would, for instance, have been no use whatever to any British citizen anxious to know how he ought to use his vote at the last General Election. Before voting for the Labour candidate or the Conservative candidate a man certainly ought to ask himself whether he would be doing right by voting for either, or again by abstaining from using his vote, but no "universalising" of any maxim would decide that very pertinent question.[50]

Actually, the two questions mentioned above--and which are considered in their separateness by commentators on the Kantian system--are very closely related. If the universalized maxim were capable of specifying the narrower duties, that in itself is virtually identical with a deduction of the specifics from the universal.

There is an uncertainty in Kant, however, at the point where it is asserted that positive duties are deducible from the categorical imperative. It sounds as if Kant did indeed yield himself to this actual deduction--in principle if not in fact. For example, when Kant declares that "...the pure philosophy of

---

50. Alfred Edward Taylor, "Some Features of Butler's Ethics," PHILOSOPHICAL STUDIES (London: Macmillan & Co., Limited, 1934), p. 319. Frankena agrees. "Kant's view," he writes, "would be more defensible if he held merely that maxims which cannot be willed to be universal laws are immoral, rather than that maxims which can be so willed are duties." William K. Frankena, Op. cit., p. 27.

morals...can be distinguished from the applied...just as pure mathematics and pure logic are distinguished from applied mathematics and applied logic,"[51] there is at least a strong suggestion that even as every application of mathematics can be foreseen in principle, as a possibility, so every application of morality can be similarly foreseen (and hence deduced), in principle. It can at least be affirmed with some certainty that the intimacy between what Kant calls "the supreme principle of morality" and his hope that that principle could be applied to a living ethical situation gives ground to the supposition that Kant intended the possibility of a deduction _in principle_ if not in fact. And so Taylor takes him to have meant and remarks that "Where Kant went wrong...was...in inconsistently proceeding to write as though the matter of our various specific duties could be deduced from the formal principle of dutifulness.."[52] This manner of writing, however, Taylor concedes, may be a matter of

> question whether Kant really meant what his language has been held to imply. His illustrations may be intended not as deductions of specific rules of duty from the general principle, but merely as evidence that these rules, taken to be already known, will all fall under the principle. Since he professedly presupposes as the basis of the whole reasoning the "common notion of morality," he may fairly be assumed to have taken it for granted that his reader would not need to learn for the first time from him that a man must not defraud, steal, commit murder or adultery.[53]

Taylor finds this to be true in Kant's treatment of adultery. Kant rules out adultery

> since adultery--breach of bed-vow--is only possible where marriage, as a status with definite rights and duties, exists, and thus he who wills to permit himself an act of adultery is willing

---

51. Immanuel Kant, FOUNDATIONS OF THE METAPHYSICS OF MORALS, p. 24.

52. Alfred Edward Taylor, "Science and Morality," PHILOSOPHY, XIV (1939), p. 41.

53. _Ibid_.

at once that there shall and shall not be respect for the rule of marriage.[54]

To this Taylor replies that

the advocate, or practicer, of complete sexual promiscuity would come out unscathed from the application of the test. His "maxim" is simply that the sexual side of human life should be, like many other sides of it, left unregulated to the "inclination" of the parties concerned, and there is no more logical absurdity in such a maxim than there is in the proposal to leave men to please themselves at which end they will break their breakfast-eggs, or whether they will starch their collars.[55]

And Taylor asks, "How, then, comes he never to have reflected that his highly extolled criterion of right and wrong cannot well be sound, since it fails in so obvious a case?" And the answer: "The only answer I can find is that Kant all along tacitly assumes that he already knows what sort of acts are right, before he resorts to his criterion."[56]

I sense that the difficulty to which Taylor is drawing our attention in Kant is that of Kant's tendency to make symmetrical the relation of rationality to morality. Entirely alert to the need of placing ethics upon a basis of universality and necessity--always the first principle of the rational--he is led to assume that one may begin with the rational and deduce an ethics from it. If, perhaps, he had really attempted to do just that, the impossibility of the effort might have been clearer. Taylor observes that "his analysis has yielded the equation: right = rational."[57] And Taylor continues,

...to justify his own claims for his criterion, Kant ought to have done something very different.

---

54. Taylor, THE FAITH OF A MORALIST, Series I, pp. 58-59.

55. Ibid.

56. Ibid.

57. Ibid.

He ought to have shown that by applying it we can
work out an unambiguous moral legislation in
vacuo for a community of human beings destitute
of all tradition. If we recognize that this task
is insoluble in principle, and that consequently
pure "rationalism" in the strict Cartesian sense,
rigid deduction of conclusion, through a chain of
"clear and distinct" ideas, from principles "evident by the natural light," is as impossible in
ethics as in other fields of thought, we must admit that it is a matter of moment for morality
itself what the unproved "synthetic" postulates
of a moral tradition are. In point of fact,
these postulates which give a moral tradition its
distinctive individual quality are not found, in
the history of civilization, existing apart from
the religious tradition of the community; they
are part and parcel of it.[58]

Such being the case, it is Taylor's position, as
against Kant, that

The injunction of the good will, to which we must
at all costs be loyal, cannot be digested, in advance of experience, into an articulated code of
precepts sufficient to guide the upright man's
steps, no matter how slippery the places where
they have to be set.[59]

Instead, Taylor adopts a middle position as touching
the central affirmations of both Mill and Kant. Kant
is right, according to Taylor, in looking for the
principle of obligation above experience--for how else
can it command experience? But Kant was wrong in
thinking (if indeed he did) that he could deduce the
particulars of an applied morality from his "Imperative." And Mill (as we have noted above) is wrong,
according to Taylor, in not seeking in any sense a
principle of obligation above experience.

Taylor, believing that "There could probably be
no worse preparation for right action than careful

---

58.   Ibid., p. 60.

59.   Ibid., p. 156.

anticipatory study of systems of casuistry,"[60] yet
holding to an a priori principle of obligation, is
left with the hope of being able to make dutiful application of this transcendental principle of right
when the moment arrives for decision in a particular
situation. Analogous to someone whose ability in
chess is very great, and in whose general ability to
make a strong move you have great confidence, but
whose specific move you may not be able to anticipate,
is the ethical situation in which you have complete
assurance of the existence of a universal standard of
right but must await the emergence of a situation in
experience before you can know precisely how the moral
principle will be applied in detail. Or again, as
Taylor states it,

> ...I may and do often feel a justified confidence
> that my friend will acquit himself as a man
> should in some situation of great "difficulty"
> and grave responsibility....In many cases, es-
> pecially when my friend is a man of riper experi-
> ence and higher moral wisdom than myself, his de-
> cision may take me by complete surprise. He may
> do what I expected he would refuse to do, or may
> take a line different from any of those which pre-
> sented themselves to me in anticipation. My con-
> fidence is not that I know what he will do, but
> that I know that whatever he does will be seen,
> after it has been done, by myself or by others of
> more penetration, to be the act of an upright and
> honourable man.[61]

There is something about Taylor's repeat warning
that you cannot know in advance of "some unrehearsed
contingency" what particular line of conduct will be
forthcoming as the right ethical response that is reminiscent of what contemporary analysts in the field of
ethics call "Act-deontology." It would be misleading,
however, to allow this extreme ethical nominalism to
suggest the real position of Taylor. Undoubtedly, his
position--to continue the contemporary nomenclature--
is a "Rule-deontology," but it is at least worth noting that much of the claimed merit of both positions

---

60. Ibid.

61. Ibid., p. 157.

is preserved by Taylor in that while <u>radical</u> "Act-deontology" is always false--on the grounds that it is devoid of that universal without which facts have no assignable meaning--it may truly be only upon the occasion of a specific circumstance that the "rule" has opportunity to manifest itself. Although it is true, according to Taylor, that

> Whatever our agreements or disagreements with Kant, there is one lesson which we have all learned from the CRITIQUE OF PURE REASON, that logic, functioning in vacuo, can tell us nothing of the course of events,[62]

it is equally true that brute facts are mute facts and the position of the "Act-deontologist" is condemned as having no standard to which it can appeal except the act itself.

It may very well be the case that the specific positive duty differs with circumstance even while the formal aspect of duty remains undeviating. Duty, in this sense is abstract but only in the formal sense that all universals are abstracted from their particular representations.

> What is the one thing "fitting and proper" in one practical situation may be the very thing which is least fitting and proper in another, and the very same principle may therefore demand sharply contrasted courses of action.[63]

Taylor compresses the principle of his argument into this formula: "A principle implied in all rules of right action cannot itself be identical with any of the rules."[64] Applied,

> Two men, for example, may have exactly the same conception of the obligations imposed by marriage and the same respect for them, yet the one may be led to regard it as his bounden duty to marry and leave children behind him, the other, on the same

---

62. <u>Ibid.</u>, pp. 152-153.

63. Taylor, "Science and Morality," p. 38.

64. <u>Ibid.</u>

principles, to hold it his duty to live in life-long celibacy, and both may be right. A king, for instance, who knew that his death without a son would probably lead to a war of disputed succession would be doing wrong not to marry, even though all his strongest personal preferences were for the life of virginity; a soldier, an explorer, a Christian missionary, whose work could be ruined by the cares and distractions of domestic life, would be equally doing wrong in marrying, however difficult he found the practice of continence. Since the principle of dutifulness (or whatever other name we may give to our ultimate moral principle) is equally illustrated by the marriage of the one and the celibacy of the other, the principle, taken by itself, cannot prescribe either.[65]

Taylor is giving recognition to the governing presupposition of duty--a moral category without which the specifics of genuine ethical action lose their ethical meaning. It is in the light of this abstractly governing universal that ethical meaning is preserved for specific actions--regardless of how conflicting these specifics may be. That is to say, an action that is adjudged morally right (even though in fact it may be morally wrong) derives the alleged meaningfulness of its moral predication from a quietly presupposed fountain of moral meaningfulness. The ultimate principle, however, is never captured as a direct object of inspection like the specific act to which it allegedly pertains; rather, it becomes validated as a presupposition in a kind of indirect awareness when appeal is apparently inevitably made to it in the countless implicit and explicit appeals of ethical discourse.

Taylor has recognized the rational element in the Kantian imperative as a necessary condition for the moral life. But, being a universal, transcending human experience, prescribing the law of duty to us, it

is not ours in possession; it is a reason which is only communicated to us in part and gradually, and that in proportion to our faithfulness to the

---

65. Ibid.

revelations already received. We do not make the
law, we discover it and assent to it, and it is
for that reason that no attitude to the source of
the law is adequate, unless it has passed from
mere respect into that unqualified reverence
which we know as adoration and worship.[66]

Thus does Taylor's willingness to bow before what he
considers to be a true principle of obligation, a
moral mandate that is the source of every genuine ethical impulse, take him across the line of the merely
ethical to the side of what Taylor considers to be
that presupposition of all ethical concern: God.

Ethics as "emotive." We have noted that within
the schools of thought that attempt to preserve for
moral value a normative significance, two divisions
are outstanding: the teleological and the formal.
There is, however, another school of thought that has
surveyed the claims of writers on ethics regarding the
normative aspect and returned a negative verdict.
Thus, for example, A. J. Ayer, speaking for a school
that Taylor refers to as the "Logical Analysts,"
writes:

> we shall set ourselves to show that in so far as
> statements of value are significant, they are or-
> dinary "scientific" statements; and that in so
> far as they are not scientific, they are not in
> the literal sense significant, but are simply ex-
> pressions of emotion which can be neither true or
> false. In maintaining this view, we may confine
> ourselves for the present to the case of ethical
> statements. What is said about them will be found
> to apply, mutatis mutandis, to the case of aesthe-
> tic statements also.[67]

Ethical philosophy is permitted by Ayer only when it
consists of "propositions which express definitions of
ethical terms, or judgements about the legitimacy or

---

66. Taylor, THE FAITH OF A MORALIST, Series I, p. 159.

67. Alfred Jules Ayer, LANGUAGE, TRUTH AND LOGIC,
     (New York: Dover Publications, Inc., (N.D.),
     pp. 102-103. /First edition published in 1936;
     second edition, in 1946/.

possibility of certain definitions."[68] Propositions describing the "phenomena of moral experience, and their causes" Ayer assigns to psychology or sociology. Exhortations to moral virtue are "but ejaculations or commands which are designed to provoke the reader to action of a certain sort," and "actual ethical judgements"--however they are to be classified--"are certainly neither definitions nor comments upon definitions, nor quotations,"--with the resultant conclusion that "we may say decisively that they do not belong to ethical philosophy."[69] This allows Ayer to say, "What we are interested in is the possibility of reducing the whole sphere of ethical terms to non-ethical terms. We are enquiring whether statements of ethical value can be translated into statements of empirical fact."[70] Such, Ayer understands, is the effort of both subjectivism and utilitarianism. The first reduces ethical terms to non-ethical feeling; the latter, to non-ethical pleasure, happiness or satisfaction. And he rejects both attempts as fundamentally inconsistent with the conventions of our actual language. "Our contention," Ayer says, "is simply that, in our language, sentences which contain normative ethical symbols are not equivalent to sentences which express psychological propositions, or indeed empirical propositions of any kind."[71] Ayer wants to be clear that it is the normative aspect that is suspect in any attempted translation.

> It is only with normative ethics that we are at present concerned; so that whenever ethical symbols are used in the course of this argument without qualification, they are always to be interpreted as symbols of the normative type.[72]

Though admitting that an "absolutist" or "intuitionist" theory of ethics would undermine the whole of the argument, Ayer finds a difficulty so formidable

---

68. _Ibid._, p. 103.

69. _Ibid._

70. _Ibid._, p. 104.

71. _Ibid._, p. 105.

72. _Ibid._, p. 106.

within their position as to eliminate it completely as a competitor. It is the fact that conflict of opinion about what is a genuinely ethical position among the absolutists or intuitionists has no recourse by which it can be settled. As Ayer puts it,

> A feature of this theory, which is seldom recognized by its advocates, is that it makes statements of value unverifiable. ...unless it is possible to provide some criterion by which one may decide between conflicting intuitions, a mere appeal to intuition is worthless as a test of a proposition's validity.[73]

Fundamental ethical concepts, therefore, are declared "unanalyzable" and "mere pseudo-concepts."[74]

The "emotivist" character of this analysis comes most clearly to the fore in Ayer's explanation of a typical ethical "proposition":

> ...if I say to someone, "You acted wrongly in stealing that money," I am not stating anything more than if I had simply said, "You stole that money." In adding that this action is wrong I am not making any further statement about it. I am simply envincing my moral disapproval of it. It is as if I had said, "You stole that money," in a peculiar tone of horror, written it with the addition of some special exclamation marks. The tone, or the exclamation marks, adds nothing to the literal meaning of the sentence. It merely serves to show that the expression of it is attended by certain feelings in the speaker.[75]

The implication of this, for Ayer, is that no factual statement has been made and, therefore, there is no question possible about the rightness or wrongness of the declared sentiment.

Taylor's comments on the "Logical analysts."
Ayer wrote the first edition of LANGUAGE, TRUTH AND

---

73. Ibid.

74. Ibid., p. 107.

75. Ibid.

LOGIC in 1936[76] and Taylor, writing in January of
1939, while not mentioning anyone by name, had his eye
on "The thesis of our contemporary 'logical analysts.'"[77]

"Can there be such a thing as a moral science, or
a science of morality?"[78] asks Taylor, and in so asking, raises Ayer's issue of a normative science in
ethics. Provisionally, Taylor answers that a science
must satisfy two conditions: "the assertions which
compose it must be true, and they must be systematically interconnected by logical interrelations."[79] It
appears certain that Ayer would deny both. He plainly
declares that

> If a sentence makes no statement at all, there is
> obviously no sense in asking whether what it says
> is true or false. And we have seen that senten-
> ces which simply express moral judgements do not
> say anything.[80]

Neither could Ayer's position admit of a systematic interconnection of logical interrelations because "emotive" or "feeling" responses do not admit the linkage
possible to genuine proposition, and Ayer insists that
"in every case in which one would commonly be said to
be making an ethical judgement, the function of the
relevant ethical word is purely 'emotive.'"[81] The issue is sharply drawn.

Taylor states the issue succinctly when he summarizes:

---

76. Revised in 1946 to which was added an introduction
    in which Ayer amended certain of his views in the
    light of criticism.

77. Taylor, "Science and Morality," p. 45.

78. Ibid., p. 24.

79. Ibid.

80. Ayer, LANGUAGE, TRUTH AND LOGIC, p. 108.

The very possibility of moral science, then, depends on our ability to make assertions about
right, and wrong, moral good and evil, which are
(a) true, and (b) systematically interconnected.
It follows that "moral science" must at once be
confessed to be an impossibility unless we can
dispose of a doctrine which is beginning to be expressly formulated by some of the more thoroughgoing of our "logical analysts."[82]

Taylor scrutinizes the strong disjunction employed by the "Analysts." Why may it not be possible
to have a language that while possessing emotional
overtones still admits of truth and falsity? Is this
so much different than what almost all of our language
accomplishes?

A sane man in the waking state does not commonly
make any statement, however true it may be, unless it is relevant to a situation which interests him, and interest has always its emotional
side, though it may not always be very prominent
in consciousness.[83]

This observation calls attention to a virtual uniformity of conjunction of the "emotive" with any "normal
sane utterance." The purpose, however, is not to call
attention to the speaker's emotion, but to some objective fact. It appears to be close to obvious that I
can become emotionally involved with any number of objective situations without undermining the objectivity
of the situation itself.

So much, I think, would be admitted by Ayer. The
real question is whether sentences with ethical predicates may claim objectivity within the range of merely
ethical predication. Taylor, assured that the mere
presence of an emotional element in our utterances
does not preclude the element of thorough objectivity,
now proceeds to narrow the inquiry to whether the ethical predicate, as such, excludes such objective reference.

---

82. Taylor, "Science and Morality," p. 25.

83. Ibid.

Ayer concedes that ethical terms have more function than that merely of expressing feeling. "They are calculated also to arouse feeling, and so to stimulate action."[84] To this suggestion, Taylor makes the reply that "...if a discourse of moral exhortation or rebuke proves effective in arousing the 'emotive' reactions desired by the speaker, it succeeds only because the listeners assume the ethical predicates employed to have a meaning and to be truly applicable to the conduct to which they are being applied."[85] And, continuing this thought, Taylor remarks,

> Your audience will not be got to "boo" at a man by describing his conduct as wicked if they either attach no meaning to the word wicked, or give it a meaning which is not true of the conduct you are describing. I shall not be wrought to a frenzy against a Nero by denunciation of his cruelty unless I already believe that evil is a word with a meaning, and that cruel deeds have the character, whatever it is, meant by the word evil. If I thought it simply unmeaning to call any conduct evil, or false to call cruelty in particular evil, your eloquence would leave me unmoved. Purely meaningless language, recognized

---

84. Ayer, LANGUAGE, TRUTH AND LOGIC, p. 108.

85. Taylor, "Science and Morality," p. 30. Taylor writes, "I happen just to have re-read John Grote's EXAMINATION OF THE UTILITARIAN PHILOSOPHY. I have found myself often agreeing with the 'ethical' propositions of the writer, sometimes dissenting from them, but only rarely perplexed by a sentence which appeared to make no assertion, true or false. And in these rare cases I seemed always to have reason to believe that my perplexity was due merely to some failure in the author to put his thought into unambiguous language. It is possible, of course, both that I may have mistakenly thought some of his assertions true when they were actually false (or vice versa), and that I may have thought his meaning ambiguous where it is not really so, but is it credible that through a work of 350 pages I should have been deluded into the fancy that there was meaning, true or false, when in fact there was none at all?" Ibid., p. 29.

as such, will have no "emotional" effect on the hearer, except possibly to bore him.[86]

Taylor's recognition of "morality in conduct as the subject-matter of a possible science" does not in itself commit us to any particular view or any particular approach on "methods appropriate to that science."[87] In general, the nature of the field of inquiry will determine the method appropriate to the science of that field. The implied criticism of the "analysts" by Taylor is that this distinction has not been kept clearly before them--with the result that they have made the unreasonable demand that the field of ethics conform to the physical sciences in matters of what constitute meaningfulness and verifiability. The question becomes, "whether a moral fact and a natural, or physical, fact are facts of the same kind."[88]

The question that appears to be essential to the field of natural fact (or physical fact) "has always the form quid eveniet si....? If events of a certain kind occur, then what?"[89] In contrast,

> The orientation of "reason in its practical use" is entirely different. Here the question to be answered is never quid eveniet, but always quid mihi faciendum, quod vitae sectabor iter? The moral problem, which even the most resolute logical positivist can never ignore in the management of his daily life, however stoutly he may deny its existence in his speculative theory, is never what will happen "of itself" if a given situation is allowed to develop itself, but always what kind of a change I am to introduce into it.[90]

Out of a mere cause and effect phenomenon in the physical world, one can never derive a moral maxim. It may very well be true that the moral maxim arises upon the

---

86. Ibid., p. 31.

87. Ibid.

88. Ibid., p. 32.

89. Ibid.

90. Ibid., p. 34.

occasion of the cause and effect event, but it is never identical with it--nor is it meaningless because it cannot be reduced to the physical components.

> No precept or maxim of any conceivable moral code is a mere answer to the question what will come of it if certain persons are placed in a situation of a certain type; the question which even the most "naturalistic" of moral theories sets itself to answer is the very different one in what situations I am to place myself and others, what direction I am to give to any initiative. I want to know, for example, not what will come of it _if_ I revenge affronts and what if I pardon them, but _whether_ I am to pardon them or to revenge them.[91]

The principle that we instinctively seek as the directive in questions of what ends I ought to seek cannot be identical with our particular desires of the moment--desires that are frequently brought before the tribunal of questioning as to _whether_ they are worthy of that principle instinctly recognized to dominate.

> If we are to have any rules we can trust for the direction of life, there must be a discoverable standard of "appropriateness" wholly independent of the particular tastes and antipathies of any of us or all of us. ...And this clearly means that our knowledge of this standard must be strictly _a priori_; it cannot be derived from any information furnished by experience about the ends which men actually set themselves to attain, since it is itself the standard by which we adjudicate on the "fittingness" of all of them.[92]

The distance then, that yawns between the scientific mood on which the positivists would build and the ethical mood which they cannot treat without distortion, according to Taylor, is formalized when Taylor introduces their contrasting principles as follows: "the scientific law is...a 'universal' which is strictly immanent in the particular instances and in each of

---

91. _Ibid_.

92. _Ibid_., p. 37.

them";[93] the moral principle (as stated above) is "a
priori" and (here, Taylor, quoting approvingly from
the work of Professor Augusto Guzzo), "'separate' and
'transcendent' εἶδος which Plato ascribes in the RE-
PUBLIC to the 'good' and in the SYMPOSIUM to the
καλόν ."[94] And of this latter principle of transcendence Taylor concludes by emphasizing that

> relevant moral fact is inherently different in
> character from relevant natural, or physical
> fact, and that, on this ground, it is idle to
> look to the procedure of the natural sciences for
> light on the methods proper to a moral science.[95]

Taylor had begun by asking whether there can be
such a thing as a moral science and, in general, he
limited his answer to the restrictions that a science
depends upon our ability to make assertions that are
true and that are systematically interconnected. He
is now ready to answer the question: "Morality can be
the subject-matter of 'science' only if 'science' be
understood in the widest sense of the word to mean inquiry into the systematic interconnection of
truths."[96] The "interconnection" is not disputed:
that is simply identical with our interlaced, interwoven social system; the possibility of ethically predictable events being also "true" is, Taylor believes,
attested by the ordinary consensus of mankind who make
appeal both expressly and by implication to what Taylor explains is the universal and a priori and transcendent presupposition of the moral life. Either a
priorism may legitimately be admitted into the language and meaning of ethical discourse, or we must be
satisfied to have morality reduced to mere description
of human behavior. But, to the latter no one appears
to yield in practice. Therefore, for Taylor, a priorism may legitimately be admitted into the language and
meaning of ethical discourse--an admittance that is a
fulfilling condition of the presupposition of ethics
as a normative science.

---

93. Ibid., p. 39.

94. Ibid., p. 37.

95. Ibid., p. 43.

96. Ibid.

CHAPTER III -- MORAL VALUE AND EXISTENCE

A persistent effort continues through nearly all
of the writings of Taylor to establish the relevance
of standards by the aid of which the rationality of
philosophic effort can be maintained in every human
concern. Not least is the effort to show the presence
of objective norms in the area of a value-philosophy.
To that end, Taylor endeavors to re-establish the conjunction of value with actuality for only by so doing,
Taylor believes, can the variously expressed relativ-
isms in ethical philosophy be overcome. Nor is this
an easy undertaking: the allegation that value knows
a conjunction with existence is threatened by a cru-
dity of identification at one level and a vaporous
mysticism at another. Taylor's effort, therefore, will
be that of elucidating the meaning of conjunction.

"Value" is virtually indefinable. "In its widest
use," writes Frankena, "'value' is the generic noun
for all kinds of critical or pro and con predicates,
as opposed to descriptive ones, and is contrasted with
existence or fact."[1] Something of this range is indicated by Frankena when he notes that

> Philosophers from the time of Plato had discussed
> a variety of questions under such headings as the
> good, the end, the right, obligation, virtue,
> moral judgment, aesthetic judgment, the beauti-
> ful, truth, and validity. In the nineteenth cen-
> tury the conception was born--or reborn, because
> it is essentially to be found in Plato--that all
> these questions belong to the same family, since
> they are all concerned with value or what ought

---

1. William K. Frankena, "Value and Valuation," THE
ENCYCLOPEDIA OF PHILOSOPHY. Edited by Paul
Edwards. VIII (1967), p. 229.

to be, not with fact or what is, was, or will be.[2]

Thus value manifests its ubiquity even as it defies definition.

Value, as understood by Taylor, is a measuring device, a norm, a yardstick, a standard, a universal. And while it is apparently essential for human discourse and, at a deeper level, meaning itself, it cannot itself be caught within that ray of illumination that it sheds upon the above mentioned concerns of human experience. It may be used--indeed, it must be used--but our most perfect knowledge of it is gained through an indirect awareness of its true nature. This "true nature" is revealed indirectly and always in part, but even the indirect awareness of its necessary involvement does not permit an exhaustive knowledge of its full nature.

But Frankena noted another aspect of value that is also given a universal recognition--though the final decision concerning the proper assessment of this peculiarity is by no means equally agreed upon: the distinction between value and existence. Thus Frankena distinguishes "critical...predicates" from "descriptive ones" and "what ought to be" from "what is." And, in an important sense, this is a helpful distinction because it calls attention to the normative significance of value that no empirical fact can be said to claim. For Taylor, it is as important to be able to distinguish where fact and value differ as it is important to avoid that ultimacy of disjunction that is frequently insisted upon.

The primary importance in the difference between value and existence lies in the normative aspect that is unique to value and is the sole means of interpreting existence. Thus, in principle, interpretations of existential situations that call for esthetic, ethical, or logical distinctions must invoke the normatively separate domain identified by Frankena above by the "aesthetic judgment" and "the beautiful," by "moral judgment" and obligation," and by "truth" and "validity." At the same time, however, the danger to which

---

2. Ibid.

Taylor will call attention is in that rigid disjunction of value from existence that would prohibit anything from being called beautiful, good, or rational.

Taylor begins his discussion of actuality and
value by asking,

> Does morality...involve any presuppositions which
> point beyond itself? Does it supply its own
> raison d'etre? If not, does it receive its miss
> ing completion in the activities, however we de
> fine them, which are commonly called religious?[3]

Clearly, if the disjunction between existential and
ethical meaning is to be granted, ethics must be abandoned as a normative science. Or, as Taylor puts it,

> If this absolute and rigid divorce between fact
> and value can be maintained, it must follow at
> once that there can be no religious, and a
> fortiori no theological implications of morality.
> ...Premises drawn from ethics, being wholly non
> existential, can never yield an existential con
> clusion.

The disjunction between "fact and value"[4] would destroy what is germane to the essence of the religious
affirmation.

> The possibility of genuine worship and religion
> is absolutely bound up with a final coincidence
> of existence and value in an object which is at
> once the most real of beings and the good "so
> good that none better can be conceived," at once
> the Alpha, the primary and absolute source of be
> ing, and the Omega, the ultimate goal of desire
> and endeavor.[5]

Continuing the look at what is the clearest presupposition of religious practice, Taylor writes,

> Religion...certainly rests on the conviction that
> something is absolutely real, or, in plainer

---

3.   Taylor, THE FAITH OF A MORALIST, Series I, p. 24.

4.   Ibid., p. 29.

5.   Ibid., pp. 31-32.

language, is "bed-rock fact." It may be hard to say just what that something is, but it is clear that some existential proposition or propositions must be at the foundation of every religious faith. Every such faith is faith in someone or something, and so presupposes at least certain conviction that this someone or something <u>is</u>, and is a very active reality.[6]

It would appear entirely clear that common practice both declares that esthetic, ethical, and rational evaluations are in fact applicable to existential situations and, further, assumes that communications regarding these conjunctions will be readily understood as fitting and proper. The question will arise whether these commonly held assumptions of mankind correspond to what is defensible at levels of philosophical analysis. It leads Taylor to consider at length the disjunction that is so frequently affirmed between value and reality.

Morality, we are often told, /Taylor writes7, has to do exclusively with values or ideals and is unconcerned with fact or reality. It deals entirely with what "ought to be" to the complete exclusion of what is. A moral conviction is a belief not in the actuality or reality of anything. ...In a word, no ethical proposition is ever existential and no existential proposition ever ethical.[7]

<u>The</u> <u>case</u> <u>for</u> <u>disjunction</u>. Taylor is forced to examine the considerations that possibly have led to this rigid disjunction of fact from value and to evaluate their strength. One such consideration Taylor finds in

Kant's first CRITIQUE, where the purpose of the smashing assault on speculative theology, and, indeed, of the whole DIALECTIC OF PURE REASON, is to divorce value completely from fact by denying that the "ideals" of speculative reason have any contact whatever with genuine knowledge.[8]

---

6. <u>Ibid</u>., p. 28.

7. <u>Ibid</u>., p. 33.

8. <u>Ibid</u>.

It is observed that Kant, in making this denial, breaks with both the Socratic tradition (that taught that "the good and the ought," -- "the supreme principle of evaluations"--provides the structure of the existent) and "the Christian doctrine that God, the source from which all creatures proceed, is also the good to which all aspire and in which all find their justification." But Kant may not have been utterly committed to disjunction, and Taylor remarks,

> ...we all remember Kant's own dismay at the apparent success of his undertaking, and his strenuous efforts, after putting asunder what "God and nature" had joined, to bring the disconsolate halves together again by invoking reason "as practical" to undo the work of reason "as speculative."[9]

Indeed, it is a distinct possibility that the first Critique contained a deliberate preparation for the later work on the "practical" reason--never closing the door to the possible re-conjoining of fact and value when it became necessary to account for the wider range of human experience. Nevertheless, Kant's great contribution may well have suggested to those more sympathetic to the message of the CRITIQUE OF PURE REASON greater justification for the retention of the disjunction of fact and value than did Kant's other contribution in the CRITIQUE OF PRACTICAL REASON suggest their reunion.

Another consideration is the allegation that mere actuality as such does not automatically entail either positive or negative value. Conduct, science, art: some of it we call good, some of it we call bad; nor will the most analytic scrutiny reveal the presence of value in the objective sense that the actuality itself compels assent. Further, our experience of the totality of actuality is far too small to justify with any confidence the generalization that the bad is dependably instrumental in the production of the good. Even assuming much of what evolutionary science would have us assume, about all that we have a right to conclude is that a "fairly steady development along continuous

---

9.   Ibid.

lines"[10] may be observed without that fact in the least implying even a desirable state of affairs to say nothing of moral improvement. And when even the greatest amount of time to which we can justifiably appeal in our evolutionary premise is contrasted with the possibly infinite backdrop of space and time, the conclusion of moral progress becomes a mere expression of optimism, an expressed desire to be guided by our ideals rather than by nature's reals. Progress must, indeed, involve change, but change does not automatically entail progress, and even less so when that progress is of a moral kind. The conjunction of fact with value therefore is at best an "accidental" relation with no clear guarantee that from either fact or value you can cross necessarily to the other. That values are commonly predicated of the actual may be true enough, but that this fact allegedly cannot be depended upon to enforce a conjunction is what backs Taylor to say that he regards it "as the most important problem in the whole range of Philosophy."[11]

The case for conjunction. On the one hand, we have actuality, being, existence, reality; on the other hand, goodness, value. In the total experience of man of which we have knowledge, these groups interfused in a manner suggestive of the fact that they, in some sense, are deeply constitutive of an order of reality that makes their relation more than merely "accidental." Indeed, it is this connection, this relatedness, of actuality and value that is virtually the warp and woof of human experience--with the corollary that he who forgets the intimacy of this conjunction and opts for singleness of treatment in which rigid and radical disjunction is performed upon fact and value is guilty of a false abstraction. In yielding to this disjunction, Taylor says, one abandons, in effect, the truer dimensions of the philosophical effort, aborted are the genuine concerns of man, and descent to trivia is the fruitless and logical outcome.

We noted above that Taylor asks, "Does morality ...involve any presuppositions which point beyond itself?" We note further that Taylor declares, "To

---

10. Ibid., p. 35.

11. Ibid., p. 36.

think of the moral life adequately, we must think of it as an adventure which begins at one end with nature, and ends at the other end with supernature."[12] Whether Taylor can make a plausible case for these goals or not, it remains that an effort will be made to attack the problem of the relation of fact and value from a point of view that is broader than that espoused by the analyst who, however carefully, merely scrutinizes the existential object and concludes that value is no part of its meaning. There is an intimacy between values and reality that, as remarked, makes up the warp and woof of mankind's existence and it is this vital concern that is forced upon the philosophical enterprise that leads Taylor to remark concerning his own participation as follows:

> I cannot reconcile myself to the view that philosophy is a simple pastime for the curious, with the same attractiveness, and the same remoteness, from all the vital interests of humanity, as the solution of a highly ingenious chess problem. If philosophy were really that and no more, I confess I should have small heart for the devotion of life to such "fooling." I am content, with Plato and Kant, to be so much of a "common fellow" as to feel that the serious questions for each of us are "what ought I to do?", "What may I hope for?", and that it is the duty of philosophy to find answers to them, if she can. If none can be found, so much the worse for philosophy, but her incompetence is not to be assumed lightly.[13]

The case for conjunction (continued): Re: concreteness and abstraction. A consideration on the way back from the rigid disjunction of value from fact takes note of the implications of concreteness and abstractions as possible objects of value-predication. Virtue, art, science, health, may be considered in their concreteness or in their abstraction. In their concreteness, we mean "actual virtuous conduct, artistic production, true thinking, healthy bodily functioning of persons conceived as existent, either in fact

---

12. Ibid., p. 124.

13. Ibid., p. 37.

or _ex hypothesi_."[14] These same designations, conceived purely as abstractions, are never the objects
of value-predication. As abstractions, they speak for
the first principle of virtue, or art, or science, or
health, and they possess the merit of possibly contributing a "clear and distinct" idea, but, in themselves, they possess no value, and other than the
clarification that they perform in the act of understanding what the common principle of virtue, or art,
or science, or health is, they perform no service.
This is not to despise their function: they are the
universals needed to sort out the essential and first
principle of particulars and, as such, perform a necessary good that epistemology cannot do without. As Taylor states it,

> These, as the logician studies them, have been
> mentally isolated from the relation to the con-
> crete individual existents in whose lives they
> appear, but it should be evident that in this
> process of abstraction they have been deprived of
> their specific value by being, legitimately
> enough for the logician's special purpose, cut
> loose from "existence."[15]

Thus we might say that while virtue and vice, in their
existential embodiments, have nothing in common, in
their abstractions they do have something in common,
viz., both are "clear and distinct ideas." Thus Taylor states,

> What we commend is not courage or temperence "in
> the abstract," an "universal" concept, but the
> characteristic life of a courageous or temperate
> man. What we condemn is not cruelty or adultery
> "in the abstract," but the characteristic acts
> and desires of cruel or adulterous men. Adultery
> "in the abstract" is good with the only goodness
> an "abstraction" can have; it is an admirable ex-
> ample of a "clear and distinct idea," and that is
> all there is to be said about it.[16]

---

14. _Ibid._, p. 38.

15. _Ibid_.

16. _Ibid._, p. 41.

Does health have a value not shared by disease? If it does, if it is meaningful so to speak, it can only mean that there are living organisms of which this is true or can be true. A universe in which there were no living organisms would be a universe in which there would be no meaning possible to the value of health-- with perhaps the exception that, in abstraction, one might be able to grant meaning to health, but only as then applicable to possible (perhaps future) existen- ces of actual living organisms. As Taylor puts it,

> Health is good is only an abbreviated way of say- ing it is good that organisms should live in a state of health... Pleasure is good means noth- ing, or means that pleasure enjoyed by existents who can feel is good.[17]

At this point, one is led to see that without the existent, there is no real way of retaining the mean- ingfulness of value. The intimacy of that conjunction should begin to make clearer what Taylor means when in the final summary he will plead for the conjunction of value and actuality as a necessary conclusion of that more concrete philosophy of wholeness that has escaped the disabling effects of the abstractions of disjunc- tion.

Care must be taken, however, to note that the in- timacy of conjunction of value and actuality does not issue in a mere identity. "Right" behavior does not arise except upon the occasion of behavior, but beha- vior in itself is not "right" or "wrong." "Health" of body does not arise except upon the occasion of a body, but a body in itself can exhibit neither health nor disease. We may generalize, therefore, and say that though values arise only upon the occasion of ex- istents, the existents in themselves do not exhibit values.

The next step in clarification is to note the role that "knowledge" plays in this intimacy of con- junction. Acknowledging that it is only upon the oc- casion of existents that values arise, we next note that it is only upon the occasion of knowledge of these existents that values arise. "Knowledge," for Taylor

---

17. Ibid., pp. 38-39.

is not the same as "truth." "In a sense," Taylor says, "if there could be, or ever has been, a world without minds or persons, there is a truth about that world. But this is not the 'truth' of which we can intelligently say that it has value."[18] A doubt may be entertained whether this application of "truth" to a mindless world is tenable--a mind seemingly being necessary to give meaning to truth--for to what otherwise would it be "truth"? However, not pausing to dispute Taylor's right to refer to a mindless situation as "true" in some sense, there would appear to be no difficulty in acknowledging that for knowledge itself, there is no question but that a mind is involved. It would therefore appear to be Taylor's position that meaningful predication of values arises only upon the occasion of knowledge of existents, and because minds are a necessary assumption for the possession of knowledge, we can now say that minds are a necessary condition for the meaningful predication of values. And because minds are themselves existential in some sense, we have a doubly reinforced reason to note the conjunction of value and actuality.

"Knowledge of" truth is so much a necessary condition for value that, for Taylor, the value of any of the great writings would immediately cancel upon the cessation of mind. Knowledge of the truth may have value, but in a mindless world there is no knowledge. Taylor writes,

> There would be no reason to ascribe any special value to a printed copy of Newton's PRINCIPIA surviving in a world where there were not, and never would be, any minds to apprehend the meaning of the printed marks, or to the noises made by a gramophone repeating the propositions of the PRINCIPIA on a mindless planet. If we could suppose the gramophone to be started on its work and all existent minds then to be annihilated, we should, I take it, not judge that it made any difference to the goodness or badness of such a state of things whether the event which annihilated the minds also affected the working of the gramophone or not. It would be as reasonable to ascribe "economic value" to a mass of precious

---

18. Ibid., p. 39.

metal supposed to be located somewhere on an unin-
habited and wholly inaccessible planet.[19]

If we are tempted to ascribe value to such worlds, it
is out of deference to some future situation in which
minds again are present.

Taylor has denied that abstractions of virtue,
health, science, art, have any value but that of a
"clear and distinct idea." There is a sense, however,
that such universals do have value: "The only stipulation is that the universal be embodied in rebus, not
the universal post res of the nominalist logicians."[20]
And this "stipulation," it will be seen, is again to
return to the conjunction of value and existents. In
this context, meaningful value-predications will be of
existents that unify under a universal in which they
participate. This recognition of the logical priority
of the universal is fundamental to Taylor's Platonism.
Such universals, or ideas, or forms, are true universals the knowledge of which arises upon the occasion
of an experience with individuals.

What is meant by the conjunction of value and actuality should by now be clearer. Because value is
not to be considered identical with nor entailed by
actuality ("we cannot argue straight away from the actuality of the actual to its goodness"), the position
taken by some for disjunction is understandable even
though it is to be regarded as erroneous and its proponents as "victims of an insidious fallacy of diction, a false abstraction due to convenient but ambiguous habits of speech."[21] Also, because valuation,
of necessity, begins with some person making a value-
judgment, it is understandable that a subjectivism
might have been endorsed as the best explanation of an
involvement of mankind that has so many variations
among the values that are honored. However, the tacit
assumption of those who discourse on ethical, esthetic, or rational themes is that they are communicat-
ing--arguing even!--an assumption that counters a
strict subjectivism by its presupposed, shared norms.

---

19. Ibid., pp. 39-40.

20. Ibid., p. 41.

21. Ibid., p. 34.

More positively, the conjunction of value and actuality involves that sort of "wholeness" that includes existents (perhaps conceived as particulars), universals (but present in rebus), knowledge (that grasps the meaning of the particular by the aid of the universal), and mind (the most prior of all the necessary conditions and active subject in evaluations at whatever level). Noting that we have said that value is predicable only of existents and that mind is a necessary condition for such predication, Taylor now confirms this by saying,

> My point...has a double edge. It is (1) that the truth, beauty, goodness to which we ascribe worth are in all cases "concreted," embodied in individuals of which they are the constitutive forms, and that our ascription of worth is only significant in view of this embodiment of the "universal" in the individual; (2) that in all such judgements of value the reference to personal activities is always more or less explicitly present.[22]

The close relation of the above elements involved in value-judgments contributes to a proper conception of the value-actuality relation. It furthermore permits Taylor to return to the before-mentioned suspicion that values are of an "accidental" character. At this point, Taylor, upon the basis of his developed argument, says, "If value always involves some kind of reference to the activities of persons, it cannot be true that value and existence (or actuality) are only accidentally conjoined."[23] An "accidental" characteristic is one that can be denied without contradiction. But value-judgments cannot be declared of an "accidental nature per se when it is of the very nature of intelligence and appetition to pass (as virtually an essential part of their natures) on those values that are their normal concerns. Borrowing from Aquinas, Taylor affirms, "If there were no intelligence, nothing could have 'truth-value,' if there were

---

22. Ibid., pp. 44-45.

23. Ibid., p. 47.

no appetition, nothing could have value at all."[24]
There is no other function of the rational, the ethical, the esthetic faculties, than that of discriminatory appraisals among value-situations representing
these universes of discourse. What is essential to
the nature of such faculties cannot be considered "accidental"--even though the pronouncements may actually
be in error. Indeed, the very possibility of error
counts on the side of objectivity--as the Ayer-type
explanation of normative ethical value would be the
first to affirm.

   The case for conjunction (continued): Implication of knowledge of value. As we have seen, Taylor
has made a provision for a barren sort of truth--the
kind that describes a mindless planet which he thinks
must be permitted to bear the predicate "true." But
it is not this sort of "truth" (that may be conceivably be permitted) that Taylor includes within the
scale of values. Rather, he speaks of "knowledge of
the true"[25] as the situation that possesses value.
And now he asks us to consider "some of the consequences which seem to follow immediately from the admission of either truths or the knowledge of them into
the list of values."[26] We have already seen that
knowledge itself is a necessary condition for value,
and since all knowledge has some object, that object
may properly be called a truth. Here truths that are
known need not share the barren ignominy of the
"truth" of the mindless planet but partake fully of
that value-scale that is indicated by the fact that
knowledge is involved. Taylor writes,

   A truth, even a truth as yet undiscovered, is a
   proposition, and it should have been quite evident, ever since Plato wrote the Sophistes, that
   to be significant at all, and therefore to be a
   proposition, an utterance must always be, directly or indirectly, an assertion about τὸ ὄν, what
   is.[27]

24. Ibid.

25. Ibid., p. 39.

26. Ibid., p. 48.

27. Ibid.

Taylor's commitment to the Sophistes position is considered of sufficient importance that he elaborates it in some detail. That is to say, if all propositions are about what is, it would follow that value is (at least in some cases) conjoined to existence, because some propositions are about value. Thought, for Taylor, no less strongly than for Parmenides, is about being. It is unfortunately true that when thinking being, the thinking is too frequently disharmonious and confused, but, so runs Taylor's argument,[28] if thought could purify itself of this disharmony and confusion, it would be seen that there is a one-for-one correspondence between thought and thing.

The reason, for Taylor, that values have been imagined to be utterly disjoined from existence is comparable to that other suspicion that formal logic and mathematics are disjoined from existence. To the end, then, of making good the claim for the conjunction of value and existence, Taylor pays some attention to both logic and mathematics. His analysis concludes by declaring: All propositions are about what is. This is easily the case with singular propositions (Legendre is a mathematician) or with particular propositions (some men are mathematicians) for these "are equivalent to groups of singular propositions whose subjects--Legendre, Gauss--are as yet unspecified. But what of universal propositions--from which it is generally agreed subalternate propositions cannot be inferred because universal propositions are said to lack existential import. Does not this conflict with what was said above, viz., that a proposition is an assertion, directly or indirectly, about what is? Taylor's reply is that the "universal"

> reduces to something less than an actual proposition. It becomes what Russell and Whitehead call a "formal implication" not between propositions but between propositional functions. That is, the true meaning of the statement "all men are mortal" can only be given without excess or defect in the form that x is a man implies that x is mortal. This again means, to state it more

---

28. This reasoning is used in Chapter VIII--"Moral Value and God"--where it becomes the basis for a clarification and defense of the ontological argument.

precisely, that "is mortal" is true of any subject of which "is a man" is true. To make a
genuine proposition out of this blank form it is
necessary that we should replace the symbol x,
on both its appearances, by one and the same name
or denoting phrase, indicating one individual
this. Only when we have done so have we passed
from asserting a relation between mere "propositional functions" to asserting a relation between
propositions. And when we take this step, the
propositions which figure in the (now "material")
implication are seen at once to have existential
import.[29]

If the above treatment of universal propositions
is sound, Taylor's thesis that all propositions are
assertions, directly or indirectly, about what is is
unshaken.

The subject of which something is asserted in the
universal proposition /Taylor declares/ is thus
neither a definite collection of determined individuals, nor yet the "universal" or "concept" of
which such individuals are "instances." It is
any individual, known or unknown, of whom a certain statement is true, and what I assert is that
a second statement also will be true of such an
individual. If there should be no such individual, if, for example, there never should be any
actual man, the statement (in this case, that all
men are mortal) seems to me to lose its claim to
be regarded as true.[30]

Indeed, Taylor finds in the statement often made by
logicians that all assertions are equally true of the
null-class an indirect confirmation of his thesis that
only of an existential situation can predicated truth-
value be meaningful. If, that is to say, all assertions are equally true of the null-class, then contrary
assertions are equally true and, therefore, "the distinction between truth and falsity loses its meaning
so far as that subject is concerned; truth and false-
hood cease to be opposed values, and so cease to be

29. Ibid., pp. 48-49.

30. Ibid., pp. 49-50.

values at all."[31] We return to an old dictum that of
nothing nothing may be predicated and, therefore, if
there is to be any predication of value whatsoever, it
must be of an existential situation.

Returning once more to Taylor's assertion that
all propositions are assertions, directly or indirectly, about what is, the question about the status of
mathematical propositions must arise. Serving as they
do in the character of their pure formality and abstraction, in what sense, if any, can they be declared
to conform to the demand that all propositions are
about what is?

This has been a much agitated question from the
days of Pythagoras to the present. It was Pythagoras
that raised the question by asking about the status of
mathematical entities. The problem arises in consideration of the fact that mathematical entities are in
some sense independent of all space-time restrictions
and, at the same time, applicable to space-time reality. It may appear that the answer that Pythagoras
gave was crude and overly simple, viz., that "number"
was the ultimate reduction to which the content of
perceptual experience referred, but, at the same time,
it can hardly be contested that something of the modern development has followed closely the direction of
Pythagoras' thought. It is not merely that mathematical entities are "applicable" to space-time reality;
they appear to be necessary to its interpretation--
especially in physics. This intimate relation between
pure mathematics and the world of experience is testified to by Whitehead.

Nothing is more impressive than the fact that as
mathematics withdrew increasingly into the upper
regions of ever greater extremes of abstract
thought, it returned back to earth with a corresponding growth of importance for the analysis of
concrete fact. The history of the seventeenth
century science reads as though it were some
vivid dream of Plato or Pythagoras. In this
characteristic the seventeenth century was only
the forerunner of its successors. The paradox is
now fully established that the utmost

---

31. Ibid., p. 50.

abstractions are the true weapons with which to control our thought of concrete fact.[32]

In keeping with the direction of Whitehead's thought above may be found Taylor's answer to the question of whether mathematics, too, is expressible in terms of propositions about what is. In principle, we may recognize with regard to mathematics what we have been forced to recognize with regard to universals in general: universals are the ultimate Ideas, Forms, Norms, Standards, by which particulars receive their meaning, their interpretation.[33] In every case, the universal is a formal principle and our grasp of it is by an a priori intuition. Without committing oneself entirely to a defense of the entire structure of the Kantian interpretation of the synthetic-a priori bond in experience, it may at least suggest a general principle, viz., that the knowledge of this a priori dimension comes before us upon the occasion of experience though it is not reducible to the experience.

For Taylor, actuality is sometimes more than perceptual experience; the universals are at least as real as the experience that they interpret and unify. Indeed, because they are the first principles of all interpretation, all meaning, it may be said that they are more real. This does not deny reality to the world of space-time experience, but it indicates the direction that interpretation must take in the universal-particular relation: the particular always looks to the universal for its meaning and interpretation, not the reverse.

---

32. Alfred North Whitehead, "Mathematics as an Element in the History of Thought," THE WORLD OF MATHEMATICS. Edited by James R. Newman. (New York: Simon and Schuster, 1956), p. 412.

33. While rejecting the "'pan-mathematism'" of Leibniz as "incompatible with a full sense of the 'historical,'" Taylor confesses, "I am keenly conscious of the attraction and cannot avoid thinking it the right and proper goal of the sciences of physical nature." "Biography," CONTEMPORARY BRITISH PHILOSOPHY. Second Series. Edited by J. H. Muirhead. (London: George Allen & Unwin Ltd., 1925), p. 271.

The answer, therefore, must be that mathematical propositions--despite their formality and abstraction --are propositions about what is. Because universals are the formal principle of existents, they, too, share "existential" status though (for Taylor) in a manner only analogous.

In the remarks made on the subject of mathematical entities and--more generally--any universal, we have bordered on the question of "Ideals." For Taylor, ideals are values. And because values ground in existential status, it follows that ideals ground in existential status. Taylor notes that the objection that since ideals do not exist in a spatio-temporal sense, they do not exist at all stems from a "source of confusion...the old and deadly error of supposing that a word must be either simply univocal or merely equivocal."[34] It will be seen that in principle some of the restrictions placed upon metaphysics by logical empiricism borrow of the allegedly "fatal error" that Taylor is attacking. Taylor writes,

> Under the baneful influences of an evil nominalistic tradition, inherited from the senility of a scholasticism which had lost its vigor, the great Aristotelian conception of the "analogous" use of predicates has been allowed to fall out of our modern thought, with disastrous consequences. It is simply not true that the alternatives, univocal predication-equivocal predication, form a complete disjunction.[35]

There is a sense in which the "unity of being" must be recognized. At the broad horizontal level of experience, though no two things are identical, no two things are utterly dissimilar. There is a word that most nearly describes this situation: analogous. Too, we have seen that Taylor's doctrine of universals permits him to find universals grounded in existence. This, we might say, allows us to mark a broad vertical level within which span of being and meaning we can again say that while no two aspects are precisely identical neither are they utterly dissimilar. Thus a

---

34. Taylor, THE FAITH OF A MORALIST, Series I, p. 51.

35. Ibid., p. 52.

doctrine of analogy is broadly and quickly sketched as holding for the entire domain of existence. It is meaningful to speak of a wise counsellor as a physician of souls even though "physician" is not identical in meaning with a Fellow of the Royal College of Surgeons. It is meaningful to speak of a wise statesman who guides his country through its many problems as a pilot of the Ship of State even though he is not a pilot of a literal ship and even though the State is not a seagoing vessel. It is meaningful to speak of both the implement and the operator as surgical even though they are not identical with each other. And so with the claim of individual values or ideals. It would appear that neither their individuality nor their existence is automatically impugned because their particular type of individual existence is in some sense other than space-time categories. Taylor writes,

> It is conceivable that individuals may be of many types and that "existence," as asserted of them, may have as many shades of meaning as there are types of individual. This possibility forbids us to assume that the existent is simply that which can be located and dated, and consequently forbids us also to assert that "values" and "ideals," since they have admittedly no date or location, must merely be non-existent, non-actual, "what is not."[36]

The case for conjunction (continued): "any such severence falsifies the facts of real life."[37] Taylor makes the discerning point that although existence and value are always distinguishable, they are never disjoined. It is this ability to view existence and value as logically separable for purposes of analysis that leads some to the conclusion of a real separation. The confusion is understandable but not to be seriously permitted as a description of a real situation. Indeed, this confusion comes about in a most natural way if we adopt "the attitude of a super-physicist or super-chemist to a laboratory problem."[38] Here the

---

36. Ibid., p. 55.

37. Ibid.

38. Ibid.

75

facts of behavior are observed as "on a screen" and only then an interpretation is given them from the outside. Thus, not only is the separation of fact from value suggested but there is also suggested a subjective, personal, arbitrary, aspect of valuation that carries the strongest impulse to deny all objectivity to values. But in the ordinary business of human living, facts and valuations are conjoined--in the analyst no less than in the individuals observed. Man is at once both actor and spectator. He is, in a manner of speaking, his own environment in that the moral traditions that he honors are at once his own responses as well as responses to a value-saturated environment. As Taylor puts it,

> The living moral tradition of the scientific, artistic, or religious group into which we have been initiated, are embodied schemes of evaluation, but they are also as much facts and part of the given to which we have to make our response as the pressure of the atmosphere, or the gravitational "pull" of the earth.[39]

As a supporting consideration to Taylor's position, one might appeal to the historical ubiquity of the moral sense and say of it that it appears to be deeply constitutive of man's very nature. Moral discourse has continued down the centuries of human history in a manner strongly to suggest an essential part of actuality. So, to repeat: it is possible for purposes of analysis to separate the factor of value from actuality, but nature abhors the disjunction and the disjunction is only logical and is not real. Analogous to the value of beauty of which Taylor remarks,

> At least the artists of the world have commonly spoken and borne themselves as if it would be the death of artistic endeavor to discover that their work has been a process of inventing and not one of finding,[40]

it has been an equally suggestive fact that the moralists of history have seemingly appealed to already

---

39. Ibid., p. 56.

40. Ibid., p. 60.

76

existing standards rather than invented them. In
part, at least, it has been this uniform assumption
that moral value is actualized in some objective order
that has invested doctrines of natural law with such
plausibility as they possess. And Taylor asserts,

> ...any tradition of living would soon cease to be
> a living tradition if men could be persuaded that
> it consists of "valuations" manufactured by them-
> selves and imposed on the "real facts" of life
> from outside. A tradition thus degraded would
> lose all its power of inspiring to fresh endeavor
> and better actions. ....The mere suspicion,
> phrase it as you will, that "divinity gives it-
> self no concern about men's matters," that "the
> universe is sublimely indifferent to our human
> distinctions of right and wrong," that "facts are
> thoroughly non-moral," when it comes to be enter-
> tained seriously, regularly issues in a lowering
> the general standard of human seriousness about
> life. Serious living is no more compatible with
> the belief that the universe is indifferent to
> morality than serious and arduous pursuit of
> truth with the belief that truth is a human con-
> vention or superstition. In short, if one is
> thoroughly in earnest with the attempt to sepa-
> rate the given, the fact, from the super-added
> value, one will discover, on the one hand, that
> what one has left on one's hands as the bald fact
> has ceased to be fact at all by the transference
> of every item of definite content to the account
> of the added, and, on the other, that the "value"
> has lost all its value by its rigorous exclusion
> from the given. What confronts us in actual life
> is neither facts without value nor values attached
> to no facts, but fact revealing value, and depen-
> dent, for the wealth of its content, on its char-
> acter as thus revelatory, and values which are
> realities and not arbitrary fancies, precisely
> because they are embedded in fact and give it its
> meaning. To divorce the two would be like trying
> to separate the sounds of a great symphony from
> its musical quality.[41]

---

41. Ibid., p. 61. For Taylor, the attempted sever-
     ance of value from fact finds its parallel in the
     attempted severance of secondary qualities from
     primary qualities. "In spite of the utterances

And so Taylor aims at emphasizing that whatever be the route of the investigation, or the subject matter of the investigation, it is never the case that we end investigating the merely given. The ever-present addendum is that of interpretation, and, although in an important sense the interpretation must originate from "the outside," in an equally important sense it must "fit" the facts. Thus, while the recognition of its systemic meaning-structure begins in a mind, the justification of that interpretation reflects an objective systemic meaning-structure in actuality. This is generally true at epistemological levels, and, because moral interpretation has not surrendered its claim to be an epistemological enterprise, the claim for objective moral status is a part of epistemology's general and genuine concern.

"To think of the moral life adequately," Taylor has declared, "we must think of it as an adventure which begins at one end with nature, and ends at the other with supernature."[42] To make this point, Taylor, as we have seen, argues for the coincidence of value

---

of a whole series of eminent philosophers, from Galileo and Descartes down to our own age, it ought to be patent that, whatever the ontological status of the greenness of the leaf and the redness of the rose-petals, they are no 'psychic addition' made by the percipient subject to a given consisting simply of so-called primary qualities. The green colour of the grass, the crimson of the rose, are there in the world as it is given to us through the eye, no less than the shape of the blade or the petal. It is not my mind which, in knowing the grass or the rose, puts into it a green or red which was not there; on the contrary, it is from an indefinitely rich and complex given that I come to single out these particular elements for separate contemplation." Ibid., pp. 56-57. It is not necessary to add to the controversy of secondary and primary qualities in order to use Taylor's conviction in this matter as an illustration of that other conjunction that as ethical analyst he is most desirous of making clear.

42. Ibid., p. 124.

with actuality. In the chapter to follow, Taylor argues again for "supernature" by considering the relation of temporality to eternity. In each of these attempts, difficulties of one kind or another are encountered that require attention. As noted in the preceding, Taylor attacks unsparingly the disjunction that declares the actual to be worthless and value nonexistent. It appears to be Taylor's recoil from this rigid disjunction of value and existence that impels him to speak in words that may be stronger than required to support his real thesis. Thus, we find him saying,

> What confronts us in actual life is neither facts without value nor values attached to no facts, but fact revealing value, and dependent, for the wealth of its content, on its character as thus revelatory, and values which are realities and not arbitrary fancies, precisely because they are embedded in fact and give it its meaning. To divorce the two would be like trying to separate the sounds of a great symphony from its musical quality.[43]

Thus, Sterling Lamprecht demurs, asking, "Does this statement not imply a greater degree of coincidence of actuality and value than we are entitled to assert? Indeed, ought we to speak of the coincidence of actuality and value without qualification?"[44] Facts, to be sure, have structural differences, characteristics that distinguish them from other facts. And if this were what is asserted by the statement that facts are not without value, there could be little reason to resist it. But this is not a case of ethical value. So much is certain. But it appears to be a case of straining to make Taylor guilty of declaring that factuality everywhere is a case of entailed value every time. Taylor's assertion that "What confronts us in actual life is neither facts without value nor values attached to no facts," means very evidently merely to

---

43. Ibid., pp. 61-62.

44. Sterling Lamprecht, "Morality and Religion: A Critique of Professor A. E. Taylor's Gifford Lectures," INTERNATIONAL JOURNAL OF ETHICS, XLI (July, 1931), p. 497.

deny that factuality as such cannot be possessed of value. Taylor does not here admit to holding the absolute conjunction of all factuality and value. He declares, "Plainly...we cannot argue straight away from the actuality of the actual to its goodness."[45] But, having conceded that one does not move from actuality[46] to value, he, nevertheless, maintains that the move from value to actuality is justified. The actuality-value relation, in other words, is not at the experience level a symmetrical one. Where there is value, there is actuality in which it grounds; but we do not automatically find a value-entailment in the premise of actuality.

Lamprecht, however, comes nearer the heart of the Taylor thesis when he says that Taylor "makes unguarded use of his statement that we are not confronted in life by 'values attached to no facts.'" Lamprecht continues: "The statement is not entirely clear. If it means that we are not confronted by goods attached to no facts, it is quite true. If it means that we are not confronted by ideals attached to no facts, it is quite false."[47] The suggestion that we may indeed be in the service of "ideals" that have no basis in fact, no basis in actuality, is a challenge to the Taylor

---

45. Taylor, THE FAITH OF A MORALIST, Series I, p. 34.

46. I think that Taylor is accurately depicted as not intending a symmetrical relation of value and existence. There are multiplied millions of facts that are ethically indifferent. But Taylor's agreement would be at the level of the ability of experience to determine when the fact had value and when it did not. It is not at the level of experience that one can determine the ethical value of a grain of sand on the shore of the sea. However, at a different level, the symmetrical relation of fact and value can be affirmed. This is the level of a creator-creature relation—which relation Taylor accepts as true of the larger involvement of reality. As an implication of such an hypothesis, every aspect of reality has some purpose and with the purpose may be said to be its value-function.

47. Lamprecht, Op. cit., pp. 498-499.

thesis. It is a challenge because Taylor plainly builds on the allegation that ideals are values. And if values demand an existential situation, ideals equally demand it if they are to be meaningful. In a different context, Taylor declares,

> It is fundamental to the view I am trying to present that there should be no division of the knowable into two disjunct realms, one of the merely real or actual, and another of ideals, or values, or goods.[48]

So what are these alleged "disembodied ideals" which might and sometimes do claim our allegiance? The categorical imperative? Code Napoleon? Some ideal yet future of enactment and hence not yet actualized--like Plato's perfect city? All of these fail of providing illustrations of ideals that have no understood ground in actuality. Without arguing the merit of any of them, the fact seems inescapable that to each the full meaning of the ideal itself is precisely that meaning's ability to actualize itself in the concreteness of human action in society. Lamprecht remembers that Socrates may be quoted in support of the contention that ideals do not have to be actualized in order to retain their full persuasion:

> Socrates takes occasion to rebuke those who inquired whether his ideal was practicable with the reply that "our purpose was not to demonstrate the possibility of the realization of these ideals." Yet he later insists that the good man who has envisaged the disembodied ideal of a perfect city will "organize his life accordingly."[49]

The unlikelihood of this perfect city emerging in Greek society at that time was great indeed. But the ideal was, after all, engineered to apply to an earthly society and the law of contradiction would not have been broken if it had been capable of being applied.

---

48. Alfred Edward Taylor, "Is Goodness a Quality?" ARISTOTELIAN SOCIETY, Supplementary Volume XI (1932), p. 155.

49. Lamprecht, Op. cit., pp. 498-499.

Thus, it becomes a commentary upon the defective fabric of society that an ideal for its structuring should have been incapable of application. In short, the ideal was calculated to find its proper identification with the society (the _matter_) to which it was the articulated form. Compare the following remark by Taylor.

> ...if a man were to say that the imaginary society of Plato's REPUBLIC is better (or worse) than London society today, I could only under⸗ stand him by taking this for an abbreviated way of saying that if there really were such a society as Plato depicts, it would be better (or worse) than that of contemporary London.[50]

Further, an _ideal_ _that_ in _principle_ cannot be _applied_ to _some_ _realization_ is totally vacuous and incapable of sustaining any loyalty of commitment to it by any who realize this fact of internal impotence. Such is Taylor's total commitment and understanding of the nature of the ideals of human action.

A summary word to sharpen the significance of Taylor's declared conjunction between value and actuality may help to clarify important distinctions. (1) Value may not be said to inhere in space-time actuality as an intrinsically necessary property. Here, the positivist is quite correct. Mere sensory inspection of space-time actuality can never reveal value. (2) Value, as fundamentally a universal, is recognized for the unification it performs upon the occasion of particular experiences. Here, Taylor is neither the extreme realist nor the nominalist of medieval tradition, but settles for the Aristotelian compromise that declares that forms (universals) have their being only "in" things, _in rebus_. (3) The sense, then, of the alleged conjunction of value and actuality is similar to the Kantian formula. Just as knowledge of the space-form and the time-form never arises except upon the occasion of experience, so, for Taylor, knowledge of value never arises except upon the occasion of actuality. This is the sense of their declared conjunction.

---

50. Taylor, "Is Goodness a Quality?", p. 155.

CHAPTER IV -- MORAL VALUE AND TIME

Whatever may be thought of the ultimate value of Kant's famous treatment of time and space as forms of sensibility and as necessarily presupposed in any knowledge that can be claimed of experience, at least this much seems evident, _viz._, that, however it be explained, the intimacy between these "forms" and experience is guaranteed. To remark that "Nothing happens outside of time" is virtually to seize upon a defining characteristic of any happening. And though this connection of entailment is recognized universally, it is Taylor's interesting and valuable suggestion that "time is the characteristic form of the life of moral endeavour."[1] All purposive activity or intentions, indeed, every case of goal-activity, cuts through time and affords a backdrop for Taylor's relating of time to _moral_ purpose. Taylor states,

> ...time is the expression in abstract form of the fundamental nature of an experience which has as yet attained only the partial fulfillment of its purpose and aspirations...[2]

This is not to deny that time may be viewed under many other fruitful categories of analysis. The perceptual and conceptual aspects of time; the question of time's infinity, divisibility, continuity and relativity; the problem of the antinomies; these, and others, suggest some of the avenues for inquiry. But Taylor's treatment, within the category of value, will largely avoid digression into these physical and metaphysical areas. Rather, there will be emphasized what

---

1. Taylor, THE FAITH OF A MORALIST, Series I, p. 87.

2. Alfred Edward Taylor, ELEMENTS OF METAPHYSICS (London: Methuen & Company, 1903), p. 335.

Taylor will call the "conative" function of man's endeavor. This approach, as the etymology of the word suggests, emphasizes effort, endeavoring, striving, volition, and always with added emphasis on the end that is the goal of such effort and volition. Such an approach is largely to be expected from a philosophy that is so overwhelmingly teleological in its general outlook.

"It is manifest," declares Taylor, "that 'self' is a teleological concept."[3] It is also a teleological unity. For Taylor, to will a habit or desire to be otherwise "is already, in principle, to expel it from the teleological unity which makes up our inner life."[4] And, in the very act of attempted or willed expulsion there is evidenced but another kind of goal-seeking. The teleological character of man's deepest nature finds witness, for Taylor, in Bentham's two sovereign masters, pleasure and pain. Thus feeling itself is essentially teleological in that, on the one hand, there is an attempt to gain an end, and, on the other hand, an attempt to avoid it. For Taylor,

> ...one thing seems clear, that pleasure is essentially connected with unimpeded, pain with impeded, discharge of nervous activity. Pleasure seems to be inseparable from successful, pain from thwarted or baffled, tendency.[5]

Indeed, it is the conjunction of ends sought and ends approved that becomes an occasion for the recognition of that other dimension of reality: moral value.

> Only a being /Taylor writes/ whose behavior is consciously or unconsciously determined by ends or purposes seems capable of finding existence, according as those purposes are advanced or hindered, pleasant or painful, glad or wretched, good or bad.[6]

---

3. Ibid.

4. Ibid., p. 338.

5. Ibid., p. 55.

6. Ibid., p. 56.

There would be no need, Taylor declares, to go beyond the merely mechanical, the behavioristic, psychology, if there were no need to satisfy the dual interests of our nature. In the nature of the case, a _merely_ mechanical account, from one point of view, will have no need of teleological modes of thought. But, from another point of view, the fact that "an account" has been given at all is itself an essentially purposive, thoroughly teleological, undertaking.[7] Taylor's first-level complaint concerning the purely "mechanical" view of the self is that in such a reduction, there is really no ground to claim explanation at all. It would be as though the "explanation" of Socrates in prison could be found in terms of his bones, sinews, and joints, or his conversation, in terms of sound and air and hearing.[8] Both the mechanical _and_ and teleological hypotheses baffle each other if either is taken as a final and only explanation. However, to Taylor, as to Plato, if the teleological is admitted, the mechanical recognition can be returned for what it is worth to them who have need of it. And this is what Taylor refers to when he opts for the broader inclusion: "...according to our view," Taylor writes,

> the interest to which Psychology owes its creation is not single but double. We have an interest in the mechanical forecasting of human action, and an interest in its ethical and historical interpretation, and Psychology, as at present constituted, has to satisfy both these conflicting interests at once. Hence the impossibility of confining it either to purely mechanical or to purely teleological categories.[9]

Undoubtedly Taylor enters here upon the defense of a thesis that has been sharply challenged. That human conduct, conceived broadly as historical and ethical, may be interpreted entirely without reference to teleological categories, has been the determined

---

7. This aspect of a teleological involvement is elaborated at length in Chapter VI -- "Moral Value and Freedom."

8. PHAEDO, p. 98 c-e.

9. Taylor, ELEMENTS OF METAPHYSICS, p. 307.

effort of many writing in defense of a naturalistic philosophy. In the narrowest view of empirical analysis, Taylor would grant that every so-called teleological function can be re-written in non-teleological terms. This is very little different than saying that what passes for teleological involvement (from one point of view) can, under mere description, be reduced to a vocabulary that has no need of a purposive or a goal-seeking recognition. And this same narrowed point of view is fructified by Hume's denial of the validity of any claimed theoretical insight of uniformity and intrinsic bond. Purpose, like causal connection, can never be captured as a percept. Kant is right--in principle--in saying that all principles of unification are conceptually apprehended if at all, and the notion of purpose is clearly a deeply unifying notion. It would be sorely stultifying to the breadth of view that Taylor is defending to descend to the experiment of trying to express the broad assumptions that have unified interpretations of ethics and history in the narrow descriptive terms of a purely empirical analysis.[10] It is, therefore, in deference to a larger and allegedly truer conceptual scheme that Taylor pleads both ethics and history as conceivable only in teleological categories. He writes,

> It is manifest...that neither the ethical appreciation of human conduct by comparison with an ideal standard, nor the historical interpretation of it in the light of the actual ends and ideals which pervade it and give it its individuality, would be possible unless we could first of all describe the events with which Ethics and History are conceived in teleological language.[11]

It is the unwavering assumption of the moral mandate as deeply constitutive of human nature and about which it is so much the concern of history to report

---

10. Morton Beckner writes that "...the rejection of functional concepts /here, teleologically understood/ would amount to the rejection of a powerful and fruitful conceptual scheme." "Teleology" THE ENCYCLOPEDIA OF PHILOSOPHY. (VIII). (New York: The Macmillan Company and The Free Press, 1967), p. 91.

11. Taylor, ELEMENTS OF METAPHYSICS, p. 305.

that leads Taylor to observe that if psychology were
not as much concerned with the teleological as it is
with the mechanical there would have been "nothing...
for the moralist to applaud or blame, or for the his-
torian to interpret."[12] But this issue, having been
kept perennially alive throughout total human history,
becomes a fulfilling condition of that view of psychology that Taylor defends. Suitable attention can never be given to this moral dimension "by any branch of
physical science which remains rigidly consistent with
its own postulates."[13] That devotees of physical science do concern themselves with moral issues, and may
even regard teleological concern at every level as important, is true only, Taylor repeatedly declares, because the fuller nature of their own psyches is such
as to involve this dualism, but "no science which describes the processes of human life in purely physical
terminology can indicate their purposive or teleological character in its descriptions."[14]

Taylor finds it highly confirmatory of his thesis that ethics in pronouncing verdicts of "good" and
"bad," "right" or "wrong," so frequently finds it
perfectly natural to predicate these values of the
"acts," "feelings," "tempers," and "desires" taken
over from psychology, and adds that

History would have nothing left to appreciate if
a record of merely physical movements were sub-
stituted for accounts of events which imply at
every turn the psychological categories of "desire," "purpose," "intention," "temptation," and
the rest.[15]

---

12. Ibid.

13. Ibid., p. 306.

14. Ibid.

15. Ibid. Taylor notes that "Professor /Henry/ Sidg-
     wick has observed /that/ the whole vocabulary
     used to characterize human conduct, apart from
     the specially ethical predicates of worth, is
     purely psychological." Ibid.

Ethics, moreover, in concerning itself with the good life, must recognize that there is a teleological aspect to the good. It is first, and minimally, never an atomized experience. That is to say, the value of esthetic and ethical goods never reduce to or are satisfied by infinitesimal moments. This is a part of the presence of the universal in every otherwise particular aspect of the good. But genuinely felt good--in any experience--seems to carry with it a propriety, if not, indeed, a demand, for extension of its quality into successive moments. And, as we have seen, mind--one of the necessary conditions for value--keeps pace with the demand for value's extension to the end that greater self-realization is accomplished. This underscores a teleological aspect of the good.

With regard to time, Taylor begins with what might be called the empirical or perceptual awareness. This is the time of experience. It is the "feeling" of duration. It is that intimate experience that gives rise to the ideas of a before and an after and a now. But there is something paradoxical and frustrating about this ever-vanishing "now," this razor's edge of a present that is sandwiched in between what Taylor calls the "no longer" and the "not yet." The "specious present," when scrutinized, virtually disappears. It reduces to a moment that has no duration. It becomes a mere infinitesimal and immeasurable, or, in the language of the mathematician, a variable having zero as a limit.

But, Taylor observes, however much such analyses may admit of paradoxes and antinomies, the evident dependence of experience upon larger dimensions makes it possible to redeem this present, this time-aspect of human experience, or, as Taylor prefers the word, this "temporality." He notes that there is a larger claim made by experience that refuses to be frustrated and denied by what it "knows best." And what experience may be said to "know" in this sense of "largeness" is how to extend the infinitesimal quality of the present into an infinite quality that becomes identical with an essential aspect of the proper environment of human concern.

To be aware of our life as temporal, /Taylor affirms7 is already to transcend the form of temporality. All human creation is an attempt to

88

experience the fruition of good in a now where
there is no consciousness of the no longer or not
yet.[16]

Much of the argument of Taylor depends upon the
allegation that the meaning of fact must be found
within the universal.

Even in the artificially isolated "physical realm"
of natural science, /Taylor writes/ what we study
is never a mere Werden, a mere succession of bare-
ly particular events which just "happen"; we are
dealing everywhere with successions which exhibit
pervasive "universal" characters, or patterns,
events in which, in the terminology of Whitehead,
objects, that is, "universals in re," are situ-
ated.[17]

And, thus, by analogy, of the moral life, Taylor declares,

Still less is any morally significant act a mere
event which happens. The piquancy of the dis-
paraging epigram that human life is "one damned
thing after another" is wholly due to its glaring
falsity as a description of any life but one
which would be morally worthless.[18]

The relation of the particular act to its universal dimension is different in an important sense from
the relation of merely physical facts to the universals from which they derive their meaning. In both
cases, we have particulars deriving their meaning from
universals. But in that relation from which the explicitly moral life is derived there is the consciousness of the person to whom the particular act belongs.
This consciousness is also evaluative, speculative,
interpretative of its own acts in which effort it dis-
covers not merely that universal which properly confers meaning upon the specific acts but that universal

---

16. Taylor, THE FAITH OF A MORALIST. Series I, p. xi.

17. Ibid., p. 68.

18. Ibid.

which confers meaning upon the total complex of personal consciousness. It is in this sense, according
to Taylor, that every aspect of the particular act--
its temporality and personality--finds its corresponding attribute of universality in an eternal God.

If, as Taylor the Platonist would say, it is
epistemologically impossible to find meaning in a
brute fact without appeal to some universal, just so
is it impossible to find meaning in a brute event of
moral category without appeal to some universal. But
there is an important difference between a particular-
universal relation in general epistemology and that
narrower specification of particular-universal in moral epistemology. To the extent that ethics concerns
itself with the question what ought I to do? there is
an identification of knowledge with action. If,
therefore, the knowledge-aspect drives beyond the
brute fact to seek meaning in a universal, the action-
aspect no less seek its meaning beyond its particularity. This does not deny the particularity of events.
It merely asserts the necessity of their conjunction
with universality. Something of particularity and universality are ever conjoined in meaningful philosophy.
This conjunction Taylor sees as

> the most patent and universal characteristic of
> explicitly moral life wherever it is found. ...
> As morality becomes conscious of itself, it is
> discovered to be always a life of tension between
> the temporal and the eternal, only possible to a
> being who is neither simply eternal and abiding,
> nor simply mutable and temporal, but both at
> once.[19]

But action (an essential of ethics) is always toward
some end, or, as Taylor would say, some interest.
With this word added, "the task of living rightly and
worthily" "is the task of the thorough transfiguration
of our interests, the shifting of interest from temporal to non-temporal good."[20]

For Taylor, as we have seen, the status of a

---

19. Ibid., p. 69.

20. Ibid.

"non-temporal good" exhibits a conjunction of value
with actuality, of axiology with ontology.[21] And the
declaration that our genuine moral concern takes us
past temporal interests to a non-temporal good rests
upon the consideration that neither change nor fragmentariness can be a logically satisfying object. Change
itself cannot be ultimàte; it necessarily presupposes
some constant in terms of which it derives its meaning.
Fragmentariness, like particularity, or brute facts,
points beyond itself to some significant universal.
Thus, for Taylor, there is a dialectic that steers the
mind through all change and particularity, nor can it
halt until temporality has given way to eternity and
particularity to a supreme universal. It cannot be
too much emphasized that a "first principle" of Taylor's entire philosophical system is the alleged recognition that finitude in its every form--as alsò for
Plato and Descartes--implies an already-present universal. That is to say, every finitude is a "limitation
of." Nor can any finite addition to this limitation
eliminate the result from being another "limitation
of." That, therefore, that gives necessary and sufficient meaning to every limitation is precisely that
concrete universal that is presupposed in every meaningful finite judgment--itself being in the nature of
the case <u>beyond</u> <u>all</u> <u>limitation</u>. It is also in the nature of the case that we never have a "clear and dis-
tinct" idea of this concrete universal--other than
that it is necessarily presupposed in all of our judg-
mental activity. Our failure to comprehend it exhaustively rebukes dogmatism even as our inability to dismiss it rebukes skepticism. Regarding this concrete
universal in the sense in which it is presented within
ethical discourse, Taylor says,

> The "Form of Good" may be "the master light of
> all our seeing," but if we are asked <u>what</u> it is,
> though the better men we are, the less hopelessly
> vague our answer may be expected to be, the best
> of us has nothing like a "clear and distinct
> idea" of what he would be at. Really to say what
> "the good" is, we should need to be in fruition
> of it, and if we had the fruition, our life would
> have become, in Aristotle's language, no longer

---

21. Chapter III--"Moral Value and Existence."

that of a man, but that of the "divine something" in man.[22]

Or, to translate this into its philosophical equivalent, we find, Taylor says,

> the thesis on which T. H. Green has so much to say in the PROLEGOMENA TO ETHICS, that in all moral progress to a better, the driving force is aspiration after a best of which we can say little more, at any stage of the process, than that it lies ahead of us on the same line of advance along which the already achieved progress from the less to the more good has been made.[23]

We are concerned in this chapter with "Eternity and Temporality" and we are reminded before we attempt to make clearer what time and eternity--"the most tormenting of philosophical questions"--mean that the Taylor thesis is committed to this proposition: "To be aware of our life as temporal is already to begin to transcend the form of temporality."[24] It will be seen that the finitude implicit in the notion of temporality, in accordance with the dialectic referred to above, does indeed constitute that condition from which we "begin to transcend the form of temporality." But more precisely: "time," Taylor says, "is the characteristic form of the life of moral endeavour."[25] In so saying, Taylor distinguishes sharply between what he calls "the mere fact of successiveness" as one finds this fact "in the course of physical events" with that other succession, past, present, and future,[26] to which is attached a meaning derived from

---

22. Ibid., p. 70.

23. Ibid., p. 71.

24. Ibid., p. xi.

25. Ibid., p. 87.

26. Taylor acknowledges a similarity here to John McTaggart Ellis McTaggart's work THE NATURE OF EXISTENCE. Taylor summarizes: "McTaggart begins by distinguishing carefully between the distinctions earlier-later and past-present-future. A set of terms related only as earlier-later forms

the "emotional and conative life of individual experients."[27] Taylor concedes that in a world where there are no experients there might be earlier and later events, but, he adds, "no event would ever be present, past, or future."[28] Taylor's distinction looks fundamentally to the lack of any theoretically discernible connection or intrinsic bond between or among events viewed as out of any relation to an experient in contrast to a past, present, and future that are united by conative disposition involving striving, aspiring, desire and volition. It is precisely this conative exhibition that does in fact contribute the binding thread to a past, present, and future, vouchsafing to them the humanly moral value of time. Thus, man is understood as never wholly relinquishing hold on the past nor wholly awaiting a future, but, with memory meeting anticipation, the present is impregnated with a linked succession that no mere physical succession can claim nor have claimed for it. Taylor speaks of the past as "no longer" and of the future as "not yet," but he does so by noting that "the 'not yet' is that towards which I am endeavoring, or reaching out. Its opposite, the 'no longer,' is that from which I am turning away."[29]

Again, recalling Taylor's thesis that "to be aware of our life as temporal is already to begin to transcend the form of temporality," we are permitted by now to see that as sheer temporality gives way constantly by that backward and forward reference of conation to an enlarged present--indeed a present that has in principle already borrowed for its meaningful vitality from past and future and has, moreover, done so by virtually uniting them into an expanded present, we have in principle an incipient eternity.

---

what he calls a B-series; terms related as past-present-future form an A-series. Time, if there is Time, requires the reality of both A- and B-series, and of the two the A-series...is the more important. On these points...I am in full agreement with him." Ibid., p. 114.

27. Ibid., p. 72.

28. Ibid., p. 73.

29. Ibid., p. 74.

Taylor remarks of the past, "When remembered, it lives again in 'ideal revival.'"

> In the world of intelligent human action, the re-
> membered past seems to be able to mould the fu-
> ture directly and immediately, striking, so to
> say, out of its own remote pastness, even though
> there has been no continuous persistence of it-
> self or its effects through the interval.[30]

This is to say that the efficacy of this remote past-
ness does not derive from a series of physical effects
through an interval of time, but, almost in opposite
manner, the mind, sorting and interpreting among a
category of events classified as past--as over against
the present--registers a moral decision as partially
determined by those very events. Thus, time becomes
for us "the characteristic form of the life of moral
endeavor,"[31] "the form of the life of conscious appetition."[32]

> Altering the approach only slightly, the merely
temporal good is declared already transcended when we
endeavor to intensify and prolong that good.

> To endeavor even to keep an agreeable condition
> of bodily well-being, like that of the cat be-
> fore the fire, steadily in consciousness, is al-
> ready to be trying to transcend the merely tem-
> poral form of the experience.[33]

All purposive activity, all purposive intentions, in
short, every case of goal-activity cuts through time
and affords a backdrop for Taylor's relating of time
to moral purpose. And because such goal-seeking is
inseparable from time and is an implicit declaration
of attempting a more worthwhile situation, we have
the combined elements of time and value interwoven.
It is to this conception of self as value-seeking and
purposive in what is virtually its total being that

---

30.   Ibid., p. 87.

31.   Ibid.

32.   Ibid., p. 88.

33.   Ibid.

94

Taylor adds the assertion that "time is the expression in abstract form of the fundamental nature of an experience which has as yet attained only the partial fulfillment of its purpose and aspirations."[34] Increasingly, as the values of life relate to man's essential dimensions do they become concerns about which we are never indifferent as to their continuity. The sometimes interpreted reductio of Hinduism, viz., that the genuine concerns of man are for being, knowledge, and joy and these in infinite degree, are interpretative and perhaps corroborative of Taylor's thesis. Blake is quoted: "More! More! is the cry of a mistaken soul; less than all cannot satisfy Man."[35] Those values (especially that we feel relate to our well-being) are best realized, not in a past that is gone, nor in a future that is uncertain, but in that present that is now, "where," to use Taylor's words, "we are not conscious of a no longer or a not yet."[36] It is this limitlessly extended now that is the felt character of that implicitly desired end of a moral conation that aims at man's chief end, his genuine concern, his true well-being. Herein is found fulfilled "the famous and classic definition of eternity by Boethius, that it is interminable vitae tota simul et perfecta possessio, 'whole, simultaneous, and complete fruition of a life without bounds.'"[37] And Taylor adds,

> What the definition excludes, as being proper to temporality, we note, is not the before and after but the not yet and no longer which would mark an experience as not the "whole and complete" satisfaction of endeavour.[38]

34. Taylor, ELEMENTS OF METAPHYSICS, p. 341.

35. Taylor, THE FAITH OF A MORALIST, Series I, p. 118.

36. Ibid., p. 89.

37. Ibid., p. 91.

38. This argument of Taylor's from "function" to an adequate environment within which the function can find adequate support is detailed in Chapter VII - "Moral Value and Immortality."

From the character of what Taylor has observed as the deep seat of moral aspiration--the "emotional and conative life of individual experients"--he feels prepared to draw a conclusion.

> If we are justified in treating our own existence and peculiar So-sein as moral beings as capable of throwing any light whatever on the character of the actual and real as a whole, we might then reasonably infer that we may argue, here as elsewhere, from the existence of a function to the reality of an environment in which the function can find adequate exercise. If the pursuit of temporal and secular good must inevitably fail to satisfy moral aspiration itself, we may fairly infer that there is a non-secular good to which moral endeavour is a growing response. In so far as such a good can be apprehended and enjoyed at all, temporality, with its antithesis of not yet and no longer, is itself progressively relegated to a secondary place in the life of enjoyment, time is actually swallowed up in eternity, the natural life is one which is, in the strict and proper sense of the word, supernatural, morality in religion.[39]

For Taylor, there is a glaring contrast between the serious preoccupation of moral concern for some ground that will satisfy the search for man's well-being and the temporal and fragmentary character of every object and dimension short of an infinite one. And so Taylor asks,

> Now, is secular good, obtainable under strictly temporal conditions, an object really adequate to

---

39.   Ibid., p. 93. Taylor states this in the following slightly different words, viz., that if "... all secular good is defective, since it cannot be enjoyed as a whole simultaneously, and one part can only be enjoyed at the cost of surrendering others," and if, in addition, secular goods can neither be denied as to their real--though approximate--goodness, nor completely satisfy, "we may reasonably infer that the ultimate good of man is non-secular and eternal, and that the facts of our moral being point to the Christian conception of the transformation and completion of nature by 'grace.'" Ibid., p. xi.

evoke and to sustain this aspiration which gives the moral life its specific character as moral? In plain words, can a satisfactory morality be anything but what is sometimes called by way of disparagement an other-worldly morality?[40]

Here, Taylor declares, we make a contact with the sphere of religion. The logic of this allegation is primarily the fact that the characteristics identified as belonging to moral aspiration are religion's fulfilling conditions—along with those other elements traditionally identified with classical theism. These "fulfilling conditions" are principally as follows: that we aspire toward a good the nature of which temporality in none of its moods can supply; that the meaning of brute fact is always found (if found at all) by reference to a universal and this is also true of the brute facts of moral aspiration; that the nature of this universal must, in conferring meaning upon the particular, possess, at least analogically, as much meaning and as much reality as the particular—in which case, the particular, being of a combination of moral and conscious character, the universal, corresponding to these characteristics, is revealed as the conscious ground and presupposition of human moral concern; that the meaning of time with its past, present, and future as experienced by moral conation is more than mere succession and actually involves that purposiveness that is itself the binding thread, the intrinsic bond, of successive moments; that this binding thread of the successive moments of moral conation is the "Form of Good," the yardstick and norm of all moral value but which itself is known only indirectly, yet necessarily, as the presupposition of significant moral discourse and significant moral action; and lastly, that the meaning of good that we predicate of our separate moral aspirations is univocal and identifies that other unity in which ideal good is realized—even God.

We have so far tried to find the inmost meaning of the moral life of man by regarding it as an endeavour towards an eternal good made by a creature who, in so far as he achieves the end of his endeavour, achieves also a derivative, or communicated, eternity. The point on which I

---

40. Ibid., pp. 94-95.

propose now to lay stress is precisely the communicated or derived character of the eternity thus
attainable by man.[41]

And because eternity is the completion of temporality,
where temporality has been declared the form of the moral life, it follows, Taylor believes, that two aggressive competitors to a true ethical view are to be recognized and disqualified as significant contributors
to an ethical dimension: he who would make us gods to
begin with and hence render of negligible consequence
what kind of effort one makes, and he who would espouse a thoroughgoing naturalism and hence know no
higher goal than "a roaming in a wilderness where he
is destined to lay his bones."[42] "In plain language,
we break with the presuppositions of the moral life
equally whether we eliminate the natural or the supernatural from our conception of things."[43] If, for Taylor, the moral life is "an adventure which begins at
one end with nature, and ends at the other with supernature,"[44] how is this transition effected? By refusing to treat the moral dimension with indifference or
as an illusion. And so, "morality transcending itself
and passing into religion and worship,"[45] is what Taylor takes to be, in principle, the transition from nature to supernature. But how is this effected? For
Taylor, it is somewhat like Brightman's "Dialectic of
Desire":[46] one begins with what is perhaps the immediate and relatively trivial but proceeds through a
series of steps of increasingly greater involvement
until the beginning desire for things ends with a desire for God. For Taylor, "Any earnest sense of the
necessity for putting anything to rights can lead you,
if you are logical and resist sloth, to the remaking

41. Ibid., p. 118.

42. Ibid., p. 119.

43. Ibid., p. 124.

44. Ibid.

45. Ibid., p. 144.

46. E. S. Brightman, A PHILOSOPHY OF RELIGION. (New
    York: Prentice-Hall, Inc., 1940), pp. 251-259.

of life as a whole."[47] This movement begins with a
desire for a little greater freedom and ends with the
discovery that "nothing less than complete freedom
would satisfy the impulse which led us to break the
first link."[48] But this "complete freedom" lies "beyond the horizon of temporality."[49] The beginning impulse to adjust, to alter, to amend, to rectify, does
not merely grow out of dissatisfaction with our environment, but with a dissatisfaction with ourselves, our
conduct, our character. There can be lesser dissatis-
factions, but moral dissatisfaction does not merely
assess the situation to be uncomfortable; it assesses
it to be other than it ought to be and, as such, one
that ought to be remedied. Fundamentally, it is man
himself who is the occasion for recognition of a dis-
location that needs righting and it is this recognition that may begin the dialectic of action that
rises, in principle, above temporality. And Taylor
adds, "Hence the superficiality of all attempts to
identify true moral progress with any mere scheme of
'social amelioration,' or the moral ideal with a
well-constructed 'social system.'"[50] For Taylor, if
the deep-seated impulse that sends the utilitarian
and the pragmatist to engage in social reform were
recognized for what it really is, manhood would triumph over these lesser philosophies by announcing its
recognition of that presupposition that saves a genuinely normative ethic from becoming a mere description of what men feel and do. The designations of
Taylor's Gifford lectures emphasize the dialectical
role that is played as the "temporal" and "natural"
man, in obedience to "time" as the "characteristic
form of the life of moral endeavour," is lifted above
"temporality" to eternity and above the "natural" to
the supernatural.[51] The important point for Taylor's

---

47. Taylor, THE FAITH OF A MORALIST, Series I, p. 145.

48. Ibid., p. 146.

49. Ibid.

50. Ibid., p. 147.

51. The lecture headings were: "Eternity and Temporality," and "Further Specification of the Good:
Nature and Supernature." Ibid., p. 67 and p.
118.

thesis is that neither "eternity" nor "supernature" are to be viewed as out of all relation to man, but rather they combine to provide not only a proper goal but in an important sense they may be regarded as the continuation of those qualities that make man a being who even in his "natural" and "temporal" state is constituted necessarily by the commanding norms of the esthetic, the ethical, and the rational--though incompletely. While it is man's ability to recognize these binding norms and to apply them, still the norms themselves testify to the bond between supernature--whence they derive their authority--and nature. And the slow recognition of the relevance and authority that these norms have for man comes only through the time that Taylor has called "the characteristic form of the life of moral endeavour." It cannot be, therefore, Taylor declares, that time is a mere accidental backdrop to the outworking of the endeavor that is man's duty, but in a manner analogous to physical evolution's moving to its development through time, so man's intellectual, ethical, esthetic and spiritual evolution should also find in time what is perhaps its necessary period of incubation. Meanwhile, man is forced by all of the reasons that already have been urged against human autonomy to recognize the dominance of the sovereignty of the norms that derive from "supernature."

In close connection, Taylor recognizes that despite certain ambiguities in Kant's endeavor to objectify and universalize his principle of ethical mandate, there are remaining evidences that Kant did succeed and, further, that the success helpfully confirms Taylor's own position that opts for the necessary recognition of just such objectivity. Examples are as follows: (1) Kant's "happiness" "means a state in which the rational will is actually realized in the course of events"--the "rational" aspect being a strong reason to see an objective, necessary and universal principle of command clearly maintained; (2)

> Kant himself allows that a will which could effect the subordination of the whole course of history to a moral demand that the happiness of individuals shall be a consequence of their moral worth, and proportionate to that worth, cannot be the will of any finite creature. It must be a will backed by omnipotence, or, at least, a will which is supreme over the whole temporal order and wields every part as a wholly plastic instrument

for a moral end. Thus it must be a living supreme divine will into conformity with which our
own wills grow in proportion as we become what we
ought to be;[52]

and (3)

> Kant guards himself...by an important distinctio.
> My will, according to him, is legislative in the
> moral world, but it is not sovereign, for the
> very reason that it is bound by its own commands.
> The moral world of persons...is...a monarchy in
> which God is the constitutional monarch. (In any
> case, Kant is clear on the point that I am not
> the monarch.)[53]

Thus, Kant's possible intentions join to Taylor's own
to underwrite the fundamental thesis that in morality
becoming aware of its own tendencies, it reveals a disposition towards an eternal good that is simultaneously both the object of moral aspiration and its commanding principle. It is a continuing commentary on how
the moral life begins "at one end with nature, and
ends at the other with supernature." There is, however, a consideration that no longer can be claimed to
find the joint endorsement. Taylor speaks of that
"nobly ethical attitude to affliction" that "makes
trouble itself the direct means to further enrichment"
--an attitude, Taylor adds, "possible only on one condition: the affliction must be regarded as 'God's mes-
senger.'"[54] ("Is such an attitude possible in a life
directed by the Kantian maxims? To my own thinking it
is not.")[55] As a fact, Taylor observes, there are
"thousands of humble souls" who "make acceptance of the
worst fortune has to bestow a means to the development
of a sweetness, patience, and serene joyousness which
are to be learned nowhere but in the school of sharp
suffering."[56] ..."The sting of the afflictions lies
just in their apparent wantonness, their seeming utter

---

52. Ibid., p. 150.

53. Ibid., p. 151.

54. Ibid., p. 154.

55. Ibid., p. 155.

56. Ibid., p. 154.

unreasonableness."[57]   And then, with regard to Kant's heavy endorsement of reason in his analysis of the moral experience, Taylor declares,

> Unless I mean by the "reason" I worship with unqualified reverence something more than the "reason I have now in possession," I own I do not see that we could admit this morally most fruitful attitude towards afflictions into a scheme of morality which is, ex hypothesi, to be a life "by the sole dictate of reason," and I note that I have found nothing in Kant's writings of any period to suggest that he himself dreamed of any attitude towards such visitations which goes beyond the "Stoic" retreat of the tortoise into its shell. Yet, if he did not, he was blind to the highest.[58]

In this consideration, Taylor claimed,

> a concrete illustration of the way in which the moral life itself, at its best, points to something which, because it transcends the separation of "ought" from "is", must be called definitely religion and not morality, as the source and inspiration of what is best in morality itself.[59]

The question natural to arise--whether there can be ethics without religion--is answered by Taylor: it can exist.

> An atheist who has been taught not to steal or lie or fornicate or the like is, probably, no more nor less likely, in average situations, to earn his living honestly, to speak the truth and to live cleanly, than a believer in God. But if the atheist is logical and in earnest with his professed view of the world, and the believer equally so with his, I think I know which of the two is the more likely to make irreparable and "unmerited" grievous calamity a means to the

---

57.   Ibid., p. 155.

58.   Ibid.

59.   Ibid.

purification and enrichment of personality.[60]

That ethics without religion can exist at all is
not, as the remark above might indicate, due merely to
example; its existence is due fundamentally to an essential characteristic in the nature of man--to which,
Taylor would add, total history testifies. Nor is it
different in principle with regard to the characteristic so universally exhibited in rationality. The argument seems to be as follows: if the universe is in
fact the kind that reason and conscience can approve,
then there must be a pervading evidence of intelligibility and moral purpose. Such characteristics are evident. Therefore a presumption is established that the
universe is in fact the kind that reason and conscience
can approve. And so committed are we to the fact of a
universe that supports both intelligibility and moral
purpose that through total recorded history man has
everywhere assumed that both characteristics hold and
demonstrated his complete confidence in that fact by
suiting action to belief in scientific investigation
and by keeping alive the ethical imperative as a goad
and corrective of man's moral dimension. But in an
important sense, one cannot disjoin moral purpose and
intelligibility: moral purpose must be intelligible,
must commend itself to analysis, to evaluation, to
comparison with such standards as it may claim, must
honor consistency and coherence, and must respect the
need for universality and necessity. Thus Taylor can
assert, "There must be a moral purpose in the world's
history, and moral purpose must be universally good,
if the world is really intelligible."[61] Such considerations lead naturally, for Taylor, to a claim for
Theism as the consciously or unconsciously held presupposition of a thoroughly rationalized ethics. The
argument carries, logically, the prediction that an
ethics deliberately and consciously attempted on a basis of secularism and humanism must fail.

Noting again that Taylor claimed

a concrete illustration of the way in which the
moral life itself, at its best, points to something which, because it transcends the separation

---

60. Ibid., pp. 155-156.

61. Alfred Edward Taylor, THE CHRISTIAN HOPE OF IMMOR-
    TALITY. (New York: Macmillan, 1947), p. 41.

of "ought" from "is," must be called definitely
religion and not morality, as the source and inspiration of what is best in morality itself,[62]

we are forced to note the importance that Taylor places
upon obligation (the "ought") as one of the touchstones
of religion. It is here--as we have seen in the earlier remarks of Chapter II where Utilitarianism as a proposed ethical position was tested on the basis of its
ability to answer the question of obligation--it is
here, that the claim of the secularist to provide an
ethics without religion will have its severest test.

The secularist finds that there are any number of
good things in life that he can pursue and obtain without the least thought of religion: the pleasures of
mind and sense, the many attractive goals of personal
and social endeavor, self-directed and other-directed
programs of action. Undoubtedly these constitute some
of the many facets of pleasure--and pleasure by no
means in any lesser or invidious sense. We may note
in passing, however, that while these pleasures may be
goods in some perfectly acceptable sense, they are not
necessarily moral goods. And the distinction may de-
tract from an early and easy victory for the secularist. From the premises that the fulfillment of moral
obligation is good, and that the above mentioned secularist goals are good, it does not follow that the
above mentioned secularist goals are in any sense the
fulfillment of moral obligation. Yet, the sense of
need to rise to the demands of an obligation-fulfill-
ment is universal. "Morality requires," "We must be
fair," "Requirements of justice are..." These refrains
are everywhere. They are strongly reminiscent of the
Natural Law philosophers and the Judeo-Christian apologists who have spoken of the transcendent law of morality that bears down upon man's nature to the end of
producing a virtually unbroken testimony of recognition of obligation. Kant writes,

There is...one thing in our soul which, when we
take a right view of it, we cannot cease to regard with the highest astonishment, and in regard
to which admiration is right, or even elevating,

---

62. Taylor, THE FAITH OF A MORALIST, Series I, p.
    155.

104

and that is the original moral capacity in us generally. What is that in us (we may ask ourselves)
by which we, who are constantly dependent on nature by so many wants, are yet raised so far
above it in the idea of an original capacity (in
us) that we regard them all as nothing, and ourselves as unworthy of existence, if we were to indulge in their satisfaction and opposition to a
law which our reason authoritatively prescribes;
although it is this enjoyment alone that can make
life desirable, while reason neither promises anything nor threatens.[63]

For Kant, it is out of this "original moral capacity"
that the overarching sense of moral obligation arises.
And to Taylor, this same "original moral capacity"
finds its proper ground, interpretation, and validation
in that identification of eternity and supernature to
which dialectically our epistemological handling of
temporality and nature points.

---

63. Immanuel Kant, "On the Radical Evil of Human Na-
     ture," Kant's CRITIQUE OF PRACTICAL REASON AND
     OTHER WORKS ON THE THEORY OF ETHICS. Translated
     by T. K. Abbott. (London: Longmans, Green and
     Co., 1923), p. 357.

CHAPTER V - MORAL VALUE AND EVIL

Although at the first level of its connotation evil is fundamentally disruptive of the moral dimension, its effects are not infrequently extended to all other categories of the person and of nature. Thus the alleged effects of the postulate of the fall of man in the Judeo-Christian tradition are found at every level of man's personality and, extending beyond the person, are alleged to appear in the "natural evils" to which nature is subject. In the former are found those disabling effects of body, mind and spirit issuing in disease, death, error, and subordination to false ideals; in the latter, the natural disasters of famine, flood, and other catastrophies. Natural catastrophies, viewed as in some sense judgments upon sin, together with the more directly moral affronts, justify the passage quoted from Augustine's AGAINST FORTUNATUS to the effect that "'There are two kinds of evil, sin and the penalty for sin.'"[1] Taylor's treatment of the problem of evil, however, declares that

> ...for the purely ethical attitude of mind the world has to be thought of as essentially imperfect, essentially out of accord with what it ought to be in order to correspond to our demands on it. ...That the world, as it comes to us in the temporal order, contains imperfection and evil which must be done away with, is a practical presupposition without which morality itself would have no raison d'etre.[2]

---

1. John Hick, "The Problem of Evil," THE ENCYCLOPEDIA OF PHILOSOPHY. Edited by Paul Edwards. (New York: The Macmillan Company & The Free Press, 1967), III, p. 137.

2. Alfred Edward Taylor, ELEMENTS OF METAPHYSICS. (London: Methuen & Company, 1903), p. 391.

In this observation, Taylor makes way to transfer the burden of "the problem of evil" from considerations of a purely ethical nature to that presupposition on which ethics itself grounds, viz., the religious dimension--and ultimately the person of God. "Thus there is not for morality, as we...see there must be for religion, such a thing as the 'Problem of Evil.'"[3] That "the problem of evil" arises in its most vexed form within the religious dimension is due to an "inevitable tendency of Religion...to identify its object with ultimate Reality, conceived in its timeless perfection as a complete and infinite individual whole."[4]

Suggestions concerning the possibility of God being finite are usually made out of deference to the dilemma suggested by this identification of the Absolute and God. In this identification, "it would appear," Taylor observes, "that evil itself must be, like everything else, a manifestation of His nature. And if so, can we say that God is strictly speaking 'good,' or is the complete realization of our ideals?"[5] But if the identification is not insisted upon, if a distinction is made between the Absolute and God, then there is some possibility--so reads the argument--that evil may be made to stop short of the Absolute and receive its explanation within the finitude of God.

There is some plausibility in the doctrine of a finite God. Both Absolutists and Finitists agree that God is a person. But our own intimate experience with what passes for personality and persons at the finite level of our associations leaves us with an equally intimate experience of finitude in every form: in intellectual power, in physical strength, in ideal commitment and behavior. Personality, to whom there is no challenge, no problem, no temptation, is not a part of our knowledge in any experiential sense. That God is both a person and faces problems some of which he cannot solve is a conjunction that our own experience as persons equips us to understand all too well. Further, it might appear that God is limited--even in the

---

3. Ibid.

4. Ibid., p. 392.

5. Ibid.

conception held of him by the Absolutists--in at least two ways: he cannot abdicate from existence and he cannot alter (and hence is subservient to) the laws of rationality. There is a difference between existence and non-existence, but God cannot choose the alternative of non-existence. It would appear therefore that he is subject to an Absolute greater than himself. The same subservience is manifested with regard to rationality's fundamental laws. Even God cannot assert contradictories as simultaneously true. Again, it would appear that deference is thereby being paid to an Absolute that transcends God.

The finitude thus envisioned brings us into the human dimension sufficiently to employ analogical illustration. Human persons know how error and evil crowd in upon the heels of the limitation that is identical with finitude. We cannot foresee contingency and we make blunders; we are powerless to effect our clearest insights; we lack the iron determination to eschew unrighteousness. Evil and error overlap and intermingle in the wake of human weakness. Such reportings are almost as certain as the experiences themselves. And while they are being recognized for their characteristic failings they are at the same time and for that reason being interpreted as failings by comparison with norms that to some extent at least may be said to transcend us. In an analogical sense, the finitude of God--together with whatever manifestations of lack of control of which he is allegedly chargeable--looks up to the Absolute, the ultimate and total identification of Reality with itself.

Taylor, in the light of the attempted solution of the problem of evil from the point of view of limiting God, proposes "not so much to offer a solution of this time-honored puzzle, as to make some suggestions which may help to put the issue at stake clearly before the reader's mind."[6] Rejecting the solution with the remark that "the finitude of God does not appear in any way to remove the difficulty about evil; in fact, it renders it, if anything more acute,"[7] Taylor notes that evil

---

6. Ibid., p. 393.

7. Ibid.

must now appear in the universe in a double form. On the other hand, it admittedly is taken to exist outside God, as a hostile factor limiting His power of shaping the world to His purpose. But again,...every finite individual, because finite, falls short of complete internal harmony of structure, and thus contains an element of defect and evil within himself. Thus evil will be inherent in the nature of a finite God, as well as in that of the existence supposed to be outside Him.[8]

It would appear that, as Taylor declares, every case of finitude is a case of defect in some sense, but it would also appear that only in those cases of the finitude having reached the possibility of moral status can the defect qualify as an evil one. In the case of finitude in general the allegation of defect looks fundamentally to the fact of the particular finitude's dependence upon external circumstances. Take any finite subject for analysis--a plant, an insect, a fish, a man--each one in turn is in a state of continuous dependence upon its environment. The environment is not the subject, but the subject cannot survive when cut off from environmental support. This fact is even dramatized by the consideration that the subjects chosen above for illustration were all organic and (from the points of view of Aristotle and Taylor) are possessed of a sort of built-in entelechy that confers a certain autonomy upon them that the pure passivity of inorganic objects cannot claim. Nevertheless, even these relatively autonomous subjects are in vital dependence both for the principle of their relative autonomy--even the principle of entelechy is passed on from parent stock--and for the nurture that is continuously and necessarily drawn from external sources. But the inorganic world also is in dependence upon the forces that shape the characteristics that it bears. No particular object of the inorganic world can claim that its sole explanation is to be found intrinsically --as though it existed in an isolation unaffected by the least force outside its own field of influence. It would appear therefore that Taylor is probably correct when, as he observes, "every finite individual,

---

8. Ibid.

because finite,...contains an element of defect."[9]
But, as remarked above, only in those cases of the finitude having reached the possibility of moral status
can the defect qualify as an evil one. Thus it does
not ordinarily appear to be a meaningful use of language to call plants, minerals and animals _evil_: they
are not generally regarded as meaningfully participat-
ing in that category in which the moral predicates belong.

I would have to conclude therefore that when Taylor declares that "every finite individual, because
finite,...contains an element of defect and evil within itself," he is correct as touching the allegation
of "defect," but not correct if he includes evil as a
part of the defect. Perhaps, of course, Taylor means
"evil" only in the sense of some non-moral defect,
some lack of "complete internal harmony of structure."[10] But, if so, this is to confuse quite need-
lessly when the need is to keep separate moral from
non-moral elements. It should be clear that not every
defect in man is a moral defect and this is even clearer when we are tracing defects of the kind that we
identified with that necessary dependence of finitude
upon its external environment.

Taylor's main effort, however, with respect to
the finite-God discussion was to evaluate the contention that the postulation of a finite God "solved" the
problem of evil. Not only does the finite-God postulate fail to solve the problem of evil, but, as we noted, it may actually compound it. And even at the
level of the suggestion that God's finitude may bring
him closer to the human need, Taylor finds that this
is nothing more than to postulate another person in
the universe, greater than human persons, but not perfectly in control, frustrated by his limitations, uncertain of the future: "a fit object only for moral
respect and sympathy, not for religious adoration."[11]

If, then, God is to be brought into Taylor's system finitude denied, the question must be faced whether we can worship the Absolute. This question--and

---

9.   Ibid.

10. Ibid.

11. Ibid., p. 394.

particularly the answer--is not to be placed against a merely psychological background. It is true enough that some persons can be found who will confess to having found worship possible of the most diverse objects --objects that for their particular psychic structuring are acceptable in some probably truly religious sense of personal dependence. But Taylor's insistence is that if the Absolute be admitted as a justifiable object of worship, there must be, in principle, that sort of rational validation that will support such an Absolute regardless of the personal determination to accept or to reject.

For Taylor, the Absolute "contains all finite existence," is "a perfectly harmonious system," "the concrete individual reality in which our ideals have actual existence," and therefore "all finite aspiration must somehow be realized in the structure of the Absolute whole," though, Taylor adds, "not necessarily in the way in which we, as beings of limited knowledge of goodness, actually wish it to be realized."[12]

There is some illustrative advantage at this point to take note of certain implications of the Judeo-Christian system which may seem to favor the general conclusions to which Taylor is directing us. Whatever the doctrine of creation ought to mean it has been at least almost of one voice in declaring that a state of absolute dependence is involved such that the appearance-aspect of things must relate back to that reality on which it depends. If this may be taken provisionally as essential to the Judeo-Christian doctrine of creation, we might say in addition that there must be as much reality in God as there is in any creature. Thus it has been remarked that if cows were to have a God, it would be a cow-God; and if spiders were to have a God, it would be a spider-God. The position adopted by Taylor would justify these positions. That is to say, there must be as much reality in God as there is in any cow or any spider. And because the position can be generalized, we can say that for every creature there is the same logical need to refer its own existence with all of its positive attributes to the source, the ground, of their being.

---

12. Ibid.

And what is decreed for finite existence in general is
ipso facto decreed for our ideals as well. It is in
this compound sense of totally referring back to God,
back to the Absolute, as the ground, the ultimate
cause, the supreme principle of all reality, that Taylor's hope seeks justification. The Absolute becomes
a proper and indeed necessary object of worship. Taylor is aware of the complaint often voiced that the
Absolute is a poor substitute for the living God. But
this is really to betray a lack of understanding of
what the terms mean. For Taylor, to know truly what
God is, to understand truly what should be meant by the
Absolute, is to realize that these are simply two different words for the same reality. So much is this the
conviction of Taylor that the Theistic Absolutism here
endorsed becomes for him the fuller explanation of
which many lesser words are merely approximations.
Thus from this point of view there is discovered an
element of truth in pantheism, namely, the absolute
dependence of every particular in the universe on God
and that God is everywhere at the same time. Similarly, there is an element of truth in agnosticism and
atheism due to the fact that no particular aspect of
reality can comprehend the ground of its particularity
exhaustively. Thus, defect of knowledge becomes agnosticism's and atheism's "element of truth."

Returning now more specifically to the problem of
evil, Taylor admits that "the detailed solution of the
problem is out of the question" but adds that "it is
at least possible to make suggestions which may show
that the problem is a mere consequence of the inevitable defects of our insight, and that it would disappear with fuller knowledge."[13] That is to say, not
everything of which we would be tempted to predicate
evil is necessarily evil. That we are tempted to ascribe evil to situations that are not evil may be due
to at least two considerations: (1) we may not know
many times what our real concerns, our real purposes,
are, with the result that we feel in the pinch of
frustration a situation that we denominate evil. When
this variance is between our imagined ideals and the
reals of existence, we are led to see evil in the opposing circumstance. With multiplied wants and desires, the growth of frustration keeps pace with the

---

13. Ibid., p. 395.

all but settled conviction that our environment is largely that of defect and even hostility. Out of these the other evils of pessimism and cynicism are born. (2) Also, the effects of our acts, as well as the effects of others' acts, are only dimly apprehended. Some of the sought-for goods of life that we have had to forego have been means to greater goods in the long-term reckoning, while some of our short-term triumphs have proven to be, not merely of short duration, but seed-plots of disaster. As Taylor puts it, "Existence appears to be in part evil, because we cannot take it in at once and as a whole in its individual structure."[14]

Taylor warns against the hope of an easy answer to questions that may tie in with the very ultimate nature of the universe.

> For it is surely certain that when science, philosophy, and theology have done all they can do, the world still remains a mysterious and surprising thing; any account of it which really eliminated all the mystery from it would be proved by that one consideration to be a false and superficial account.[15]

Such declarations by Taylor indicate that he will not underwrite a complete dogmatism; neither, however, -- as the earlier discussions show--does he yield to a complete skepticism. It would appear that his general position is that man knows too much to know nothing and too little to know all. In this in-between position is defined at once in principle the limits and prospects of general epistemology.

Because Taylor later will measure--and thus validate--the significance of the ethically good and the ethically evil by comparison with an absolute standard that he will claim to be the inescapable norm, the universal presupposition, of moral value, the question arises whether we can regard the Absolute as "Good," and whether, more narrowly, we can regard it as

---

14. Ibid., p. 396.

15. Alfred Edward Taylor, THE PROBLEM OF EVIL. (London: Ernest Benn, 1929), p. 5.

"ethically good."

To the first question, that is, may we regard the Absolute as Good, Taylor returns the answer, <u>Yes</u>. The Absolute is Good because it is the embodiment of all our ideals, or, more accurately, all that our ideals should be. There is no fuller meaning for Good than this meaning. Here the fulfillment of all partial goods is concentrated. Here is <u>the Idea</u>, <u>the Form</u>, <u>the Norm</u>, of Good--wherever that term has <u>any</u> use. It is <u>The Ideal</u> that "we are trying amid our ignorance and confusion to realize."[16]

But, to the second question, may we call the Absolute ethically good, Taylor returns the answer, "...we can hardly say without qualification that the whole is good....it is better not to call the Absolute 'moral.'"[17] "Ethical goodness" means the goodness of "gradual assertion of the ideal against apparent evil."[18]

This contrast between the Absolute that is Good without qualification and the Absolute of which it is "better not to call /it/ ...'moral,'" would find its parallel in the consideration that the Decalog which might be considered the command and the measure of man's moral stature, is not applicable to God himself. Ethical <u>endeavor</u>, simply because it is endeavor, is not the completion of the ideal which is its goal. And, for Taylor, this situation is repeated in all of experience and becomes to a marked degree one of the fundamental meanings of experience. For, as Taylor puts it, "...we have, as in all the experience of finite beings, a process which is throughout directed upon a result that, once attained, would transcend the process itself."[19] This is true in the areas of the intellect and the will. We strive for knowledge. But the striving ceases when the knowledge is attained. And if, theoretically, all knowledge could be attained, the learning experience itself would be no more.

---

16. Taylor, ELEMENTS OF METAPHYSICS, p. 396.

17. <u>Ibid</u>.

18. <u>Ibid</u>.

19. <u>Ibid</u>., p. 397.

Morality, then, Taylor affirms, "...would not be content with anything less than the total abolition of
the evil in the world; and with the disappearance of
evil, the struggle against it would itself disappear
in some higher form of experience."[20] So, we may conclude that the reason why we would not call the Absolute ethical is because "it is already all that ethical life consists in striving to become."[21]

Before turning to what is Taylor's more defini-
tive discussion of the ramifications of the problem of
evil, let us note that the following have been acknowledged: the universality of evil in its historical,
geographical, and personal in-depth manifestations;
that, strictly speaking, there is no "problem of evil"
for morality--for morality presupposes the defect that
is evil as the only baffle that is to be overcome, but
that the problem of evil does arise in its fullest in-
tensity when God as the Absolute is introduced; that a
finite God--as distinct from the Absolute--only postpones the solution of the problem of evil--for such is
only another person in the world and it is out of the
domain of finite persons that the problem is generated; that finitude is itself in some sense a defect
due to its essential dependence upon some reality external to itself; that, although we cannot promise a
solution to the problem of evil in detail, we are
helped by noting that not every case of imputed evil
is necessarily one, but is possibly due to our not
knowing whether our frustrations are real indexes of
evil's presence or only our failure to know our own
true aspirations, and, too, we cannot always know the
effects of our or others' acts--whether in the long
calculation they are really evil or good; and, lastly,
however much inability we may experience in answering
in detail questions relating to evil's origin and
(possible) purpose, we are persuaded of its presence--
which calls attention to that Norm or Ideal by which
it is identified and measured. It is to this conception of a presupposed Ideal that Taylor will now direct attention as he takes note of the unique standard
that is presupposed in order to account for the

---

20. Ibid.

21. Ibid., p. 398.

uniquely differentiating characteristics of evil as it is met and exhibited in human experience.

It is a defect of many of the writers of modern ethics, Taylor believes, that, ignoring the norm by which alone moral good and evil can be truly and adequately identified, their writings are said to reveal only a surface awareness of the problem. That moral evil has not received adequate treatment in the "ordinary philosophical treatises on ethics" is their "most outstanding defect."[22] True, they write of the good for man, of virtue, of obligation, but they do not write of sinfulness, or wickedness.[23]

It might not be going much too far to say that, of the major philosophers who have dealt expressly and at length with the moral life of man (independently of a theological tradition), there are only two, though they are two of the greatest, Plato and Kant, whose language reveals a keen and constant sense of human sinfulness. Certainly, one would look in vain for such a sense in the work of most of the best-known of these philosophers. It is not in Aristotle, nor in Descartes, nor in Spinoza, nor in Leibniz, nor in Hegel; least of all in the breezy and easy-tempered David

---

22. Taylor, THE FAITH OF A MORALIST, Series I, p. 163.

23. As Taylor remarks of Kant, he /Kant7 does not spare the human person from the strongest indictments of moral failure. That the world is advancing from worse to better, Kant describes as an "heroic opinion," an opinion, he adds, "certainly not founded on experience." (Immanuel Kant, "On the Radical Evil of Human Nature," KANT'S CRITIQUE OF PRACTICAL REASON AND OTHER WORKS ON THE THEORY OF ETHICS. Translated by T. K. Abbott. London: Longmans, Green and Co., 1923, p. 326). "The depravity of human nature" is actually, Kant says, "perversity of heart," (Ibid., p. 344) and "the propensity to evil amongst men is universal, or, what here signifies the same thing,...is interwoven with human nature." (Ibid., p. 337). For Kant, although we may speak of man's "natural propensity to evil, ...man must," Kant adds, "always incur the blame of it," and the evil itself may be declared a radical badness in human nature, innate..." (Ibid., p. 339.)

Hume. It is not even prominent in such vigorous champions of an "eternal and immutable" morality as Cudworth, Clarke and Price.[24]

A tendency that Taylor notes in many of the philosophers of ethics is to treat evil as essentially of one kind--and particularly not noting that aspect of evil that has contributed its most sharply differentiating character, viz., wickedness.

Among the "great philosophies of profoundly ethical inspiration" Taylor includes Christianity, Plato and Kant. Taylor writes,

The Platonic position, as we may conveniently call it after one of its most eloquent assertors, is that evil is not of one kind but of several. Want, for example, is really an evil thing, so is bodily disease, so is the moral disease we call sin. But they are not all equally evils. Disease, which has its seat within the person, is an intenser and more typical evil than want, which has its seat in his circumstances; and incomparably worse than either is sin, which has its seat in the inmost citadel of his personality, his soul. The supreme and typical evil is neither want nor bodily disease, but the moral sickness of sin. Suffering is bad, and may be very bad indeed, but sin is incommensurably worse.[25]

Plato's remark on the evil in the soul in GORGIAS 477 is perhaps typical of Plato's attitude toward that specific evil of which Taylor speaks, viz., that "injustice and the evil of the soul in general" is "the most shameful." And again, "its superlative shamefulness must be due to a harm and viciousness immeasurably and surpassingly great." In the LETTERS vii. 335, the materialistic Philistine is declared "blind and does not see that consequences attend the abominable wickedness of his acts of violence, for each wrongdoing adds its weight to a burden which the sinner must drag with him." Again in the LAWS v. 731, Plato observes

24. Taylor, THE FAITH OF A MORALIST, Series I, pp. 163-164.

25. Taylor, THE PROBLEM OF EVIL, pp. 12-13.

that "no man...will of set purpose receive the supreme
evil into this most precious thing /i.e., his soul/
and live with it there all his life through"; yet, despite this, there is the "unqualified and incorrigible
offender, the utterly corrupt." In the REPUBLIC x.
608, we read that evil is "That which destroys and cor-
rupts in every case," and we are urged in THEAETETUS
176 to recognize that "Evils...can never be done away
with...but they must needs haunt this region of our
mortal nature." We are bidden therefore "to take
flight from this world to the other, and that means becoming like the divine so far as we can, and that
again is to become righteous with the help of wisdom."[26]

For Taylor, the "exceeding sinfulness of man" is
an aspect of moral evil that is not adequately emphasized by regarding evil as a merely regrettable inci-
dent of human life, as misdeeds that should be put
right and avoided in the future, as something merely
morbid as to subject matter and better dismissed in
the interest of healthy-mindedness. "Amendment," Taylor remarks, "attended perhaps with confession, virtually becomes...the whole of penitence; the contri-
tion which makes itself heard in the 'penitential'
Psalms seems almost unknown to 'philosophical'
ethics."[27]

It is the deep, permanent, insistent meaning
within the moral reaction that must be dealt with as a
first concern and, as such, indicts as inadequate all
naturalistic explanations. Kant remarks on the can-
celling effects of any attempt to reduce ethics to a

---

26. The above quotations from Plato are taken from
     THE COLLECTED DIALOGUES OF PLATO. Edited by E.
     Hamilton and H. Cairnes. Bollingen Series LXXI.
     New York: Bollingen Foundation, 1961. The var-
     ied publisher sources represented in this antho-
     logy of Plato's writings indicates the propriety
     of acknowledging the various translators. Thus,
     GORGIAS, translated by W. D. Woodhead; LETTERS,
     translated by L. A. Post; LAWS, translated by
     A. E. Taylor; REPUBLIC, translated by Paul
     Shorey; and THEAETETUS, translated by F. M. Corn-
     ford.

27. Taylor, THE FAITH OF A MORALIST, Series I, p. 165.

naturalistic basis. To "naturalize" what we ordinarily call ethically predicable actions is to lose for those actions their moral quality. "...nature, ...if it meant...the opposite of the source of actions from freedom, would be directly contradictory to the predicates morally good or evil...."[28] It is this same meaning that dialectically points beyond the de facto experience of ethical reaction to what is at once the epistemological ground of that meaning and the ontological cause of ethical aspiration.

> Our moral reaction to "wickedness" appears to me to be a genuinely ethical reaction, and yet to bear witness to the impossibility of preventing the ethical habit of mind, once thoroughly awakened, from developing spontaneously into a habit which must be regarded as specifically religious. It is not, so far as I can see, theology which has contaminated ethics with the notion of sin; it is morality which has brought the notion into theology.[29]

Taylor is forced to measure the coherence of his account of ethics by considering the naturalistic explanations. Thus, evolutionary accounts of man's long development teach that judgments of every kind--ethical, esthetic, rational, practical--are themselves, in course of development, necessarily untrustworthy due to their trial and error advances, and in no case is their process of correction ever fully completed. Moral judgment (and corresponding moral action) is regarded as measured by the standard(s) already reached by our society. "The bad man may be regarded simply as a 'barbarian' among civilized surroundings, or an 'animal' among men."[30] Good and evil fluctuate with circumstances of time and place, and the doctrine of cultural relativism is fructified by the wide disparity of mores. Here, evil, viewed broadly, is like growing pains; or, it is identical with the tensions of development; or, it is "a relapse into ways of

---

28. Kant, "On the Radical Evil of Human Nature," p. 327.

29. Taylor, THE FAITH OF A MORALIST, Series I, p. 169.

30. Ibid.

120

response which have become inappropriate as the 'environment' develops."[31] But evil appears to be much more than an epiphenomenon that attaches to slaved or arrested development like a shadow following a man; evil, to be sure, arises upon the occasion of personal and societal tensions, but is not identical with them, and still less is it the purely passive phenomenon exercising no causal force of its own. If evolution's account of evil is to identify it with the latent savagery of developing man, that account, Taylor believes, is reversed by the consideration that "it takes high intelligence to be greatly wicked, no less than to be greatly good," as was evidenced in the world-war: "impossible except to a world in a 'high state of civilization.'"[32] "When we give the reins to human wickedness," Taylor writes, "we run a far worse danger than that of sinking back into the state of 'animals'; we risk becoming something like 'devils.'"[33]

In THE PROBLEM OF EVIL, Taylor takes note of "Some Typical Theories, Ancient and Modern" that purport to explain the nature of evil. One such "Typical Theory" is that "when I call anything bad or evil, I mean no more than that I personally happen to feel a dislike for it, and personal likes and dislikes are merely arbitrary and capricious."[34] Because this position is implicitly a disclaimer of all objectivity in evil, Taylor notes that it prevents any _rule_ of "choice and avoidance"--a prohibition that the advocate of this theory cannot put into practice. The "practice" would be a type of passivity that is denied by the very decision to adopt it. Further, the attempt to equate evil with personal dislike does not obviate the distinction between _experienced_ good and evil. And though this experience may be written off as illusion the illusion itself now must bear the burden of a besetting evil.

Another "typical theory" is that "taught in the

---

31. Taylor, THE PROBLEM OF EVIL, p. 10.

32. _Ibid._, p. 11.

33. _Ibid._, p. 12.

34. _Ibid._, p. 7.

ancient world by the Stoics, and often repeated by optimists of later times, that though evil is not a pure illusion, it is only relative."[35] The element of recognized "optimism" lies in the interpretation of particular evils contributing to universal goods.

> As Chrysippus put it, the worst sufferings, blunders, and crimes of men are, in the life of the universe, what rants, doggerel, and bad grammar may be in a good plan, sorry stuff, considered in themselves, but an actual beauty when taken in their setting as contributing to a total effect. To find fault with their presence in the world is like censuring Shakespeare for the blunder of Dogberry, or the vapourings of Ancient Pistol.[36]

Taylor recognizes the hazardous quality of the attempted analogy. There is simply no proof whatsoever that the particular evils with which experience is so much concerned do in fact contribute to this universal good. And even if, Taylor adds, we had the faith so to believe, it really does not solve the problem of evil at that narrow point where evil is so conspicuously unwanted. "It is not clear that all 'partial evil' is productive of good, and, if it were, to be productive of good is one thing, to be good another."[37] There is no guarantee that the particular sufferer will be solaced in a subsequent unveiling of universalized good.

Although Taylor is ready to recognize a genuine ethical situation arising upon the occasions pointed to by the naturalist, he is not prepared to see the uniquely differentiating character of the ethical dimension reduced to and identified with this natural event. Neither in what may be man's evolutionary prehistory, nor in any of the descriptively delineated human actions of real history, does the genuinely ethical residue appear.

---

35. Ibid., p. 8.

36. Ibid., pp. 8-9.

37. Ibid., p. 9.

The point I am anxious to enforce, /Taylor
writes/ is that, in more ways than one, our human
expression of wrong-doing and guilt is so singu-
larly unlike anything we can detect in the pre-
human world that we are bound to treat it as
something strictly sui generis and human, not
generically animal.[38]

Taylor now proceeds to give an account of these "more
ways than one" in which the uniquely differentiating
aspects of moral evil are manifest.

First, our human sense of guilt is not a mere discontent with our surroundings, but a condemnation of
what we are and what we do. Thus, a man who stands to
inherit a fortune is disappointed by the unexpected
eccentricity of the testator, but self-condemned if he
knows he was cut off "for his idleness, profligacy, or
ingratitude."[39] The first is unfortunate; the latter,
punished. Taylor comments, "We should not even remark
it, as we do, as a common feature of human nature,
that men so regularly try to awaken our pity for their
misfortunes by dwelling on the theme of their being
due 'to no fault of their own'."[40]

Secondly, guilt possesses a sort of indelibility,
a lingering reproach and dissatisfaction with our
past. Thus, our past keeps pace with our present,
misdeeds are never wholly obliterated, and, in contrast to our debt to society which may be considered
to be paid, our debt to the more categorical demands
of moral awareness are not thus put to silence. Of
him who has paid a debt to society, Taylor says, "We
may have lost the right to reproach him; he does not
cease to reproach himself."[41] These remembered ne-
glects, cruelties, unfair advantages taken, even the
relative trivialities now gone, forgotten by those of-
fended, their harm, if any, now absorbed in the social

---

38. Taylor, THE FAITH OF A MORALIST, Series I, p. 170.

39. Ibid., p. 172.

40. Ibid.

41. Ibid., p. 174.

123

cosmos' infinite ability of adjustment, even these,
haunt and torment, and if they produce no further than
a silent wish that we had not done them, it is sufficient to mark the moral reaction as exhibiting a
uniquely differentiating characteristic of our abiding
sense of wrongdoing. And as such it becomes a peculiar but trenchant witness to an objective moral value-
complex. So nearly universal does Taylor regard this
sense of indictment by our remembered past moral failure that he is emboldened to reply to charges of "mor-
bidity" and "superstition" by reminding his critics
that

> if you allow yourself to dismiss any universal
> characteristic of life as "morbid," you lose the
> very basis for an intelligible distinction be-
> tween health and disease. If we cannot take quod
> semper, quod ubique, quod ab omnibus as the stan-
> dard of health and normality, what is to be our
> criterion of the normal and the morbid? If all
> men without exception are mad, how are we to draw
> the distinction between the sane man and in-
> sane?[42]

But is the sense of past moral failure with its
present gnawing indictment a universal experience?
Taylor can have only one answer: "Each of us must ask
himself whether there are not some episodes in his own
past about which he himself feels it."[43] But this
answer is deceptively simple. It calls forth both denials of fact as well as proffered explanations if the
fact must be affirmed. As for denials of fact, Taylor
is too persuaded of the virtual ubiquity of the moral
sense in its exhibition throughout the totality of
written history to be much deterred by this argument.
It is safe to say that a pinpoint cannot touch down on
the flow of human history but that it should alight
upon conflict where the claims and counterclaims of
justice and injustice are being challenged. It is an
all but sufficient empirical proof that man's essential nature is deeply constitutive of an ethical dimension. Civilization exhibits this uniquely differentiating aspect of moral evil both in the individual

---

42. Ibid., p. 176.

43. Ibid.

124

and in the larger groupings of society--even to the
level of sovereign states. Kant indicts both by remarking,

> if one is disposed to think that human nature can
> be better known in a civilized condition (in
> which its characteristic properties can be more
> perfectly developed), then one must listen to a
> long melancholy litany of complaints of humanity;
> of secret falsehood, even in the most intimate
> friendship, so that it is reckoned a general max-
> im of prudence, that even the best friends should
> restrain their confidence in their mutual inter-
> course; of a propensity to hate the man to whom
> one is under an obligation, for which a benefac-
> tor must always be prepared; of a hearty good-
> will, which nevertheless admits the remark that
> "in the misfortunes of our best friends there is
> something which is not altogether displeasing to
> us"; and of many other vices concealed under the
> appearance of virtue, not to mention the vices of
> those who do not conceal them, because we are
> satisfied to call a man good who is a bad man of
> the average class. This will give one enough of
> the vices of culture and civilization (the most
> mortifying of all) to make him turn away his eye
> from the conduct of men, lest he should fall into
> another vice, namely, misanthropy. If he is not
> yet satisfied, however, he need only take into
> consideration a condition strangely compounded of
> both, namely, the external condition of nations--
> for the relation of civilized nations to one an-
> other is that of a rude state of nature (a state
> of perpetual preparation for war), and they are
> also firmly resolved never to abandon it--and he
> will become aware of principles adopted by the
> great societies called States, which directly
> contradict the public profession, and yet are
> never to be laid aside, principles which no phil-
> osopher has yet been able to bring into agreement
> with morals, nor (sad to say) can they propose
> any better which would be reconcilable with human
> nature; so that the philosophical millennium,
> which hopes for a state of perpetual peace,
> founded on a union of nations as a republic of
> the world, is generally ridiculed as visionary,
> just as much as the theological, which looks for
> the complete moral improvement of the whole human

race.[44]

As for explanations of this fact that purport to escape the uniquely differentiating character of the ethical dimension by employing naturalistic alternatives, Taylor's reply is that of distinguishing the _form_ from the _matter_ of ethical discourse. Thus, if sense of sin should be likened to the discomfort one feels in having committed some "social blunder," the one making this reply, Taylor says,

> is really bearing witness against himself. He is testifying that he has the feeling all the time, though it may, in his case, be attached to the wrong objects, exactly as the man who is thrown into transports of delight by the second-rate in literature or music really has a sense of beauty, though an untrained and ill-regulated sense.[45]

This is Taylor's recurrent Platonism and calls attention to "the Ideas" of justice, beauty, good, as the antecedently present _norms_ by the aid of which we identify _approximations_ appearing in the relative impurity of experience. To reverse this epistemology and to "explain" the Idea as a consequence of a non-moral aspect of experience, for Taylor, "is a pure fallacy of _hysteron proteron_."[46] Third, Taylor names as a "further peculiarity of the genuinely ethical attitude towards sin" a demand for punishment noting that in doctrines of demands for punishment and doctrines of retribution, though open to misunderstanding, we find "a doctrine really indispensable to sound ethics."[47] Not to be confused with revenge--"essentially a personal gratification"--a truer doctrine of retribution as exhibited in law "depends on the withdrawal of the initiative in bringing offenses to punishment from the parties immediately concerned and the lodging of it with bodies representative of the

---

44. Kant, "On the Radical Evil of Human Nature," pp. 340-341.

45. Taylor, THE FAITH OF A MORALIST, Series I, p. 177.

46. _Ibid_.

47. _Ibid_., p. 183.

community at large."[48]   Nor is this transfer from the
hands of the private to community representation a
repetition of a revengeful motivation: "...when the
murderer and the forger are brought to justice, no
section of a civilized society enjoys the pleasant
feeling of gratified personal revenge."[49]   Rather,
with a sort of Rousseau-like flavor of "general will,"
Taylor explains:

> What we all feel at bottom, I believe, is that
> the sentence of society, or of a court of law,
> inflicting punishment on an offender, if it is
> really a just sentence, is only the repetition of
> one which the offender, if his moral being re-
> mains sound at the centre, must already have
> passed against himself.[50]

---

48.   Ibid.

49.   Ibid., p. 186.

50.   The "retributivist" position is possessed of many
      difficulties. It is said, for example, that
      there is no absolutely just way in which a punish-
      ment can be made to fit the breech of conduct--
      whether the breech of conduct is legal or moral or
      both; again, it is said that breech of conduct
      does not automatically entail punishment--the for-
      mer being conceivable without the latter without
      contradiction; again, the historical fact that
      legal and extra-legal punishments have been used
      to regulate society is (on the surface at least) a
      utilitarian consideration and does not in itself
      show that the breech of conduct "demands" punish-
      ment--at least not in a tightly logical sense. It
      would appear that, once again, Taylor is distin-
      guishing between the form and the matter of pun-
      ishment--a distinction that permits him to agree
      to the difficulties of application of a just pun-
      ishment while adhering to the principle of a just
      retribution. This is, in principle, a Platonic
      position that recognizes that, though none of the
      great determining norms that make up the unity,
      the cement, of experience are capable of exact ap-
      plication, they may not be dismissed because of
      that difficulty. In a manner of reasoning not
      dissimilar to Kant's principle of universalization

A fourth characteristic claimed as identifying
moral experience is its polluting quality. Appeal is
here made to the fact that "all languages" are made to
bear a dual message, viz., that which most offends
sight, touch or smell and is described in words such as
filthy, dirty, stinking, in turn, serve to describe
that which is offensive to the conscience as well.
Thus, defilement is an idea carried by some similar set
of words and made to apply at both physical and moral
levels. One can feel unclean at both levels and much
of ritualistic practice consists of ceremonial wash-
ings and other purifyings strongly suggestive of the
thesis of a moral pollution.

Taylor sees the retention of the "dirtiness" of
dirt at both physical and moral levels as an implicit
protest to a naturalism which, if successfully carrying its philosophy to completion in daily human thinking, would eliminate our preoccupation with "dirt" as
an emotionally charged and offensive thought. So, at
the physical level, "dirt" is a subjective illusion.
There is no "dirt" to the scientist; to him, it is
chemically what it is and nothing more, and even "refuse" in one place is valuable in another. Similarly,
should not the same application of naturalistic explanation relieve us of this virtual legacy of felt
moral-pollution and in the wake of the rationalized
purge of our morbidness grant us rather an objectivity
and healthy-mindedness? Taylor notes that in the case
of physical "dirt" "the progress of science does not
seem to have...(the) result...of banishing the notion
of 'dirt' and the emotional reaction against it from
men's lives,"[51] and, regarding moral "dirt": "What
actually happens is rather that our notion of the
'polluting' is transferred to fresh types of action."[52]

---

of a true maxim or of Plato's writing justice
large upon the State, Taylor sees "punishment"
as, in principle, the manifest fruit of the violation of true moral value. It is the interior
aspect of the immoral act coming to its own natural fruition.

51. Ibid., p. 198.

52. Ibid., pp. 198-199.

The "transfer," that is to say, follows our deepening sophistication of what is to be included among moral values. Increased consciousness, greater coherence in our value-philosophy, progressive "rationalization" of ethical meaning: these are the dialectical promptings that indicate the greater range of possibility for what Taylor here calls evil's "polluting" characteristic. If this slowed emancipation from an older moral scruple is not merely due to our human inertia, it may well be that Taylor's appeal to the fact of man's felt involvement with physical and moral pollution points out a true fulfilling condition of his general thesis of the uniquely differentiating character of moral reaction. It is not only acts themselves but the causal fount from which these effects emerge to which Taylor draws attention, remarking,

> As the range of applicability widens, the principle itself acquires a deeper inwardness at every fresh stage in the process. It is not the overt act alone, but the unworthy desire or thought, even the desire which is regularly repressed before it can influence action, the thought which arises only to be dismissed, that our "honour" feels as a stain.[53]

Premising this deep moral disturbance as too universally insistent for successful denial, Taylor turns to the utilitatian interpretation with the observation that we have

> plain proof that the identification of the moral good with mere beneficent social activities is a superficial falsification of moral experience. If the whole of our aim as persons with moral aspirations were merely to act for the promotion of "social welfare," I can see no reason why our discontent with our own character should demand the purification of the inner man with all this intensity. So long as our unworthier thoughts and contemplations lead to no consequences in overt action, I cannot see why, on such an interpretation of morality, they should not be regarded as exempt from judgement of conscience.[54]

---

53. <u>Ibid.</u>, p. 199.

54. <u>Ibid.</u>, p. 200.

That they may not be "exempt from the judgement of conscience"--on Taylor's basis of reckoning--is due to the fact accepted that "As a man thinketh in his heart, so is he." The intimacy of conjunction between man's thought and man's being amounts to a practical identity and, therefore, if man's being is never exempt from the scrutiny and critique of conscience, neither is his thought. Hence, quite independently of consequences of man's thought, the thought itself is seen to be the natural object of censure for an illumined and sensitive conscience.

A last point in the census of uniquely differentiating characteristics of moral reaction concerns the subject that is felt to be defiled and polluted. This "subject," for Taylor, is not the "person as it actually exists that is the object of this unqualified and solicitous reverence"; still less, primitive and elemental human nature, there merely "natural" man, "not yet caught up in the advance of the moralising process, if such a creature ever existed;"[55] the subject that is acknowledged as defiled and polluted is the true self, or, in other words, the ideal self. In Taylor's words, "What is defiled by sin and dishonour is the self I aspire yet to possess as my own, quando che sia."[56]

Taylor's idea of the "good," as well as his idea of what constitutes the "good self," or "good person," uniformly possesses a teleological overtone. Thus we find Taylor, in another connection, emphasizing this aspect of the "good": he writes,

> The change of expression from this is good to this is what it ought to be brings out in high relief a genuine fact, the teleological reference implied in the use of the predicate good, and it further indicates that when the word good is used in its proper sense, and not as a loose equivalent of useful, the teleology is internal, inherent in the very nature of the thing which is pronounced good. The "nature" of the person or thing in question is not merely to have certain

55. Ibid., p. 206.

56. Ibid., p. 207.

characters, but to <u>tend</u> <u>to</u> a certain completion or fulfillment. In <u>this</u> sense, what I may call a <u>forward-looking</u> reference is embedded in the very structure of the subject of the predication.[57]

This implies that the ideal self must be present <u>now</u>, though enslaved, weakened, and rendered impotent to actualize its own recognized ideals by the accident of the disabling effect of that poison that has attacked "the very fountain of our moral personality."[58] It is this contest between the real and the ideal self that enables us to become acutely aware of the character possessed by each. If we, as persons, are censured by an ideal that appropriately and relevantly addresses itself to the essential matters of our moral personality, a presumption is created that the fuller nature of that ideal identifies with "a person of supreme excellence, entitled to wholehearted devotion."[59]

We catch analogies of this fuller ideal when we "personify" a cause or principle. Loyalties (or treasons) become significant only when <u>a person</u> is being thus served. But when we are asked to evaluate the explanation of our loyalties, or the extent of our culpability in treason (when <u>persons</u> have been the direct object of either), to what norm and ideal do we appeal--except that norm and ideal that is itself personified: "of that ideal as already embodied in the living and personal God."[60] Here, Taylor is somewhat like Kant in that to neither can the hard fact of the moral ought be minimized. The result of taking it with supreme seriousness is to end with equal seriousness with that ideal, that norm, that presupposition by which it is measured, and to note that the nature of those human selves that are thus directed and rebuked by this ideal--human selves that individually unify life, will, intellect, and moral aspiration--cannot properly consider the ideal by which they are

57. Taylor, "Is Goodness a Quality?", pp. 154-155.

58. Taylor, THE FAITH OF A MORALIST, Series I, p. 207.

59. <u>Ibid</u>.

60. <u>Ibid</u>., p. 208.

131

thus directed to be other than "that ideal as already embodied in the living and personal God." That is to say, the norm by which some particular is to be measured cannot be the particular itself. Thus, when the particular to be "measured" is itself a person, the norm must include at least all that "person" includes in addition to supplying the essentials of a person at an appropriately universal dimension.

We get closer to the uniquely differentiating characteristic of evil when it is viewed (as Taylor believes Plato, Kant, and Christianity combine to teach) as "something which absolutely ought not to be."[61] Such an imputed characteristic, if true, would separate evil from all naturalistic interpretations: of none of the tensions of evolutionary development-- however unsatisfactory they may be when experienced-- can it strictly be said they ought not to be. Strict naturalism must eliminate as meaningless the "ought not" from its interpretations of reality. Whatever opinions may be held regarding the total structure of Platonic, Kantian, or Christian systems, it appears, with respect to man's sense of the conflict between justice and injustice, as evidenced throughout the near-totality of human history, that these three systems of thought and man's general sense of justice have maintained a very close approximation to a doctrine of condemnation of evil as "something which absolutely ought not to be."[62]

The paradox that emerges--whether on naturalistic or supranaturalistic grounds of explanation--is that generated by the consideration that in one sense some things ought not to be and therefore might not have been, while in another sense it would seem, everything must in some sense have been decreed by whatever is the ultimately governing power of the world. Now, it is the contention of Taylor that any decision--implicit or explicit--to settle the moral issue by pleading an ultimately governing cause for human action other than an autonomously generated cause of human free will is, in principle, to destroy the ethical dimension and, with that destruction, to deprive human nature of an essential attribute. If, Taylor believes,

---

61. Taylor, THE PROBLEM OF EVIL, p. 13.

62. Ibid.

no true account of the ethical dimension in human history can evade personal responsibility, then the naturalist must be accounted as having given no true account of the ethical dimension because he transfers responsibility to some power or powers over which he has no control. Indirectly, man's very determination to account for his moral failure by reference to all sorts of causes behind the act shows his sensitiveness to the claim that ethical responsibility has upon him. Taylor remarks,

> Augustine, in his CONFESSIONS, treats his own early Manicheanism as a heinous moral fault rather than a mere intellectual mistake. He feels that his secret reason for being so ready to believe in the limitation of the divine power by the existence of an opposing evil principle lay in his own pride; he wished to ascribe the worst in his own life to lack of power in God rather than to rebelliousness in his own will. [63]

In contrast, for Taylor, men who take seriously the moral dimension prefer the pain of acknowledgement of personal moral failure to the subterfuge of referring their moral acts to a power or powers that lies behind them.

> They are acutely sensible that, whatever excuses we may try to make to ourselves and for ourselves, wickedness is not the same sort of thing as a wretched memory or a weak heart, a misfortune which we "cannot help," and they prefer intellectual honesty about the matter to self-compliments, as they all at heart prefer the criminal who owns his crime candidly to the commoner type who represents himself as the sympathetic victim of circumstance. [64]

The importance that Taylor gives to the moral dimension in general and to personal responsibility in particular together with his repudiation of naturalism as adequate to explain this area of human experience

---

63. Ibid., p. 16.

64. Ibid., p. 17.

leads to a defense of the proposition that "there is nothing inherently self-contradictory either in the notion of a free agent or in that of the creation of free agents. The one," Taylor adds,

> contradicts only the crude prejudice that an intelligent agent is related to the "motives" of his contemplated acts precisely as a balance is related to the weights put into its scale-pans, the other only the mere assumption that a Creator can only create puppets. To use such argument is simply to assume the very points which are at issue.[65]

That there is nothing inherently self-contradictory in the notion of a free agent, and that, moreover, the allegation of such freedom is both supportive of our deepest sense of moral awareness and coherent with all else that we must admit concerning both nature and man is the position that Taylor now takes. Here, Taylor is indebted to the Augustinian location of evil in the will. Indeed, it is not generally denied that if moral evil exists at all, it correlates so perfectly with human volitions as to suggest a thorough causal relation. But, Taylor argues,

> on the supposition that...the root of moral evil is in the will, the question how the earliest act of rebellious will come about becomes an illegitimate one. To ask it is to presuppose that there is still some further and more ultimate root of evil behind the sinful volition and thus to deny ones' own professed assumption.[66]

Is the volitional act without a cause? Is it uncaused? Taylor would say no: it is self-caused. And no cause need be admitted nor sought behind the self-caused act. The act is spontaneous, and, though it may relate to various motivations--such relating being helpful in the determination of the moral worth of the act--it need not be admitted that the motivations are its sufficient cause. Taylor says,

---

65. Ibid., p. 19.

66. Ibid., pp. 22-23.

in reaching the spontaneous choice we have
reached a _first_ cause and cannot go behind it.
As Kant puts it, when we find ourselves trying to
say _how_ freedom is possible, we have reached the
limit of practical reason. This strikes us, who
have the tendency always to ask for a reason behind every assigned reason, as paradoxical, but
it is not absurd or contradictory. What would be
contradictory would be that there should be a
remoter cause behind a spontaneous act.[67]

In a manner reminiscent of Aristotle's denial of
infinite regression, Taylor remarks that moral choices
are not the only examples of spontaneity, declaring
that

> it is, indeed, obvious that in the inanimate
> world itself, however far we may go in accounting
> for movements as communicated from outside, there
> must be movements which have to be assumed to be
> original and spontaneous, and of which we cannot
> ask the question from what quarter they were com-
> municated; _all_ the movements in the universe can-
> not have come there by being "passed on" from
> somewhere else.[68]

The "spontaneity" of Aristotle's Unmoved Mover--assum-
ing the validity of the argument employed by him--is a
description that almost suggests itself in that very
individualized case of a source of the movement of the
entire world itself unmoved by anything than its own
nature. The analogy to what is allegedly human spontaneity is at least illustrative if not demonstrative.
And Taylor, returning to his thesis of the autonomous
human will, declares,

> however much I may have been influenced in making
> that choice by the example or suggestion of some-
> one else, the fact remains that I made the choice,
> it was not made for me by others, or the
> responsibility would be theirs and not mine.[69]

67. _Ibid._, p. 24.

68. _Ibid._

69. _Ibid._

Taylor puts a great burden upon the experienced confrontation with a moral ought--as, indeed, did Kant. Taylor writes,

> we are confronted by a dilemma; either the acts for which an agent is morally fully responsible have his choice for their _first_ cause, and then the question "What other agent caused him to choose so?" is senseless, or there is really no such thing as moral responsibility at all. And, as Kant used to insist, though we cannot _demonstrate_ that moral responsibility is real, we know what to think of the character of a man who seriously denies its reality.[70]

In passing, if freedom of the will is granted as at least a possibility another possibility there is that cannot be denied, _viz._, that of going wrong. "A finite creature incapable of voluntarily going wrong would be equally incapable of voluntarily going right."[71]

We have noted that Taylor (on rather technical grounds) declares that evil is no problem for morality. This, because morality presupposes the fact of evil as its _raison d'etre_. But a deeper and more important question now arises, _viz._, whether the essence of the moral life is merely a struggle with evil. And if such is the case, does Bradley's alleged "antinomy" of morality really hold, _viz._, that because morality is fighting against evil, and if evil were destroyed by reason of morality's successful battle, there would remain nothing to fight against, with the result that morality must be looked upon as endeavoring to destroy itself? "It is thus of the first importance," writes Taylor, "to consider whether, after all, the fundamental aspiration of morality is

---

70. _Ibid._, p. 25.

71. _Ibid._, p. 23. Taylor's more thorough analysis, however, of the meaning of freedom must await the next chapter where the conjunction of freedom and rationality will reveal the better ground of Taylor's conception of freedom as it is pleaded to support the moral dimension.

self-destructive."[72]

   We are led thus to consider the essence of morality as possibly independent of its struggle against evil. And in such consideration we are guided rather naturally toward what is Taylor's expected reply by the previous unfolding of Taylor's insistence upon the conjunction of value and actuality. Morality is not only a name given to certain actions of men; it is a postulated complex of norms that are uniquely suited to the identification, interpretation, and command of the "practical reason." But we have seen that Taylor invests all such norms, such ideals, with the status of reals. Therefore the <u>essentia</u> of morality, by reason of such treatment, becomes independent of the actions which it may happen to approve or disapprove.

   This is the point at which a remark should be made regarding the alleged coordinate aspect of good and evil. For Taylor (as for Plato) the idea of the good arises upon the occasion of evil. The idea of justice arises upon the occasion of injustice. For the Judeo-Christian system, the ideas of good and truth arise upon the occasions of evil and error. But for none of these positions is there a strict parallel of actuality. As some might style it, this is a one-way street. That is to say, the idea of evil implies <u>the actuality of good</u>; it does not follow that the idea of good implies the actuality of evil. Similarly, the idea of error implies <u>the actuality of truth</u>; it does not follow that the idea of truth implies the actuality of error. One may, however, say that the idea of truth or the idea of good implies the <u>possibility</u> of error or evil.

   The corollary that follows (and to which Taylor subscribes) is the doctrine that evil and error are privations. That is to say, they are not substantively real. Their "reality" while not an illusion depends substantively upon another. Error and evil are, strictly speaking, <u>inconceivable</u> apart from that substantive reality that gives them their support.[73]

---

72.   Taylor, THE FAITH OF A MORALIST, Series I, p. xix.

73.   In discussing Augustine's doctrine of moral theory, Copleston asks, "...what is evil in itself, moral evil? Is it something positive?" And he

There is another sense in which the "positive" side of morality can be understood--a sense analogous to the general concern of science which may be thought of as enjoying a proper goal that far transcends the correction of error. There is a proper side to science that is positive and aims at the penetration of reality to whatever limit is made possible by the structuring, interpreting, investigating, power of mind. That this effort is of necessity attended by the uncovering of error and the elimination thereof need be regarded only as a side-effect of the natural work of intellectual exploration. The correction of error is an accidental, not as essential, aspect of the mind's genuine concern. Similarly, Taylor affirms,

the moral life would not disappear even from a world in which there were no wrongs left to be righted. Even a society in which no member had

---

answers, "It cannot, first of all, be something positive in the sense of something created by God: the cause of moral evil is not the Creator but the created will. The cause of good things is the divine goodness, whereas the cause of evil is the created will which turns away from the immutable Good: evil is a turning-away of the created will from the immutable and infinite Good. But evil cannot strictly be termed a 'thing,' since this word implies a positive reality, and if moral evil were a positive reality, it would have to be ascribed to the Creator, unless one were willing to attribute to the creature the power of positive creation out of nothing. Evil, then, is that which falls away from essence and tends to non-being. ...It tends to make that which is cease to be. /De moribus eccl., 2, 2, 2./ Everything in which there is order and measure is to be ascribed to God, but in the will which turns away from God there is disorder. The will itself is good, but the absence of right order, or rather the privation of right order, for which the human agent is responsible, is evil. Moral evil is thus a privation of right order in the created will." Frederick Copleston. A HISTORY OF PHILOSOPHY. Volume II. MEDIAEVAL PHILOSOPHY, Part I. AUGUSTINE TO BONAVENTURE. (New York: Doubleday & Company, 1962), pp. 99-100.

anything more to correct in himself, and where
"thou shalt love thy neighbor as thyself" were
the universally accepted rule of social duty,
would still have something to do; it would have
the whole work of embodying the love of each for
all in the detail of life. It is this, not the
mere abolition of abuses, or the elimination of
unfavourable circumstances from the environment,
which is the paramount business of the moral
life.[74]

Morality's positive side, therefore, Taylor feels, is
as clearly independent of the war against evil as is
science's positive side independent of the correction
of error. And were we to eliminate all of the blocks
to moral realization, all, that is to say, of the
temporally threatening and competing evils, aspiration
to know and to conform to the highest norm of the moral life would still remain--and remain with greater
clarity by reason of the elimination of the negative
aspects that competed with its purer unveiling. "We
need," Taylor insists,

> to employ the Aristotelian distinction between a
> "process" and an "activity." If we do so, we
> shall see that there is nothing irrational in
> anticipating a state in which the process of
> forming character is over, while the activity
> issuing from character remains. ...there would
> be room for "practice" as well as "contemplation"
> even in heaven.[75]

The "problem of evil," however, continues to be a
problem. Taylor has confessed that he cannot offer a
solution that is final--"the detailed solution of the
problem is out of the question"[76]but, at the same
time, there are broad indications that we have made
significant progress against an ethical skepticism:
in the knowledge of what is involved in the moral response of human history; in our general awareness of
the problem; in the proffered solutions to the prob-
lem--whether they are to be adjudged good or bad; in

---

74. Taylor, THE FAITH OF A MORALIST, Series I, p. 400.

75. Ibid., p. xx.

76. Taylor, ELEMENTS OF METAPHYSICS, p. 395.

the consideration that neither evil nor error can be
norms in their own right, but, on the contrary, are
adjudged as excrescenses and blots on the positive
side of human effort; in all of these considerations,
Taylor is led to feel that the problem of evil, if not
quite put to rest, is contained; and these presuppositions by the aid of which we interpret and identify
evil are at the same time the truer locus of authority
by the light of which we know truth from error and
good from evil--even while we do not know to perfection the source of our lesser enlightenments. Without
stultifying his entire philosophical position, Taylor
may never treat evil and error as illusions, nor grant
to them substantive reality, nor fail to recognize
what he calls the transcendent norms by the aid of
which evil and error are identified and condemned; yet
these norms cannot be brought under their own illumination to the end of exhaustive comprehension of their
essence.

Taylor's account of evil has run the entire gamut
from non-moral evil (conceived as the mere defect of
finitude) to that moral evil conceived as wickedness
and as something that absolutely ought not to be. It
is in the latter range of prohibition and condemnation
that the norm, the locus of moral authority, takes on
the dimension of a divine person as the only proper
final evaluation of the nature of that norm that condemns the specific evils of finite persons. If "evil"
is to be accounted more than mere mistake and more
than a description of personal frustration, if evil is
to be adjudged as competing with genuine obligation,
it would appear that Taylor's insistence upon a transcendent norm that is also personal is at least meaningful.

CHAPTER VI - MORAL VALUE AND FREEDOM

Introduction. The issues and debates that have turned about the question of freedom are legion. "Freedom" is a word that stands for something that at once is so well known as to demand no clarification other than the information of what specific application of the word is in mind, while, on the other hand, it is a word so fraught with ambiguity and uncertainty that it is safe to say 2,500 years of Western philosophy have not yet adequately defined it.

Freedom meets us at both empirical and metaphysical levels. And therein lies one of the major areas of confusion. At the empirical level, one may be said to be free when he is unhindered from doing what he may wish to do; at the metaphysical level, even unhindered empirical freedom can be denied. That is to say, one who seemingly knows no obstructions to a meteoric rise in social position, moving easily into areas of greater responsibility and honor, and fulfilling the demands of office with ease and intelligence may be thought a perfect example of the kind of freedom that we have denominated empirical, while at the same moment, it may be claimed that a deeper analysis and appreciation of those invisible causes on which one's greater and lesser destinies depend would show that the one in question was by no means free, but was merely acting out in a time-space continuum that which had been decreed by what perhaps was the thrust of the total past. Thus, Spinoza's stone, cast into the air by some person, becoming conscious in flight, affirms its freedom: an empirical fact. It knows not of the thrust of forces that precipitated it on its course before its consciousness had dawned: the metaphysical fact.

Taylor now turns to the question of freedom--in both of its aspects: empirical and metaphysical--and

141

hopes to show that in a sense both combine to testify to the reality of man's freedom in the realm of moral value. Taylor's argument will make the greatest possible use of a declared essential relation between moral value and rationality--to the end that rationality, which exhibits the clearest testimony to universality and necessity, may add its unique strength to the claims of morality as well.

Because the virtually undeviating experience of mankind has been that of assuming sets of norms that in every case transcend the narrowly empirical--norms of rationality, morality, and esthetics--because of this, Taylor, too, turns to these presuppositions for a longer, harder look, and in so doing, salutes many of the idealist philosophers who have preceded him and who like him had endeavored to set up a barrier against the various naturalists that (Taylor believes) covertly and unknowingly revealed a dependence upon those very norms that at overt levels they denied. "Green, the Cairds, Lewis Nettleship, William Wallace, Adamson, Bosanquet, Bradley":

> The chief part of their united work, /Taylor writes/ was to continue the age-long war of believers in genuine morality and real obligation against every kind of naturalistic substitute; to expose once again, with special reference to the positivists and evolutionists of their generation, the inherent flimsiness of all theories of morality which treat man simply as one part of nature, one animal among the rest, making up by cunning what he lacks in physical strength or elaborately pre-formed instincts, human good as computable in terms of purely secular satisfaction, human duty as having no authority more august than the sanctions of the law-court and the ambiguous voices of popular applause and reprobation. Like Plato, or Cudworth, or Clarke, or Butler, or Kant, they stood for an "eternal and immutable" morality against the morality of acquiescence in the fashion of an age.[1]

---

1. Alfred Edward Taylor, "The Freedom of Man," CONTEMPORARY BRITISH PHILOSOPHY, Second Series, (London: George Allen & Unwin Ltd., 1925), pp. 273-274.

And now, Taylor, "With some trepidation...venture(s) to reopen the old dispute" concerning the freedom of the will calling it "the most important in the whole range of moral psychology," and proposing "a return from the fashionable Hegelian and Leibnizian position to that of the CRITIQUE OF PRACTICAL REASON and denying the feasibility of a combination of "a genuine libertarianism in Ethics with a thorough determinism in the realm of natural science, declaring "that 'scientific determinism' has only got a foothold in the philosophy of the natural sciences...by a mistake."[2] The latter two points are against Kant favoring instead "the good old Greek and scholastic doctrine of real contingency as a characteristic present everywhere in 'nature.'"[3]

What is moral freedom? There are some rather obvious things that moral freedom is not. It is not the "free-fall" of a body in accordance with gravity's law; it is not "the mere capacity of spontaneous or internally initiated movement";[4] nor is it that "purely illusory freedom which is all Spinoza allows to man in the famous and flippant utterance that 'a stone which was aware of its falling would think itself free.'"[5] Less negatively, freedom is "to be taken as the minimum necessary condition of even beginning to live the specifically moral life; although," Taylor adds, "it is not to be the sufficient condition of morally good life."[6] Still more narrowly, the freedom here contemplated, though positive, is beneath the perfect freedom of "an absolute and final harmony of the individual with every element of his 'environment,'" and, though negative, is beyond "that mere spontaneity which we share with the animals."[7] Between these two limits, a true freedom must be found if at

---

2. Ibid., p. 278.

3. Ibid., pp. 278-279.

4. Ibid., p. 280.

5. Ibid.

6. Ibid., p. 282.

7. Ibid.

all. Moral freedom as thus delineated has the uniquely differentiating characteristic of setting a duty for
man that is beyond animal instinct but with no absolute
guarantee of perfect fulfillment. Moral freedom's
awareness of its duty parts with skepticism even as its
awareness of its imperfect fulfillment of that duty is
a rebuke to the dogmatism of claimed arrival. In an
attempt to answer the question, What is moral freedom?,
the following might be hazarded: Moral freedom is
(a) a choice or decision of some end for action, (b) in
terms of norms believed relevant, and (c) by rational
means of discrimination.

    As we shall see--and as other parts of the paper
on Taylor's position have repeated--it would be stultifying to Taylor's position to say more precisely and
definitively what moral freedom is. This is precisely
because the norm by which moral value is highlighted
and justified is that universal which, while illuminating particular moralities, is not caught in the direct
illumination of its own light. This is Taylor's "presuppositionalism." It is also an unavoidable type of
negativism which in the nature of the case must follow
Taylor's exposition through to the end.

    The relation of moral freedom to rationality.
The medieval answer that Taylor elects to defend "is
to be found in libertas arbitrii, a 'freedom of the
will'"[8] that Taylor finds to be almost the opposite of
that "motiveless choosing" with which some have chosen
to link the freedom of the will and which for Taylor
"would amount to pure haphazard or caprice, and would
thus be only another name for downright irresponsibi-
lity."[9] For Taylor, if will means anything, it means
choice, and choice "is never without a 'motive,' or,
what is the same thing, a 'reason.'"[10] Further, if
free will means anything, it means that this "motive"
or "reason" is the implicit denial of every non-rational explanation. That is to say, duly to apprehend
what rationality is, to understand what it is that

---

8. Ibid.

9. Ibid.

10. Ibid.

preserves validity for a conclusion, is, at the same
time and for the same reason, to understand that an
essential attribute of rationality is its freedom.
This is probably an ideal poorly realized, but it is
an ideal that we honor. We need only invent some hypothetical interferences with this ideal to note how
quickly and positively we condemn them as inimical to
the ideal we intuitively recognize must be preserved.
Attitudes that we believe manifest bias, prejudice,
partiality, intolerance, subjectiveness: what are
they but direct threats to the possibility of preserving what must be known by no better word than "freedom" in rational procedure? Alcohol, drugs, disease,
fever, bodily pain: are they not commonly understood
as threatening in varying degrees the truth-value and
the validity of pronouncements made under their influence? The intuitively apprehended ideal by which suspicion is generated that the above mentioned attitudes
and bodily afflictions are interfering with proper
rational processes is thus seen to bear witness to an
attribute of freedom essential to the meaning and
function of these rational processes. Nor should it
discourage one to discover that non-rational biases
are frequently at work without our being aware of it;
it remains true that, in principle, we condemn this
intrusion and the condemnation witnesses to the formal
command of the ideal of rationality's freedom.

To conjoin the allegation of freedom of the will
to rationality is high strategy. That the rationality
factor must be free, Taylor thinks, is an absolute
mandate issued by what everyone expects of truth and
validity. It would appear to be a working principle
of Taylor's that if truth- and validity-allegations
can be shown to be the result of what is virtually a
mechanical process--produced by non-rational causes--
then truth and validity lose their whole and only
meaning. A parrot or a machine can be made to recite
syllogisms and tables of factual data but the parrot
or machine is not speaking validly or truthfully--even
though the syllogisms are formally correct and the
tables of factual data verified. Some rationality,
independent of both parrot and machine, must declare
for the validity and the truth on grounds free from a
non-rational causation. It is freedom in this rational sense that tempts the will to action and it is this
same sense that preserves whatever meaning is present
in a doctrine of libertas arbitrii. Sufficient

recognition has already been given to the non-rational biases that are frequently at work without our being aware of them; but, to repeat, our implicit disapproval and rejection of their propriety is itself a testimony to our allegiance and implicit reliance upon this presupposition of rationality--a presupposition that, Taylor believes, is a necessary condition for truth, for validity, and for freedom.

The freedom of the will that grounds in rationality and ends in action is now emphasized as being not merely incompatible with "scientific determinism" but fundamental for morality and the preservation of ethical value.

If we start by recognizing that it is fundamental for morality that a "responsible" agent should be able to find an adequate motive to action in the perception of a given act as the right and reasonable thing to be done, it must follow that, on any theory which makes my present judgment of good the necessary consequence of earlier acts or events, there never is any act of unbiased comparison of alternatives on their own merits; hence the freedom demanded for moral responsibility can never be more than a dream.[11]

Regarding the allegedly "free" act and its relation to motives: If we choose between alternatives where there is no motive at all, Taylor is prompted to say that

if there are such "unmotived" choices, they must surely have no significance for our moral life, since they do not express the character of the agent supposed to be making the choice. It is just the choices which are rooted in our personal moral quality and give expression to it with which the moralist is concerned.[12]

11. Ibid., p. 290.

12. Taylor, THE FAITH OF A MORALIST, Series II, p. 425.

But all such choices must depend upon "the worth of the evidence." Implicitly or explicitly, the rational factor must be present. Thus Taylor brings this discussion of the role that motives may legitimately play back to their relation to rationality. "A _motive_, we must remember," Taylor writes,

> is not the same thing as a mere impulse which releases, or discharges, an act. To act with a motive is not merely to be impelled to act in a certain way, but also to regard one's act as justified by a certain consideration. When I say that I act thus and with this motive, I mean both that the considerations I allege are truly those which impel me to act as I do, and also that they make my acting as I do the right and reasonable thing for me to do. A motive is always something which, at the time of acting, the agent regards as a reasonable incentive. It is a "reason" in the double sense that it explains why the agent does what he does, and that, so long as he does not repent, it is held by him to justify his behaviour. It follows that a man's "motives" are rarely, if ever, present to his own mind at the moment of action in "clear and distinct" apprehension; they are usually very largely "subconscious," or "habitual." But this does not detract from their rationality.[13]

What, then, can it mean to say that choices are determined by motives? Taylor replies,

> For all that such a phrase really means is that a responsible agent, when he chooses his line of action, has what he regards as intelligible justificatory _reasons_ for choosing as he does and not otherwise. His "motive" is neither an agent nor a "driving force," nor an "antecedent event"; it is just the character of significance _in_ the choice which he is making.[14]

For Taylor, then, judgments of good, when _effects_

---

13.   _Ibid._, p. 426.

14.   Alfred Edward Taylor, "Freedom and Personality," PHILOSOPHY, XIV (1939), p. 426.

in a _merely_ causal linkage, lose their validity and
their moral importance. This is declared true even
when the effects proceeded from "acts" that are my own.
As Taylor sees it,

> It does not in the least mend the matter to be
> told...that the past to which one is fettered is
> one's own past. What morality demands is that
> the _present_ perception of an act as good and ob-
> ligatory should be a sufficient condition of its
> execution.[15]

This does not mean that Taylor would see no value for
an overall picture of morality in that "built-in"
reservoir of habitual moral responses--those virtually
automatic reflexes that continue a pattern of accepted
and largely predictable ethical behavior--but it does
mean that there must be the genuine possibility of a
"present perception of an act as good and obligatory,"
the rational endorsement which is independent of any
merely non-rational causal linkage. That is to say,
if challenged to answer for the goodness and reasonableness of an act, there must be discoverable _in_ _prin-_
ciple a "present perception" of that goodness and reasonableness that does not depend for its existence upon
a past causal sequence of events of which the present
perception is a necessary consequence. It is precisely this view, _viz_., "that the whole and sufficient
'motive' for any act can be found in its now discerned
goodness and reasonableness _per_ _se_" that "is precluded
on principle by determinism."[16]

The self-contradiction of the determinist. Taylor speaks of "the paradox" that he has heard applied
to the determinist, that he

> never applies to his own action the deterministic
> theory which he treats as valid for that of
> everyone else. He may persuade himself that all
> the apparent "decisions" of his fellow-men are no
> more than "conditioned reflexes," the like of
> which he could produce by "laboratory" methods
> which would preclude all possibility of genuine

---

15. Taylor, "The Freedom of Man," p. 290.

16. _Ibid_., p. 291.

choosing on the part of his "subjects." But he
does not think of his own imagined procedure in
instituting his laboratory experiments on his
subjects as a "conditioned reflex." That he regards as throughout controlled, not by "antecedent conditions," but, in a wholly different way,
by a final cause, or purpose, his intelligent
purpose to conduct a series of experiments which
will establish his theories, and to conduct them
on lines not prescribed for him by anything but
their relevance to the conclusion which is to be
established. On his own theory, there must be at
least one being in a universe of "robots" who is
not a "robot"--the experimenter in his laboratory. It follows that even the "scientific" determinist habitually admits the real existence of
one "free" agent--himself when he is acting in
his capacity as an experimenter.[17]

If this kind of difficulty occurs in setting up the
experiment, it does not disappear when drawing conclusions from the results of the experiment. Are the
conclusions themselves together with all of the considerations on which they are allegedly based also
determined? And if so, how do conclusions that may
repudiate the first conclusion fare? When nothing but
antecedent conditions can be pointed to--antecedent
conditions that are virtually mechanical causes--where
is the principle by which one may critically distinguish between the differences?

In the article "Freedom and Personality Again"
Taylor states the case for the determinist more systematically.

That doctrine...is that every voluntary act of an
intelligent person, being an event in time, is
subject to a law which is universally valid for
all events without exception. The law is that
every such event, or at least every event except
the first event of all, if there ever was such a
first event--is a one-valued function of earlier
events, and of nothing but earlier events.[18]

---

17. Taylor, "Freedom and Personality," pp. 260-261.

18. Alfred Edward Taylor, "Freedom and Personality
     Again," PHILOSOPHY, XVII (1942), p. 27.

Taylor reduces this argument of the determinist to the following syllogism:

(a) Every event is a fully determinate function of antecedent events, and of antecedent events only.

(b) Every decision to act in one way rather than another is an event.

(c) Ergo, every decision to act in one way rather than another is a fully determinate function of antecedent events and of antecedent events only.[19]

This account, Taylor explains, must be absolutely binding because "Any qualification of the assumed principle...amounts to a surrender of the principle of scientific determinism."[20]

But this leads to the recognition that the principle espoused is an a priori one because "it is alleged to hold good for our acts of choice not in virtue of anything which is specifically characteristic of acts of choice as such, but because such acts, whatever more they may be, are events, and every event is a one-valued function of earlier events."[21] It is this universal, a priori inclusion of all events that has no option other than to include all mental events such as drawing conclusions regarding the interpretation of data, the recognition of valid inferences, and all other

> processes of assenting and dissenting, of following the "thread" of an argument, in a word, all the processes into which the psychologist might analyze our thinking. ...Either every event of my mental life must be completely determined by antecedent events or none need be so--unless some reason for making a distinction can be given of which no determinist has as yet thought, least

19. Ibid., p. 30.

20. Ibid., p. 27.

21. Ibid.

of all the "scientific" determinist.[22]

Indetermination. This leads Taylor in his argument for the freedom of the will to mention the real meaning of "indetermination" or the "open mind" doctrine. Taylor recognizes that there has developed a sensitiveness to being identified with the doctrine of "indetermination" that is virtual embarrassment. "Too many writers," Taylor observes,

> on ethical subjects a generation ago were still, for some reason, afraid of the word indetermination, and I am not sure that the prejudice is even yet wholly extinct. One might almost suppose, from the shame-faced way in which the fact was commonly wrapped up in circumlocution and euphemism, that the incompleteness of determination characteristic of all situations where choice and decision are possible were a partie honteuse of the creation which decency forbids us to call by its plain name.[23]

The fear--if "fear" it is--that seemingly prescribed against the use of such a word is partly a reflection of that commitment to a determinism that can only view any suggestion of "indetermination" as directly antithetical to clearest insights; another inhibiting consideration might well be the suggestion within the word "indetermination" of a sort of vacuum of causal possibility out of which if there is to be asserted any action at all it would have to resemble some sort of magic. For Taylor, however, the phrases, "I will," "I determine," "I act," so nearly require the absence of any idea of the one so acting being merely the transmitting medium of the thrust of non-rational antecedent events that he quotes at length "the good sense and plain speaking" of one Richard Price.[24]

As far as it is true of a being that he acts, so

---

22. Ibid., p. 28.

23. Taylor, "Freedom and Personality," p. 262.

24. REVIEW OF THE PRINCIPAL QUESTIONS IN MORALS, pp. 305-306., cited by Taylor, Ibid., p. 263.

far he must _himself_ be the cause of the action,
and therefore not necessarily determined to act.
Let anyone try to put a sense in the expressions:
I will; _I act_; which is consistent with supposing
that the volition or action does not proceed from
myself. Virtue supposes determination, and determination supposes a determiner; and a determiner
that determines not himself is a palpable contradiction. Determination requires an efficient
cause. If this cause is the being himself, I
plead for no more. If not, then it is no longer
his determination; that is, _he_ is no longer the
determiner, but the motive, _or_ whatever else anyone will say to be the cause of the determination.
To ask what effects the cause of our determination
is the very same thing with asking who did an action, after being informed that such a one did
it.[25]

The "indetermination" is identified by two considerations. And in neither case is there the denial of
a cause. What is denied is precisely the formula of
the determinist given above that every event, including voluntary acts, "is a one-valued function of earlier events, and nothing but earlier events." The
first consideration is that of the time-interval between having decided to do something and not yet having done it. That is to say, it cannot be argued that
throughout this time-interval a causal linkage such as
that of which the determinist speaks can be affirmed
without begging the question. Taylor illustrates by
analogy:

as the very statement that I terminate certain
proceedings by taking such and such a step implies that they were not terminated until the
step was taken so the statement that I determine
to do A presupposes that before I have made my
choice it is _not_ determined whether A shall be
done or not.[26]

How does the determinist reply to this "first
consideration"? He does two things. _First_, he

---

25. _Ibid._

26. _Ibid._, pp. 263-264.

supposes that the motive to act is itself a sufficient cause. By this, he could close the gap by having found the causal linkage that extends through the time-interval. But we have already noted that Taylor regards a motive not as a cause, but as a "reason" for action that, after due consideration, may approve itself as worthy of being pressed into some specific service. As Taylor was quoted above,

> A motive is always something which, at the time of acting, the agent regards as a reasonable incentive. It is a "reason" in the double sense that it explains why the agent does what he does, and that, so long as he does not repent, it is held by him to justify his behavior.[27]

Second, the determinist supposes that one's "character" is something fixed, determinate and determining. And this position, it would appear, has great plausibility. In general, there is that predictability about a man's acts that strongly suggests that between the acts and the "character" of the man there is a uniformity reminiscent of the uniformity of nature. But, on the other hand, this may be only generally true, and when confronted by the necessity of making decisions that are not only novel but momentous, the insistence that here, too, there is nothing more involved than simply another event that is the "fully determinate function of antecedent events, and of antecedent events only" may not hold. It is Taylor's suggestion that in such novel and momentous cases one may actually be making character and not merely transmitting it.

> Pilate,...when he shirked the duty incumbent on him in virtue of his office, to give judgment in accord with the law and equity of the case, by leaving the multitude to decide an issue which he ought to have decided himself, was not merely revealing himself as an evader of his responsibilities, he was making himself one; it is conceivable that he had never been in the past the sort of man he showed himself to be at that moment. The plain fact is that, so far as we can tell, no man's character is a thing finally made and fully determinate while the life remains in him, and

---

27. Ibid.

being itself not completely determinate cannot be the source of complete determination in anything else.[28]

It would appear, however, that the above argument that character is possibly made in the act of choosing in a sense that was not there before has to manifest extreme cleverness to offset the plausibility of the all but uniform relation suggested in the predictability of one's acts. The defense, however, does appear to Taylor to be strengthened by his second consideration in favor of the doctrine of "indetermination."

This second consideration stems from a proposition that Taylor appears to regard as virtually axiomatic:

> There is plainly a sense in which the possession of rationality involves absence of complete determination. ...a rational creature, just in the degree to which it is rational, is always only imperfectly amenable to suggestion. It responds to the suggestions of the environment by assent or by the performance of an action or meets them with dissent or refusal to act, "according as it sees reason." And the more rational it is, the more thoroughly does it look into the "reason" on both sides of the alternative before it commits itself in theory or in practice. Now it could not do this unless it were strictly true that until it has "seen reason" it remains undetermined in respect of the suggestion which is yet to be accepted or rejected. If it is to make up its mind according as it "sees reason," there must be a preliminary stage in which a suggestion is there, but acceptance or rejection is not yet determined. In our possession of reason we are thus provided with an internal source of indetermination within ourselves.[29]

Here then in a word is Taylor's defense of "indetermination": first, between the decision to do a thing and the doing of it there is an interval across

28. Ibid., p. 264.

29. Ibid., p. 272.

which it is impossible to trace that causal bond necessary for the determinist to make his point; and, second, there is in the very nature of a <u>rational</u> decision that which forbids the determinist's non-rational account of the act. Again: "Reason or intelligence is in its very nature a principle of indetermination in each of us."[30]

Emphasizing the advantage that he believes man's possession of rationality gives to the defense of his doctrine of freedom, Taylor charges that

> If the determinist thesis is sound, then, it must follow that it is never possible to consider any issue, however purely speculative, with an "open mind," intending to pronounce one way or the other strictly, "according to the worth of the evidence." The "worth of the evidence" will always be different for different minds, since for every mind which attempts to estimate it, its probative force will be a one-valued determinate function of past events private to the history of that particular mind.[31]

<u>From free thought to free will</u>. Taylor's reason for making the strongest possible case against the determinist by appeal to rationality ("only another way of saying that it is the universal in us")[32] is because he is convinced that the determinist himself holds this high view of rationality "when it is a question of belief or disbelief."[33] But why, then, should the determinist not hold the same high view of ethical value when it is a question of to act or not to act? Pairing the two positions--the rational and the ethical--Taylor notes:

> He (i.e., the determinist) always assumes that his own belief in determinism is based upon and justified by the reasons which he produces for

---

30. <u>Ibid</u>., p. 273.

31. Taylor, "Freedom and Personality Again," p. 28.

32. Taylor, "Freedom and Personality," p. 275.

33. <u>Ibid</u>., p. 272.

155

its truth; it is not, as the rival beliefs of his fellows may be, a baseless superstition or prejudice. But he is only entitled to claim as much as this if he is prepared to say that he has considered those reasons with an "open mind"; in other words, that there was a time when he was undetermined between the alternatives of determinism and indeterminism. It would be fatal to his whole case for the truth of determinism to admit that his acceptance of it was already predetermined for him in advance by his peculiar hereditary temperament and his past history. For he will have to admit that, in that case, he is in exactly the same predicament as the opponent whose views he rejects; both are victims of inevitable prejudice, and there can be no sense in asking on which side the truth lies. Yet the same man persistently refuses to admit that one can come to the practical question whether to do A or to leave it undone with an "open mind," undetermined to either alternative until one has judged that one course is better than the other. Here, according to the consistent determinist, we are all of us and always at the mercy of the prejudices due to native bias and past history. Yet if the "open mind" is really ever possible towards a speculative problem, what ground can there be for holding that it is never possible in relation to action?[34]

Taylor's point here and elsewhere is a two-pronged attack. The attack is first at the level of mere rationality which he declares threatened by a thoroughgoing determinism. But because the determinist is merely inconsistent here (according to Taylor) and actually holds to an "indetermination" (without which he could not justifiably argue the truth of any proposition), Taylor's next attack appears at the level of an applied rationality--applied, that is to say, to the task of making a choice of what is now within the ethical category.

The personality of man. During Taylor's examination of determinist reasoning he is exposing more than the mere fact of the determinist's inconsistency. He

---

34. Ibid., pp. 272-273.

is revealing that underlying any and all argumentation man as a rational being is discovered--or re-discovered. It is revelatory of man's personality, of man's meaning, of man's essential character.

> That intelligence, or rationality, is a principle of indetermination within us is, in fact, only another way of saying that it is the universal in us, in virtue of which each of us transcends his own particularity.[35]

Nor is it different with regard to man's involvement in the ethical dimension: when man does specific acts and counsels specific programs, those are merely empirical manifestations of the ethical dimension; but when he declares that these specific acts and programs ought to be done, he is again recognizing human personality as exhibiting its true character as a universal.

> Free will is not impeccable, and free thought is not inerrant. But our very ability to recognize both the possibility and the actuality of error testifies to that rational norm by which both truth and all departures therefrom are meaningful. Similarly, our restlessness before the self-imposed or other-imposed charge of wrong-doing and our readiness to add to the virtually ubiquitous fact of human concern throughout history for justice testifies in its turn to that ethical norm by which moral right and all departures therefrom are meaningful. Thus is the human person analyzed and identified as a creature who in a very meaningful sense is a citizen of two worlds.

> Contingency. It is, I think, natural to wonder whether the arguments that have been employed--arguments calculated to safeguard the special concerns of rationality and ethical value--were adequate to offset the special claims of the determinists. This suspicion may be strengthened by the fact that the causal relation is a universally applicable category and is at the same time the first principle of determinism. It may be added, in addition, that the empirical aspect of determinism is as ubiquitous a fact as the empirical aspect of freedom. But we saw that as freedom

---

35. Ibid., p. 275.

can be called into question when its metaphysical status is raised, so can determinism be made to appear a little less obvious when its a priori assumption is made explicit.

When the "intrinsic bond" that allegedly unites events in the mood of what is called cause and effect is called into serious question, the events stand to lose their best claim to be exhibits of determinism. History records that it was called into serious question--by one who thereby awoke more than one from his "dogmatic slumber." David Hume's challenge to show the impression from which ideas could be validated, when directed to the relation of cause and effect, had the revolutionary effect of introducing contingency in what is perhaps its most radical form. When events in sequence give no more than a sense of orderliness along with their sensory impressions, the claim to a causal bond must either be retired or defended at a level other than that of a purely empirical one. Having been awoke from his "dogmatic slumber," Kant endeavored to answer this difficulty by recourse to an other than purely empirical reference. But to Hume and his followers, the hope of securing empirical fact with transcendental moorings was not promising. The result is that for him who depends upon an unequivocal support from experience, the radical contingency that empiricism thus reveals can only challenge his faith in determinism's alleged total interlock of events. True, Hume explains, the repetition of events in an orderly sequence builds up in us a powerful sense of expectation, and it is manifestly easy to convert this sense of psychological expectancy into a claimed theoretical insight. But such an inference is clearly invalid. It is thus that the events of experience are revealed as having no necessary claim upon each other in any way that can be detected and defended by inductive techniques. This is a picture of radical independence rather than radical dependence. Contingency, it would appear, was found to be a permanently predicable characteristic of nature. It is true that contingency may be said to imply a dependence, but the difficult feature of this "dependence" is that while it appears to be a necessary part of its meaning, one can never say with quite the same finality what it is that it depends upon. The Humean account clearly demonstrates that the dependence cannot be grounded in any of the contiguous events that may happen to generate the expectation of such a causal relation out of the mere fact of their experienced association. The unsettling conviction begins to dawn that all order in any theoretically defensible sense has been destroyed. "But," Taylor remarks,

> Indeterminism, unlike Determinism, is not wedded to the view that the natural order is the only order there is. Its windows are open to the spiritual sun, if spiritual sun there be, not shuttered and barred against it.[36]

Kant, too, would have agreed in denying that "the natural order is the only order there is" if by "natural order" were meant that constriction of "natural" to a point of a pure empiricism. The "transcendental" aspect of Kant and the transcendental aspect of Taylor agree at least in their repudiation of the possibility of finding coherence in the explanation of Hume. The "spiritual" aspect of the Taylor "transcendental" has to be argued as over against the Kantian interpretation, but it is at least suggestive in passing over the point that in the larger Kantian context, God was eventually thought necessary to be included as an ultimate ground of the moral order of the universe.

That Taylor takes some satisfaction in Kant's eventual recognition of God as necessary to taking the moral life seriously was recognized in the above chapter on the relation of value to existence wherein Taylor was noted as saying,

> we all remember Kant's own dismay at the apparent success of his undertaking, and his strenuous efforts, after putting asunder what "God and nature" had joined, to bring the disconsolate halves together again by invoking reason "as practical" to undo the work of reason "as speculative."[37]

This observation was prompted by Taylor's conviction about the inseparability of value and existence.

---

36. Taylor, "The Freedom of Man," p. 304.

37. Taylor, THE FAITH OF A MORALIST, Series I, p. 33.

I cannot, however, feel that in Kant himself, in any explicit manner, the breech was healed. "The dualism of Nature and morality /that/ appears with Kant in its baldest form in his PHILOSOPHY OF RELIGION"[38] continued, it seems to me, to be the truest explicit fact of Kant's treatment of these two realms.

Taylor is ready to speak of a certain behavior of nature's parts that justifies our speaking of them as "tied down by the fact of the collocation and the laws of their interconnection to a determinate course of behavior,"[39] but on the other hand, "contingency is found to be a universal character of whatever is temporal and mutable."[40] It is as though the fragmentary and flux-aspect of the physical world--where uniformities can create psychological expectancies but never theoretical insights of necessity--bespeak in a very radical sense a denial of that very rigid necessity of interconnection on which the "scientific determinist" is in dependence. Contingent events do not carry the impress of necessity upon their particularity; they can be thought of as not-being without contradiction. Taylor applies this characteristic to a very wide range of physical nature noting that on the hypothesis that physical nature is totally contingent a number of narrower phenomena are explained, viz., that the recoverability of the past and the anticipation of the future appear to be impossible; that there is no cyclical recurrence or periodic rhythm to "the whole movement of things"; that "explanation" of particular phenomena leads to higher generalizations that, in turn, require explanation; that a species of the "irrational" is introduced in such sweeping revisions as that occasioned by the desertion of the old Euclidean conception of space with its dependable uniformities in favor of a space-time of the new physics that is "variegated and non-uniform."[41]

---

38. The phrase is that of Wilhelm Windelband, A HISTORY OF PHILOSOPHY (New York: Dover Publications, 1958), p. 556.

39. Taylor, "The Freedom of Man," p. 301.

40. Ibid.

41. Ibid., p. 300.

In these observations, Taylor does not conclude
to an irrationality, but sees that predicate as belonging to a physical nature that is attempted of explanation in terms of its own immanent categories.
When this is attempted, Taylor concludes, the various
fulfilling conditions of a deep and radical contingency are everywhere revealed. The conclusion thus
forced in terms of this "loosening" of the events of
physical nature places further strictures against denials of freedom. The emerging doctrine appears to be
favorable to Taylor's defense of freedom of the will.
But Taylor really makes no use of it. He writes, "...
I do not appeal to the assertion of a 'principle of
Indeterminancy' in the physical at large as an argument for our moral freedom," but adds, "I believe it
to be an important step in the direction of a sounder
metaphysic and cosmology."[42] To the view that the
doctrine of contingency is "an illusion begotten of
our ignorance of the details of becoming," Taylor replies by saying that there is misunderstanding as to
what "contingency" really is. It is not caprice in
the occurrence of events; it is not random or cause-
less happenings; rather, it is precisely a caused
event but one for which the true cause is never to be
found in contiguous association or proximate causes.
This is, of course, a Thomistic counter and finds its
fuller explanation in locating the "true cause" in the
divine purpose, the "superessential" cause. And Taylor
finds this point of view--when divorced from

> the precise form in which it was used by the great
> schoolmen, who inherited Aristotle's unfortunate
> and perverse crotchet of a radical distinction
> between terrestrial and celestial "matter" and
> their respective dynamics[43]

--one to which we are "driven."

> If we are to retain the distinction between neces-
> sary and contingent causation, (then, it must be
> admitted that) ...God...is the only cause which
> causes with complete necessity...all other causes,

---

42.   Taylor, THE FAITH OF A MORALIST, Series II, p.
      417.

43,   Ibid., p. 419.

remote or proximate, "celestial" or "terrene,"
being infected with contingency.[44]

It appears that there is something of a consistency in Taylor's theistic system; it works from both
ends to emphasize the aspect of contingency that he
teaches. As we have seen from the starting-point of
experience, the Hume analysis declares for no necessary connection between and among the discrete impressions; and from the side of the hypothesis that God
stands to the world in the role of creator and sustainer, the very fact that full causal power is exerted downward vertically (to use a metaphor) would indicate why it might be predicted that one would not find
the same causal connection exerted laterally. As a
matter of fact, this is almost exactly what Berkeley
must have meant by his assertion that ideas were purely passive. Movement one could see, but the principle,
the cause, of the movement one could not see: hence
the passivity claimed. And so Taylor evidently understands it:

> ...the doctrine (of contingency as argued above)
> seems to me to be perfectly intelligible. It
> means, in effect, that while everything that hap-
> pens in cosmic history happens as God ordains or
> permits, no event is a perfectly determinate
> "one-valued function" of other specific events,
> and that when we say that the occurrence of X may
> certainly be inferred from the occurrence of A,
> B, C, ...there is always an understood Deo
> volente.[45]

The question arises, Must there be contingency in
nature at large as a requisite for human freedom?
There are some causes in which it clearly appears that
nature can be affected by the direct result of my
choices. In these situations at least Taylor takes
the position that we may not extend any denial of contingency "to those physical events which are the expressions of our responsible choices."[46] Non-contin-
gency, admitted at this point, would have the indirect

---

44. Ibid., p. 420.

45. Ibid.

46. Ibid., p. 422.

effect of making a free choice impossible--even in those cases where the empirical evidence of true freedom is clearest. As Taylor states it,

> If it is true that the movement of my hand is ever the result of my choice, then that movement cannot be a determinate one-valued function of previous events of the physical order; these events must leave it an open issue whether my hand is to move or not. Consequently, the same consideration must apply to all events of the physical order which depend causally, no matter at how many removes, on the choice of a moral agent.[47]

And if, Taylor adds, there should prove to be no natural events at all that are not the choice of a moral agent, then perfect contingency must be admitted into the total sphere of nature. That this is at least a possibility is due to Taylor's willingness to consider other agents than man--though, of course, they must be created moral agents. But, in the event that there were some natural events that are never the choice of a moral agent, to these Taylor would allow the denial of contingency to apply.

This latter acknowledged possibility calls for a remark on the further meaning of contingency. Under the dominance of the hypothesis that there is God who sustains a creator-preserver relation to the world, it would appear to follow that contingency in nature is entailed by that very fact. That is to say, the total control over the world as well as its total meaning refers fact to God absolutely and any actual or conceivable immanent forces are themselves effects of God's direct power. The principle, then, is that the doctrine of creation entails the doctrine of contingency.

May there, then, be admitted a 'secondary causality'? The answer is 'yes,' but with qualifications. We have seen that, in a manner reminiscent again of Berkeley, the human person may be considered as truly effecting events and is, therefore, causal. But what of the natural events of the world that must, in the

---

47. Ibid., pp. 422-423.

nature of the case according to the theistic hypothesis, be intrinsically and ultimately dominated by a principle of dependence and contingency? The answer is that they exhibit only a phenomenal causality. That is to say, because natural events are acting in obedience to a divine causality, the fact of a cause cannot be denied. But, as in Kant, the fact of the causal relation cannot be discovered by a reduction to the minimal experience itself. Nevertheless, because the causal control is really there, the scientist can (and most often does) substitute the corresponding epistemological equivalent for the transcendental ontological relation. It is the result of the scientists' success in areas of control and prediction (the entire exhibition of the induction effort), accompanied as it must be by no direct confrontation with that mysterious 'intrinsic bond' called cause, that has led to an emphasis being placed on the epistemological side of scientific explanation.

But this (sometimes) pointed disregard of the scientists' deeper assumptions has not escaped notice. Russell writes of the principle of induction: "The principle itself," he declares,

> cannot, ...without circularity, be inferred from observed uniformities, since it is required to justify any such inference. It must therefore be, or be deduced from, an independent principle not based upon experience. To this extent, Hume has proved that pure empiricism is not a sufficient basis for science. But if this one principle is admitted, everything else can proceed in accordance with the theory that all our knowledge is based on experience. It must be granted that this is a serious departure from pure empiricism, and that those who are empiricists may ask why, if one departure is allowed, others are to be forbidden. These, however, are questions not directly raised by Hume's arguments. What these arguments prove--and I do not think the proof can be controverted--is that induction is an independent logical principle, incapable of being inferred either from experience or from other logical principles, and that without this principle

science is impossible.[48]

The spirit as well as the substance of this remark by Russell is supportive of Taylor's arguments in favor of freedom--when these arguments are considered in their fullest range of reference. Taylor asks repeatedly that we recognize those presuppositions without which rationality and morality are impossible, but he warns that these presuppositions are of the conceptual variety that cannot, in the nature of the case, become amenable to direct approach and inspection. Our dependence upon them is a sure and steady fact of human experience but their reality is most dramatically emphasized when we resolutely endeavor to execute a way of belief and action without them.

---

48. Bertrand Russell, A HISTORY OF WESTERN PHILOSOPHY. (New York: Simon and Shuster, 1945), p. 674.

CHAPTER VII - MORAL VALUE AND IMMORTALITY

The many values and concerns in life that men honor are intimately dependent upon life itself, a fact that is not debated or debatable. And the narrower particularization of human personality may be declared at the very least a necessary condition for exercise of these concerns and the honoring of these values. As Taylor succinctly puts it,

> ...the whole question is at bottom one of values. ...Even the most anti-religious man of science must go at least part of the way with us in our conviction. For he at least believes that truth is in itself a thing of more value than error, a thing it is worth our while to spend and be spent in seeking for. And he does not usually think this belief in the worth of truth a mere personal peculiarity of his own, like relish for the taste of olives or a dislike of the taste of port wine. He holds that Science does reveal something of the real character of the common or objective world in which we all live, and that, for that reason, men ought to prize scientific knowledge and seek after it.[1]

It is in connection with this same point of the scientific man's serious commitment to searching out that structuring of the universe that permits of prediction and control that reveals him in dependence upon an assumption of uniformity that, strictly speaking, he cannot prove. Taylor says,

---

1. Alfred Edward Taylor, "The Belief in Immortality," THE FAITH AND THE WAR, edited by F. J. Foakes-Jackson (London: Macmillan & Co., 1915), pp. 136-137.

He cannot _prove_ that Science might not some day issue in a tangle of insoluble contradictions. He accepts his conviction that truth is worth having and that those who seek it will not be disappointed. ...His belief that Science will never finally contradict herself is really an act of faith, faith in the rationality or reasonableness of the Universe, in the sense that the Universe answers our human demand that _it_ shall not contradict itself. We who go further than the anti-religious man of science, and ascribe the same degree of value to the moral and religious as he does to the physical order, are simply carrying out this same act of faith more consistently and thoroughly. We, too, believe in the reasonableness of the Universe, but when we call it reasonable we mean that it answers not one but all of our fundamental human demands.[2]

Or, as Taylor otherwise states it, "If the order of the Universe is to be pronounced truly reasonable, it must not be at hopeless variance with the foundations of the moral order."[3] Nor does there appear to be any assignable time when man's interest in such matters turns into disinterest and indifference. This fact may well characterize and introduce the question of immortality as a "genuine option" (to use William James' phrase) --combining as it does elements of the momentous, the necessary, and the vital. In contrast with whatever hope this approach might seem to justify, Taylor notes what appears to be the grand indifference of nature to man's temporal existence and understands that, perhaps quite unconsciously, man's otherwise tendency to regard the belief in immortality favorably is weakened. He writes,

This apparent insignificance of the human person by comparison with the lavish and inexhaustible fertility of Nature which seems to care nothing for the fate of any individual life, this ruthlessness with which what we account the most precious of human lives are daily cut short by what looks like the senseless sport of circumstance,

---

2. Ibid.

3. Ibid., p. 145.

--these, rather than any specific arguments, seem to be the consideration which, inevitably perhaps, weaken men's belief in an unseen future when that belief is no longer kept alive by the vigorous assertion of ecclesiastical authority. When the poet cries out against God

Thou has fed one rose with dust of many men,

which of us, in a scientific age, can help saying in his heart, "Yes, that is the truth"?[4]

In keeping with the emphasis carried by the other pages of this paper, Taylor's argument will be from the point of view of the nature of moral obligation. That is to say, no appeal will be made to the metaphysical argument for the immortality of the soul from the alleged fact of its simplicity, nor will appeal be made to the alleged evidences of life beyond death offered by "spiritualism" and necromancy through the medium of certain empirically applied demonstrations. It may be granted, Taylor concedes, that if the soul is indeed simple--that is, without parts--it cannot suffer disintegration because there are no parts to separate. This would not, however, avoid the soul's passing out of existence instantaneously; even "simple" existence does not guarantee imperishability. As for the experimental appeals of the "spiritualists," Taylor does not regard their evidence sufficiently compelling to coerce assent to their larger conclusion.

Regarding this "witness of spiritualism and physical research," Taylor remarks,

The actual occurrence of the alleged "facts" is often next to impossible to establish, and as for the interpretation, there seems no doubt that conscious or unconscious fraud plays a large part in the "phenomena," and it is at least likely that, where fraud is excluded, much that seems at first sight to be communicated by the dead is really derived by thought-transference from the living. If there remain any "facts" which cannot be accounted for in these ways, there is still always the open possibility that the "spirits"

---

4. Ibid., pp. 126-127.

from whom the spiritualist medium obtains a message are mischievous, or absolutely evil, beings fraudulently adopting an alias for their own purposes. The traditional belief of the Church in diabolical possession, it may reasonably be held, explains many of the "phenomena" as well as, if not better than, the theory of the spiritualist.[5]

But, in any event, neither of these arguments is strictly a moral argument and the effort pursued in these pages is that of noting the probably implications of moral concern. As Taylor states it,

> A genuine moral argument for immortality must be one to the effect that the destruction of human personalities would make the moral end unattainable. If this can be proved, the proof will be sufficient for those who believe in the absolute objectivity of moral obligation, though for no others.[6]

The further indication of the direction that Taylor's argument will take may be found in his statement of conviction that

> Apart from an adequate doctrine of God, it is, as I believe, impossible to find any secure foundation for a doctrine of human immortality, or any ground for thinking the prospect of such immortality attractive.[7]

This joining of the moral dimension to immortality is what Taylor understands to be its "attractive" and compelling character. It is the moral and intellectual character that has been long in building and it is precisely this characteristic of man that gives him his unique meaning and his sense of worth and his hope for commensurate goals along the line of the same advance. It is not mere immortality as such but an immortality that is structured with the essential moral thrust of its earlier beginnings to which will now be added the promise of continuance in that very

---

5. Ibid., p. 131.

6. Taylor, THE FAITH OF A MORALIST, Series I, p. xvi.

7. Ibid., p. 256.

value-participation that has given man essential meaning.[8]   Taylor writes,

> What has made the hope of immortality precious to
> mankind in its hours of peril and bereavement is
> precisely that immortality, in the great reli-
> gions, has always been taken to mean that it is
> the best features in our personality which endure
> in spite of the mortality of all earthly things,
> that in "the world to come" the soul will retain
> its interests in Truth, Beauty, and Goodness, and
> will be able there to pursue these ideals as it
> cannot while it is hindered at every moment by
> the limitations imposed on its endeavours by its
> connection with its present body, and exposed to
> all the chances and changes of this mutable
> world.[9]

It is an immortality structured by a continuation
of what is essential moral concern that differentiates
it from lesser defenses that a doctrine of immortality
may have suffered under--even when the arguments employed have escaped the above mentioned metaphysical
and empirical ones. For example, it is not mere desirability for an immortal state that justifies our
hope; nor is it the alleged fact that extinction of
human personality is an inconceivable event; nor is
the argument one from the consensus of mankind which,
though perhaps not perfectly universal, is so wide-
spread as to demand some kind of adequate explanation;
rather, Taylor says, "It is plain...that we do not
seriously judge immortality to be good at all, unless
we have some guarantee of its quality,"[10] and that
"quality" is to be revealed in Taylor's argument as of
one piece with what we here and now honor by our recognition of the norms of value-predication.

---

8. The above two sentences are so nearly identical
    with the general attitude of Taylor as touching
    the relation of moral value and immortality as to
    suggest an actual quotation, but I am unable to
    verify the reference.

9. Taylor, "The Belief in Immortality," p. 130.

10. Taylor, THE FAITH OF A MORALIST, Series I, p. 263.

As we have noted in the section on the relation of value to actuality, Taylor does not exempt ideals or norms from being grounded ontologically. It would therefore follow that in the measure that the "norms of value-predication" must be admitted as effectually operative in value-judgments, and in the further measure that they cannot be validated on the basis of experience, that their transcendental character is at the same time seen to ground in actuality. At this level, the "actuality" can only be called God. But if one has ab initio excluded God in principle from his metaphysics, the above argument must be frustrated all down the line until once again the preoccupation of man with judgments of value--logical, esthetic, and ethical--re-raises the question of proper standards, standards for which, Taylor has argued, experience cannot give us, and thus once again to raise the question of whether we will resolutely abandon the claims of the ethical dimension in toto or, not being able so to do, end again with the necessity of finding a proper locus of those values above experience.

The strength of Taylor's argument for immortality then, rests upon two assumptions: (1) that "the moral life is identical with the truly human life";[11] and (2) that there is "absolute objectivity of moral obligation."[12] To these assumptions is added a principle of argument, viz., "We may fairly argue from the reality of a function to the reality of an environment in which it finds its use." To this, Taylor adds,

> The question at stake is whether the moral life
> presents us with functions which demand the
> "other world" as an environment, i.e., whether
> the "good" is such that it cannot be obtained "in
> this life."[13]

"Function" suggests that sort of relation that is fundamentally one of dependence. Even in mathematics, a function is "a variable quantity whose value depends on and varies with that of another quantity or

---

11. Ibid., p. 281.

12. Ibid., p. xvi.

13. Ibid.

quantities."[14] (Italics mine) Less narrowly, function is "the normal or characteristic action of anything; especially, any of the natural, specialized actions of an organ or part of an animal or plant: as the procreative function."[15]

The intimacy therefore involved between "function" and its "environment" is clearly understood and Taylor offers comment as follows:

> The real problem to be faced is not whether reasoning of this kind from the reality of function to the reality of the environment in which it can function is valid. To raise doubts on that point would be fatal to the admission of enough rationality into the cause of things to make science itself possible. The real question is rather whether in fact examination of the moral life reveals the reality of any such functions.[16]

Here, of course, the "functions" would be commonly accepted moral acts. And the question being asked is whether these acts find an appropriate "environment" totally within the secular-temporal dimension. Taylor searches the secular-temporal scene to note whether there are implications of dependence upon the larger dimension of right--one that transcends the secular-temporal, whether, that is to say, the purely secular and temporal environment is an environment proper to the function being enacted within it. Taylor takes away from his scrutiny a conviction that there are abundant "intimations of immortality."

a) More subtly insistent that explicit formula, there is a _feeling_ abroad in human experience, a _feeling_ of an imperative that we ought to make the best of ourselves, to practice virtue, to abstain from cruelty, never to testify knowingly against another falsely,

---

14. WEBSTER'S NEW WORLD DICTIONARY OF THE AMERICAN LANGUAGE. (Cleveland and New York: The World Publishing Company, 1966), p. 586.

15. _Ibid._

16. Taylor, THE FAITH OF A MORALIST, Series I, p. 282.

et cetera. But every imperative is a moral imperative. It is, once again, the uncompromising categorical imperative of formalism. It is the "ought" of moral obligation. It sanctions the stands that we take in our conscience--whether these conscience-stands are objectively right or wrong. It is an ultimate presupposition that so far transcends experience as to permit condemnation or justification of experience. And, as we are found living out our function within an environment that condemns (or justifies) the secular-temporal act, it follows, Taylor says, that the environment proper to the function, being here an "other-worldly" one, permits a rational belief in an immortality appropriate to the function.

b) Much of life calls upon man for sacrifice. Something is given up that another might benefit. There are many acts that demonstrate a sacrificial spirit that are susceptible of no adequate interpretation other than that the author of the act is in dependence upon that "larger" environment that is the unconsciously assumed necessary condition for the validation of the sacrificial act or "function." That is to say, there are sacrifices that are justified just because they are right--a declaration that must sound perfectly vacuous were it not for the combined considerations that experience cannot quite justify them and yet there is the conviction that they are not only "right" but many times a matter of felt duty.

c) Instinctively nationalism hesitates before it boldly announces, "My country, right or wrong!" And what means this hesitancy? Taylor replies, in effect, that the hesitancy derives from the (again) unconsciously held presupposition of a norm of right that transcends time and place. If the country is to be adequately defended, its defense must be that of rendering explicit the implicit presupposition and declaring that its alleged "rightness" is justifiably claimed because the country participates to an appropriate extent in the norm (or form) of the right that transcends the country. As Taylor styles it,

> The rule of all wise and profitable love of everything that passes is to love without losing one's heart. He who wishes for the true good of wife or child or country must love them dearly, but there will be something he loves more: if

174

there is not, his love will carry in it the seeds of a curse for the very beings he loves most. To make a god of one's child is to spoil the child of your idolatry; to make "my country, right or wrong," the principle of your action is to do what lies in you to turn your country into one which is not worth loving. ...The true secret of life is to love these things well, but to love something else better. And we have only to think of the various names we give to that something else the love of which keeps all our loves for particular things sane and sweet, to see that, whether we call it "God," or "beauty," or "the right," or "honour," by all these different names we mean something which is "not of this world," but stands above and untouched by the temporality and mutability it transfigures.[17]

d) That virtue is to be honored is so nearly a universal conviction as to amount to a tautology. It is just another of the "functions" of a largely uncritically held part of the common morality. But its "environment"? The appeal of the immortality argument is not merely that "Virtue shall receive its reward," but rather that the intrinsic meaning of virtue shall not be artificially stifled by its secular-temporal appearance. It is again the case of the idea of virtue arising upon the occasion of experience, but not being identical with the experience. For how can the act justify itself? As long as the virtuous act hopefully receives its justification by some principle other than the act, the principle is established of looking to some implied universal. It is Taylor's conclusion that such a validating universal cannot be found in the secular-temporal dimension.

e) The above considerations (a through d) are really only so many recognitions of right and wrong that are ordinarily referred to conscience. And Taylor now introduces this word in order to speak further of the authority that the moral mandate has for man and, moreover, of the locus of this authority.

The main question for us at the moment is whether we really are unavoidably driven, when we consult

---

17. Ibid., pp. 303-304.

175

conscience, to admit that the ideal of good which has inspired our historical moral achievements proves on examination to be something not included in good as good can be legitimately conceived by the humanitarian. Is devotion to the temporal welfare of human society the sufficient justification of the imperatives of morality? If it is not, then, unless we admit--and the admission would be fatal to all moral philosophy--that moral imperatives cannot and need not be justified at all, and so have no genuine obligatoriness about them, we must be prepared to admit that there is good rational ground for anticipating a destination of human persons which is ignored when such persons are thought of as merely transient; morality will thus bear a real witness of its own to the presence of the seeds of immortality in us.[18]

The appeal to conscience, for Taylor, is actually a case of finding authority that is not formal infallibility. "Conscience," Taylor tells us, "is not infallible; yet its authority constitutes a strict obligation."[19] Here is an authority "the reality and worth of...which...is not the same as a formal inerrancy... (but is) a life which is more than merely natural and yet not fully and consciously supernatural."[20]

Here, Kant is thought to have claimed too much:

If he is to be tied down to the letter of his teaching, (he) appears to confound the authority of conscience with a formal inerrancy. In his anxiety not to weaken the sense of obligation in man he actually maintains that an honestly mistaken judgement on the morality of an act I am contemplating is impossible; "an erring conscience

---

18. Ibid., p. 293.

19. Ibid., Series II, xvii.

20. Ibid., p. 237.

is a Chimaera"[21] an imaginary danger not to be met with in the real world. ...The only "conscientious difficulty" he (Kant) contemplates is that of the man who knows quite well that what he is proposing to do is a violation of positive moral law, but is looking for some plausible "colour" for the transgression.[22]

To this, Taylor offers the rejoinder that

Had he considered the kind of decision which is really critical, choice between alternative lines of conduct where there is no traditional rule to afford any guidance, and the whole responsibility of deciding right or wrong thus actually falls on the individual conscience, the decision, for example, to accept or refuse an offered post, to make or not to make a proposal of marriage, he must have seen the extravagance of maintaining either that in every such case we pronounce one alternative right and the other wrong, or that when we do with difficulty arrive at such a pronouncement, its honesty is sufficient guarantee of its correctness.[23]

Let us then grant that not every specific of morality can be deduced from formalism. What of Taylor's insistence that in spite of this lack of infallibility there remains "strict obligation"? Before considering the reasons that may justify this position, Taylor, in passing, notes that "most moralists" have tended to agree with this position.

Most moralists, after all, have admitted that an erring conscience is only too common in actual life, but have not held that the possibility that my conscience may be in error diminishes my obligation to follow it. St. Thomas, for example, is as convinced that an erroneous conscience

---

21.   Translating Unding in WERKE (Hartenstein, iv. 251, vii. 204. Taylor's note. THE FAITH OF A MORALIST, Series II, p. 237.

22.   Ibid., pp. 237-238.

23.   Ibid.

absolutely obliges as he is that it does not relieve from responsibility.[24]

And Hutcheson is noted to have distinguished "between
the material goodness of the act which is in fact demanded by the situation and the formal goodness of the
act which the agent honestly believes to be demanded."[25] Sidgwick is also noted to have thought that
conscientiousness, though not a sufficient, is always
a necessary, condition of virtuous action."[26] Something of the same distinction is offered by William
David Ross[27] in contrasting actual with prima facie
duty--where in the latter only does one find a notion
of duty that transcends exception.

The reasons to which Taylor appeals have already
been given in principle when we were charged to recognize that only unless the entire moral dimension be
surrendered can we avoid acknowledgment of an ethical
mandate that is above the mere fact of descriptive behavior and by the light of which behavior is accounted
justified or condemned. And practice confirms the
above in the sense that of all dispositions that might
be singled out to identify what is truly man the ethical disposition is as nearly constant throughout man's
history as any. The idea of right--with its negative
of wrong--is apparently present everywhere. And whether objectively right or not, the governing commitment of right is there and may be said to be the only
standard that conscience knows. Conscience therefore
manifests itself as a strong feeling (Mill is right
here) that acts, as it believes, rationally (Kant is
right here) out of deference to a locus of

---

24.   Ibid., p. 238.

25.   Ibid., p. 238-239. Taylor adds: "Though, to be
      strictly accurate, Hutcheson expresses himself
      rather differently about formal goodness; an act
      is formally good 'when it flows from good affec-
      tion in a just proportion.'" (SYSTEM OF MORAL
      PHILOSOPHY, i. 252). Ibid., p. 239.

26.   Ibid.

27.   THE RIGHT AND THE GOOD. (Oxford: The Clarendon
      Press, 1930).

transcendent authority, a concrete universal, that is continuous in principle with man's moral concern and confers upon the particularities of man's ethical judgments that meaning and justification that in principle is the function of every universal in relation to the particulars properly subsumed beneath it.

If now, it is indeed "a legitimate inference from the reality of a function to the reality of the environment where the function will find its use,"[28] Taylor is willing to marshall the above considerations of "functions" as evidences that they do indeed depend upon an "environment" and such an environment as must of necessity transcend the secular-temporal dimension. The "feeling of the moral imperative," the natural response of man to sacrifice, the hesitancy to identify nationalism or any other moral good with the de facto situation, the near-tautology that everywhere decrees that "virtue should be honored," the implicit and explicit obediences to "conscience," are all "functions" within the meaning of the word as employed by Taylor and, as such, testify to their proper "environment" which, in the nature of the case, in order to the preservation of their very meaning and worth, mark that environment as fulfilling human nature and as pointing human nature to its proper goal beyond the death of the body. Thus Taylor finds at the least a necessary condition for the full assertion and defense of personal immortality.

Although Taylor presses his argument for immortality with vigor and conviction, he does not regard his conclusion in the nature of a demonstration. He clearly states that "the question of a future life must remain an open one for metaphysics,"[29] while holding that the argument for life-continuance from the natural concern of the self is essentially valid within the assumption--as we have seen--of the relation of "function" to an adequate "environment." This more general appreciation for "the various special forms which the desire for immortality takes," is related to

---

28. Taylor, THE FAITH OF A MORALIST, Series I, p. 282.

29. Alfred Edward Taylor, ELEMENTS OF METAPHYSICS, (London: Methuen & Co., 1903), p. 357.

the larger teleological consideration in the following observation.

> Normally, as we know, the extinction of a particular teleological interest is effected by its realization; our purposes die out, and our self so far suffers change, when their result has been achieved. (And incidentally this may help us to see once more that dissatisfaction and imperfection are of the essence of the finite self. The finite self lives on the division of idea from reality, of intent from execution. If the two could become identical, the self would have lost the atmosphere from which it draws its life-breath.) Hence, if death, in our experience, always took the form of the dissolution of a self which had already seen its purposes fulfilled and its aims achieved, there would probably be no incentive to desire or belief in future continuance. But it is a familiar fact that death is constantly coming as a violent and irrational interrupter of unrealized plans and inchoate work. The self seems to disappear not because it has played its part and finished its work, but as the victim of external accident. I think that analysis would show, under the various special forms which the desire for immortality takes, such as the yearning to renew interrupted friendships or the longing to continue unfinished work, as their common principle, the feelings of resentment against this apparent defeat of intelligent purpose by brute external accident.
>
> Now, what is the logical value of this feeling as a basis for argument? We may fairly say, on the one hand, that it rests on a sound principle. For it embodies the conviction, of which all Philosophy is the elaboration, that the real world is a harmonious system in which irrational accident plays no part, and that, if we could only see the whole truth, we should realize that there is no final and irremediable defeat for any of our aspirations, but all are somehow made good."[30]

---

30. Ibid., p. 356.

There is little doubt but that Taylor is committed to rationality as a part of the essential nature
of things and understands irrationality as a privation
and mere negation of the rational. For Taylor, there
is no surd of irrationality in the universe; indeed,
there is no irrationality that is incapable of reduction to its rational components. It must be recognized that however much Taylor's inclusion of God,
soul, freedom, immortality, and other such non-empirical terms may win rejection by some on the grounds of
their alleged "irrationality" or "meaninglessness,"
for Taylor, this is not true in principle and, as his
arguments are calculated to show, neither is it believed to be true in fact. For Taylor, the principle
that would limit possibility is that of the law of
contradiction. That is to say, if a proposition does
not in fact exhibit internal formal contradiction,
then its possibility must be admitted--its actuality
awaiting the convergence of such evidence as may be
brought to bear upon its central allegation. By the
same line of reasoning, faith is never merely blind
faith. Faith always has some object that it names as
proper for belief and some kind of relation between
that object and the world that it defends on the basis
of some sort of analogy that in turn promotes an alleged maximum coherence. This is the position that
Taylor may be depended upon to defend, and whatever
its outcome as judged by its ability to sustain a coherent account of things, it cannot be adjudged as a
commitment to a program that separates from rational
process in principle.

In keeping with these thoughts and these principles, Taylor notes that there is no a priori need for
the dissolution of the self. "It is manifest," Taylor
writes,

> that "self" is a teleological concept. The self
> whose quality is revealed in Biography and Histo-
> ry, and judged in Ethics, has for its exclusive
> material our emotional interests and purposive
> attitudes towards the various constituents of our
> surroundings; of these, and of nothing else, our
> self is made.[31]

And though, as we have acknowledged,

---

31. Ibid., p. 335.

...we clearly cannot have any positive demonstration from the nature of the self of its indes-
tructibility, and it would therefore be vain to
demand that philosophy shall prove the permanence
of all selves, ...On the other hand, if the permanence of a self is ultimately a function of its
inner unity of aim and purpose, there is no a
priori ground for holding that the physical event
of death must necessarily destroy this unity, and
so that the self must be perishable at death.[32]

In a manner somewhat reminiscent of Butler's defense of immortality, Taylor finds nothing either in
experience or in a priorism that disproves the soul's
(or self's) existence beyond death. It clearly is not
the case that the very meaning of the self entails its
ultimate cessation with regard to its personal consciousness. "The utmost," writes Taylor, "that even
the Roman Church demands is the admission that 'proof'
of immortality is not intrinsically impossible."[33]
As for arguments from experience, as Butler taught,
the fact of death merely removes the empirical evidence of life, not permitting one to follow further
the possible itinerary of the self beyond death. Or,
as Taylor states it,

The observer can satisfy himself that something
is now perceptible which was formerly impercepti-
ble, or something formerly perceptible now imper-
ceptible; he cannot actually observe non-existence passing into existence, or existence into
non-existence.[34]

Taylor is not impressed with the reductions of
body to mind or of mind to body. In fact, his position is strongly dualistic as far as the present time-
space man is concerned offering "a defense and a modified restatement of the old doctrine of Interaction as,
at present, the most satisfactory theory of the

32. Ibid., p. 354.

33. Taylor, "The Belief in Immortality," pp. 129-130.

34. Taylor, THE CHRISTIAN HOPE OF IMMORTALITY, p. 30.

connexion between body and mind."[35] Indeed, to some
form of dualism it would appear, virtually every discussion of the problem of the mind and body must return. Even discussions that have no thought of capitulating to dualism, in their very retention of the
terms, give some sort of recognition to the apparent
permanence of the difference.

> If is, of course, clear, /writes Taylor/ that the
> question how mind and body are related presuppo-
> ses the previous recognition of some distinction
> between the two; only from the standpoint of some
> kind of relative dualism has our problem any mean-
> ing.[36]

As we saw in Taylor's treatment of human freedom,
to free the rational faculty from the grip of an irrational determinism is a necessity unless we relinquish
all title to critical distinction between valid and
invalid argument. Now, similarly, the identification
of mind and body--and the current tendency is that of
a reduction in favor of body--appears to destroy that
independence that, for Taylor, is a necessity for the
preservation of rational discrimination and the elimination of illusion. "If mind and body," Taylor argues,

> are to be two aspects of one thing, then we must
> have rigid one-to-one correspondence of each ele-
> ment of the psychical manifold with one definite
> element of the physical manifold. ...Now such
> complete correspondence, as Ward argues, is pre-
> cisely what we have not got.[37]

The dualism that emerges in the Taylor argument--
together with the "interaction" involved--preserves
the common-sense attitude that virtually every man
takes toward mind and body as well as offering an explanation of why it is so difficult to eliminate these
dualistic tensions even when the applied reduction is

---

35. Alfred Edward Taylor, "Mind and Body in Recent
    Psychology," MIND, XIII (October, 1904), p. 476.

36. Ibid., p. 477.

37. Ibid., p. 483.

attempted by minds eminently capable of performing the
subtlest analytical dissections. As Taylor puts it,

> The philosophical value of the interaction theory
> is thus, to my mind, that without necessarily
> proving purposive human activity ultimately real,
> it logically permits of our regarding it as at
> least a phenomenon bene fundatum, whereas paral-
> lelism, strictly interpreted, seems to reduce it
> to something unpleasantly like a mere illusion.[38]

Taylor appears to notice the paradox that the very
sharpness of antithesis that Descartes drew between
mind and body, and which in turn drew objection from
many sources, continues to be exactly the same sharp
antithesis in the very writings that are dedicated to
the elimination of the dualism. Taylor declares that
"Descartes was fundamentally in the right in opposing
the 'physical' and the 'subjective' to one another as
ultimately irreducible modes of being. Nothing that
is physical is 'subjective' and nothing that is 'subjective' is physical."[39]

It is clear that these various examinations of
positions inimical to the preservation of a dualism
together with their rejection, are at the same time
preparations for further defense of immortality by
establishing the necessary conditions for the doctrine.
It is the same concern that leads Taylor to remark on
the question of "personal identity." Such an "identity" cannot be maintained if the mind's reduction to
the body were successful, and it is, at least, annoy-
ing for the success of the undertaking to separate
them that we never appear to meet the separation in
experience--not, at least, in any manner other than
the dialectical one that has been pursued in the analysis of that meaning that is alleged to be necessary if
the function of the mind is to be preserved in its rational and purposive character. But what the mind is
permitted to think without contradiction may be true.
And so Taylor asks whether personal identity resides
solely in the soul or mind, or does it involve

---

38. Ibid., p. 508.

39. Alfred Edward Taylor, "Back to Descartes,"
     PHILOSOPHY, XVI (1941), p. 127.

identity of the physical organism? In actual practice, of course, life does not present us with cases in which personal identity is found apart from some body. But we can at least imagine such a possibility.

"Suppose, for example," Taylor writes,

> that the Pythagorean doctrines were true, and that the soul of man could become associated with the body of a parrot. If it were possible for the supposed parrot to convince us that it retained the psychical character which we had previously known as that of a friend, it is difficult to see how we could refuse to believe that we were dealing, not indeed with the same man, but with the same person. We should, e.g., be morally bound to treat the parrot, not as a mere parrot, but as having the same moral claims and rights as our friend, and we should hardly regard the belief in personal immortality as capable of refutation by the mere consideration that there can be no identity of organism between an embodied and a disembodied spirit.[40]

And the reason that impresses Taylor that there "can be no identity" is, as we noted above, the fact that we are dealing with "ultimately irreducible modes of being." It is this "irreducibility" in fact that perpetuates itself in both the non-reflective attitudes of the man on the street as well as the marked tendency of even critical discussion of this subject to return in principle to the tacit recognition of the real difference between mind and body. And so Taylor concludes that "Personal identity would thus seem to be essentially psychical and, in its concept (whatever the full concrete facts may be), independent of bodily identity."[41]

Personal immortality, then, depends upon a clear separation of the psychical from the physical. But in what does the psychical identity consist? The answer that Taylor gives is that it does not consist in some

---

40. Alfred Edward Taylor, "Identity," ENCYCLOPEDIA OF RELIGION AND ETHICS, 1912, VII, p. 98.

41. Ibid.

sort of "substratum" but is, rather, "formal." This
endorsement of "formal" identity is opposed to both
the identity of content and the identity of matter.
What is "content"? It would be our thoughts, memo-
ries, imaginations, desires, et cetera. But these
change. They change as much as many of the bodily
characteristics. Therefore if there is to be any sort
of meaningful "identity," it must not be identified
with either the content of the psychical or physical.
"It is no more required," writes Taylor,

> in order that a man may be the same person as he
> was twenty years ago, that some mental "content"
> should have persisted unchanged during the twenty
> years, than the sameness of his body requires
> that some of its particles should still be the
> same as twenty years ago. What is required is
> that the succession of changes in mental and moral
> character should be linked together as a continu-
> ous development according to a law of growth
> which in its concrete fullness is characteristic
> of the person in question and of no other being
> in the universe. A man's present experience is
> his experience, because it fits on to his past
> experiences as it does not fit on to any other
> series of individual experiences. It is thus an
> abuse of language, which may easily lead to the
> gravest confusion of thought, to speak of person-
> al identity as involving anything in the nature
> of an unchanging psychical "substratum."[42]

This explanation which makes use of a "succession
of changes in mental and moral character...linked together as a continuous development according to a law
of growth" is reminiscent of Aristotle's entelechy--a
sort of built-in blueprint that the "law of growth"
follows in the development of the living form. And it
is necessary to plead such a "law" of continuity in
order to overcome that otherwise looseness of mental
states that characterizes Hume's account of the person.
Taylor's is a dynamic view of the human person and contrasts with the inert view that is implied in the "substratum" theory that he rejects. Indeed, it is worth
noting in passing that Taylor refuses the "substratum"
theory in both psychical and physical identities. The

---

42.   Ibid.

"identity" is defended in both, but is kept "formal."

The "personal" aspect that Taylor is defending
demands appeal to memory as an essential (though not
sufficient) condition of identity. An identity could
be defended without memory, but it would not be "personal." Plants, and perhaps animals, would illustrate
such an impersonal identity. But the very meaning of
a person, for Taylor, demands that his unique characteristic of being "personal" requires that that narrower particularization and exhibition of identity be also preserved by some suitable linkage. "...it seems,"
Taylor declares, "...that memory is essential to personal identity, and that there is ultimately no sense,
e.g., in speculations which represent the same person
as passing through a succession of lives in each of
which he is absolutely precluded from all possible memory of the events of those which have gone before. If
all links of memory are destroyed at death (or at re-
birth), on what ground do we pronounce a given man A
to be a reincarnation of another man B rather than an
entirely new creation?"[43] Taylor thinks of a case in
Spinoza where "memory and imagination are excluded
from continuance after the death of the body" and
feels that this "proves that Spinoza cannot be thinking of anything that can properly be called 'personal'
immortality."[44]

Hume, too, sensed a necessary relation between our
sense of identity and memory. But empiricist Hume cannot grant himself the advantage of a "law of growth"
postulate (or some equivalent) as the more fundamental
principle by which memory is explained. Hume must
start with memory--and endeavor thereby to account for
our sense of identity. He ends--as might be expected--
with a denial of personal identity. And Taylor observes,

> If personal identity were the fiction that Hume
> asserted it to be, such a statement as "This is
> my long-lost son" would always be false. Hence,

43. Ibid., p. 99.

44. Alfred Edward Taylor, "The Conception of Immor-
    tality in Spinoza's Ethics," MIND, V (April,
    1896), p. 156.

wherever a statement of identity in diversity is made, it will be found to include as part of its meaning an assertion of the form a = a. This is not to deny that physical things change or that organisms grow; it is merely to state that, unless the change or growth is a process within something permanently self-identical, the very statements "This changes," "This grows," cannot be true.[45]

That Taylor's argument for personal identity is believed to contrast most informatively with the Humean account dictates the wisdom of a longer look at Hume's argument and to ask whether our persistent idea of unity among the perceptions is well accounted for in Hume. It must be remembered that when the perceptions are completely released from any sort of interconnectedness, that any subsequent idea of connectedness would seem to involve us in the doctrine that the disunified perceptions somehow become conscious of themselves as a unity. This is a recognition that at least belongs to Kant. The fact to be accounted for is not a succession of awarenesses, but an awareness of succession. That this loosing of all our perceptions involved even Hume in a quandary when he came to explain the ideas of simplicity and identity is evident from his own confession. He writes

> ...having...loosen'd all our particular perceptions, when I proceed to explain the principle of connexion, which binds them together, and makes us attribute to them a real simplicity and identity; I am sensible, that my account is very defective.[46]

However "defective" this account of simplicity and identity may appear to the later reflections of Hume, it is certain that he made a pronounced effort to explain (and thus at the same time to explain away) our persistent idea of a self-identity. The word he

---

45. Taylor, "Identity," p. 96.

46. David Hume, A TREATISE OF HUMAN NATURE, edited by L. A. Selby-Bigge, (Oxford: At the Clarendon Press, 1888). Bk. I, Pt. IV, Sect. VI.

seized upon to account for our false sense of personal identity was <u>memory</u>. Hume writes,

> Suppose we could see clearly into the breast of
> another, and observe that succession of percep-
> tions, which constitutes his mind or thinking
> principle, and suppose that he always preserves
> the memory of a considerable part of past percep-
> tions; 'tis evident that nothing could more con-
> tribute to the bestowing a relation on this suc-
> cession amidst all its variations. For what is
> the memory but perceptions? And as an image nec-
> essarily resembles its object, must not the fre-
> quent placing of these resembling perceptions in
> the chain of thought, convey the imagination more
> easily from one link to another, and make the
> whole seem like the continuance of one object?
> In this particular, then, the memory not only
> discovers the identity, but also contributes to
> its production, by producing the relation of re-
> semblance among the perceptions.[47]

And again,

> As memory alone acquaints us with the continuance
> and extent of this succession of perceptions,
> 'tis to be consider'd upon that account chiefly,
> as the source of personal identity. Had we no
> memory, we never shou'd have any notion of causa-
> tion, nor consequently of that chain of causes
> and effects, which constitute our self or per-
> son.[48]

It must be confessed that there is nothing that gives quicker impulse to the retention of the doctrine of the self than the notion of memory. But memory, like perception, impression, imagination, is all but totally meaningless <u>unless</u> a <u>self</u> is <u>posited</u> <u>which</u> re-members. Recalling again what Hume's doctrine of the mind is, <u>viz</u>., "...nothing but a heap or collection of different perceptions, united together by certain re-lations, and suppos'd tho' falsely, to be endow'd with

---

47.   <u>Ibid</u>., Bk. I, Part IV, Sect. II.

48.   <u>Ibid</u>., Bk. I, Part IV, Sect. VI.

a perfect simplicity and identity,"[49] or, as stated in the Appendix to the 'Treatise,' "...all our distinct perceptions are distinct existences, and that the mind never perceives any real connexion among distinct existences," it will be seen that if there is to be any "knowledge of," at all (and hence "memory of"), and if Hume's account is true, it follows that the only knowledge of memory possible is one generated by the perceptions themselves and from within the perceptions. Practically, this means that the percept blue has knowledge of and possibly remembers the percept loud. It means that the whole series of passing states, each distinct from the others, becomes conscious of itself as a series. It means that, in spite of the radical disunity, a sense of practical unity is discovered. It means that, in spite of the "certain relations" that unify the perceptions, "real connexion" is not among them. And yet, in spite of this radical disconnectedness and disunity and denial of a substantial self that stands over against the perceptions, memory can still arise to make a permanent contribution to "the fiction of person and personal identity."

Taylor believes it safe to risk the criticism of such an empiricism, knowing the labor that it must expend to render coherent its own doctrine. Taylor's position would appear to be consistent with both the common-sense approach to the mind-body relation as well as with the recurrent suggestions of latently assumed dualism that appear even in the writings of those most anxious to be rid of it. Rather than derive a pseudo-knowledge of the self through the instrumentality of memory, the position that Taylor prefers to accept is that without the self there could be no memory whatsoever. Hume has reversed his order of being with the correlative result that knowledge, which should grace the end-term, has allowed skepticism to become enthroned.

In support of what Taylor calls "our natural and reasonable anticipations"[50] of immortality, the preceding pages of this chapter have dealt with certain considerations that may now be profitably summarized.

---

49. Ibid., Bk. I, Pt. IV, Sect. II.

50. Taylor, THE CHRISTIAN HOPE OF IMMORTALITY, p. 47.

Two things must be remembered: (1) Taylor does not claim to be able to demonstrate the truth of the doctrine of immortality, yet he takes the position that if the truth of the doctrine is assumed for the sake of the argument, it will throw light upon certain of man's experiences that in turn will strongly suggest that the assumption is a valid one, (2) It is of the nature of the immortality doctrine defended by Taylor that man's nature, as exhibited particularly in his commitment to moral purpose, is a function that demands nothing less than immortality as its proper environment. The tentative assumption of the above points as explanatory of what we mean by immortality and particularly the intimate relation and claim that it exerts upon our living moments will now be seen to gather these summarized points together and exhibit them as pointing with high probability toward the truth of Taylor's larger thesis.

1. Man possesses a natural and aggressive interest in life and there seems to be no point beyond which indifference sets in. It is true that men weary of life and even take their life, but there is the clearest evidence that their concern is with some set of distressing circumstances over which they know no control. Their disposition, therefore, has no reference to life itself, but only to the accidental circumstances that beset them. That these circumstances are 'accidental' is clear because life can be both conceived and experienced without them. If therefore there is in fact no point where indifference to life sets in, it corroborates the thesis that man's concern is to go on and realize a continued life that knows no necessary limits.

2. Remembering Taylor's formula that "We may fairly argue from the reality of a function to the reality of an environment in which it finds its use,"[51] we note that man's present moral concern is partially satisfied in this life--which shows that to some extent there is a natural adjustment of the function to its environment. This establishes the reality of the relation. But because the function is only partially satisfied, the relation of function to its

---

51. Taylor, THE FAITH OF A MORALIST, Series I, xvi.

environment goes on to demand the larger fulfillment in an environment suitable to the function's full completion. This (as in Kant) must go beyond the limit imposed by an earthly life span.

3. The entire dialectical thrust of the moral "ought," implying as it does a reliance upon norms that in the nature of the case cannot be merely psychological or empirical, transcends experience thereby establishing that our normative concerns not only correct us and guide us but offer at the same time a proper goal for moral endeavor. The moral mandate that guides and corrects cannot be less than the man that is thus corrected and guided. It is thus that the personality of man, in obedience to the normative command, moves toward a personal locus of transcendent moral value.

4. The goal of the moral life is thus argued to find its natural, its dialectical fulfillment in a state of affairs that go beyond the limit of man's earthly existence. But the truly human life identifies in such a way with the moral life that it, too, is carried on to the same goal that is indicated as proper to moral aspiration. In this, the moral dimension is regarded as an essential part of man--with the result that the natural destiny (environment) of this moral dimension is at the same time and for that reason the natural destiny (environment) of the whole man.

5. If man is in fact as deeply constituted with such moral aspiration as finds its proper goal only in the transcendent, evidence of this relation should be observable in the experience and behavior of men. Taylor claims that there is evidence of this relation in the experience and behavior of men. Specifically, it is observable in man's feeling that he should practice virtue; it is observable in man's practice of sacrificial living; it is observable in man's practice of judging the rights and wrongs of particular situations by standards that are not identical with the particulars themselves; it is observable that there is widespread willingness to concede that virtue, while arising upon the occasion of specific experiences, may not be reduced to the experience itself. For Taylor, these "evidences" of living in a relation to a transcendent locus of values is analogous to the presence of a foreign accent's revelation that the owner

sustains a relation to another country. Because Taylor assumes it to be proved that a "this-worldly"
philosophy is incapable of producing such norms as
regulate our lives in the manner in which they are
largely unconsciously regulated, it follows that man
sustains a vital relation to a transcendent locus of
values. Only, Taylor repeats, if one were to repudiate the moral dimension totally, can this conclusion
be voided.

6. Conscience is a closely related phenomenon.
In man's acknowledgment of conscience as a non-
infallible source of strict obligation, he avoids the
pitfalls of casuistry while maintaining that there is
nevertheless present some invading sense of formal mandate that explains why men have no option but to regard the urging of conscience with the respect that is
naturally due to the highest behest of duty. This
phenomenon transcends "conditioning" in that conditioning will be made to answer whether its course is right
or wrong. To defend conditioning in a moral context
is to appeal above the condition for its justification
to call itself right.

7. Ethical analysts have frequently enough incorporated distinctions between the material and the
formal goodness of an act to indicate that it is not
alone the man-on-the-street in his unsophisticated
conditioning that preserves these distinctions. That
is to say, there are those with professional compe-
tence who make the distinction with full awareness of
that to which they are committing themselves. (They
are not to be confused with the more empirically ori-
ented who inconsistently are revealed as borrowing
from a dimension of normative significance that is actually transcendent without being aware of their dependence.) Taylor's point is that when ethical analysis admits the formal element, it necessarily abandons
secular-temporal experience as not capable of providing a meaningful ethical norm.

8. It is Taylor's conviction--and he believes
that it is also the implicit assumption of all men--
that the universe is deeply constituted by teleology
and intelligibility and that therefore death which
would seem to frustrate this teleology must be an accidental feature and not capable of ultimately frustrating man's natural function to seek an environment

beyond the secular-temporal dimension. This assumption of a general and ultimate intelligibility, Taylor feels, is manifest at two levels: man himself is essentially rational, and the external world is essentially rational. And this accounts for man's ability to apply rational techniques to the penetration and formulisation of nature. Even attacks on this alleged intelligence and intelligibility are of necessity forced to employ the very assumptions under attack.

9. There is no a *priori* need to invest the soul with impermanence or destructibility. It may be true that the soul is impermanent and destructible, but the claim must be made good by synthetic means; the predication is not analytic. The claim of immortality, not violating, therefore, the law of contradiction, must remain an open question subject to the determination of other means of confirmation than that of formal logic.

10. Neither can empirical means by employed to deny the soul's active continuity beyond death. Butler has noted approvingly that all that empiricism can tell us is that the empirical means available up to the time of death to confirm the fact of life are now no longer available--it remaining an open question as to the soul's existence, a question for which empiricism has no certain information.

11. The most determined "reductions" of the mind to the body by whatever means cannot avoid a remaining recognition of some permanent distinction between the two. It would appear that the grammatical distinction of a mind observing, controlling, "having" (?) a body, may well have its correspondence in fact with the result that a permanent dualism may be assumed as the best explanation of a problem that is as permanent as the distinctions are persistent.

12. The reduction of mind to body has precisely the effect of determinism generally, viz., that of rendering critical discernment impossible. Every mental act becomes a one-valued function of a bodily event and therefore responsible to no norm other than the non-rational movements of the body itself. Movements of a body are nothing but particulars and there is implicity denied in this reduction the possibility of relating and categorizing these particulars with

the result that knowledge becomes impossible. To interpret, to relate, to categorize, one must transcend
the realm of particularity. This is the traditional
function of mind. Under the reduction of "identity"
theory, the mind loses its last opportunity for logical discourse. The particulars of the body's movement
cannot even assert their impotence.

    13. The dualism that emerges preserves the com-
mon-sense attitude as "the most satisfactory theory of
the connexion of body and mind"[52] even as it reappears
inadvertently in the more sophisticated discussions of
the mind-body problem.

    14. The "identity" of the soul may be defended
if the distinctions between the material and the formal aspects of the soul are maintained. In the case
of the alleged maintenance of the soul's identity beyond death, it is the formal aspect that endures--a
"formal aspect" identified with a "law of growth"[53]
reminiscent of Aristotle's "entelechy" and providing
a solution to Hume's defective account of simplicity,
identity, and memory.

---

52. Taylor, "Mind and Body in Recent Psychology,"
    p. 476.

53. Taylor, "Identity," vii, 98.

CHAPTER VIII - MORAL VALUE AND GOD

We remember...the saying of Jacobi, that a God capable of proof would be no God at all; since this would mean that there is something higher than God from which His existence can be deduced. But this applies only to the ordinary reasoning of the deductive logic. It does not apply to that higher kind of proof which may be said to consist in the mind being guided back to the clear recognition of its own ultimate presuppositions. Proof in Theism certainly does not consist in deducing God's existence as a lower from a higher; but rather in showing that God's existence is itself the last postulate of reason --the ultimate basis on which all other knowledge, all other belief rests.[1]

It is recognized that the gradual emergence of God as the ultimate presupposition of thought has been the eventual point to which each of the preceding chapters has come. Chapters I and II emphasized the dominance of the moral factor in the experience of mankind with the insistence that if this factor is taken seriously, a break with naturalism is required in order to preserve the normative aspect of the moral imperative. Chapter III, in its requirement that value ground in actuality, declares for an ultimate ground of value that unifies the esthetic, the moral and the rational. This unity is declared to be that concrete universal which is God. In Chapter IV, man's essential purposiveness necessarily coincides with time-- "...the characteristic form of the conative,

---

1. James Orr, THE CHRISTIAN VIEW OF GOD AND THE WORLD. The Kerr Lectures for 1890-91. (Grand Rapids, Michigan: Eerdmans Publishing Company, 1948), p. 94.

forward-reaching life"[2]--and the contemplation of such
temporality leads dialectically to temporality's proper universal which is eternity and God--the appropriate presupposition of temporal purpose. Chapter V
notes the uniquely differentiating character of evil--
a privation that points up the good as the norm by
which it is recognized and identifies the good with a
Person in which character alone the authority of conscience can be explained. Chapter VI defends the freedom of the will by identifying it with its most fundamental and necessary condition: rationality. Rationality, in turn, is seen to be the presupposition of
all argument--including every attempt to "naturalize"
it--to the end that the intimate conjunction between
rationality and mind again leads to the naming of God
as the more appropriate characterization of that concrete universal that is at the same time the locus of
ultimate rationality. In the same chapter, in a manner reminiscent of Aquinas and Aristotle, the contingency of the world is seen meaningful only against the
backdrop of a necessary being. Chapter VII urges that
we may argue validly from the reality of a function to
that proper environment in which it finds its use.
The "function," in this case, is that of man's teleo-
logically-oriented nature, his value-seeking purposiveness, his rationally-dominated inquisitiveness.
Because death cuts short this natural "function" of
man, it may be argued, Taylor believes, that the proper fulfillment of man's function lies beyond death.
But remembering that the proper goal of such purposive
value-seeking must be that of some existence, some
actuality, in which the values ground, we are led to
God as both the inspirer and the goal of the immortal
desire.

The purpose then of this chapter will not be to
reiterate the several arguments that have already been
employed to relate the various aspects of value to the
existence of God, but, in view of the continued allegations throughout these several chapters that God is
the ultimate presupposition that validates value-
claims wherever made, it will be this chapter's effort
to show Taylor's supporting reasons for viewing God's
existence as indeed the capstone of philosophic
thought generally.

---

2. Taylor, THE FAITH OF A MORALIST, Series I, p. 76.

For Taylor, both atheist and theist occupy common ground in important areas of consideration. Both recognize that they have been thrust forth on the crust of this spinning planet by a force or forces independent of themselves. No man has created himself nor does he preserve himself. And that all but necessary backward look to what Tillich has styled "the ground of our being" is an essential characteristic of the religious attitude. Further, the reflection that from the consideration that something exists one cannot avoid the inference that something exists necessarily leads on to the further question of what other characteristics or attributes this necessarily existing something possesses. Here, the atheist and the theist part ways. The former must deny intelligence to this necessarily existing something; the latter must affirm intelligence.[3] The theist sees a continuum between the intelligence of man in the world and the postulated intelligence of the necessarily existing something. The atheist must deny this continuum in the sense that although he will prize his own and others' intelligence in the contribution it makes to any and all conclusions, ultimately he must reduce this particular manifestation to something that is non-intelligent in order not to betray his essential atheistic commitment. In keeping with this general principle of maintaining a continuum of analogically unified realities--the human and the divine, the world and God--Taylor has hoped to create the general conception of such a

---

3. "Ionian science, without intending it, prepared the way for the atheism which holds that there is no purpose or intelligence behind the scheme of physical nature." Alfred Edward Taylor, PLATONISM AND ITS INFLUENCE. (New York: Cooper Square Publishers, Incorporated, 1963), p. 102. The apparent reason why the scientist of whatever period can progress without reference to "purpose or intelligence behind the scheme of physical nature" is due to the fact that no amount of purely descriptive effort has need of this further reference. Even the purpose and intelligence of the investigator is hid from a purely empirical concern--a fact which may explain why naturalism has tended to treat purpose as irrelevant and the self as an entity dualistically separable from the body as ghostly.

Weltanschauung that does not have to reduce value to
non-value, intelligence to non-intelligence, rationality to the non-rational. He endeavors to preserve in
his system of presuppositions a hope that ultimately
our preoccupation with the many value-forms is not in
vain and may indeed be a light, however feeble, that
points back to what he fondly refers to as the "master
light of all seeing."

"We shall probably not depart far from the implications of current language," Taylor writes,

> if we agree to define theism as the doctrine that
> the ultimate ground of things is a single supreme
> reality which is the source of everything other
> than itself and has the characters of being (a)
> intrinsically complete or perfect and (b), as a
> consequence, an adequate object of unqualified
> adoration or worship.[4]

Taylor recognizes the long historical endorsement of
theism as a meaningful philosophical pursuit, noting
that "Theology, as a body of doctrine about God claiming to be capable of proof, was /Plato's7 ...own creation and first appears in the tenth book of the
Laws."[5] Undoubtedly many of the strongest minds of
Western philosophy have seen in theism the better
answer to the need for an ultimate synthesis of the
multifold aspects of total experience. And Taylor remarks,

> If we look at the history of European philosophy,
> it may be said in the main the general trend of
> philosophic thought, even independently of the
> influence of positive religions, has been theis-
> tic, at least from the time of Plato to our own
> day.[6]

And though Taylor is led to observe that "...this tendency to theism is a direct consequence of the permanent influence of Plato on all subsequent developments

---

4. Taylor, "Theism," ENCYCLOPEDIA OF RELIGION AND
   ETHICS, 1912, XII, p. 261.

5. Taylor, PLATONISM AND ITS INFLUENCE, p. 97.

6. Taylor, "Theism," p. 262.

in philosophy,"[7] it is "only in Neo-Platonism that [8] Greek philosophy succeeds in being fully theistic."

What has disputed this reign of theistic philosophy, this "general trend of philosophic thought...from the time of Plato to our own day"? In principle, the challenging restriction has been that associated with the alleged limitations of reason when reason is said to go beyond experience. As Kant nicely styles it,

> The light dove, cleaving the air in her free flight, and feeling its resistance, might imagine that its flight would be still easier in empty space. It was thus that Plato left the world of the senses, as setting too narrow limits to the understanding, and ventured out beyond it on the wings of the ideas, in the empty space of the pure understanding. He did not observe that with all his efforts he made no advance.....[9]

It is to Kant and Hume that Taylor quite naturally turns to remark upon the critique of the theistic proofs. Taylor writes,

> In dealing with Kant's drastic assault on speculative natural theology in the CRITIQUE OF PURE REASON, we may perhaps distinguish two questions which Kant himself naturally treated as one. It is one question whether Kant has proved that the demonstration of theism is impossible on the assumption that the special doctrine of his CRITIQUE as to the limits of human knowledge is true, but quite another question whether that doctrine is true, and consequently whether Kant has proved the fallaciousness of natural theology unconditionally.[10]

---

7. Ibid.

8. Ibid., p. 263.

9. Immanuel Kant, CRITIQUE OF PURE REASON. Translated by Norman Kemp Smith. (New York: St. Martin's Press, 1965), p. 47.

10. Taylor, "Theism," p. 276. "It would be wholly unjust to Kant to confine our attention to the destructive side of his treatment of philosophic

In passing, it may be remarked that "experience" is by no means a word with perfectly cut-and-dried meaning. The complexity of experience has been attested throughout the entire history of philosophy. It has run the entire gamut from attempts to reduce it to the discrete impressions of the five senses to identifying it with the total content of our consciousness. Considerations that militate against an easy solution for the reduction of experience to discrete impressions involve relations, categories, and space-time. It was the insistence of Kant that these can neither be reduced to pure experience nor dismissed that led to the famous "second Copernican revolution." "Experience," for the Kantian solution, became a compound of the categories (the "a priori" element) and the material supplied in sensation.11

Taylor recognizes, as did Kant, that experience is a curiously compounded affair and rejects the reduction of experience to the discrete and radically disconnected impressions of Hume. He agrees with Kant that the fuller account of experience must recognize

---

theism; even more important is his positive teaching, which will be found most fully expressed in the KRITIK DER PRAKTISCHEN VERNUNFT. If Kant's object was to destroy the old speculative natural theology, it is even more his purpose to replace it by a positive moral theology, and it is probably true to say that it is primarily due to his influence that in our own time it is mainly upon the moral argument that popular theistic philosophy continues to base itself." Ibid., pp. 279-280.

11. This "material supplied in sensation" is a curiously embarrassing feature of the Kantian analysis. It has supplied the occasion for the paradox of Jacobi that without the presupposition of realism one cannot enter Kant's system and with it one cannot stay there. It would appear that the entire CRITIQUE OF PURE REASON moves through a contradiction that simultaneously must affirm in some meaningful sense a real that is independent of the compounding action of the mind while at the same time maintaining the impossibility of any such real that is at the same time a legitimate object of knowledge.

that there is a principle of unity that cannot be found in sensory analysis. Without the presupposition of a unifying bond even the "discreteness" loses its meaning for the allegation of discontinuity is a mere negation of continuity. This principle of an ultimate unity, for Taylor, is therefore an integral part of experience. And the question of whether one may legitimately "go beyond" experience is itself a failure to recognize that experience in its particularized aspects has already been transcended in the barest attention given to its fuller involvement.

In keeping with this analysis of experience, it may be anticipated that Taylor would look upon the ontological argument for God's existence with somewhat less distrust than that usually generated by the Kantian criticism. That is to say, somewhat in similar vein to Taylor's philosophy of experience which views experience as saturated with its own transcendent ground, the genuine kernel of the ontological argument is viewed as a forced concession to a transcendent real.

It will be recognized that the main point of Kant's criticism of the ontological argument was that it endeavored to conclude to real existence from a premise that was purely intelligible. Without discussing here the question of whether existence is a predicate, it is enough to note that according to Kant if the "proposition" God exists is synthetic, then the predicate (existence) may be denied without contradiction; if, on the other hand, the proposition God exists is analytic, then, though the predicate cannot be denied without contradiction, there would be no contradiction if one were to deny both subject and predicate. And Taylor concedes this restriction. He writes,

> ...if "existence" is originally included among the perfections by which the subject "God" is defined, the proposition God exists is certainly necessary, but is also tautological, and amounts, in fact, to the mere assertion that "an existing perfect being is an existing perfect being." But if the "existence" spoken of in the predicate is something not included in the definition of the subject, then you cannot infer it from that

definition.[12]

And Hume's remark is similar in restriction when he
writes, "Whatever we conceive as existent we can also
conceive as non-existent. There is no being, therefore, whose non-existence implies a contradiction.
Consequently there is no being whose existence is
demonstrable."[13] Taylor's reply to this traditional
criticism, conformable to what has been said already
in these pages about "presuppositions," follows generally in the wake of Hegel and perhaps more particularly the position of Bradley in APPEARANCE AND REALITY.

The ontological argument cannot validly be
claimed to prove the existence of space-time particulars. Therefore the argument is not upset by Gaunilo's "perfect island" nor by Kant's "hundred dollars
in the pocket." In neither does the idea prove the
reality. "It is manifest," concedes Taylor, "that
Kant is perfectly right when he contends that taking
existence to mean presence in the space-time order,
you cannot reason from my possession of any idea to
the existence of a corresponding object."[14] "But,"
Taylor adds, "the principle of the ontological proof
is perhaps not necessarily condemned by its failure to
be thus universally applicable."[15] This "principle,"
as Taylor understands and states it is as follows:

> The idea and the reality outside its own exis-
> tence as a fact in the time-order which it
> "means" or "stands for" are mutually complemen-
> tary aspects of a whole Reality which include
> them both. For there is, on the one side, no
> "idea" so poor and untrue as not to have some
> meaning or objective reference beyond its own
> present existence.[16]

---

12. Taylor, ELEMENTS OF METAPHYSICS, p. 401.

13. David Hume, DIALOGUES CONCERNING NATURAL RELI-
    GION, part 9.

14. Taylor, ELEMENTS OF METAPHYSICS, p. 402.

15. Ibid.

16. Ibid.

The important qualifying words are "<u>some</u> meaning."
(italics mine) The fallacy alleged of the ontological
proof by Gaunilo in his criticism of Anselm was that
the <u>full</u> <u>meaning</u> of an island finds no correspondence
in an equally <u>full</u> <u>reality</u>. Taylor's position is that
the idea of an island finds "<u>some</u> meaning or objective
reference" in reality. (italics mine) This is what
Taylor means by saying that no idea is "so poor and
untrue as not to have some meaning or objective reference beyond its own present existence." So, on this
basis, every thought means something, and, meaning
something, implies by that fact that the "something"
that is "means" is correspondingly in existence. The
ontological argument then, for Taylor, "in its most
general form""is simply a statement that reality and
meaning for a subject mutually imply one another."[17]
From this we are encouraged to understand that while
every thought means something and has some corresponding reality, "it does not follow that every thought is
equally true and significant."[18] This observation
quite properly lays the basis for the fairly obvious
fact that there is a great deal of conflict among the
multitude of thoughts on differing subjects. These
thoughts therefore cannot claim a one-for-one correspondence between their idea-aspect and reality; neither, however, can it be said that they are wholly false.
And it is in the latter aspect that the truth-element
of the ontological argument is found--even as it is in
the former aspect that the fallacy of the same argument is revealed.

   It may not be possible to refine human thoughts
sufficiently to overcome this remainder of confusion
and falsity. But--so Taylor teaches--the principle is
implicit within the above argument that <u>if</u> <u>one</u> <u>could</u>
refine human thought to eliminate all confusion and
falsity, if one's thought were <u>thoroughly</u> "internally
harmonious and systematic,"[19] then one might lay claim
on a corresponding reality that possesses the same
characteristics. And anywhere along the line of advance of the mind's becoming more aware of its genuine

17. <u>Ibid</u>.

18. <u>Ibid</u>.

19. <u>Ibid</u>.

concerns, "the more adequately it represents the true nature of that which it means."[20] And Taylor notes,

> How freely we use this ontological argument in practice will be readily seen by considering the way in which, e.g., in the interpretation and re-construction of historical facts, the internal coherency of a systematic and comprehensive interpretation is taken as itself the evidence of its truth. Hence it may be argued that if there is a systematic way of thinking about Reality which is absolutely and entirely internally coherent, and from its own nature must remain so, however the detailed content of our ideas should grow in complexity, we may confidently say that such a scheme of thought faithfully represents the Reality for which it stands, so far as any thought can represent Reality.[21]

It is most natural that a defense of the ontological argument should appear within the context of a general idealist philosophy. The one-for-one correspondence claimed by Taylor between thoughts--however minimal in truth and significance--and the reality which they are said to "mean" in some sense is merely a reassertion of that idealism that alleges a natural affinity between thought and thing. Thus the mind is never pictured as a stranger in the world, but rather the world of nature is pictured as open to the penetration of the mind precisely because in some sense it is made of the stuff that minds are made of. This "confidence"--if we may so style it--in the power of the mind to hope in every case of confrontation with nature for an eventual solution is perhaps borrowed unconsciously from an assumption that in the world there are no areas the penetration of which is denied to the mind in principle. This may be claimed as the practicing attitude of the scientist: for every event there is its sufficient explanation, behind the particulars of experience there is the interlock and the universal and the unity; and it appears to be the unique prerogative of mind to write the formulae of a structured universe thereby confirming through its

---

20. Ibid.

21. Ibid., pp. 402-403.

successes the confidence with which it began. This
confidence of the mind in its powers of penetration of
nature and its subsequent writing of the hierarchy of
formulae of increased generalization, from Taylor's
point of view, is at once a defense of a broad idealistic philosophy and, more specifically, a theistic
one. "If thoroughly systematic coherent thought,"
writes Taylor, "may be mere misrepresentation, our
whole criterion of scientific truth is worthless."[22]
Indeed, the thrust of Taylor's whole philosophy of science is to establish the extreme likelihood of that
one-for-one correspondence of thought with thing that
automatically lays the basis on the broadest possible
scale for the deeper truth of the ontological argument.
If rational processes are the sole means of rendering
explicit the underlying structure of the cosmos, then
the cosmos may be declared to that extent and for that
reason <u>rational</u>. And to declare for the rationality
of the <u>cosmos is</u> to name perhaps its chief fulfilling
condition for the truth of the hypothesis of the existence of God.

While the rationality of the cosmos, for Taylor,
may be its chief fulfilling condition under the hypothesis of God's existence, the transition from what is
believed to be a valid defense of the ontological argument to the affirmation of the God of religion is
recommended to be accompanied with extreme caution.
The two conclusions are not necessarily identical.
With respect to the ontological argument itself, Taylor says,

> ...the ontological proof appears, in any sense in
> which it is not fallacious, to amount merely to
> the principle that significant thought gives us
> genuine knowledge; and therefore, since the tho-
> roughgoing individuality of structure of its ob-
> ject is presupposed in all significant thought,
> Reality must be a perfect individual.[23]

But then, "That this perfect individual must further
be 'God,' <u>i.e.</u> must have the special character
ascribed to <u>it</u> by beliefs based upon specifically

---

22. <u>Ibid.</u>, p. 402.

23. <u>Ibid.</u>, p. 403.

religious emotions, does not follow."[24] The validity
of the ontological argument--if granted--includes the
God of religion only if the God of religion may be
equated with the Absolute. But, Taylor warns, "...it
is obvious that if by 'God' we mean anything less than
the Absolute whole, the ontological proof ceases to
have any cogency."[25]

In a Preface to DOES GOD EXIST? written in 1945
Taylor declares,

> My purpose is not to demonstrate "the being of a
> God," but only to argue that some alleged and
> widely entertained "scientific" objections to
> theistic belief are unsound, and that it is un-
> belief (not belief) which is the unreasonable at-
> titude.[26]

The business of science, for Taylor, when not deserted
for excursions into what science is not, simply has
nothing to say one way or another about God's existence.

> Natural science....is exclusively concerned with
> the detection of "laws of nature," uniformities
> of sequence in the course of events. The typi-
> cal form of such a law is the statement that
> whenever certain definitely measurable events
> occur some other measurable event will also be
> found to occur. Any enquiry thus delimited ob-
> viously can throw no light on the question which
> is really at stake when we ask whether God exists
> or not, the question whether the whole course of
> events among which the man of science discovers
> these uniformities of sequence is or is not guided
> by a supreme intelligence to the production of an
> intrinsically good result.[27]

---

24. Ibid.

25. Ibid.

26. Alfred Edward Taylor, DOES GOD EXIST? (London:
    Macmillan, 1945), p. v.

27. Ibid., pp. 13-14.

If science could validly deduce a result of the existence of God and then show that the result was not in
fact forthcoming, then science might conclude properly
that there was evidence against God's existence. As
Taylor states it,

> ...if you could say, "if there is a God, the as-
> tronomical constitution of the solar system must
> be such-and-such, and we see that it is not," or
> "if there is a God, certain statements about the
> past history of the earth or of man must be true,
> whereas geology, or anthropology, has shown that
> they are not true," these would be "scientific"
> arguments against Theism. But in actual fact it
> is impossible to say things of this kind, and
> such reasoning consequently proves nothing what-
> ever against the existence of God and His control
> of the world's history.[28]

A principle that is supportive of the above allegations about the limitations of science is found in
Taylor's contention that exact science and knowledge
are not coextensive, that science is the smaller word.
That truth is not merely identical with the methods of
laboratory experiment is strongly hinted at in the
reasonableness of the question how one knows that the
methods of laboratory experiment are true. This dialectical thrust acknowledges a distinction between the
methods of laboratory experiment and the "truth" that
they are presumably hopeful of approximating. Partial
understanding of this "truth" that goes beyond the
narrower confines of scientific method, or, better,
this "truth" that is presupposed by scientific method,
this "extra-scientific knowledge,"[29] is gained by
acknowledging certain assumptions that the scientist
makes and without which he cannot get on with any sort
of coherent account of his subject matter. And in
this enlarged view of science Taylor does find reason
to believe that support is found for theism. Thus:

> Even if it turns out to be true that our scienti-
> fic knowledge, taken by itself, affords no ground
> whatever for theistic belief, it may still be

---

28. Ibid., pp. 10-11.

29. Ibid., p. 20.

true that the extra-scientific knowledge, apart
from which science itself could not exist, provides the theist with sufficient justification
for his assertion.[30]

This enlarged sphere of dependence is evidenced for
Taylor in a number of assumptions that the scientist
(in the narrower view of that word) makes of necessity
as he engages in the activities peculiar to his pro-
fession. Following are some of these alleged dependencies.

1) Realism. The conclusions of the scientific man
are, of course, personal experiences of his own; what
he has seen and heard and touched; what he has measured and recorded; and, of course, the grand conclusion to which all of these particular appeals allegedly point.

> But, /Taylor says,/ in his conclusions he always
> takes it for granted that he is telling us some-
> thing that is true not about himself and his own
> experiences of vision, hearing and the like, but
> about something that actually exists or has
> existed, independently of his experiencing.[31]

There is temptation here to stop with the epistemological successes gained through those exact observations,
measurements and generalizations and refuse to go on
to anything as non-empirical as the ontological dimension identical with what Taylor calls "realism."
There is something so immediate, indubitable, and
verifiable, about experience considered in its radically empirical form that any attempt to vouch for a
wider dimension of ontology on which this immediacy of
experience allegedly depends seems pale by comparison
if not positively an illusion. Still and withal there
is a compulsion about Taylor's enlarged sphere of
knowledge's involvement that is hard to overcome. The
very fact of the assumed communicability between and
among practicing scientists is itself justifiable only
upon the basis that there is in some sense an

---

30. Ibid.

31. Ibid., p. 21.

independent reality that each can share by participation. The acceleration of freely falling bodies, the relative atomic weights of elements, the calculating of planetary motions, the predictability of natural events,--all of these in their differing ways are assumed to be participant in some sort of reality that is independent of that epistemological formula that describes their activities. Indeed, individuality being what it is, the academic attempt to reduce the successes of epistemological analysis and calculation to merely personal responses staggers under the virtually infinite improbability of any unified language of communication being possible. The necessity for some postulate that accounts for the unification of knowledge would repeat what Taylor is urging under his assertion that in the assumption of "realism" the scientist is revealing a dependence upon an enlarged aspect of knowledge that the narrower empiricism cannot give.

2) The knowing act. The fundamental problem that leads naturally to the solution espoused by Taylor is that generated by that radical lack of theoretically discernible connection left by Hume's epistemology. Hume's strict empiricism precluded the discovery of any intrinsic bond that unites the impressions of sense. That a steady expectancy was generated by experience for certain events to follow other events Hume never denied. But because one may not cross from psychological expectancy to the claim of a theoretical insight of connectedness, Hume was left with an ultimate reduction of the knowable to numerous impressions radically disconnected from each other. It is in precisely this situation of the ultimate disconnectedness of the impressions that was born the observation--many times repeated--that a series of conscious states never from itself yields an "awareness of succession." This awareness of succession is truly a mode of knowledge different from anything found in the series of discrete impressions and considered as merely one of the impressions. As Kant states it,

> There can be in us no modes of knowledge, no connection or unity of one mode of knowledge with another, without that unity of consciousness which precedes all data of intuitions, and by relation to which representation of objects is

alone possible.[32]

To this dependency Taylor refers as a further indication of epistemology's involvement with a dimension of reality that transcends the phenomenology of the scientist's narrower concern. Taylor remarks that "...all the time, every bit of the scientific man's knowing is something more than...one of the occurrences which make up what we call 'nature'; it is also a knowledge of itself and of its relation with the rest of the series."[33] This is an acknowledgement that reintroduces the subject-object relation commonly asserted of the knowing-act. And it must be kept in mind that Taylor is making use of this dualism (that he believes is forced) to demonstrate a transcendence over the object of knowledge in its narrower aspect. For Taylor, this knowing is itself a fact. The knower is itself a fact. And both of these "facts" transcend the narrower fact of the thing known. "The reality of this unique relation," writes Taylor, "between two events or facts (that the one is the knowing of the other and of itself in relation to the other) is, of course, presupposed by the very raising of scientific questions, but no scientific question is raised about it."[34]

Without this reflected reference back to the act of knowing and to the knower behind the act there can be no real account of knowledge, and, Taylor remarks,

> ...this is why psychology, the "natural science of the mind" or "mental processes," has no account to give of knowledge. ...It has been said, both epigrammatically and truly, of scientific psychology that the "human mind" it describes is an artificial abstraction which "knows nothing by its knowledge."[35]

For Taylor, therefore, in order for there to be

---

32. Op. cit., p. 136 (Reading at A 107).

33. Taylor, DOES GOD EXIST? p. 28.

34. Ibid., p. 29.

35. Ibid.

knowledge, it follows that "the knowing mind is something more than, or other than, 'a part of nature' among other parts."[36] Taylor has (again) returned to something very like the dualism of Descartes.

3) The witness of language. Not infrequently the thought is aired that the proposals of David Hume are so in violation of our basic assumptions that speech itself will not properly accommodate the expressions. Taylor follows this line of criticism with special attention to Hume. Thus when Hume refers to the mind as "'a heap of perceptions succeeding one another with incredible rapidity,'"[37] Taylor remarks that "...strictly speaking,...Hume should not have called the 'heap' a 'heap of perceptions,' since the word inevitably suggests that the constituents of the heap are apprehensions of an object which is distinct from the perceiving of it."[38] And when Hume speaks of "'impressions'" and "'ideas,'" the words suggest, in the first case, "something which impresses the impression on something else," and, in the second case, "to talk of an 'idea' suggests that it is an 'idea' of something not itself."[39] And Taylor adds, "We are really left with a 'heap' of states which are not states of anything and convey no knowledge of anything. The determination to recognize no knowledge but 'scientific' knowledge has destroyed knowledge itself."[40] Indeed, the very grammatical structure of language--whether explicitly evident or merely implicitly--testifies to the dualism that Taylor insists is a necessary part of the fuller account of true knowledge. Thus the familiar paradigm structure of the sentence "I know x" (where x is any object) testifies to all of the parts of knowing to which Taylor is calling attention. The "I" is the agent in the knowing-act; the "know" is the act itself whereby the object is possessed by the agent as knowledge; the "x" is the object. So Taylor

---

36. Ibid., p. 30.

37. Ibid., p. 32.

38. Ibid.

39. Ibid.

40. Ibid., pp. 32-33.

calls attention to the fact that in the business of
knowing there is much more than that to which an attempted thoroughgoing empiricism is wont to effect reduction. "...we have still to remember," says Taylor,

> that a complete survey of the situation must in-
> clude reference not only to the existence of the
> "object," but to the existence of the observer
> and the fact that he knows certain things about
> the "object." When anything is known, there is a
> triple presupposition: there must be that about
> which something is known, the person who knows
> this something, and the knowing of it. All three
> are constituent factors of the concrete world of
> our experience, and we have no right to treat the
> second and the third factors as insignificant.[41]

The inclusion of this discussion on the nature of
knowledge in a book entitled DOES GOD EXIST? has relevance from two different points of view. First, it is
at least illustrative of what Taylor means by "presuppositions." Presuppositions are larger areas of involvement on which narrower specifics depend. They
are mostly apprehended conceptually and frequently
have the character of a universal. The "forms" of
Aristotle, the "ideas" of Plato, the "categories" of
Kant: these illustrate what, for Taylor, may be called
"presuppositions." To use a Kantian terminology, these
"presuppositions" arise upon the occasion of experience
but are not to be reduced to or identified with the
narrower aspect of experience that gives rise to their
reality. In the above discussion of the larger aspect
of knowledge, the "knower" or "agent" is considered a
presupposition in the analysis of knowledge. Again,
the knowledge of this active agent arises upon the occasion of knowledge in its narrower form but transcends that narrower aspect. The full account, however,
of the knowing act may not omit this involvement of
the fuller analysis of knowledge. Taylor, too, has a
place for the transcendental apperception!

The second relevance that may be claimed for this
inclusion of knowledge in an argument for God's existence is the fact that the fuller meaning of knowledge

---

41. Ibid., p. 34.

involves a reference to personality for validation. "Knowledge," like "perception," "impression," "idea," carries with its meaning an almost inescapable reference to <u>someone</u> who knows. For Taylor, this is no accidental feature, but an essential one. If there can be no assigned or assignable meaning to knowledge that does not refer eventually to personality, there may indeed be reason to consider that knowledge in that hierarchical structure of ascending generalization may carry with it the suggestion of both an ideal summit of generalization as well as a divine personality to whom the ultimate ideal of knowledge is meaningful. "What physical science leaves ambiguous," Taylor writes, "<u>may</u> become certain through study of the intellectual and moral nature of man."[42]

The relation that Taylor has labored to establish between the narrower and the larger aspects of knowledge--with the target of his endeavor being the establishing of mind as fundamental as a presupposition in the ultimate validation and meaning of knowledge--he now continues with attention paid to what is essentially a variant of the teleological argument.

A first movement in the direction of validating the claim of teleology is that of showing that "brute fact" is a mute fact and requires that enlargement of reference, that inclusion within some universal that confers meaning upon it. "Brute fact" is thus considered really an abstraction from its wider context and, as such, divorced from the only source that can confer meaning upon it. This complaint of Taylor that science in its narrower involvement--"exact science" as it is called--cannot, in the nature of the case, offer <u>philosophical</u> explanation finds support from different quarters. Philip Wheelwright remarks,

Philosophy...pays attention to the larger relatedness of things; it is the attempt at harmonizing and integrating the various provinces of human interests and activity. Thus where each of the sciences is abstract in its own

---

42. <u>Ibid.</u>

characteristic way, philosophy is, or should be, concrete.[43]

And Frederick Copleston, commenting on certain aspects of Augustinean tradition, notes that "man in the concrete is man with a supernatural vocation," in contrast to man "considered in the 'state of nature'"--a legitimate abstraction."[44] Taylor would agree that these narrowed studies of man--psychology, sociology, anthropology--are legitimate areas for investigation. He counsels only against the supposition that the fuller range of meaning and values can be discovered within the same narrowed range. It is in the determination of the fuller meaning and value of man that one must, according to the Taylor thesis, go beyond the particularity of the scientific abstraction.

Under the hypothesis that reality is totally interconnected, it would appear that no isolated aspect of that reality could be autonomously interpreted or evaluated. It would appear that such an isolated aspect would present baffling problems and leave unanswered questions--unless one were permitted to seek out answers within (at first) its nearer environment and then extend the reach of the environment in order better to understand its fuller meaning. This has been the Taylor thesis. We might compress this aspect of his thesis to say: The meaning of the minimal aspect of experience cannot be confined. This approach is not new. It is at least as old as Plato and has been nurtured within all forms of neo-Platonism. But now Taylor puts it to a test asking whether the "bedrock fact" of the scientist's concern does not in some sense point beyond itself in order to justify explanation. "Do the facts of the world-order," Taylor asks, "...so far as the sciences take them into account, disclose, or even suggest, the presence of a

---

43. Philip Wheelright, THE WAY OF PHILOSOPHY. Revised Edition. (New York: The Odyssey Press, 1954), p. 8.

44. Frederick Copleston. A HISTORY OF PHILOSOPHY. Mediaeval Philosophy. Volume 2, Part I. (Garden City, New York: Image Books, Doubleday & Co., Inc.), p. 272.

directing purpose..?" and "Does nature exhibit recognizable traces of what Paley called 'prospective contrivance'?"[45]

In answering his own question, Taylor is forced to distinguish between the inorganic and the organic realms--both of which have furnished out subject-matter for scientific comment. And it is not conspicuously in the inorganic realm that Taylor finds the easiest opportunity to exhibit his claim on teleology. This is because, "Taken by themselves, the laws of physics and chemistry reveal only one type of order in the natural world, a <u>causal</u> order."[46] Of this order Taylor confesses, "...we are forced...to admit that, taken by themselves, those /facts/ which can be detected in the inorganic realm do not go very far to provide the theist with any confirmation of his belief."[47] That such a world--exhibiting only the characteristic of causal connection--is thoroughly compatible with a theistic overview Taylor would grant; he merely means that from the sheer presentation of a causality operating within a purely inorganic realm one cannot infer any kind of personal control. "...if all we knew," Taylor says, "about the actual world were only what we can learn in the physical or chemical laboratory, so far as I can see, atheism might conceivably be true."[48]

But even this inorganic world is redeemed to some extent from its intrinsic inability to suggest with greater clarity the character of its ultimately causal principle. It is redeemed by the fact that it interconnects with the organic world at (practically speaking) an infinite number of points. And it is to this organic world--"...the actual world in which all of us live": "living beings, sentient beings, intelligent and purposively contriving beings"--that Taylor turns-- as countless other apologists have turned before and since--to find the evidence that will speak for a teleological interpretation.

---

45. Taylor, DOES GOD EXIST?, p. 41.

46. <u>Ibid</u>, p. 43.

47. <u>Ibid</u>., pp. 42-43.

48. <u>Ibid</u>., p. 44.

It is not, however, to the practically limitless illustrations of adaptation of means to ends in the organic realm of plants and animals that Taylor finds his strongest evidence; it is rather in the mind--as "something completely and utterly novel, not to be connected with its supposed antecedents by any permanence of measurable 'natural constants.'"[49] Taylor, largely following the argument of G. F. Stout's MIND AND MATTER,[50] resists the offer of emergent evolution to include mind as one of the emergents. It is true that water possesses characteristics that cannot be found as such in the elements of oxygen and hydrogen that compose it. Similarly, salt possesses characteristics not found as such in its supporting sodium and chlorine. And, by a parallel argument, it has been said that a consistent materialism may explain the emergence of mind with its peculiar characteristics of contriving and purposive and evaluative behavior by referring it to its origination in material elements. Taylor finds "no real parallel" between the water and salt illustrations and the peculiar "prospective contrivance" and "intentionality" of mind. The water and salt illustrations--and the many others like them--are cases

> of transformation of something already in existence, which persists under the new conditions, and reveals its continuity with what had gone before by the constancy throughout the transformation of definite measurable characteristics (the atomic weights of the ingredients).[51]

It would be less than satisfactory to leave as complicated an issue as that of emergent evolution with no more recognition than that given above. In spite of a certain seeming irrationality about emergent theories and in spite of the fact that they tend to end with a descriptive effort rather than an explanatory one, there is such complexity surrounding any total causal involvement as to counsel hesitancy

---

49. Ibid., p. 45.

50. G. F. Stout, MIND AND MATTER, (Cambridge University Press, 1931), pp. 94ff.

51. Taylor, DOES GOD EXIST? p. 45.

in laying to rest any hypothesis that offers tentatively to deal with it. Mind, however, as a prime exhibit of teleology can occupy the forefront of analysis and speculation without doing violence to anything that may be claimed for emergent evolution at lower levels. Even if one were to discover the invariable occasions upon which mind were to "emerge," it would hardly follow that the totality of its characteristics could be identified with the non-mental event that was the occasion for its emergence. This is a point easily overlooked and perhaps was overlooked by Hume when he pointed out that there are other causes equally potent with intelligence to explain the universe: "natural," generation, instinct, vegetation--any of which, Hume said, might offer us a theory by which to explain the origin of the world. Or, referring to the spider, Hume remarks, "Why an orderly system may not be spun from the belly as well as from the brain, it will be difficult...to give a satisfactory reason."[52]

It is Taylor's considered reply to this sort of reduction of mind, reason, intelligence, to some status that is non-mind, non-reason, non-intelligence that it really begs the question. Granted that an orderly though small universe can be spun from the belly of a spider, has this explained the performance of the spider? If, by hypothesis, intelligent purpose in the universe is the primary principle by which spiders spin webs, we have clearly short-circuited explanation by stopping inquiry with the de facto spinning of the web. And this observation can be generalized: however successfully one may be led through the virtually infinite gradation of evolutionary changes it is by no means clear that we have done anything more than record with descriptive accuracy that which now awaits explanation as well.

There is something at once temptingly obvious and disconcertingly baffling about purposive behavior. The "obvious" aspect is perhaps due to the fact that the alleged ends that are being achieved are closely analogous to ends that we in our personal purposiveness can attain. The baffling aspect is due to the fact that in no case is "purpose" writ large upon the

---

52. David Hume, DIALOGUES CONCERNING NATURAL RELIGION. Part VII.

surface for a sensory experience to report. Perhaps
the paradigm example is that of the alleged telic behavior in nature as taught by Aristotle. The elaborate analysis of causality when applied to a growing
tree emphasizes that formal element that cannot be apprehended by sense perception. There is, Aristotle
assures us, a "built-in" blueprint--entelechy--which
upon the occasion of the effective causation of elements directs development to the end (telos) of a ma-
ture tree.

Taylor finds it helpful to his thesis of purpose
in nature to point out that purposive behavior not
only works in harmony with the laws of physics and
chemistry but, while so doing, exhibits a contrast to
anything that the laws of physics and chemistry may
demand. On the one hand, Taylor recognizes that

> It is not that the processes taking place in liv-
> ing organisms appear in any way to violate the
> causal laws of physics. On the contrary, it
> seems that, so far as can be ascertained, the be-
> havior of the components of the living organism
> conforms throughout to these laws. Thus transfor-
> mation of energy taking place within the organism,
> like similar transformations in the realm of the
> inorganic, appear to conform strictly to the prin-
> ciple of Conservation of Energy; there is an in-
> crease or decrease of energy of a specific kind
> only at the cost of a proportional decrease or
> increase somewhere of energy of another kind.[53]

Thus Taylor's argument for purposive behavior never
knowingly breaks with the causal laws of physics. We
might, therefore, say that every case of purposive behavior conforms to and makes use of the causal laws of
physics. "But," Taylor immediately adds,

> the important point is this. There are indefi-
> nitely numerous ways in which a natural process
> can be continued in strict conformity with the
> principle of Conservation...valuable as preserv-
> ing the individual organism or making for the

---

53. Taylor, DOES GOD EXIST? p. 47.

continuance of the species...[54]

It is this "selection" from among the various conformi-
ties to the causal laws of physics that emphasizes the
distinction between purposive behavior and merely
causal behavior. Examples are plentiful. Insects'
eggs are deposited on a particular leaf which supplies
necessary food for the generation to be born. Muscu-
lar exertion that requires an added amount of oxygen
receives the needed amount from a membrane that acti-
vates at that moment to force oxygen inward. A cat
watching a mouse-hole adjusts its actions to an anticipated future moment. And Taylor observes,

> It is this event yet to come which gives the whole
> series its distinctive character. As far as the
> working of the machinery which I call the cat's
> body is concerned, there might as well have been
> any one of a hundred other series of movements
> and arrests of movement which would have been in
> equal conformity with all the laws of physics,
> only none of these would have been equally suc-
> cessful in leading up to the capture.[55]

If one is permitted to introduce the factor of purpose,
the recognition of "adaptation" is meaningful; if one
is denied the right to introduce the factor of purpose,
"...so far as the laws of physics alone are concerned,
processes of 'prospective' misadaptation stand on the
same footing with, and should be just as probable as,
those of prospective adaptation."[56] And Taylor, noting
that Whitehead has thought along similar lines, remarks,

> As Whitehead has said, the electrons within the
> living organism, no doubt, run as "blindly" as
> the electrons in a lump of inorganic matter, but
> they do not run in the same way. There are count-
> less ways in which they might run, all of them in
> accord with the known laws of physics, but the

---

54. Ibid.

55. Ibid., p. 49.

56. Ibid., pp. 50-51.

actual way in which they do tend to run is always one which is "prospectively" adapted to the preservation of the individual organism or the species to which it belongs.[57]

With literally "thousands of alternative ways"[58] in which the electrons might run and still conform to the laws of physics, there is only one way in which they must run in order to accomplish precisely the end that is the normal expectation won by countless thousands of repeat experiences. With all controls removed, there is a virtually infinite improbability of the precise end normally associated with a purposed end being realized in the organic realm. Therefore, Taylor contends, it is not enough to say that the laws of physics are sufficient to account for such uniform repetition of organic ends, and is led to declare: "...there is just one known condition which, if we suppose it to be present, would remove this improbability, and that is the presence of mind as somehow determining the course of events."[59] And this declaration brings Taylor to appeal to the testimony of personal experience, to the introspective evidence that he feels every man will corroborate. "The one case," Taylor says,

> in which the existence of mind as a fact is directly and immediately disclosed to us is our own, and nothing is clearer than that, in our own case, the distinctive character of mind is that, by its very nature, it is forward-reaching and shows its presence by the devising of adaptations to situations not yet present, but anticipated.[60]

The argument is reminiscent of Aristotle's analogy. The ends of human fabrication are, for Aristotle, clearly the effects of intelligent purpose. The ends of organic nature resemble the ends of human fabrication. Therefore a presumption is gained that the ends

---

57. Ibid., p. 50.

58. Ibid., p. 52.

59. Ibid.

60. Ibid.

of organic nature are the effects of intelligent purpose. So far Taylor would find himself generally sympathetic with the Aristotelian position. But the disjunction of mind from its effects is clearer in Taylor
(as it is in Plato) than in Aristotle. And in our own
life, Taylor says, "...the evidence of its presence is
direct and unmistakable" and "it is impossible to escape recognizing that it guides and shapes present action with a view to a future which 'does not yet appear.'"61 So necessary for the success of Taylor's
thesis is the disjunction of mind from the matter it
directs that any "identity" theory would go far to
wreck both his argument for teleology and for freedom.
The chapter on Moral Value and Freedom contains Taylor's replies to determinism and naturalism and they
will not be repeated here other than to remark that if
mind is allowed to become "naturalized," ...it loses
its every claim to distinguish between truth and error,
between validity and invalidity. It is this peculiar
and unique property, according to Taylor, that provides
"compelling reason for the view that mind is not itself an effect called into being by the action of physical agents, but at least a primitive underived con-
stituent of the real world, at the very least as real
as 'matter' and 'energy.'"62

The mind or self for Taylor is everywhere given a
treatment that consistently separates it not only from
the status of "an effect called into being by the action of physical agents," but from any and all of its
perceptions. That is to say, the mind, for Taylor,
stands as an agent behind its perceptions to which it
relates as subject to objects. The act of knowing, or
perceiving, is by no means as simple as it may appear.
There seems to be a highly justifiable sense in which
it can be said with Kant, that the self is that which
is always subject. We confuse that which clamors the
loudest for distinction when we make the self and the
most intimately conjoined of its perceptions the same
thing. It is this unfortunate gross identification of
which many are guilty when, in the reading of Descartes, they make the self of Descartes and the thinking
of Descartes the same thing. Granted that there is

---

61. Ibid., p. 54.

62. Ibid.

some justification for this slurring over the distinctions even in Descartes himself---("But what then am I? A thing which thinks.")[63]---there is not the same justification for continuing the identification once the distinction is made clear. It is, paradoxically, just here (again) that Hume is at once so helpful even while believed to be wrong. He enables us to see that the most intimate and recurrent acts, by the aid of which we find the mediation of consciousness, are themselves distant from any self. Here Hume confesses that he is amazed to find that others lay claim to having found the self while he has been unable to find anything but some perception or other. But here arises that distinction between the self and its perceptions to which Taylor points as a distinction that must be made in the interest of coherence and yet such a distinction as leaves this "true self" only a presupposition, yet a necessary one. The perceptions are not the self (Hume is right here), but neither is the awareness of the succession of the perceptions the perceptions! Behind the perceptions must be postulated the self in that very permanence of distinction that the grammatical form suggests and that analysis confirms. The self emerges as the presupposition of the knowing acts.

Taylor's "presuppositionalism" again finds illustration in this analysis of the self. If our analysis is of any value it has affirmed that a "knower" of perceptions is never caught as a perception itself, yet cannot be dismissed from the census of involvements that make up a true account of the knowing act. The self is never the direct object (and therefore is never identified with that sort of objectivity at all), but in the very act of naming any object as object thereby presupposes itself as subject. Never an object, yet never retiring into nonentity, the mind emerges as representative of a dimension of reality that is at the same time an introduction to a type of "presuppositionalism" as well as a plea for a significant metaphysics.

---

63. Rene Descartes, MEDITATIONS ON FIRST PHILOSOPHY. Meditation II.

In emphasizing the identity and significance of the mind as a purposive factor in the world, Taylor is strengthening the case for teleology. He now continues toward the same goal by emphasizing another unique characteristic of the mind: its involvement with the future. "Mind is, in its very nature, forward-looking,"[64] Taylor writes, and illustrates this by what he alleges is

> "prospective" adaptation to the future running through the whole of organized nature, though the lower down we go in the scale of organisms the simpler such adaptations are, and the less remote and more immediately impending the "future" to which the present behavior of the "organism" is seen to be adapted.[65]

There is, of course, great distance between the higher organism who "can adapt the whole scheme of his life to the realization of a future that he will never live to see, which perhaps generations of his descendants will not live to see," who can "build for 'remote posterity'"[66]--in contrast to the lower animals. Yet there is some not too remote analogy between the purposiveness of man and the behavior of insects wherein we find "a thorough-going adaptation of the behavior of one generation to the needs of a fresh generation which will only come into being after the death of the present."[67] If this is an "intelligence," it must be interpreted so in the light of a larger reference than that immediately evident to the introspective analyses of persons. For Taylor, this "prospective" adjustment of the lower animals is no less intelligence though conceivably without consciousness of its present plans for future alternatives than is that sharp awareness of future goals that so characterizes the actions of men. In both there is that selection of one set of actions from among tens of thousands of possible actions that ends with fruitfulness of endeavor rather

---

64. Taylor, DOES GOD EXIST? p. 54.

65. Ibid.

66. Ibid., pp. 54-55.

67. Ibid., p. 55.

than fruitlessness.

For human experience, there is a difference between the effects of intelligence and the effects of non-intelligence--when both are engineered by human volition--that is virtually self-evident, axiomatic. Contrivances--small and great, simple and complex-- brought into being by planning, applied techniques, careful guarding against that departure from limited routes of progress: one and all can be destroyed in a "moment" by just enough intelligent purpose to select this object as its target of destruction. The sand castle by the sea shore, built by hours of careful planning and execution, can be destroyed in a moment by a kick. A human life into which has been poured years of disciplined preparation for a place in the parliament of nations can be destroyed in a second by just enough ability of an assassin to aim and fire. We know with what almost approaches absolute certainty that there exists a difference between planned and random behavior. And though we may not always know when behavior is not random, we are able to conceive that there is the difference in principle. If this were not so, the difference between planned results and non-planned results would not occur to us. In short, the meaning of the difference between ends that are the result of purpose and those that are the result of no purpose is a difference that is forced upon our attention both at levels of mere conceivability and in experience. This difference, then, for which conceivability prepares us and which experience would appear abundantly to confirm is Taylor's premise in an argument that leads to a teleological view of the world and of man. Even if, Taylor argues,

> ...we could suppose that the inorganic world has either existed all along or come into existence independently of intelligence, I do not see how we could avoid at least adding that with the advent of life we find intelligence somehow seizing upon and getting the direction of inanimate nature and its forces and turning them to its own account.[68]

But this concession to a world partially contributing

---

68. Ibid.

to the doctrine of pre-human purposelessness knows little or no support by analogy. True, applied intelligence of man frequently has for its tools those not of her personal manufacture nor indeed of a manufacture of which many are capable. Thus we employ many contrivances by the aid of which we accomplish our ends and perhaps none of the contrivances have we nor could we have devised for ourselves. This is as far as the analogy goes in support of the concession that an inorganic world might have existed prior to the appearance of intelligence and to which later intelligence applied itself. The weakness of the analogy is precisely where it should be strong: that is to say, the tools of contrivance by the aid of which we have fashioned later effects were invented, fashioned, manufactured, by someone if not ourselves. Whatever merit there may be in the suggestion that the inorganic world came into existence--or at least into its present structure--independent of intelligence, the final conclusion of the hypothesis does seem more than a little contrived. Consider: first, the inorganic world comes into its present structuring independent of intelligence; then intelligence "emerges" in this same world independent of a prior intelligence; then the coincidence is discovered, viz., that the intelligence that has emerged from the non-intelligent appears to be uniquely fitted to penetrate, classify, categorize, formulate, generalize, predict, and, in general, control, the inorganic world. It is this success that we noted earlier as justifying to some extent the idealist's claim that whatever the world of nature is it appears to be nearer to what minds are made of--thus offering a possible explanation of that affinity that exists between mind and the object of its exploration and interpretation. And so Taylor takes it, remarking,

> Either we must be content to take it as an unexplained and inexplicable miracle that our environment should be one which has made the appearance of increasingly intelligent and purposeful species of organisms and the development of scientific knowledge possible, or we must carry back the presence of controlling and directing intelligence beyond the appearance of living species and admit that it has been at work throughout the whole history of the formation of the environment which is their indispensable background. If there is

"design" in nature at all, design must be woven into the whole fabric of nature.[69]

This inferred design "in nature" is actually what the "designing" mind of man depends upon as he "modifies the environment in all sorts of ways into conformity with his own demands upon it." And Taylor adds, "The history of the application of science to the purposes of medicine and industry is one grandiose illustration of this."[70] And the endorsement that Taylor is most anxious to underwrite is the natural affinity that the mind finds in an environment that it appears to recognize as in some intimate sense its own--in opposition, perhaps, to the allegation sometimes made that man's control of nature is in answer to his purely practical needs. Rather, Taylor sees this ceaseless preoccupation with exploration as a natural by-product of man's virtually limitless curiosity--a thesis not significantly disturbed by the many times that man's intellectual successes have been rather directly concerned with matters of practical invention. The intellectual curiosity that Taylor feels is more "The distinguishing characteristic of man"[71] is the larger motivation and is not discredited by the fact that it sometimes can be harnessed within practical molds.

> Man did not first feel an imperious need for rapid communications over great distances, /Taylor writes/ next invent the telegraph and telephone to meet this need, and finally elaborate a theory of electromagnetism as the outcome of these inventions. The theory came first, and was developed in response to the purely intellectual desire to understand the processes of nature; the telegraph and telephone are the results of commercial exploitation of theories already worked out by men who were not for a moment thinking of these applications of their discoveries.[72]

---

69. Ibid., p. 57.

70. Ibid., p. 64.

71. Ibid.

72. Ibid., pp. 64-65.

To separate man's motivations that stem from allegedly "pure" intellectual curiosity from those other motivations that stem from man's multiplied practical needs is not an easy task. So intimately do the two work together, either one supplying an opportunity for the other; the other, in turn, supplying reason for the extension of the one: this interplay of cause and effect merely serves to illustrate the need for "wholeness" in our treatment of priorities in motivation. And Taylor recognizes this fact. He remarks with justice to the other side of the debate,

> If men had not long ago had to fashion elementary machinery to serve the purposes of the industrial arts, the discovery of the principles of mechanics would have been at least longer delayed and more difficult; anatomy would hardly have reached the development it had already attained among the Greeks of the fifth century B.C. if fighting had not been a major practical concern of the Greek citizen, and the successful treatment of the wounds inflicted a need of the first magnitude.[73]

But there comes an end of this nice balancing of "practicalities" against "intellection." Taylor's major contention in this defense of a teleological view of the world is not practicality against intellection, but intelligence against forces of non-intelligence as an explanation of the universe. And to this basic priority Taylor returns again and again--feeling that to reduce intelligence to something non-intelligent and to claim for this reduction the support of an intellectual insight is to veer very close to a working contradiction.

Taylor now faces another aspect of the difficulty of maintaining that sort of teleological defense that takes us "outside" the realm of experience. "The unexpressed presupposition of the reasoning," Taylor says, "is that we can know nothing except what is a part of 'nature,' in the sense of being part of the field of 'objects presented to our notice.'"[74] Thus we may claim to know "design" within some natural

---

73. Ibid., p. 65.

74. Ibid., p. 107.

order to events, but may not thereby claim to know
that the order of events itself is the product of design. Cause is treated similarly in that the interconnection of causal events within nature is said to
be no ground for the inference that nature as a whole
depends on a cause outside of itself.

In a manner that is an enlargement of what was
recognized earlier in this chapter under the caption
"The knowing act," Taylor now argues that no part of
science or investigation is or can be limited to the
"objects presented to our notice" in that minimally
limited sense of a "world of bodies."[75] In short, "We
are self-conscious; we not merely know that there are
bodies and that there are transactions taking place between them, but also that we are aware of the existence of these bodies and the occurence of these transactions."[76] It is not illegitimate to ignore the observer for the purposes of the natural sciences, but
when the larger questions and issues of philosophy are
raised the role of the observer may not only be included but may be introduced in a way to indicate that
this wider inclusion is at the same time an introduction to what is genuinely a separate order of reality.
As Taylor strongly puts it, "...myself and my own
states and activities as conscious self or person,
though the most indubitable of realities, have no
place whatever in 'nature,' in the sense of the field
of facts and events presented to my observation."[77]
And even when the self and its states is itself made a
legitimate field for inquiry and observation, the
truer self "that is always subject" may be said again
to have retreated to a post of observer and interpre-
ter that is not identical with "the self and its
states" considered as object. By such a recognition
of the "transcendental" self without which there could
be no science Taylor again paves the way to reaffirm-
ing the separable feature of intelligence--even at
that moment when it would appear that the only legitimately verifiable object of inquiry is the materials
of the empirical world. "Hence I fully agree with Mr.

---

75. Ibid.

76. Ibid.

77. Ibid., p. 108.

Bowman,"[78] remarks Taylor, "that the 'subjective' is a unique 'modality' of being entirely unlike that of physical things and events and irreducible to it."

There thus emerge two realms that while not reducible to one another are not closed to one another. (This is to reaffirm Taylor's Cartesianism in psychology once again.) "Nothing," Taylor declares, "which is a member of one can be a member of the other. ... But the two realms are not closed against each other in the sense that the course of events in the one is unaffected by events which belong to the other."[79] That physical events draw our attention, cause modifications of interpretation of them, force reactions all out of keeping with the hypothesis that we are sole cause and director of their being and condition is a situation that few would be willing to question. But that "...in some cases...a strictly physical event depends on conditions which are not themselves physical but belong to the subjective order,"[80] may be considered ground for hesitation--especially those who would reject Taylor's dualism. "The clearest illustration," Taylor affirms, "is the relation between a man's desires and purposes and the events in the physical order to which they give rise."[81] That the explanation of how the mind can influence matter may still elude us may be true, but, for Taylor, "That this relation exists is really quite obvious and undeniable."[82] and remarks that

> ...even those men of science who profess to hold that "consciousness" is totally incapable of influencing the course of physical events never really succeed in believing their own doctrine.

78. Archibald Allan Bowman, A SACRAMENTAL UNIVERSE. (Princeton, New Jersey: Princeton University Press, 1939), particularly chapters IV through VII.

79. Taylor, DOES GOD EXIST? p. 110.

80. Ibid., p. 112.

81. Ibid., p. 111.

82. Ibid.

They write essays and books in support of their view, and not one of the writers seriously doubts that his treatise or essay was written "on purpose" to destroy a "mediaeval superstition" which he dislikes. The author of an exposition of scientific "epiphenomenalism" would probably be offended--and reasonably offended--if I maintained in his presence that his conviction of the truth of his theory and its hatred of "mediaeval superstition" had nothing whatever to do with causing the train of events in the physical world which we call the writing of his book. And yet on his own theory this is neither more nor less than the fact.[83]

This chapter has called attention to the natural affinity that the mind finds in its environment (supra, p. 228) to which was added the further recognition of the "'subjective'" as "a unique 'modality'" (supra, p. 231). In larger compass, the chapter has elicited from ontological and teleological considerations a confirmation of the existence of God as that ultimate presupposition of concerns relating to moral value. These several considerations now combine to offer a characterization of ultimate reality that identifies with the unique modality of mind.

In the structuring of knowledge, Kant's system of explanation frequently raises the question of the relation of private minds to each other. The contribution that the mind is alleged to make in the Kantian epistemology is never so subjective as to justify the suspicion that the account was not meant to hold universally. That all minds impose the same categories upon the business of knowing is an implicit thrust in the direction of the recognition of a unified mind which is actively engaged in structuring identical patterns in the knowledge of all persons.

Nor is it necessary to start and stop with Kant in order to be confronted with the broadest possible exhibition of belief in the ideal of a unified knowledge. The entire effort of analysis, synthesis, speculation, hypothesis and correction wherever found, proceeds on the tacit assumption that a common

---

83. Ibid.

knowledge is possible to all, and, indeed, that an ultimate disunity in which the parts are in principle incapable of synthesis and reconciliation with each other is everywhere tacitly repudiated.

It would appear that the mind never encounters the utterly opaque, the inscrutable, the impenetrable --never, that is, in principle, and, in the nature of the case, never as known fact. Factual blocks to the mind's further penetration of nature are always mere difficulties of the moment--to be circumvented when more time and analysis are given to the problem. It might, therefore, be claimed an insight as to the nature of the world in general when what is evidently the faith of the scientist in the endless penetrability of nature by mind is actually confirmed by every scientific advance. It may fairly be claimed to be a breakthrough in the endeavor to categorize at the broadest possible levels when it is claimed that a decisive clue to the nature of the world is offered by the discovery that the only forms and categories which the mind knows are precisely the forms and categories that prove fruitful in scientific analysis. If Schopenhauer could offer in his DIE WELT ALS WILLE UND VORSTELLUNG the idea that the various particularizations of the world are objectifications of will, by an even more commanding parallel of reasoning can it be maintained that the various particularizations of the world are objectifications of mind. It would appear that the mind of man is so much "at home" in the world and so little has to yield to the suggestion that there is the utterly nonrational to contest its powers of penetration and analysis, that the grander conclusion seems to be the sole remaining alternative, viz., that there is nothing encountered nor encounterable save that of a cosmos that not only is thoroughly saturated by mind but is mind. This is but to say that God it is that identifies with the nature of ultimate reality.

CHAPTER IX -- "THE MAJOR DISPUTED ASSUMPTIONS"[1]

Although the preceding chapters of exposition carry also commentary, evaluation, and a recognizable support of Taylor's position, it is thought that a concluding chapter written in the spirit of a deliberate defense, a rejoinder to criticisms that have been or could be made to Taylor's doctrines, might be helpful in rendering explicit that central contention on which the narrower as well as the broader aspects of his value-theory depend.

Having uncovered the fact of a deliberately endorsed theism in Taylor's overall position, the claim must be expected that only that account of reality--in all of its aspects--that ultimately bears either covert or explicit reference to the theistic ultimate can hope to escape serious internal tensions and a nagging incoherence.

But Taylor does not merely start with an announced assumption of deity and then proceed to adjust the manifold of experience to this assumption as best he can; indeed, it may be said that in an important sense, Taylor's entire philosophical effort is begun in experience. But it is not the experience of naive realism to which Taylor appeals, but rather that experience that is articulate with the meaning brought to its interpretation from universals that transcend it. In a grand gesture, reminiscent of the entire range of Platonism of which Taylor is so eloquent a spokesman, universals that transcend all particularization are seen as the necessary presuppositions for

---

1. The phrase is borrowed from Edwin A. Burtt, TYPES OF RELIGIOUS PHILOSOPHY, Revised Edition. (New York: Harper & Row Publishers, 1951), pp. 139, 166, 196, 235, 278, 396.

the retention and defense of meaningful predication in any of its forms.

For Taylor, as presumably for Plato, there is a sense of ultimate mystery in that apex of hierarchically structured reality that begins with the least aspect of experience and ends with God. But it is the mystery that is invested with that ultimate universal to which all lesser experience stands in the role of particular participant. It is not a disjoined locus of ultimate mystery; rather it is the ultimate presupposition of all meaningful conjunction, providing the principle of unity so notoriously lacking in a radical empiricism.

Nevertheless, it is this break with experience that occasions the chief hurdle that any serious transcendentalism must overcome. It is often said with confidence: "Experience we know and understand, but that which allegedly transcends experience loses its every opportunity to speak a language that is verifiable." Strictly speaking, it is claimed, that which is "above" or "beyond" experience cannot be meaningfully called either true or false. And fundamentally, it is this claim of not only the possibility but the necessity of transcendental reference that Taylor's type of theistic value-theory must make good. It is this claim that the remainder of this concluding chapter must engage, because it foundations and explains his entire theory.

The controlling thesis then of this chapter is that there is a transcendental and that its reality is discoverable as immanently present behind the varying modes represented in experience. More narrowly, the norms crucial to the maintenance of value-claims in esthetics, ethics, and rationality will be the norms that are necessary to the interpretation of experience and which therefore cannot be identified with the experience they are called upon to interpret. This will give them their transcendent status. It may be further anticipated that this transcendental reality will necessarily exhibit itself under analysis as a hierarchy of logical dependencies.[2]

---

2. As de Burgh observes, "As against the doctrine of the plurality of intrinsic goods, he /Taylor/ appeals to the principles of analogical unity and of

The burden of Part I of this chapter will be to affirm that being is the most ultimate category and is to be regarded as the final referent of epistemology. The fact that <u>being</u> is deserving of this recognition of ultimacy does not prevent recognition of its categorical structuring by the aid of which the mind may rise from the narrowest specification of experience to the hierarchically-fixed apex of being. This apex is then regarded as the ultimate nature of the transcendental and the supremely enabling presupposition of epistemology.[3]   Indeed, the point of view defended

----

hierarchical order..."   W. G. de Burgh, THE FAITH OF A MORALIST, by A. E. Taylor. Review. PHILOSOPHY, VI (1931), p. 232.   Or, as Warner Fite expresses it, "The word 'hierarchy' expresses for him /Taylor/ the necessary form of the universe." THE PHILOSOPHICAL REVIEW, XL (1931), p. 483.

3.   There is a not uncommon interpretation of Plato that favors this hierarchical aspect of reality. Thus, Stace writes, "There is, in fact, a hierarchy of Ideas. Just as the one Idea presides over many individual things of which it is the common element, so one higher Idea presides over many lower Ideas, and is the common element in them. And over this higher Idea, together with many others, a still higher Idea will rule. For example, the Ideas of whiteness, redness, blueness, are all subsumed under the one Idea of colour. The Ideas of sweetness and bitterness come under the one Idea of taste. But the Ideas of colour and taste themselves stand under the still higher Idea of quality. In this way, the Ideas form, as it were, a pyramid, and to this pyramid there must be an apex. There must be one highest Idea, which is supreme over all the others. This Idea will be the one final and absolutely real Being which is the ultimate ground, of itself, of the other Ideas, and of the entire universe. This Idea is, Plato tells us, the Idea of the Good." W. T. Stace, A CRITICAL HISTORY OF GREEK PHILOSOPHY. (London: Macmillan & Co., Ltd., 1962), p. 198.

would not differ essentially from the epistemology
espoused in Plato's doctrine of the divided line and
the allegory of the cave.[4]

PART I - GENERAL EPISTEMOLOGY

Why is transcendence disputed as a legitimate
involvement? Fundamentally, the answer to this is
found in the alleged limitations of reason--an allegation coinciding with the delimiting of meaningful discourse either to propositions whose subjects already
contain their predicates--Kant's analytic judgment--or
to existential propositions whose truth can be confirmed by some technique of empirical verifiability.
With such allegiance paid to epistemology's strict empirical reduction, any variant of a synthetic-a priori
nature--with its implication of transcendence--would
be sharply contested. The complaint would always take
the form that in the measure in which departure from
empirical reduction was attempted, in that same measure the ensuing claims for transcendental reality are
left strictly without meaning.

How is transcendence affirmed as a legitimate involvement? In principle, transcendence is affirmed by
broadening epistemology's genuine concerns and dependencies to show that even the most radically reduced
exhibitions of empirical recognition are already saturated with a meaning-complex that transcends sensuous
experience. In brief, this rebuttal would involve the
contention that in no case does a minimal reduction of
experience give any meaning whatever, but, rather, in
every case, where meaning may legitimately be claimed,
there is a necessary involvement beyond the attempted
reductions to empirical particularity. The specific
discussion of how transcendence may be justly claimed
to be a necessary involvement in meaningful experience
will now become the continued effort of this chapter.
Undoubtedly, Taylor engages this issue in declaring
that one not only may go beyond experience but actually does go beyond experience and indeed must go beyond
experience if experience is to become a meaningful object to the inquiring mind. Experience, for Taylor,

---

4.   REPUBLIC, VI (509e--511e) and VII (514ff.).

238

will be found to be saturated with overarching principles of unification which cannot be denied and which cannot be reduced to sensuous content. This domain of overarching principles is identical with that to which Taylor's "presuppositionalism" refers and will be defended in what follows in this chapter. _This same thesis not only promises that the ethical life if taken seriously will point to a transcendent dimension of reality, but, mutatis mutandis, the esthetic and rational categories may be said to yield to a similar dialectic._

There is a dialectic that uncovers a crucial difficulty in any attempt to postulate an ultimate empirical particularity. Without intending to defend Kant's "synthetic-a priori" contention, it is at least fruitfully illustrative to call attention to the larger consideration that Kant provides as against Hume. Here, Hume's reduction of knowledge to "impressions" becomes the ultimate plank of his empiricism. And it should be remarked how strangely unsuccessful is this attempted ultimate reduction. There is something about ultimate particularity, ultimate matter, ultimate potentiality, that appears to verge upon a perfect nihilism. The point is that particularity can never be carried to an ultimate reduction without either remaining partially informed or simply passing beyond the last possibility of formation into nothing at all. And because Hume did not regard the impressions as being "nothing at all," it appears to follow that the formation, the structuring, left to them makes them strictly-speaking incapable of exhibiting the ideal limit of a truly radical empirical reduction. It is precisely this resident formation or structuring that cannot be denied and cannot be squared with 'the ideal limit of a truly radical empirical reduction' that introduces an immanent transcendental. If this resident form cannot be captured by radical empiricism, and if it cannot be denied, it would appear to follow that a dimension of reality is indicated that comes to our attention upon the moment of any and every attempted reduction of reality but which itself is never subject to the same sort of empirical categorization.

There is something teasing and tempting about the prospect of honoring experience that leads one to try for that _ultimate reduction_. Kant's own postulation

of the thing-in-itself--a truly ghostly presupposition
of realism--is virtually a fulfillment of that condition remarked above of 'simply passing beyond the last
possibility of formation into nothing at all.' But
Kant is not alone in holding to some assumption of
realism: Plato and Descartes, also, share the conviction that in some sense something less than a fully
articulated or articulatable impulse contributes to
the beginning of a knowledge-situation. In some sense,
there is a first moment in which the jar of experience
calls down the appropriate universals, and the union
of these is at once knowledge and to some extent the
interpretation of knowledge. It might be thought ad-
missable to speak of the shock of experience beginning
this further movement into a recognition of universals
appropriate to the interpretation of experience: Plato is frequently enough interpreted as allowing experience to introduce our "prior" knowledge of the Ideas.
But, on the other hand, for each of these thinkers
there is something that forbids recognizing experience
in an ultimate irreducible sense. The above remarks,
therefore, that highlight the near-contradiction in
any attempted postulation of an ultimate particularity, may be taken as pointing with legitimacy to a larger domain of reality that may properly be called
transcendent.

Change implies a constant: a paradigm example of
how the transcendental dimension is introduced when we
analyze the meaning of experience. An illustrative
way of seeing the emergence of what in principle is
common to the 'overarching principles' (so named on p.
239) that are claimed to unify experience may be found
in that presupposition believed necessary to account
for change. The synthesis of Aristotle which may be
said to placate the essential demands of Parmenides
and Heraclitus--demands respectively emphasizing being
and becoming--and which declare in effect that no meaningful account of change or becoming could be given
that did not postulate being as a sort of underlying
constant,[5] this synthesis, with the postulate of a constant thus incorporated, becomes a sort of paradigm

---

5. A fundamental plank of Aristotle is that there
   must be a subject in every change. /Physics, Book
   I, Chapter 7/ This concedes whatever may be demanded of both change and its underlying constant.

example of how the mind is forced <u>beyond</u> sensuous experience in order to retain experience in any <u>meaning-
ful</u> sense. Actually this going 'beyond' is not to introduce a dualism; it really reveals that experience
is not the utterly and ultimately simple thing that
might be inferred from the casual and confident manner
in which the word is used. It is worth noting in passing that <u>flux</u> and <u>experience</u> stand very intimately re--
lated to each other. To report any aspect of experi-
ence is to imply either that the experience reported
is itself in process of change or, if at rest, the
rest is meaningfully contrasted with the possibility
of its movement or the possibility or actuality of
movement around it.

To follow the itinerary of the mind outward and
upward, it is well to note that this dialectic that
sees in <u>the very meaning</u> of flux some constant--a constant, that <u>is to say</u>, that supplies a subject for the
verb, substance for the act, being for the becoming--
has called attention to what must be grasped by the
mind <u>conceptually</u>. It is safe to say that there is an
important sense in which the concession of a constant
cannot be denied if one is to deal meaningfully with
change, but neither can the constant be captured by
sensuous experience. It would appear that here we
find an illustration of how experience becoming aware
of its deeper involvement transcends its narrower limits. It is recognized that this principle is essentially a Kantian one to the extent, at least, that in
some important sense it is true that percepts without
concepts are blind. It further serves to emphasize
that whether one feels committed wholly to the enlarged Kantian epistemology or not, there is, nevertheless, rendered manifest the distinction between a perceptual field that may be said to be the limited commitment of experience and the conceptual field that is
outside of sensuous experience but required to preserve
the varied senses of unification that the meaningfulness of experience demands. Transcendence is implied
in this conceptually-oriented reference.

<u>No epistemology without ontology</u>. The above em-
phasizes the need for a conceptually apprehended constant in order to render meaningful any aspect of
change. Thus far, however, the implication was at the
surface level of epistemology. The relation of flux
to the constant which preserves for flux its meaning

was offered above as illustrative of how experience under analysis is seen to direct the mind to a conceptually apprehended presupposition. The illustration chosen, however, turns out to be more than a merely accidentally instructive example; in its own right, it provides substance and foundation for that sort of transcendental philosophy which for Taylor merged into a theism.

Here it must be remembered that it was the objective, existent, world of experience--in contrast for the moment with the subjective world of experience--that forced the mind to that conceptually apprehended presupposition of a constant. It is therefore within the same claim of objective existence that the constant--already admitted at the epistemological level--may now be admitted at the ontological level. And the question naturally arises, what is the nature of this objective existence thus far identified only as a necessary presupposition of epistemology and ontology? Is it one or many?

The instability of pluralism. There is a difficulty about pluralism that tends toward solution only in the direction of a monism. It would be presumptuous to assume that this question of what has been styled "The One and The Many" can be answered with that finality that is a prerogative of divine intelligence. It may well be that in some sense this formula speaks for one--if not the one--of the profoundest problems in philosophy. Nevertheless, it does appear that pluralism--at least in the form that it has known in Greek atomism--is helpless before the question of the relation of the supposed differences to each other. As Roland Hall states it,

> ...the dualistic position is inherently unstable and puzzle-generating. Once we have divided the world into two (or, we might add, into many)... we have on our hands the problem of the relation between the resulting worlds.[6]

---

6. Roland Hall, "Monism and Pluralism," THE ENCYCLOPEDIA OF PHILOSOPHY. Edited by Paul Edwards. (New York: The Macmillan Company and the Free Press, 1967), V, p. 364.

And when Hall further remarks that "A striving for
unity in a world description...is a perennial urge in
human thought,"[7] it may very well be that the 'urge'
goes well beyond psychological impulse in the direction of logical necessity. The unifying bond, however,
may not be less real than the particular instances
that constitute what we have called the "instability
of pluralism"; neither, on the other hand can it avoid
the categorization of abstraction.

BEING as a constant and ultimate category of meaning. There is this category--there is perhaps no better word--that may without great inaccuracy be designated as "being," "existence," "reality," "substance,"
"actuality," or, to use Weedon's phrase--actually employed of Spinoza--"that which 'is,' preeminently and
without qualification--the source and ultimate subject
of all distinctions."[8] This category--hereafter
called "being" for convenience--appears to be so utterly pervasive that no pluralism in any attempted ultimate sense can withstand its claim. Its 'pervasive-
ness' is revealed simply in the way in which the entities of the claimed pluralism, in their respective and
individual claims of existence, do thereby claim a participation in this category that goes beyond their individualized limits. The very seriousness with which
the pluralism in its every part is said to exist is
itself a concession to participation in a category
that transcends the differences. And if it is claimed
that this category as thus used is without meaning, it

---

7. Ibid.

8. William S. Weedon, "Being," DICTIONARY OF PHILOSO-
    PHY. Edited by Dagobert D. Runes. (Totowa, New
    Jersey: Littlefield, Adams & Company, 1966), p.
    36. As Aristotle declares, "It is clear...that it
    is the work of one science...to study the things
    that are, qua being.--But everywhere science deals
    chiefly with that which is primary, and on which
    the other things depend, and in virtue of which
    they get their names. If, then, this is substance,
    it will be of substances that the philosopher must
    grasp the principles and the causes." METAPHYSICS,
    Book IV, Chapter 1. THE BASIC WORKS OF ARISTOTLE.
    Edited with an introduction by Richard McKeon.
    (New York: Random House, 1941), p. 732.

can only be because it is impossible to get behind the category to a genus more ultimate. This would be a case of failure to understand what is meant by a presupposition the postulation of which illuminates many particulars but which is never similarly caught in the beam of its own illumination. But this category does have meaning: it is the meaning that is preserved and testified to by the distinction between something and nothing. Being, in the light of this distinction, is preeminently something. Indeed, it is so utterly and ultimately and pervasively something that it may be said that being is that category that makes redundancy impossible to avoid. In attempting to define it--whether connotatively or denotively--one is forced to repeat a series of variations on the same essential meaning and without improving upon the elusive though pervasive demand of the category with which we began. As Hall remarks, some "like William James, may find they have a temperamental objection to monism, with its emphasis on the totality and its exclusion of individuality and quirkiness,"[9] but it is believed that the claim against pluralism overrides 'temperamental objection,' and grounds deeply and seriously in a last category of meaning that is identical with a last category of being. It is a case of unavoidable transcendence, of ultimate presupposition conceptually apprehended, and outside of sensuous particularity: an ultimate reference in which being and meaning fuse in an inseparable and indistinguishable unity. In this ultimate reach of the mind, the formula, "no epistemology without ontology," finds validation.

A complaint from Logical Empiricism--and its weakness. For Herbert Feigl, the above classifies under "the seductive fallacies of metaphysics," which he deplores along with "the reductive fallacies of a narrow-minded positivism" both of which to their detriment are contrasted with what he hails as a

> Full maturity of thought /which/ will be attained when neither aggressive destruction nor fantastic construction, both equally infantile, characterize the philosophic intellect.

The "alternative left," for Feigl, "between a

---

9. Hall, Op. cit., p. 364.

philosophy of the 'Nothing But' and a philosophy of the 'Something More' is a philosophy of 'What is What.'"[10] The strong dissatisfaction that is felt with metaphysics emphasizes the respect that is paid to empiricism--an empiricism that tends to stop with phenomena even when deductive proof and inductive evidence are pleaded as principles of justification.[11] That is to say, Feigl, for example, in answering the question of what "justification" can possibly mean finds that

> the surprisingly simple answer is that the only clear meanings of that term in common life and science are deductive proof for one thing and exhibition of inductive evidence for another,

and adds,

> The "great problem of induction," therefore, consisted in the impossible demand to justify the very principles of all justification. If, /he continues7 we must have a Principle of Induction ...it had better be formulated not as a piece of knowledge but as a rule of procedure.[12]

But this tends to subsume the principles of logical procedure under nothing but a pragmatic assumption. It is guilty of making fullest use of these principles without thinking it necessary to raise the question of what kind of world it is that supports this possibility. How different is the challenge of Bertrand Russell when he notes this procedure as "a serious

10. Herbert Feigl, "Logical Empiricism," TWENTIETH CENTURY PHILOSOPHY. Edited by Dagobert D. Runes. (New York: Philosophical Library, 1943), p. 375.

11. "This phenomenalistic empiricism," remarks Frederick Copleston, "is a strongly marked characteristic of Professor Ayer. Adopting Russell's theory of 'logical constructions,' he reduces mind and matter to sense-data or sense-contents." CONTEMPORARY PHILOSOPHY. (Westminster, Maryland: The Newman Press, 1956), p. 10.

12. Feigl, "Logical Empiricism," p. 389.

departure from pure empiricism" and names induction as "an independent logical principle, incapable of being inferred either from experience or from other principles, and that without this principle science is impossible."[13]

The conceptual bond of experience. It is understandable why a stop is called at what is considered the foundational concern of philosophy, viz., the discrete elements of sensuous data. Equally understandable is the impatience that must be generated when mystery and mysticism appear to threaten the no-nonsense attitude that identifies with fundamental appeals to experience. Still and withal, there is good reason to regard "pure empiricism" as merely introductory to a wider and fulfilling involvement. In addition to the claim above that the particular aspects of an attempted pluralism cannot withstand the claim to participation in a wider and over-arching unity--that of being--there is the narrower specification of being sometimes illustrated under the doctrine of relations that undeniably serves to unite the particulars of sensuous experience yet in such a way as not itself to fall within the narrower domain of sensuous experience. The causal bond is such a one.

Epistemological dependence on the causal bond is one thing; the recognition of an ontological background is another. There are abundant indications that the idea of an ontological ground for the retention of causality is thought superfluous and that its extrusion from philosophic vocabularies would do no harm to a philosophy of science. The disaffection with an ontological reference when successfully plotting probable causal futures or when endeavoring to solve the host of practical problems that confront laboratory technicians is again identical with that

---

13. Bertrand Russell, A HISTORY OF WESTERN PHILOSOPHY. (New York: Simon and Schuster, 1945), p. 674. It may be remarked that Russell's observation is temptingly adjustable to the thesis of this chapter, viz., that meaningful use or interpretation of experience reveals its dependence upon an extra-experiential factor, "an independent logical principle," a transcendent dimension outside of sensuous experience.

impatience which we before recognized as almost inevitable when it would appear that practical effort is being asked to abandon the white-hot crucible of experience for something that at first blush appears to have no obvious and immediate connection. How is this disaffection overcome?

The break with phenomenological empiricism. The first and perhaps the sufficient step away from a phenomenological account of cause lies basically in the recognition that our epistemological successes are not those of a purely subjective idealism. If the position of the subjective idealist were true, there would be no reason to anticipate nor possibility of sharing in the de facto experience of agreement in causal determination. It is entirely possible that the implications of this shared experience of agreement out of which meaningful checks and corrections can be imposed upon one another have never been made fully explicit in expositions of the Kantian philosophy. If individual opinions can be accounted as approximations to a true account, objectivity is already an implicit acknowledgement of having found ground outside of the formulae themselves. That is to say, the formulae that connect events in the relation of probable cause and effect, by virtue of being adjudged right or wrong, do thereby imply reliance upon some ground outside of individuality. What the nature of the ground is is not given fully in the fact that it must be recognized--other, that is, than that it is objective to the formulae, normative to the determination of truth and error, and presupposed as necessarily transcendent to the sensuous experience that called our attention to the deeper involvement.

It would appear as a forfeiture of philosophic effort to stop either with the phenomena of experience or the language by which experience is interpreted. If "linguistic analysis" is to mean anything more than dictionary explanation or a mere census of the ways that "ordinary language" is being used, it must reintroduce the hope of arriving at the "true" meaning of a word. As Copleston remarks,

> ...this question cannot be answered without the inspection of the extralinguistic data. Hence analysis cannot be identified with a purely verbal activity. Russell rightly remarks in MEANING

AND TRUTH that "there has been a tendency, especially among logical positivists, to treat language as an independent realm, which can be studied without regard to non-linguistic occurrences."[14]

It appears to be axiomatic that language is about something. Even if the object to which language directs
us should turn out to be fully absorbed and interpreted within an idealistic philosophy, it would still remain true that language had performed its work by directing attention to something independent of the language itself. When language turns in upon itself
philosophic effort has all but expired. When the phenomena of knowledge are loosed from their metaphysical
bond, how is it any longer possible to distinguish
them from the ideas (words) that describe them? This
difficulty is emphasized when the self as agent is denied in deference to the phenomenal self of activities.
In the wake of this double denial, how are my ideas of
phenomena distinguished from the phenomena themselves?
It is this inability to afford any justification for
going beyond words that tends to promote linguistic
analysis as the sole legitimate concern of epistemology. Yet the meaningfulness of truth and validity--as
against their failures--not being discoverable within
phenomenalistic empiricism, yet not abandoned, impels
toward the recognition of what is actually the case,
viz., a dependence upon metaphysical presupposition.

---

14. Copleston, CONTEMPORARY PHILOSOPHY. p. 15. And
    Mure writes warningly, "The study of ethical lan-
    guage has proved an effective safeguard against
    any genuinely objective treatment of moral con-
    duct. The degree of dull remoteness which can be
    achieved by discussing the language of a subject
    instead of the subject itself is remarkable."
    G. R. G. Mure, RETREAT FROM TRUTH. (Oxford:
    Basil Blackwell, 1958), p. 173. And from W. R.
    Inge: "The philosophy of science in the nine-
    teenth century illustrates the danger of despising
    metaphysics. For the most part it rested on a
    very naive realism, but sometimes...it confounded
    perception with the perceptum." DOES GOD EXIST?
    by A. E. Taylor. Review. THE HIBBERT JOURNAL,
    XLIV (1946), p. 177.

It has been argued, /Copleston writes7 that ethical statements cannot be meaningless, since we
can argue, and do argue, concerning the rightness
and wrongness of actions...if two people differ
in their estimation of what are good or bad consequences, argument between them is possible only
if they are already agreed concerning wider valuations.[15]

Of these "wider valuations" of which Copleston speaks
and of the "dialectic" referred to in the beginning of
this chapter, a word of clarification might well be
attempted. Presumably enough had been said already
concerning the role that is believed to be performed
by that most ultimate of all ontological categories--
being itself--together with the narrower specifications of being in that doctrine of relations without
which there could be no unity to epistemology in any
sense and hence no epistemology.

   The subject-object relation in the knowing act.
In human experience there is an almost unavoidable
dualism. There is that which is experienced: call it
the objective part; and there is that which experiences: call it the subjective part. It would appear
that any situation that can fairly be called "knowledge" is at the same time a dualism involving the
knower and the known. The acceptance of this dualism
is already (again) a case of where epistemology's
genuine concerns take one beyond the mere objectivity
of the one-half of the dualism and show by a species
of presupposition the wider and deeper dependence.

   There is a justified passion that seeks to escape
dreams, illusions, superstitions, and fallacy generally by recourse to objectivity. The tough-minded appeals to realism, verification techniques, and, in
general, the subjecting of propositions to the screen-
ing by which they become public fact are all evidences
of healthy-mindedness. And it may be granted that even
the overmuch preoccupation with the sheer objectivity
of the above dualism has at least this to its credit:
it feels keenly enough the stifling threat of the arbitrary, the whimsical, the untestable-in-principle,
the unchallengeable dogmatism. In principle, this

---

15. Copleston, CONTEMPORARY PHILOSOPHY, p. 39.

concern with objectivity preserves place for "truth," "validity," "evidence," "proof," without which no contention could compete with its own contradictory and all argument would be supplanted by force. But sheer objectivity, in the sense of the one-sided concern for the extra-subjective, falsifies the fuller involvement of human experience. The subjective part must be included. Nor does its inclusion violate in any sense the thorough objective appeal that must be retained in order to have a sharable knowledge and interpretation of experience. Indeed, it is precisely the function of interpretation of experience that introduces this subjective part and at the same time validates it as a bona fide part of that dualism recognized above as unavoidable in any adequate account of human experience.

Interpretation comes from the subjective side. It is within the act of interpretation of experience that one moves beyond the reduction to the physical elements of man's body or the discrete impressions or ideas of man's mind. It is not in or among these same discrete reductions of pure objectivity that one finds interpretation. The external elements of man's objective world do not interpret themselves, do not announce their own formulae, do not call attention to their system of internal relations, do not endorse nor eschew any proposition whatever descriptive of their status. The truths and the system of truths, if any, must come from the subjective side of experience and this is not less so when it is added that whatever truths or system of truths may be enunciated must be tested for acceptance or rejection by a demonstrated ability to make the objective half of experience show a conformability to a maximum coherence. The subjective side of experience articulates the structure of the objective side of experience.

It is then with respect to the subjective side of human experience that one meets the great cohesive--though intangible--forces and values of life that promote a sense of propriety and unity. Outstandingly (here) are encountered the virtually ubiquitous norms that undergird the meaning and application of moral value and rationality. And of necessity they are brought together: they direct each other in virtue of their respective first principles of right action and true thought. The scandal into which philosophy has fallen to so great an extent may here be identified:

it is precisely the use that is everywhere made of the
norms that come from the subjective side of experience
in the effort of structuring experience but without
that proper and formal recognition of the role that is
played by this subjectivity. There is every propriety
in the asking of the question, What sort of world is
it in which the objective aspect of experience which
does not supply its own norms for its own interpretation nevertheless yields peaceably to a normative
structuring? Whence comes this normative structuring?
Is it not that sort of world that we have denominated
"dualistic" to the extent that the subjective-objec-
tive aspects must both be given recognition?

Philosophic effort is abandoned unless one goes
beyond "rules of procedure" as pragmatic to "rules of
procedure" as derivative. In contrast with the extreme importance of the subjective half of experience
that supplies (or at least mediates) the norms of interpretation for the objective half of experience, it
is almost a cavalier ignoring of this dimension of
reality that recognizes it only in the words quoted
above by Feigl as "a rule of procedure" instead of "a
piece of knowledge." But of course, Feigl is right in
refusing to call the "Principle of Induction" "a piece
of knowledge" if all knowledge that involves existence
must first reduce to the "What is What" of empirical
category. Such limited concern is precisely what is
here regarded as truly an abandonment of philosophical
effort refusing as it does to recognize as determinative and determining that subjective half of experience from which is derived every "rule of procedure"
necessary to the structuring of the objective half of
experience.

What is a "rule of procedure"? In formal disciplines it appears clear enough. Mathematical "rules"
are justified by their very intrinsic necessity.
What of empirical "rules"? They are seen to have
pragmatic sanction and their use raises no question as
long as no claim is made of a philosophical nature.
That is to say, they serve in the role of uncritical
dependence. They are "practical" in the pedestrian
sense of that word, in the sense of the man on the
street. But it is believed that neither in the formal
sense nor in the uncritical sense of the man on the
street does Feigl intend to use the phrase "rule of
procedure." Rather, he understands such a "rule" to

be a critically forged substitute for what he regards
as "the impossible demand to justify the very principles of all justification."[16] And why is this called
"an impossible demand"? Precisely because it cannot
be deduced from formal logic, nor, without circularity,
from experience itself. The "rule" of procedure, then,
is indeed a _rule_ and not merely procedure. It quietly
prepares for the future in the spirit of a dependence
that is never really weakened or embarrassed by its
professed recognition of radical contingency and disconnectedness. This does indeed appear to be a dependence upon a principle strictly independent of empirical
endeavor--as Russell remarked--and yet the _sine qua non_
of all scientific advance. The principle, therefore,
may be claimed as another fulfilling condition of the
truth of a transcendental type of philosophy. That is
to say, if this transcendent dimension of reality
exists, and if we are in fact drawing upon it as the
source of our every principle of interpretation, to
such would be our natural ground of referral when principles like those of induction which cannot be naturalized and cannot be abandoned rise before us for explanation. _In practice, we live in this attitude of "referral."_

PART II - MORAL VALUE

The dialectic of moral value. When the appeal is
in terms of moral value, the same dialectic (that appeared in Part I) lifts the mind _beyond feeling_ to
some sort of norm or standard that is presupposed. As
Mure puts it,

>   If the feeling expressed is one of approval, the
>   speaker is not simply ejaculating; he is very ob-
>   viously claiming to refer to something beyond his
>   own feeling and to judge it by some objective
>   standard. If there is nothing in his claim, why
>   call this feeling approval and not sheer

---

16. Feigl, "Logical Empiricism," p. 375.

liking?[17]

It may well be that the suggestion that ethical language has no reference in any meaningful sense to standards outside of the emotional state of the speaker is so diametrically opposed to the common assumptions of men that inevitably their language will betray them and bear witness to a supposed standard in spite of theories per contra. It is suspicious that only when the subject is the academic one of the logic of moral discourse does this absolute reduction to some emotional state of the speaker suggest itself.

> In passing, /observes Copleston/ one might...observe that it is somewhat strange to find a number of philosophers delivering excellent maxims concerning the value of the individual, the value of freedom, etc., when their phenomenalistic analysis of the self or their behavioristic description of man would seem to lead to the conclusion that there is neither a self to have a value nor a human freedom to be prized.[18]

It has been said of David Hume that the propositions he proposed in the wake of his attempted reduction of meaningful philosophy to "impressions" were so skeptical that language would not obey the burden placed upon it.[19] It would appear that ethical language

---

17. G. R. G. Mure, Op. cit., p. 172. In the statement "You stole that money," A. J. Ayer remarks, "In adding that this action is wrong I am not making any further statement about it. I am simply envincing my moral disapproval of it." LANGUAGE, TRUTH, AND LOGIC. (New York: Dover Publication, Inc., n.d.), p. 108.

18. Copleston, CONTEMPORARY PHILOSOPHY, p. 41.

19. It was in regard to Hume's exposition of the knowledge of the self (TREATISE, Book I, Section 2) that Robert Flint remarked, "In a word, what Hume tries to represent as the testimony of his consciousness is at this point so preposterously sceptical that his language refuses to convey it." AGNOSTICISM. (New York: Charles Scribner's Sons, 1903), p. 151. (This paper considers

similarly either must be given up entirely or one must be prepared to admit that its meaning bears a transcendent reference.

Moral purposiveness. Another strong indication of the presence of the transcendental element is uncovered in man's purposiveness. This paper's general concern has emphasized moral value and the two facts may now appropriately be conjoined under what will be called moral purposiveness.

Purpose combines two factors without exception: value and time. Purpose is a forward-looking, forward-reaching, condition and the object or goal of that forward effect is always some value. This, of course, does not automatically validate every goal as equally meritorious; there is the common enough spectacle of mistaking disvalue for value and paying too much for one's whistle. But the conjunction remains that man moves forward to attain some fancied good.

Time as the "form" of the moral life. Time is not believed to be an accidental factor in man's moral endeavor. The situation that man faces is that values, goods, that he does not possess now, yet desires, must be realized, if at all, in some future, near or remote. It is in this sense that time is declared in Chapter IV as the "form" of the moral life. And time as the "form" of the moral life is fundamentally different from that understanding of time that belongs to mere succession of non-mental events. One important difference may be remarked, viz., that in a mere succession of non-mental events there is no awareness of participation in time. If, as Kant assures us, the conception of time awakes only upon the occasion of experience, it is equally true for Kant that this same conception of time awakes only upon the occasion of a mind for which alone the temporal "form" has meaning as such. Thus, the intimate relation of mind to time is secured.

It is not mere succession, however, of which the mind is aware, nor is the mind merely aware that the form of temporality somehow has emerged upon the

---

the problem of personal identity in Chapter VII - "Moral Value and Immortality.")

occasion of a certain kind of experience; rather, the
form of temporality is seen to impregnate and to be
impregnated by (what Taylor calls) the "conative"[20]
disposition of the human being. Here, the emphasis
falls upon effort, endeavoring, striving, volition,
the total emphasis being that of a teleological consideration. There is indeed much more than a mere succession of events in the human experience; there is
virtually a constant purposiveness--and frequently an
acute consciousness of this purposiveness--that directs
toward a future while guided by the past. Thus the
"specious present" has moral significance because it
is purposively directed by what it believes to be its
own genuine concerns toward a goal of values identical in principle with those concerns. Nor does it appear that the human person is ever really indifferent
to those values that are believed to have given meaning to his future. Even the attempted non-axiological
reductions of the universe, so unimpassioned and neut-
ral and realistic and analytical: are they not accompanied by a sense of bringing the part of the universe
under investigation into some sort of secured, measurable, and understandable relation to the human spirit?
Is Principia Mathematica to be viewed as merely an end
in itself, a highly articulate expression of an attempt to demonstrate that the laws of the mathematics
of number can be reduced to logic? Would it be without meaning to inquire what the purpose of this gigan-
tic reduction might be? And if an answer were forthcoming along the lines of giving some very fundamental
explanation to the foundations of mathematics and
thereby providing at the same time foundation for all
of the disciplines identifiable with applied mathematics, would it be strictly meaningless to inquire the
purpose of this more ultimate answer?

Under this sort of goading, patience may retire
in exasperation. But I would contend that even as
there is acknowledged purpose in the beginning of such
an undertaking as Principia, a purpose that is capable
of an immediate and clearly defined goal, so there is
purpose more distant still. A declaration of impatience is no reply. If there is propriety in raising

---

20. "Conative" and "conation" are almost pure deriva-
    tions from Latin conatio (an attempt) and conari
    (to undertake, attempt).

255

the first question of purpose, there is propriety in
raising a second question about the purpose of the
purpose. And it is this not to be circumvented propriety that points along the line of the mind's genuine and immediate concerns to that ultimate presupposition of value which, denied, renders impossible the
validating of the least of claimed purposive actions.

The human act is therefore a purposive act, and a
purposive act is one ruled by future consideration.
But there is a temporality along the line of the human
advance that "mere succession" cannot claim. It is
precisely the continuum that marks past, present, and
future as a distinctly human meaning. It is like the
thread that unites and gives form to a string of
beads. The very memory of man's past, the awareness
of his present, and the prospect of his future, are,
in an important sense, temporality's differentiations
along the line of the "conative" function of man's
fundamentally unified obedience to a sense of value-
orientation. And this impulse to live as in recognition of a value-mandate is no more conspicuous when
clearly affirmed than it is when suffering under its
several forms of denial. Thus: the cries of pessimism, of cynicism, of the alleged meaninglessness and
absurdity of existence, all of these call attention in
their very negations to the norm of ideal value without which these privations would have no meaning.

Beyond temporality. It is evident that the above
thoughts tend very directly to transcend the temporal
dimension. That is to say, to know temporality meaningfully is to transcend it.[21] This is the implied

---

21. "I believe," writes Muirhead, "that we are bound
to agree with.../Taylor's7 powerful argument for
the intimate union of temporal and eternal in
man's moral consciousness. Morality commits us
to the realization of a form of good which goes
beyond anything that can be called happiness,
adaptation to environment, social progress, and
which can perhaps best be expressed as harmony
with the will of God, as that is revealed to us
in history and finds confirmation in our own conscience, however erring owing to its subjectivity that may be." J. H. Muirhead, THE FAITH OF A
MORALIST, by A. E. Taylor. Review. THE HIBBERT

dialectic of finitude. It is Plato and Augustine and Descartes. We interpret factuality by the aid of universals. Temporality is a fact. Therefore, temporality is interpreted by its universal. The finite dimension in any and every sense gives rise to the notion of infinity. The finite is always a limitation of. And regardless of the number of finite additions, one still has a limitation of. That, therefore, that is the presupposition of all limitation whatever is precisely the limitless or infinity. And in the universe of discourse to which temporality belongs as the limiting notion, eternity appears to be the proper presupposition to confer appropriate meaning to the time-limitation. We appear to be committed to an eternity already entered upon! And this is only a particularization of what is more generally true, viz., that it is necessary to find transcendent meaning already included in every instance of particularity. And if the argument appears to go beyond the dialectic that belongs purely to intellection, seemingly making an identification with action, the best reply is simply to admit it. Indeed, it is eventually to this identification of true thought with right action that the more coherent interpretation of moral value will ultimately lead. It is this same identification of thought and action that is involved in the meaning and application of the "conative" function, for here, the various involvements--man's purposive nature, future commitment, involvement in time, striving and volition, and all to the end of attaining some value or values that ground in that sort of existence in which man may hope to participate and thereby find security--unite to validate 'moral purposiveness.' And noting again the natural conjunction of value with existence, the fact of temporality may now be observed to be so intimately annexed to the striving person that the dialectic that introduces eternity also introduces the eternal Person. It is thus--when value is the consideration--that God enters Taylor's system. It would

---

JOURNAL, XXIX (1931), p. 557. Blanshard, however, finds Taylor's "struggle of a temporal being to put on eternity" a "very dark saying" though admitting it to be "the key to the whole work." Brand Blanshard, THE FAITH OF A MORALIST, by A. E. Taylor. Review. THE JOURNAL OF PHILOSOPHY, XXIX (1932), p. 131.

appear, therefore, that eternity and supernature are discernibly distinct meanings but necessarily related aspects of the same reality.

A variant of the "naturalistic fallacy." It is believed that the transcendent character of moral value comes to our attention in yet another way. There is a loose, frequent, and certainly not wholly incorrect way in which the idea of the "good" is linked with a multitude of everyday experiences. Thus: "utility is good," "pleasure is good," "health is good," "knowledge is good." It would appear that in some sense certainly these ways of speaking are in-contestably true. The sense of their truth, however, is that preserved within the logical relation of inclu-sion. We would therefore more accurately say that utility, pleasure, health, and knowledge are included within the good. This class-inclusion is sufficient to guarantee the conjunction of value within existence --the proposition maintained in Chapter III. But the admonition of elementary logic that the proposition, "pleasure is good," cannot automatically be converted to "the good is pleasure" carries by implication the warning which, if unheeded, would produce a variant of the "naturalistic fallacy." The assumed validity of the conversion of any of the above propositions that link some experience with the good has the effect of creating a logical equivalence between the terms. And it is this assumption of equivalence that leads to the variation on the "naturalistic fallacy."

The proponent of a transcendental philosophy might well attempt to bring out his main point while exhibiting the inconsistency of his opponent in the following way. He might say: we both know what uti-lity, pleasure, health, and knowledge are. Why do you complicate the issue by calling them good? Each one of these can be adequately and accurately described. That should be sufficient. And if the response to this challenge is that we do actually mean to add some-thing by the word "good" that goes beyond the mere des-cription, the only observation appears to be that this deeply felt meaning is entirely proper and we should be guided by its felt propriety to recognize the trans-cendent dimension introduced by this unavoidable lan-guage. The "going beyond" the descriptive fact is and has always been the sine qua non of normative appeal and therefore of ethical appeal. To attempt to retain

the full value of the ethical dimension by literally
identifying the predicate of moral value with that of
which it is predicated is to produce a merely non-
informative tautology or--at a different level of
thinking--to commit in principle a "naturalistic fallacy." There appears to be no real escape from these
restricting binds other than to admit the control that
transcendent reality has over the ordinary use of language.

   The Is-Ought controversy. The presence of this
alleged transcendence in reality is indicated modestly
enough by the contrasting words, "ought" and "is,"
that, in turn, suggest the normative as over against
the merely descriptive in our language. However David
Hume is to be interpreted in the famous passage in the
TREATISE, his words are almost precisely what one
would choose if one were to announce the difference
and the distance between the ought of obligation and
duty and the is of mere description. The passage in
question reads,

> I cannot forbear adding to these reasonings an
> observation, which may, perhaps, be found of some
> importance. In every system of morality, which I
> have hitherto met with, I have always remark'd,
> that the author proceeds for some time in the or-
> dinary way of reasoning, and establishes the be-
> ing of a God, or makes observations concerning
> human affairs; when of a sudden I am surpriz'd to
> find, that instead of the usual copulations of
> propositions, is, and is not, I meet with no pro-
> position that is not connected with an ought, or
> an ought not. This change is imperceptible; but
> is, however, of the last consequence. For as this
> ought, or ought not, expresses some new relation
> or affirmation, 'tis necessary that it shou'd be
> observ'd and explain'd; and at the same time that
> a reason should be given, for what seems altogeth-
> er inconceivable, how this new relation can be a
> deduction from others, which are entirely differ-
> ent from it. But as authors do not commonly use
> this precaution, I shall presume to recommend it
> to the readers; and I am persuaded, that this
> small attention wou'd subvert all the vulgar sys-
> tems of morality, and let us see, that the dis-
> tinction of vice and virtue is not founded merely
> on the relations of objects, nor is perceiv'd by

reason.[22]

The question of how to interpret Hume may be an interesting exercise but it must be regarded as irrelevant to the question raised by Hume's words, viz., "how this new relation /the ought or ought not/ can be a deduction from others, which are entirely different from it." Of course, it may turn out that it is not a case of being "entirely different"--as Geoffrey Hunter would apparently insist when he flatly declares that "Hume makes ought-propositions a sub-class of is-propositions, namely is-propositions about the causation of certain sorts of feelings."[23] But if this classification of ought-propositions as a sub-class of is-propositions is in itself invalid, then it cannot matter what Hume thought and the question for us is open regarding the proper relation between ought and is.

In a sense, the Is-Ought controversy is a paradigm example--from Taylor's point of view--of the extremes that the opposition will adopt in order to give life and promise to a denial of that transcendence alleged to hold of normative relations. Thus, Mavrodes remembers that Ought is supposed to imply Can. If so, then, he declares, the contraposition also holds that the denial of Can implies the denial of Ought--the latter implication, supposedly, a derivation of ought from is![24] Shaw's reply should prove adequate: "If it is agreed that something cannot be done, then it is agreed that no choice is involved, and the question of whether it ought to be done, may be done, or ought not to be done, just doesn't arise." And Shaw adds, "The trouble lies in saying that 'ought' entails 'can.' It is better to say that 'ought' presupposes 'can.'"[25]

---

22. A TREATISE OF HUMAN NATURE, Book III, Part I, Section I.

23. Geoffrey Hunter, "Hume on Is and Ought," PHILOSOPHY, XXXVII (April 1962), p. 149.

24. George I. Mavrodes, "'Is' and 'Ought,'" ANALYSIS, Vol. 25, No. 2 (December 1964), p. 42.

25. P. D. Shaw, "Ought and Can," ANALYSIS, Vol. 25, No. 6 (June 1965), p. 197.

Similar concern is shown by Max Black when he declares as "mistaken" the view that "no term may occur in the conclusion of a valid argument unless it occurs, or can be made to occur by suitable definitions, somewhere in the premises."[26] In the interest of his contention, Black distinguishes between valid syllogisms --here the rule holds--and valid arguments. For the latter, it is contended, the rule does not hold. Example: "A citizen is a person; therefore a married citizen is a married person." "Here," Black affirms, "the word 'married' occurs for the first time in the conclusion."[27] I would suggest that the unqualified use of citizen in the first sentence admits the possibility of any single adjective not denied by the meaning of _person_. Therefore, married could be one such possibility. In this sense, then, the adjective does not appear "for the first time" in the conclusion.[28]

Next, Black endeavors to show how from a valid syllogism that does not violate the rule above, a valid argument can be derived that does violate the rule. Thus: "Vivisection causes gratuitous suffering to animals. Nothing that causes gratuitous suffering ought to be done. Therefore, vivisection ought not to be done." From this syllogism is derived the following: "Vivisection causes gratuitous suffering to animals. Therefore, if nothing that causes gratuitous suffering ought to be done, vivisection ought not to be done." This, for Black, constitutes a "valid argument proceeding from 'is' to 'ought.'"[29] But is not this

---

26. Max Black, "The Gap Between 'Is' and 'Should,'" THE PHILOSOPHICAL REVIEW, LXXIII (April 1964), p. 167.

27. _Ibid_.

28. Even R. F. Atkinson, though holding against the derivation of a value-laden _ought_ from an _is_, remarks that "Hare himself would allow that such a sentence as 'This is an augur' might entail 'This _ought_ to bore holes.'" "'Ought' and 'Is,'" PHILOSOPHY, XXXIII (January 1958), p. 30. It would appear that this is the plainest type of enthymeme. It merely invites for completion the major that reads "All augurs ought to bore holes."

29. Max Black, _Op_. _cit_., p. 167.

merely concealing a premise--the premise containing the ought--in the form of the conclusion? In this example, the conclusion is so conjoined to the major premise and following the word therefore as to suggest that the premise itself was a part of the conclusion. The meaning, however, serves to avoid the confusion and returns the premise to its original place in the syllogism--thus preserving the rule that the conclusion may contain no new term. But Black generalizes upon the basis of this example and declares, "...in general, 'If $\underline{A}$ then $\underline{B}$' entails 'If $\underline{B}$ ought not to be done, $\underline{A}$ ought not to be done.'"[30] This is a sort of variant on Mavrodes' attempted contraposition above,[31] and glaringly makes explicit the alleged propriety of introducing new meanings in the conclusion that do not appear in the premise. Indeed, in its naked symbolism, the impropriety of so doing appears as a silent rebuke to the undertaking and an endorsement to the good sense of the traditional rule.

For Black, however, these exercises are mere "preliminaries" and "To those who claim the existence of an unbridgeable logical gap between 'ought' and 'is,'" is offered the following "counterexample." "Fischer wants to mate Botwinnik. The one and only way to mate Botwinnik is for Fischer to move the Queen. Therefore, Fischer should move the Queen." Here, for Black, both premises state matters of fact while the conclusion contains a "non-factual 'should'-statement."[32] For Black, this should of the conclusion has a "performative aspect" by which he means that "a speaker who uses this form of words counts as doing something more than, or something other than, saying something having truth value."[33] What is this "something more"? Black answers by saying that in the case of a "second-person use" of should,

It is plausible to hold that the prime function of the...formula is to urge the hearer to adopt a

---

30. Ibid.

31. Page 260.

32. Ibid., p. 169.

33. Ibid., p. 171.

course of action selected by the speaker as preferable, optimal, or correct.[34]

Thus: You want to achieve E. Doing M is the one and only way to achieve E. Therefore, you should do M.[35]

Now, it would be natural to think of this argument as an example of an enthymeme with a suppressed but understood premise. And Black recognizes that this counter would likely be brought to bear against his argument. Indeed, Black formulates the possible form that such a suppressed premise might take, viz., "Everybody should do anything which is the one and only way to achieve anything that he wants to achieve."[36] Black's rather surprising reply to this charge of a suppressed premise--and particularly to the premise as formulated above--is as follows: "...the proposed additional premise must be held to be analytic, in the sense of being guaranteed correct by virtue of the meanings or functions of the terms it contains. If so, its presence is unnecessary..."[37]

But this premise is not analytic! Even if it were granted that there are cases in experience of which we may say that there is one and only one way of achieving a given end--a dubious proposition at best! --it need not at the same time be said that one should act in that direction. And similarly, even if it were granted that one wants to achieve that end, it need not be true that he should. And even if both conditions hold at the same time, viz., that there is one and only one way of achieving a given end and one wants to achieve it, it still need not be true that he should. This is particularly true in cases of clear moral issues; it is even true in the case of a chess game where conceivably the winning of the game might

---

34.   Ibid.

35.   Ibid., p. 173.

36.   Ibid.

37.   Ibid.

prove deleterious to the welfare of the opponent.[38]
Therefore this premise is not analytic; it is clearly
synthetic, and the full burden to prove the truth of
this suppressed premise must be assumed by the one
whose argument has forced this premise into its structure. The only further remark necessary is to note
the presence of 'should' in this premise--thus qualifying under the ordinary rule of the valid syllogism
that every term that appears in the conclusion of a
valid syllogism must appear once in the premises.

But Professor Black is not really committed to a
relation of entailment between premises of pure factuality and a conclusion of non-factuality. While admitting the premises that P and if P, then Q, it is
logically impossible not to admit that Q, when these
same premises are made to stand for purely factual propositions. Black concedes that the one admitting them
might still hesitate about insisting on a should-con-
clusion. "I am reluctant to say," Black writes, "that
the practical 'should'-conclusion is entailed by its
factual premises" and adds, "the important contrast
with straightforward cases of entailment might indeed
be marked by using some such label as 'latent necessity' or 'virtual necessity.'"[39]

In this manner and by these words, Black emphasizes what most moralists would also emphasize, viz.,
that there is a sort of felt compulsion about the doing of certain acts and the withholding from others
that when fulfilled gives a sense of propriety and victory and when violated leaves a sense of guilt. But
this is not a case of strict logical entailment but
rather a case of the felt propriety of the moral act

---

38. Both Max Black (Ibid.) and a paper by D. Z. Phil-
    lips ("The Possibilities of Moral Advice,"
    ANALYSIS, 25, No. 2 (December 1964), pp. 37-41.)
    make a certain concession to the welfare of the
    opponent in a chess game as a possible circum-
    stance that might alter one's decision to win.
    But Black thinks this intrusion of consideration
    for the welfare of the player "involves a change
    of subject" and especially "to introduce moral
    considerations is to change the topic." (Max
    Black, Op. cit., p. 175.)

39. Ibid., pp. 178-179.

arising upon the occasion of the experience though not
being reducible to it. The attempt to erase the difference between the is and the ought is a case of attempted reduction. If the reduction were indeed possible, then the pure factuality emerging might lend
itself to an argument of entailment--even when the
conclusion contains a should- or ought-clause and the
premises none. Professor Black's concession of no
strict entailment is a fulfilling condition of the is-
ought controversy as signalling (in Hume's words) an
"entirely different" relation.

Without a reduction then of an ought to an is
neither entailment nor derivation in any lesser sense
is strictly possible. And the question arises (again)
whether such a reduction is compatible with the meaning of moral value and the meaning of moral obligation.

It is the implicit prediction of Taylor that any
tampering with the transcendental status will force
such compromise as virtually to obliterate the true
significance of moral obligation. John R. Searle is a
fair example of how this is accomplished. The bare
structure of Searle's attempt to derive an ought from
an is can be found in the following:

> (1) Jones uttered the words "I hereby promise to
> pay you, Smith, five dollars." (2) Jones pro-
> mised to pay Smith five dollars. (3) Jones
> placed himself under (undertook) an obligation to
> pay Smith five dollars. (4) Jones is under an
> obligation to pay Smith five dollars. (5) Jones
> ought to pay Smith five dollars.[40]

Does this demonstrate the derivation of an ought from
an is and, if so, in what sense must we consider it to
be a derivation? Searle recognizes that it will be
suspected that there is a concealed evaluative premise
somewhere but assures us that this is only question-
begging--the case of insisting that no ought can be derived from an is. To be sure, it does appear that the
evaluative premise is indeed included in the premises
and not too cleverly concealed at that. But Searle's

---

40. John R. Searle, "How to Derive 'Ought' From
    'Is,'" THE PHILOSOPHICAL REVIEW, LXXIII (January
    1964), p. 44.

defense is to distinguish between "statements of brute fact and statements of institutional fact."[41] Thus, to utter words and make gestures may be a brute fact; to make a promise by their aid is to introduce an institutional fact. A home run, five dollars, getting married, making promises, may all be considered "institutional facts," but baseball, money, marriage, and promising, are the institutions presupposed by the corresponding facts. And Searle makes his point explicit: "...the institutions...are systems of constitutive rules. The institutions of marriage, money, and promising are like the institutions of baseball or chess in that they are systems of such constitutive rules or conventions."[42]

Searle's solution, therefore, is but another sample of conventionalism in ethics. Moral obligation is referred to an institution which in turn is the result of definition and agreement--like chess. The moral imperative has been reduced to hypothetical status: if you agree to the rules of the game of chess, then you ought to move thus and so; if you agree to the rules of the institution of promising, then you ought to fulfill your promises.

But how does the alleged moral institution of promising defend itself against criticism? Suppose that the charge is leveled that the institution is wrong. What can this charge mean? Does it mean only that the institution is inefficient? But, as was argued earlier, to define a moral maxim (or institution) by efficiency is to commit the naturalistic fallacy. That is to say, we know what efficiency is. Why not stop there? Why call it _moral_? Searle, it would appear, ends either not having any title to moral obligation whatever, or, if he does, it is because of a concealed premise of genuine moral obligation that is sensed but suppressed and greatly misunderstood. It cannot be too much emphasized that every "institution"--really only a universal called upon to give meaning to particulars--short of an absolute will eventually come before the need to answer how it can possibly respond to the charge of being in the wrong. And that

---

41. _Ibid._, p. 55.

42. _Ibid._

assumption by the aid of which the inescapable meaning of 'wrong' is preserved is itself precisely that ultimate presupposition of moral evaluation without which the questions, the challenges, the defenses, of the moral dimension would never arise.

The tenuous holding to an ought-language in spite of the difficulties of deriving the ought from is-statements has evidently impelled M. Zimmerman to try for a pure is-language.[43] This, he tells us, is in order to derive "the benefit of one without the hindrance of the other."[44]

In a paragraph strongly suggestive of a species of attempted human engineering, Zimmerman writes,

> If a man wants to break promises, tell lies, rape or kill, which is better, merely telling him that he ought not to, even if it succeeds in restraining him, or telling him that if he does what he wants, he will be disliked, ostracized, punished or killed? This is not all. We can not only tell him these things, we can do some or all of these things. ...We can use all our resources of knowledge, in the sciences, in psychology, economics, sociology, etc., and the further acquisition of knowledge to get him and others to do the things we want him and others to do.[45]

It would appear that in order "to get him and others to do the things we want him and others to do," that these same things be truly desirable and that truly desirable goals ought to command us; otherwise these "things we want him and others to do" will not be those that necessarily ought to command us,--which circumlocution is to indicate the concealed presence of an ought-statement among those that Zimmerman thought to be innocent of all such! It is this kind of concealment that prompted Kenneth Hanley's remark:

---

43. M. Zimmerman, "The 'Is-Ought': An Unnecessary Dualism," MIND, LXXI (January 1962), pp. 53-61.

44. Ibid., p. 61.

45. Ibid., p. 56.

My main criticism of Zimmerman's position is that
we do not really crash the is-ought barrier by
removing 'ought' from our language. What happens
is that our 'is' statements take on a dual personality: that is, they perform not only the old
tasks which they did before the revolution, but
also all the tasks that 'ought' used to do.[46]

It should not escape the most cursory inspection
that what I have styled Zimmerman's "attempted human
engineering" is not without its long-term and large-
scale goals and that these goals for Zimmerman are
eminently worthwhile. But it must simply be seen with
a resolute inspection of all of the meanings involved
that wanting or desiring such and such ends is not the
same as identifying these ends with the values that
ought to command us. Yet, this confusion runs through
Zimmerman's entire article. He writes, "...suppose,
for example, that most people find the 'is' statement
that a man could not help doing what he did, an acceptable 'is' reason for saying that he 'ought' not to be
punished? What are we aiming for here in getting people to say that an insane man ought not to be punished,
if other than that we do not want to and will not pun-
ish an insane man?"[47] The answer, I think, is clear.
The idea of the ought arises upon the occasion of Zimmerman's is but is not identical with it. The reason
for not punishing an insane man is not found in the
state of his crippled psychology, but the reason does
come to the fore upon the occasion of our awareness of
his impotence. Zimmerman clearly has not grasped the
idea of the ought as a category transcending particular applications. "If we continue to use the 'ought'
language," he writes, "we will continue to be stuck
with finding the right 'ought' statements to begin
with..."[48] And again, "...the totalitarians will also
be using the 'ought' language for their own ends. In
the case of finding the right 'ought' statements to begin with, the totalitarians will proclaim their

46. Kenneth Hanley, "Zimmerman's 'Is-Is': A Schizo-
     phrenic Monism," MIND, LXXIII (July 1964), p. 443.

47. M. Zimmerman, Op. cit., p. 58.

48. Ibid., p. 60.

self-evident truths just as we will." But the inability to make proper use of the category of the _ought_ does not invalidate the fact claimed, namely, that a category is recognized by all parties as furnishing the ideal of ethical language.

I cannot forbear the remark that the above several pages of discussion, wherein were reviewed various attempts to derive an _ought_ from an _is_, lowered the quality of the issue suggested by the larger view of the ethical dimension. There is assuredly a loss to the fuller meaning of human experience when that experience can know no commentary other than a reduction to descriptivism. My protestations against imposed pain can carry no hint of a possible injustice--and if the cry of an injustice is raised, it can only be at the cost, on one view, of committing the naturalistic fallacy, and, on another view, that of perhaps unconsciously recognizing the existence of an ideal category believed violated. The paradigm example that the scientist may be able to tell you that cyanide of potassium will probably kill you but not that you ought not take it distinguishes clearly enough between a predictive and a prescriptive remark. As R. M. Hare writes,

> There is, indeed, a logical inference that can be elicited....Given that the toadstool would kill me, I can infer that I ought not to eat it, if I also accept a further premise that I ought not to eat what would kill me. To accept this other premise is to have one of a class of things which I shall call, in Professor Braithwaite's phrase, 'springs of action.'...In fact anything belongs to /this class/ which can, as it were, turn a descriptive statement into a reason for doing something; or, more formally, the expression of which in language, ...together with some descriptive statement, logically entails some prescription. But there is no logical link between the descriptive premise, by itself, and the prescriptive conclusion.[49]

When the descriptive statement "turn/s/...into a

_____

49.   R. M. Hare, "Descriptivism," PROCEEDINGS OF THE BRITISH ACADEMY, XLIX (1963), p. 133.

reason for doing something" the category of purposive
action is introduced and this is a category that descriptivism cannot find. And when the ends of purposive action are those of the attainment of some moral
end, purpose and moral motivation unite to endorse
what is Taylor's most insisted-upon thesis: the conative disposition of the individual.

There is, therefore a 'point' to morality, but
that point must be recognized as transcending the particular actions and conditions to which it is applicable. It is introductory of a larger dimension, of a
conceptual background, of a metaphysics, of a universal, without which the brute facts of the descriptivist remain mute facts.

> Certainly, /write Phillips and Mounce/ those who
> have insisted on the necessity of a certain con-
> ceptual background in order to make sense of mo-
> ral beliefs and moral judgements have done philo-
> sophy a service. They have revealed the artifi-
> ciality of locating what is characteristically
> moral in a mental attitude such as pro-attitude,
> or in a mental activity such as commending.[50]

And again,

> The notion of "offense" is parasitic on the no-
> tion of a standard or norm, although these need
> not be formulated. The person who wishes to say
> that the offense is a "pure fact" from which a
> moral conclusion can be deduced is simply con-
> fused.[51]

Value-relativism. The above claims against the
adequacy of a descriptionist ethic and the supporting
attempts to violate the unique category of the moral
ought may now find support from a consideration of the
failure of value-relativism. The loose, personal,
subjective relation of value to actuality has been an

---

50. D. Z. Phillips and H. O. Mounce, "On Morality's
    Having a Point," PHILOSOPHY, XL (October 1965),
    p. 310.

51. Ibid., p. 311.

allegation affirmed with a confidence that has increased with the discovery of a widespread relativity
of valuation throughout the length and breadth of time
and place. The idea is commonly enough heard that
there is no virtue anywhere but what has been considered a vice somewhere. And this is alleged to hold
not just of the trivial value-commitments, but of the
cardinal values. In the light, therefore, of this paper's thesis that looks hopefully to the defense of
transcendent and absolute values, a further consideration of this claim of relativism is desirable.

An illustration of how such an assumed necessity
for adjustment to a species of relativism might arise
is provided by C. D. Broad in a direct challenge to
Taylor upon occasion of writing a review of Taylor's
THE FAITH OF A MORALIST.

> I am fairly sure that, if I were to put the case
> to my more intelligent pupils or to my younger
> colleagues in Cambridge, a large proportion of
> them would answer somewhat as follows. "The ethi-
> cal ideals in which we were brought up were devel-
> oped by men in societies where a non-naturalistic
> view of human nature and destiny was almost uni-
> versal, and they were appropriate on such a view.
> Since then the cumulative evidence for a natural-
> istic view has become overwhelming, and it is now
> far more reasonable to suppose that the tradition-
> al moral ideals are inappropriate to our nature
> and situation than that the naturalistic view is
> false. No doubt this does make human life and
> human effort rather a sorry business, and no
> doubt the general recognition of this fact would
> tend to make most men slacker and more self-indul-
> gent than they ought to be even on a naturalistic
> view. This may be a good reason for not proclaim-
> ing our convictions from the housetops, but it is
> no argument against their truth. Our own wisest
> course is to try to exorcise, by psycho-analysis
> and similar means, the ghosts of those moral
> ideals which still haunt us from the dead past of
> our individual and racial infancy. We can then
> at least set about making the best of a bad job,
> undiverted by the lure of an impossible perfec-
> tion, and untroubled by the strings of irrational

remorse.[52]

To the above, Broad prudently defers declaring
his support allowing his "more intelligent pupils" and
"his younger colleagues in Cambridge" to bear the glo-
ry or the burden of the assumed position, but does say,

> I am sure that, if such an argument as Prof. Tay-
> lor's is to do more than impart a pleasing glow
> of self-satisfaction to the already convinced, it
> would need to deal very seriously and sympatheti-
> cally with the position which I have crudely sta-
> ted. I do not find any such attempt in Prof.
> Taylor's book, and this does seem to me to be a
> serious defect in it.[53]

It is true that no such attempt to answer the particular form of this challenge is discoverable in Taylor's treatment of the ethical question, and neither
indeed could there be without stultifying his position.
It is precisely because of Taylor's consistent contention that the ethical dimension cannot be naturalized
that an argument in defense cannot be based upon naturalistic assumptions. It would be Taylor's position
that Broad's challenge does not even raise a truly moral issue. It reduces to a form of descriptivism that
by-passes the entire question of where a normative
ethic really bases. When Broad acknowledges that on
this relativistic view most men might become "slacker
and more self-indulgent than they ought to be even on
a naturalistic view," the meaning of Broad's 'ought'
will certainly come under focus. It would appear to
be impossible to rise above a merely prudential
"ought" in the context proposed by Broad. The use of
the word, however, according to Taylor, continues the
internal witness of our allegiance to a transcendent
ethical norm.

Of a somewhat different regret is that of W. G.
de Burgh who, also commenting on Taylor's THE FAITH OF
A MORALIST, expressed the wish that Taylor had proceeded by "defining clearly and in detail the nature

---

52. C. D. Broad, THE FAITH OF A MORALIST, by A. E.
Taylor. Review. MIND, XL (1931), pp. 367-368.

53. Ibid., p. 368.

of morality as such," and, more narrowly, de Burgh adds,

> There is a further point which we should like to question in Professor Taylor's account of the moral life. He follows the historical tradition in interpreting it as a life lived sub ratione boni and motivated solely by desire of good, in opposition to the Kantian doctrine which interprets it in the light of the concept of duty, holding that an action to be moral must be done for the sake of its own rightness and for no ulterior end.[54]

There are two issues raised here. First, with regard to "defining clearly and in detail the nature of morality as such": This, strictly speaking, cannot be done by the finite intelligence. The difficulty is almost exactly paralleled by the Platonic difficulty in defining justice. What we seem to know clearest is the presence of injustice in its manifold forms, but this is possible only by having an idea (Idea?) of justice by the aid of which the true principle of justice is applied to the situation and, by this same aid, the privation detected. Now, this is Taylor's position and it is Taylor's answer to de Burgh's wish for detail in the nature of morality. The general guiding principle is there, the principle that joins to human awareness and determines man to a behavior and a language with peculiarities the full interpretation of which directs back to that (frequently unconsciously held) presupposition necessarily transcendent to the specific action which is interpreted.

The second issue raised by de Burgh is whether Taylor resolves what might be considered an opposition to the Kantian doctrine of duty for duty's sake in his espousal of the historical tradition of a "life lived sub ratione boni and motivated solely by desire of good."

Part of the difficulty in this fancied opposition lies in the strong suggestion that the words bear that on the one hand we are honoring an extrinsic good and on the other hand we are honoring an intrinsic good.

---

54. W. G. de Burgh, PHILOSOPHY, VI (1931), p. 233.

Kant's ethic is made out to be practically disjoined
from all human relation. This is very false. After
all, in Kant, it is man's duty to fulfill the moral
law. And if the formula, duty for duty's sake, appears to be overdominant, it must be remembered that
this is Kant's way of recognizing the rational character of a maxim that cannot be satisfied with less than
universality and necessity. Taylor would agree with
this aspect of moral law. Further, Kant is by no
means hostile to the inclusion of the word "good" in
his system--strictly rational though it is. "Good" is
good only when it is conjoined with something unquali-
fiedly good, viz., a good will. And a good will is
the possession of a rational being fulfilling the universality and necessity of rationality. As noted
above, this is man's duty. And therefore the rational
as a test of genuine morality is seen in Kant (and in
Taylor) to be joined essentially to the notion of good.
Taylor is not inconsistent in making his good obey the
test of universality and necessity--rational criteria;
and Kant is not inconsistent in making his rationality
fulfill the meaning of a good will. Neither the rational nor the good is meant to be a private possession for Kant or for Taylor. But both the good and the
rational may become the fruition of an individual's
moral and rational maturity.

   In the actual experience of men, neither the good
nor the rational proves to be sufficient producers of
moral or rational worth; but, as necessary conditions
of moral and rational worth, their relevance to the human situation can be demonstrated--if in no other way
--by the collapse of the society that has dared to attempt their compromise while willing to extend the compromise to universal limits. This is the message of
Plato in the famous contest between the claims of justice and injustice in the REPUBLIC. The disintegrating effects of injustice in the individual may escape
notice--especially, as in a curiously paradoxical way,
the injustice of the individual is sustained by the
larger environment of justice. (The individual liar
gains his ends because his larger environment can be
depended upon to assume that truth is being practiced.)
But when injustice is pushed to universal limits--the
"individual writ large"--then, if not before, it can be
seen that the principle of injustice is non-viable.
And this must not be confused with a teleological
ethic. The collapse of the immoral principle was

already implicit in its initial proposal; it but remained for the outcome at universal limits to render obvious the already existing fatal defect.

Returning now more directly to the question of relativism: when a situation is declared "right" by one party and denied by another, the question should arise whether the dispute is really about the predicate-term of the proposition or about the subject-term. That is to say, is it not the case that when a given situation is simultaneously affirmed and denied to be right by two parties to the dispute that what is really at issue is whether this particular situation really belongs to the category or class of things called "right." It is as though one individual to the dispute is saying, "I know what 'right' means--and this situation is a case of it," and the other, "I know what 'right' means--and this situation is not a case of it." If indeed this is a true analysis of the disputants' intentions, it is clear that the predicate of value is not being disputed at all, not, that is to say, with regard to the singleness of meaning that the value-objectivist would insist must be accorded in some ultimate sense to values. Does capital punishment, euthanasia, abortions, belong to the class of "right" actions, or not? It would appear that both he who affirms and he who denies must hold to the same essential meaning of right--for otherwise, could there be any possibility of an argument in any significant sense? With so radical a failure to meet on some ground held in common, the parties to the difference might still fight, but they could not argue. To render explicit the near-obvious, if the predicate of a dispute were really to be possessed of such divergent meanings as "long," "bitter," "green," "shrill," "distant," "large," "bright," and if, to enlarge upon the difficulty, the disputants had no idea of what meaning the others held of the predicate being used, the confusion could only be that of the miracle at Babel.[55]

The use of presuppositions. The type of argument here employed to indicate value-objectivity offers at the same time an illustration of the use of presuppositions. Presuppositions are assumptions on which we are in perpetual dependence; more, they enter into the

---

55. GENESIS, Chapter 11.

very warp and woof of our being. They are therefore
the very categories natural for the human being to
honor and on which we are in perpetual dependence both
in thought and action. They are the guides and correctives normally identified with the norms and yardsticks of human thought and behavior. Within the
broad categories of the rational, the esthetic, the
moral, unconscious behavior attests their presence and
our allegiance to them--regardless of how they may be
misrepresented by our application of them.

This hypothesis of the existence of a set of overarching Norms vitally related to the very meaning of
the human enterprise carries with it--as indeed do all
hypotheses--a prediction. The prediction is, in effect, that so essentially related to man is this complex of value-norms that aside from species of academic experiment they will never yield to repudiation in
practice. Thus, an attempted dismissal of the claims
of rationality not only will be found to have reinsti-
tuted rational procedures immediately afterwards but
the attempted dismissal itself will be found to have
moved through rational devices thus testifying to the
contradiction of attempting to escape rationality by
rational means. Nor is the all but universal tendency
to meet the world of the esthetic with critical ap-
praisal quite consistent with that other judgment that
would interpret the esthetic as strictly a case of
homo mensura--grounding all such judgments within the
eye of the beholder. Nor does the case of moral value
with its attempted reduction to an ethical relativism
seem quite secure in the wake of its doctrinal forget-
fulness, its moral outrage, and cries of Injustice!

It is not that we are being asked by the value-
relativist to recognize that as a fact we live in a
world in which appeals to values as normative do not
exist; such a denial of practice would be ludicrous.
What we are asked to recognize as the case is that the
universal practice of overt and covert appeal to such
norms is totally unsupported by the objective fact of
such norms' real existences and authority. And in distinction to this sweeping denial of the real existence
and authority of normative value, it is Taylor's eminently sensible thesis that, rather than attempt to
build a picture of coherence upon the assumption of the
total falsity of this objectification, it is wiser and
better to attempt a picture of coherence upon the assumption of its truth.

The witness of evil to transcendence. It is little less than dramatic that evil--that direct antithesis to good--should appear as a witness to the transcendent quality of moral value. It is a curious paradox that evil, though at the opposite end of the spectrum from good is fruitfully revelatory of many of the aspects of moral value. Evil makes us aware of the distance that yawns between its own negation and the positive norm by which the negation is identified as such. In the very complaint that evil generates, one catches a hint of why it is a complaint and sometimes how a cure might be effected.

In the light of such remarks--continuous with time--it may even be hazarded that however much evil may merit opprobrium, it may even be said to signal the existence of a positive transcendent dimension and that there is something virtually unique about a situation that can in all verity be called evil. This unique feature forces our attention at that point where we are simultaneously compelled to recognize evil's dislocating force in our midst and yet are unable to pinpoint it as an isolatable factor in experience. Actually, this is but another way of noting the limitations of an empirical approach while in no sense derogating from experience its proper authority.

Descriptivism cannot pinpoint either good or evil. In the many exhibitions of experience upon the occasion of which the sense of evil arises, each one of these occasions can be made to yield to an analysis such that evil will never appear as an isolatable feature nor as an empirically identifiable characteristic. Take any, take all, of the situations that have been conjoined in the evaluations of men with that perspective that may rightly be called evil and it is perfectly safe to say that evil itself will remain a sort of epiphenomenon whose presence is too sure to deny and too fleeting to identify with the raw material of the experience that introduced it. This is but to say that in the virtually limitless manifestations of evil --deeds, thoughts, events--all of these, by whatever designation, can be described without having to call in evil to aid in the description. This is to say, further, that such deeds, thoughts, events, can be described as so many actions, so many directions, so many parts--and all without bringing the notion of evil to bear upon the descriptive effort in any way. This description-analysis is the proper effort of the

277

physicist, the psychologist, the sociologist, the
biologist. And for none of these disciplines is the
notion of either moral good or evil really meaningful.[56]

     A necessary presupposition: the transcendent
Nature of the good. The unique feature then that is
said to characterize a situation that in all verity can
be called evil is that though evil cannot be identified
with the physical aspects of the case, it remains to
be recognized and affirmed in some other sense. The
sense in which it must be affirmed would appear to be
what is meant by that virtually total experience of
mankind in which values and disvalues seem to be in
constant opposition. Here, things held to be most precious are overcome by a multitude of disvalues. Here,
health, and hope, and honor are too effectively com-
bated by their opposites. Here, the cardinal principle of justice becomes conceptually evident only by
reason of the practically infinite intrusions of injustice into the human family. It would appear that
to treat this characterization of total human history
as a characterization of negligible and irrelevant
significance is to confuse what is essential and what
is accidental; it is, in short, to falsify the meaning
of human history by denying that its preoccupation
with the problem of good and evil was a concern about

---

56. A similar thought expressed by G. R. G. Mure em-
     phasizes the meaning of good as being irreduci-
     ble to the narrowed residue of empirical analy-
     sis. "An intrinsic good is...not simple and
     atomic. Its unity is the individuality of coher-
     ent system. If it is analyzed, a diversity of
     'parts,' or 'characters,' or 'aspects' will in-
     dubitably emerge. But none of these will, out-
     side the totality of their synthesis, reveal in-
     trinsic value. Analysis pushed far enough will
     even exhibit purely economic characters. If you
     analyze moral conduct (assuming it to be an in-
     trinsic good) you will in the last resort find
     bodily movements in a physical environment.
     Analysis of an aesthetic experience may lead down
     through proportion and harmony to patches of pig-
     ment, which may be in turn dissolved into their
     chemical constituents. To a purely analytical
     thinker it must remain a sheer mystery that these

278

its most essential feature. And yet, only by such a
denial can the transcendent character of that norm by
which evil becomes conspicuous as such be avoided.

It will be appreciated that any descriptivist account of evil must be rejected by the nature of this
paper's thesis. Simply to write off evil as identical with the disasters of nature or the violence of
man or the ravages of disease or the suppression of mi-
norities is precisely to fall into the trap of what
above has been designated a variant of the "naturalistic fallacy." That is to say (again), we know what
all of these things are and they can be described quite
exhaustively without having recourse to the notion of
evil. But if recourse to the notion of evil is irre-
sistibly thrust upon us upon the occasions of these
experiences, it is only because we are being compelled
to recognize a transcendent dimension of conceptually
apprehended reality.

Evil: a privation. It is appropriate to give
recognition to a further characteristic believed to
belong to that notion of the good that has been sig-
nalled by beginning with the sense of evil. Evil is
nothing in itself. That is to say, evil is not substantively real. One cannot isolate evil as one can
presumably isolate a microscopic organism. Yet evil
cannot be denied. All of this has been taken to mean
that evil--like error--is to be considered a privation. The positive reality of which evil is a privation is the good.[57] And it is this good that performs

---

products of analysis should have anything at all
to do with intrinsic value. What can he do but
deny that they have and consign value to feeling?" "The mystery remains," Mure adds, "until
it is seen that pure analysis does not lead towards the essential nature of the intrinsically
good (or to anything else), but away from it
towards some fragmentary abstraction." G. R. G.
Mure, Op. cit., pp. 173-174.

57. "I have contended," G. R. G. Mure writes, "...
that science is the privation and not the mere
absence of value." Ibid., p. 183. This is but
another way of saying that though value cannot be
identified with empirical reduction, neither can

a transcendent function in moral valuation and is apprehended conceptually only. As has been stated, the knowledge of this good arises upon the occasion of experience but cannot be reduced to it. But this transcendent, conceptually apprehended, norm of good performs such a function as to deserve a recognition that in turn confers upon it an added revelation of character. It is because this norm of the good exercises a role of correction, of approbation, of condemnation, of positive mandate, as touching the affairs of man, that its recognition for a philosophy of moral value may be said to be entirely relevant and philosophically fruitful. It is a mandate directed to persons. These combined considerations may be said to fortify the conclusion that this same dimension of transcendent reality, this positive norm of moral value, is therefore itself personal. God is thus introduced as the fuller characterization of those presuppositions believed necessary to give adequate account of the moral dimension.[58]

In summation, therefore, we may say that moral value transcends experience and must do so in order to preserve its normative function. Moral value is of the nature of a universal. It is a norm that so far transcends particulars as to qualify as the ideal by which they are identified as belonging or not belonging to moral value; as the ideal by which particular acts are corrected, interpreted, reproved; as the ideal that introduces and preserves the distinction between the "is" of description and the "ought" of an entirely different dimension. This moral norm may be

---

it be _disjoined_. The _conjunction_ witnesses to the transcendence.

58. G. R. G. Mure sees in "moral action the will of the singular individual...actively identified with a will which is beyond him as well as within him, with a will, that is, which at once constitutes the individual as a moral agent and constitutes itself in and as the individual." Mure adds, "...to ascribe moral value to anything which is less than this self-transcendence leads in the end, so far as I can see, to absurdity." _Ibid._, pp. 178-179.

said to "suffer abstraction" from particulars precisely in the sense that it lifts the conceptually apprehended essence of the moral acts from their several differences and, in the manner of all universals, clarifies the principle by which the many relate to their one.[59] The <u>real</u> status of the moral-value universal is guaranteed in the same way that all universals are guaranteed, <u>viz</u>., by noting that they begin with undisputed reals and in abstracting from the plurality the essential character of each preserves thereby their own true nature. That moral discourse is indeed involved with 'undisputed reals' is what is believed shown by the assumption of univocity in the moral predicates of ethical discourse.

In the same vein, we may also consider <u>ideals</u>. If, within the context of moral value, ideals are moral values, then ideals, too, may be considered universals, because, as we have seen, moral value is a universal. In Taylor's words,

---

59. Because "abstraction" sometimes suggests an invidious connotation, it is well to counter by noting that values <u>as</u> <u>abstractions</u> <u>introduce</u> <u>the</u> <u>status</u> <u>of</u> <u>universals.</u> It is the characteristic-denominated "transcendent"--that has generated the suspicion that we are dealing here with a certain kind of abstraction--an abstraction that has no greater reality than the words used to witness to the feeling evoked. Thus, values and ideals are regarded as less than participant in an objectively real world. We ask, therefore, are values and ideals mere abstraction, unreal, mere words--<u>flatus</u> <u>vocis</u>--with no objective status? The question is reminiscent of the mediaeval controversy between the realists and the nominalists. This paper favors the realists and affirms that universals are real and that their reality is virtually guaranteed by the particularized reals that they are called upon to unify. Thus, <u>abstraction</u>, rather than becoming a term of disrepute, is a term that designates the nature common to the particulars. The universal may then be said to have been "drawn away" from the particulars in the sense that their common and essential property was recognized and conceptualized. If, then, one <u>begins</u> <u>with</u> <u>particulars</u>, the reality of

It is fundamental to the view I am trying to present that there should be no division of the knowable into two disjunct realms, one of the merely real or actual, and another of ideals, or values, or goods.[60]

As in the case of moral value in general, ideals aim at concretizing human values, of regarding them as truly belonging to some situation wherein their intrinsically felt worth may know actualization, where, in short, moral value and the existential person may be joined in the final mode of that situation to which man's already felt aspiration tended. It is the nature of an ideal that it is capable of being realized by that person to whom it is an ideal. In distinction to value-norms and ideals that reflect man's historical preoccupation with ideas of moral worth and justice, the only ideals or values that are totally worthless abstractions are those that in principle cannot be applied to some realization, that cannot know that fruition of conjunction with persons, and wherein the aspiring individual person cannot be sealed with that value that is the central hope of his aspiration. Where moral value is given serious consideration, ideals should easily be seen to conjoin with the actual. They become the refined goal of moral endeavor, the truest form by which moral excellence is identified and interpreted. Values in the abstract are either nothing at all, or they serve merely analytically to give--as Taylor said--a clear and distinct idea of the first principles of the specific value that is under consideration. That is to say, a value not conjoined to an existent is unreal save for the possible clarity performed in analysis.

---

which is not questioned, draws away from them that essential characteristic by the aid of which the true sameness is recognized, names that characteristic as the universal uniquely appropriate to their interpretation and identity, then the imagined difficulty of conceding real status to the universal with which one ends should disappear.

60. Alfred Edward Taylor, "Is Goodness a Quality?" ARISTOTELIAN SOCIETY, Supplementary Volume XI (1932), p. 155.

It is, of course, a natural transition to a hypostatization of this locus of ideal moral value. Such
a locus is more than a focal point for the consciousness of aspiring man; it is also a locus of moral mandate. The moral obedience of persons can only be commanded by personality. As surely as the analysis of
moral value takes us into a transcendent dimension,
just as surely is the further character of that locus
of transcendent value revealed. Only by the resolute
denial of all meaning to ethical imperatives can the
dialectical itinerary of the mind be stopped short of
the further postulation of God. Such, traditionally,
it is recognized, has been the moral argument for the
existence of God. Much--perhaps its entire force--
rests upon how seriously we take the moral imperative
as it has given evidence of its existence throughout
what is virtually the entirety of human history.

PART III - RATIONALITY

Effort has been expended in Parts I and II preceding to indicate that experience, analyzed under
general epistemology and moral value, is not a self-
contained affair, but rather shows the clearest evidence of being in dependence upon a larger dimension--
called transcendent. It would appear that in view of
the interpretative and evaluative effort that accompanied this examination of the alleged immanent transcendental in moral and general epistemology that some
attention should now be given to rationality itself
which has been throughout presupposed. It would appear further that attention should be paid to the relation that rationality sustains to moral value, the relation of both in the hierarchy of being, and the nature of that apex of the hierarchy that is disclosed
by virtue of the dual relation of moral value and
rationality in the total structure.

Rationality, like the norm of the ethical dimension, protests reduction to the base ingredients of
experience that it is by its very nature called upon
to judge. It cannot be "naturalized" for what are
fundamentally the same reasons that hold for all norms
whatever, viz., the loss of critical function. It is
the function of rationality to interpret experience,
to decide upon the truth of proffered propositions, to

evaluate the claimed validity of conclusions. Because of these responsibilities, rationality must be regarded as _above_ the experience that it is called upon thus to interpret.

Essentially, this was seen to be the position taken by Taylor in Chapters V and VI. In a manner somewhat differing in detail from what immediately follows, but carrying the same message of _transcendence_, the position was taken that rationality cannot be "naturalized" without losing its critical function.

If this consideration is valid, rationality must either be abandoned, or it must be elevated to a transcendent position. But, it is virtually the total testimony of humankind that rationality is an essential attribute of their being. It is the undeviating presupposition that accompanies discourse irrespective of the subject. A presumption is thereby created that we are nearer the truth about man and his universe when we concede to such an undeviating assumption its objective position in reality and its normative claim upon human experience than when we resolutely deny to rationality this eminence. That rationality can be employed at pragmatic levels is granted; this, however, merely postpones the question of its nature, its status, and the ground of its authority. It must remain a genuine philosophic question what sort of world it is that permits the ubiquitous presence of a normative value-system which is in some sense independent of the experience it investigates, evaluates, and interprets. It would constitute such a wrench to experience to attempt the resolute abandonment of rationality and putting that abandonment into the practice of human living as would be equivalent to a total disintegration of human society.

The conclusion would appear to be that in recognizing that both moral value and rational value are necessarily to be spared reduction to the experience that they are called upon to interpret and evaluate, we are clearly conceding to them transcendent status. It but remains to see how this supra-experiential status identifies with the apex of reality's hierarchical structure and, more particularly, what character is conferred upon this apex in virtue of the identification.

Rationality, though shared by individuals, is
everywhere assumed to be perfectly univocal. The perfection of form, continuous throughout all individual
persons, is unmarred by being the immanent force that
it is. It is these multiplied characteristics--tran-
scendent in function though immanent in availability,
objective to that which it interprets, conceptually
monistic--that create a strong presumption that a personal hypostatization of rationality would at the least
be strongly suggested.

The hierarchy--in being and epistemology. This
hierarchical arrangement with the apex identified with
personality ought not appear as a mere alternative to
a philosophy of moral value that takes the categorical
imperative seriously. Even for Kant--it may be af-
firmed--the hypothetical imperative is not really a
moral imperative. The "if, ...then" type of argument
is no more applicable in a philosophy that takes morality seriously than it is in a mathematics that takes
rationality seriously. The Cartesian principle that
we may learn the enabling and illuminating presupposition of the absolute by paying attention to the implicit insufficiency and privation of experience will
either be confessed, or the alternative of being driven to a philosophic nihilism be suffered. The
diesseitigkeit Philosophie must yield to a jenseitigkeit Philosophie if it does justice to its own ability to recognize the limitations of experience. Behind the mathematics of probability there is the
mathematics of necessity, behind the disunity of percepts there is the unity of concept, behind all flux
there is the implied constant; in short, behind the
many there is the one. The principle by which the
existential-many preserves and directs itself is not
given in the observed instance and, unless every dependence upon the law of sufficient reason is abandoned, one is forced above the existential plurality
of a phenomenalistic empiricism to a transcendent
principle in which is found the fulfillment of what
otherwise remains a mere 'insufficiency and privation
of experience.'

The more precise structure within what has been
called the hierarchy of being should be made explicit.
Certain logical designations have been mentioned--
called categories--that compose the hierarchical structure with which this paper's concern has dealt. Thus,

being, rationality, moral value, having been specifically named, their relation to each other should be made clear.

It has already been made sufficiently clear that being is considered both a meaningful category and the most ultimate category in actuality and in conceptuality. Behind being one cannot go; as far as being one must go. Next, rationality must be given place. Without outside information, one might think of being as non-rational. But one cannot think of rationality without some ground. If we are forced to grant rationality, we are forced to make it belong somewhere. It does not carry its being in the concept of rationality itself although it demands that being in order to offer a full account of rationality. Moral value, would be in the third position from the apex of being. It is safely placed there because it must make use of rationality in order to give account of itself.

No account need be nor can be given of being itself--other, that is, than that it is that ultimate category without which no word is ever really fully accounted for. Rationality would appear to enjoy a similar sovereignty were it not for the fact that the concept of rationality does not carry the ground of its being within the concept. Is it the world that is rational? Is it the universe that is rational? Is reality rational? Is God rational? The point here is that whatever it is that is the ground of rationality, that ground is not rationality itself. Hence, the dependency of rationality. And moral value follows a similar reasoning. To begin, the ground of moral value is not given in the concept of moral value. Neither is the ground of moral value to be found in the rational category above it--although the rational category must be depended upon to evaluate the truth-claims or the validity-claims that may arise within ethical discourse. But the ground of moral value must go on through to being itself. Thus, moral value is dependent in a certain sense upon rationality; rationality is likewise dependent upon being; being is dependent upon nothing but its own nature. But because the ultimate dependency of moral value is upon being, as we have seen, an argument for God (conceived as ultimate Being) is possible from moral value itself. Similarly, because the ultimate dependency of rationality is upon being, as we have seen, an argument for God

286

(conceived as ultimate Being) is possible from rationality itself. Moral value will make use of rationality and--so to speak--carry rationality with it in its
proper rise to the apex which supplies its uniquely
validating norms. Rationality, similarly, grounds in
the apex, but, being above moral value in the hierarchy, does not carry moral value with it.

In the above discussion of the places that are
held in the hierarchy of being of moral value and rationality, it must be remembered that the ultimate
category of being is not conceived as fragmented or
suffering real division. It may very well be the case
that value generally, including rationality, is coextensive with all that ultimate being is. The distinctions, therefore, are not ontological, but logical,
and correspond to the ways that the mind moves upward
systematically to grasp the attributes of being in
their relation to each other. Even in the classical
notion of God as a Being in whom there are no parts or
divisions and where each attribute is infinite and
eternal, even in this case, the mind demands the being
of God as a necessary condition for the meaningful as-
cription of attributes. The fact of ontological inseparability does not prevent logical separability. And
doubtless it is the fact of ontological inseparability
that gives to the formula "the real is the rational
and the rational is the real" such truth as it can
claim.

A Weltanschauung. It is acknowledged that in this
Chapter, as in Chapter VIII, and, indeed, in much of
the argument of Taylor himself, there is a wide-ranging
appeal that moves frequently enough far beyond the narrower concerns of moral value to the entire range of
epistemology as touching upon cosmological, teleological, axiological, and ontological concepts. This appears almost inevitable in the sense that the apex of
the argument from moral value is at the same time the
apex of the arguments from the other considerations as
well. It may be claimed therefore that the wider
range of appeal gives support to the narrower concern
of moral value in the sense that the apex of the argument from moral value is not isolated from that fuller
world-view that knows no alternative to a harmony in
principle of the multivaried aspects of reality. As
we have seen with regard to pluralism, there appears
to be an enforced frustration practiced when by

definition or initial resolve on the part of the philosopher the parts are refused the possibility of subsumption under any order of higher relation. So it is
with the attempts to keep arguments that begin with
that single aspect of real experience--moral value--
separated ultimately and utterly from considerations
of the rational, the esthetic, the empirical, the ontological. Probably the overlap with the rational is
the first that meets the eye: the province of moral
value must conform to consistency and coherence; esthetic consideration may appear in emphasis on form, in
recurrent patterns, in emphasis placed on balance,
symmetry, perspective; or, to overlap categories, one
might find esthetic approval in the harmony of a moral
adjustment, or perhaps in a context of logic where the
postulational field is neither too great nor too small
to accomodate the theorems that are deduced therefrom.
Too, we have seen clearly enough that knowledge of the
moral dimension begins with experience, and the ones
to whom the experience belongs belong to the order of
being. So it is not a careless wandering over the entire province of philosophy that is being engaged in
when the subject of moral value is announced and then
it is discovered that all reality has become involved;
indeed, in any philosophy that takes the unity of
reality as impossible to avoid and ontological considerations as assumptions too fundamental to ignore, the
adequate account of any part is ultimately to be an appeal to the whole in its interrelations.

     The above remarks on the hierarchical structure
of the categories that logically comprise being are
intended to provide reason why moral-value categories
should eventually be made to join rational categories
and both to point to the character of being that is
illuminated by this dialectic.

     Part II of this chapter and Chapter IV endeavor
to speak convincingly of time as the "form" of the
life of moral endeavor. The argument whereby man's
constant search for values that lie always in his future and thus the intimate relation of time's passing
to his "conative" disposition need not be further remarked here. But it is now fundamental to the argument to note that every interpretation of the conative
function of man is an interpretation that borrows from
the categories of rationality and being. If time is
the "form" of the moral life, rationality is an even

more prior "form" because it is presupposed in every attitude that is taken towards moral value. One starts with the intimate relation of a moral endeavor that assimilates time in the pursuit of its ends; second, there is the higher category of rationality that interprets and evaluates this total endeavor; and, lastly, there is being beyond both moral value and rationality: the inspiring goal of the endeavor and the most ultimate category of all.

So great is the tendency to separate these categories--thus providing abstractionism with its partial and necessarily inconsistent account of reality--that a reintroduction to the interrelation and functional unity should prove fruitful as an account of philosophy's genuine concerns. It would appear to be very wrong to ignore the intimacy that exists between moral endeavor and time. It appears to be equally wrong to ignore the almost too obvious fact that no interpretation or evaluation of moral endeavor is without the application of the rational category. And because, as declared above, the rational category--certain conditions being stipulated[61]leads eventually to an acknowledgement of being, confidence may be generated that our understanding of moral categories will lead us through rational categories to a concrete universal the fuller character of which will have been supplied by the very subordinate categories employed to reach that ultimate position.

---

61.   These stipulated conditions are here given merely formal recognition--the substance of them having been incorporated into the general argument. They are: (1) rationality is "outside" of nature; otherwise it could not possess the critical function necessary to interpret nature; (2) rationality is one; there are not several rationalities; and (3) rationality has its ground in being. Analogous to moral value, rationality in the abstract gives only a clear and distinct idea of a formal principle; it comes into its own only when conjoined to a concrete situation. Thus, we speak of a rational person, a rational solution, a rational universe. But rationality, lifted above all particularizations, may be presumed to ground behind all particularizations--that is to say, in being.

The hierarchy-in-brief with which we are here concerned has indicated the dependence of moral value on rationality. This is due to the fact that rationality interprets its various claims. Then rationality itself was declared dependent on being which is the ultimate category. The argument toward this ultimate being and the ensuing character which it will bear has been chiefly from moral value.

But there is a different approach to this ultimate being and its proper characterization: the way of rationality itself. And, because both ways end with the same ultimate being--(there can only be one)--it is in order to recall some of the reasons for thinking that rationality does indeed perform that same itinerary for the human spirit.

The priority of the rational in the hierarchy of attributes of being appears guaranteed by that very need that discourse evidences. Regardless of the subject, the honoring of consistency and coherence and obedience to the law of contradiction are always presupposed--in ideal if not in practice. The penalty paid for repudiation of rational procedure would be the total absence of evaluation in any and every field. In such an extreme position, the repudiation itself could not be evaluated and could not be defended. One could still fight, but one could not evaluate the moral worth of the cause nor defend any reason for either continuing the fight or abandoning it. Even in esthetics, where the temptation to lapse in an attitude of subjectivism and relativism is great, even here, exposition and commentary and analysis are too seriously indulged to permit the thought that any and every proposition employed in the effort is actually of no greater worth than its contradictory. Such considerations show the top priority that is given to rationality.

Augustine, it is believed, obeyed a true philosophic impulse when he placed the Ideas of Plato within the personality of God. For Plato, the Ideas were the supreme principles of intelligibility, but they were not causal and they were not intelligent. A common interpretation of Plato is that he had to invent the demiurge, an architect of the world of space-time, to supply both causal force and intelligence. Now, either this reintroduces another example of an unstable dualism, or we must interpret Plato as unconsciously aiming at the ultimate identification of rationality, will, and being. For Augustine, ultimate being was from the beginning identified with intelligence and will. And in this identification, Augustine did not have to sacrifice any truth that belong to the Platonic insistence that the Ideas (the universals) were the supreme principles of intelligibility. For Plato, there could be no knowledge except through the aid of these eternal universals. But the universals themselves did not know this. In Augustine, one might say, the universals know the world. The wording may be awkward but the idea of a reciprocal rationality is introduced into the world-view.

At the level of human experience, there is much to suggest a harmony with this high-level view of ultimate reality. Much of scientific formulization suggests the need for a rising hierarchy of subordinate generalizations which, in its turn, suggests an ideal generalization--the apex of the hierarchical structure defended in this chapter.

With the suggestion becoming stronger, developing, that the apex of the hierarchy may be identified with personality, with will, with rationality, a further possibility occurs, viz., that the totality of reality, wherever encountered, is either itself rational or is penetrable by the advance of rational techniques and analyses. This might be said to be a sort of prediction, a deduction from the hypothesis that in the last analysis ultimate reality is itself personal and rational and, therefore, all cases of subordinate reality must partake of this essential attribute. The 'prediction' in narrower compass would be that rational man in his approach to reality in any of her forms would be unconsciously committed to the optimism that reality will never turn an opaque side to his approaches. This is what we might call the faith of the scientific investigator. It appears clear among the difficulties that he cannot help but encounter in his investigation of empirical reality there is never the difficulty of the impossible. That is to say, reality is to the practicing, the theoretical attitude of the investigator always in principle penetrable to the approach of rational procedure. This is altogether remarkable; it is not merely that man has not learned where his limitations are: he appears to be incapable of even conceiving such an absolute limit as the utterly impenetrable would have to be. And this might well be called an "observation-statement" predicted by the above hypothesis: if, in the nature of the case, there is no part of reality that is not penetrable in principle by rational analysis, the practicing optimism on the part of the investigator (the "observation-statement") is thoroughly harmonious with that larger--and transcendent!--fact.[62]

---

62. I have borrowed the phrase "observation-statement" from Copleston who, in endeavoring to meet a demand of the logical positivist, remarks as follows: "let us suppose that I make the statement that God exists. I am then challenged to show that the statement is empirically verifiable, by deriving from it an observation statement, that is, some statement which is empirically verifiable, at least in principle. Let us suppose that I answer, 'If God exists, there will be order in the world.' We can then see if there is in fact order in the world. It is to be noted that I am not suggesting that the statement that God exists implies logically the statement that there is order in the world. The reason that I derive the statement that God exists is that, as far as philosophic knowledge of God is concerned, I come to knowledge of God through reflection on some aspect of or factor in empirical reality. Supposing, then, that my philosophic reason for accepting God's existence is reflection on the order in the world. I can offer the statement that there is an order in the world as an empirically verifiable statement, which is derivable (not logically, but in view of the empirical origin of our ideas concerning reality) from the statement that God exists. It is open, of course, to an opponent to say that one cannot justifiably conclude to God's existence from the order in the world; but we are not now discussing the truth of the statement that God exists so much as the meaningfulness of the statement. And if the logical positivist would accept this sort of empirical verification, there would not be much reason for quarreling with his criterion. If it were not for reflection on empirical reality I should never

292

The world-view that has emerged from the above considerations is one with rationality predominating as a marked feature. Indeed, as intimated, it apparently cannot even be conceived that there is a situation which, in principle, frustrates by its very nature the advance of rational penetration.

It remains to remind ourselves of the intimate connection that the notion of the rational sustains to words like "reason," "judgment," "intelligence,"-- even "wisdom." This near-synonymity, taken together with the universality of rationality, now reveals with even greater plausibility the fact of a theistically-dominated universe. If the governing principle of all investigation of any aspect of reality is rationality, and if reality appears ever open to receive that same governing principle, there appears to remain no obstacle to the meaningful possibility of a theistic philosophy.[63]

---

come, as far as philosophic thought is concerned, to postulate the existence of any being transcending direct experience; and, if anyone wishes to start with the statement of the existence of such a being and challenges me to 'derive' an observation-statement, I can always offer him one of the propositions concerning empirical reality which originally led me to postulate the existence of the being in question. Indeed, the logical positivist would be quite right in demanding the production of an observation-statement or an empirically verifiable statement. And he would be right because human philosophic knowledge of the metaphenomenal must be acquired in another way." Copleston, CONTEMPORARY PHILOSOPHY, pp. 41-42. I would add that if there is any reason at all for going from nature to God, there is thereby established some reason to go from God to nature. Much depends upon the first transition, but, if valid, the idea of an "observation-statement" seems to be a not unreasonable claim.

63. Note might be taken here of the distinction between the logical and the chronological awareness of norms. Because it may appear that God has been allowed to make a very tardy appearance, it may be helpful to remark that in principle everything

A remark is called for with relation to the word "wisdom" that appeared above. Wisdom is more than knowledge; it is more than intelligence; it is different in some sense from rationality. Yet, in another sense, it belongs to all three. The difference deserves mention in a paper that is much concerned with the explication of moral value. Wisdom contains value-overtones. Wisdom is not to be considered dispossessed of rational insight, but the value-factor possessed by wisdom performs a guidance-function, a selection-operation, a discrimination among possible ends. Nor is this function of wisdom a merely subjective, personal, characteristic; rather in conformity with moral value generally, it presupposes that, in principle at least, its judgments are conformable to that objectivity in moral valuation that is the universally accepted presupposition of univocity in ethical discourse.

----

that has been argued up to this point has been in dependence upon God as the ultimate presupposition of whatever value there is. The chronological appearance of God in the course of an argument's development does not offset the logical dependence on God that has been the enabling and implicit premise of the entire effort. Such is believed to have been the principle operative in the famous contest with doubt in the MEDITATIONS of Descartes. While minutes by the clock ticked away before the announcement that God exists was heard, still the very first affirmation of the existence of a finite self already (for Descartes) carried the implicitly enabling and illuminating knowledge of infinity by the logical aid of which finitude was discerned as such. Thus, contrary to popular exposition, it is God which is the logical first of the argument of the MEDITATIONS --although God may have been a chronological second in the order of announcement and commentary. As Frederick Copleston remarks, "...what the philosopher does is to make explicit the relation of finite reality to infinite transcendent Being." Ibid., p. 5. The Cartesian dialectic is merely one way of the many ways by which the relation of finite to infinite reality is argued.

Wisdom, therefore, carries a special importance for a thesis that has everywhere maintained that ethical and rational norms cannot be forever separated.

Closely related to the prohibition imposed by logical positivism that one cannot go beyond experience is another warning that relates to the use of analogical language. Specifically, it would be alleged that there can be no genuine meaning preserved in the attempts to speak of "the mind of man" and "the mind of God," "a human architect" and "a divine architect." It is not that the allegations that purport to go beyond experience are false; they are declared to be simply without any meaning at all. Experience--in the narrowed sense of the word--having been abandoned, there is no meaningful way in which truth can be ascertained, no preservation of verifiability. Indeed, Immanuel Kant sounded the warning in his own way when he observed that Plato, feeling the restriction of the world of sense, ventured out beyond--not noting that he was getting nowhere![64] Copleston observes that

> ...the critique of metaphysical and theological propositions from a linguistic point of view has meant the reintroduction into modern philosophy of a consideration of the analogical language of metaphysics and theology. And the very fact that the criticism has sometimes taken a radical form should stimulate metaphysicians to make a more thorough investigation of analogical language and its various types than has yet been made.[65]

The break with radical empiricism which this paper has regarded as inevitable constitutes at the same time a possible healing of the same breach that analogical language has been designed to overcome. The defect with an attempted radical empiricism was precisely that it could not supply the principle of its own unification, nor could it supply the norms without which it lost its critical function, nor could it give an adequate account of its internal relations.

---

64.   Immanuel Kant, "Introduction," THE CRITIQUE OF PURE REASON.

65.   Copleston, Op. cit., p. 12.

Empiricism, therefore, is convicted of being in perpetual dependence upon an extra-experiential reality. This has been denominated the element of transcendence attendant upon the fuller account of experience. Further, because certain elements of this extra-experiential involvement cannot become "naturalized" under pain of losing their normative function, and, seeing that this normative principle is both universal and necessary to an accounting of experience, the distance has been further increased between the narrowest aspect of experience possible and those 'norms on which the meaning of experience depends.' Now, because this domain of the 'norms on which the meaning of experience depends,' is itself a part of reality, it would appear that language must be prepared to move across the line set by any of the narrower aspects of experience to that other reality on which experience depends for its meaning. When language does this, it is being employed analogically. A severe bind is placed upon the future of philosophy when analogical language is refused; it appears to signal another refusal, viz., that of recognizing the different levels of being. No qualitative difference can remain between the mineral, the vegetable, the animal, and man, other than such differences as can be detected descriptively and empirically. And though the normative principles by which experience is interpreted are everywhere employed--such has been the contention of this paper-- they are nowhere explained or justified.

It is recognized that analogy endeavors to make the best of two worlds. It contains within its meaning something of sameness and something of difference. But, if our recognition of being as an ultimate category is justified, it is from this being that the sameness is derived. And if the differences of the world cannot be denied, it is to these differences that analogy simultaneously appeals. Meaning may not be allowed to claim only sameness: one could only say the same thing about everything; nor can meaning be permitted to recognize only difference: one could not say the same thing about anything. In both of these extremes, epistemology comes to an end. But an epistemology that permits itself the use of a sameness that runs through differences satisfies a necessary condition for a meaningful epistemology. And this is the province of analogy in prediction. It would appear that discreteness is not ultimate: no two things

are utterly dissimilar; neither does it appear that
sameness is all that there is: no two things are identical with each other. If this accurately describes
the situation that exists in reality, it is necessary
and proper that a word be given that satisfies that
peculiar dualism. The word is analogy.

W. G. de Burgh is restless before the spectre of
anthropomorphism which he feels arises in the wake of
Taylor's use of analogical argument. He writes,

> While we are wholly with him /Taylor7 in his de-
> sire...to secure positive knowledge of God, we
> feel a little uneasy at his silence on the diffi-
> culties that beset his path. There is a need of
> a criterion of such analogies, to save from ille-
> gitimate anthropomorphism: and where can the cri-
> terion be found? ...What we seem to need is an
> attribute possessed alike by God and man in wide-
> ly differing measure, but without difference in
> kind. We cannot assert this either of goodness
> or of intelligence or of power.[66]

There may indeed be such a thing as an "illegitimate anthropomorphism" and it would be conformable to
the thesis of this paper to identify such illegitimacy with the suppression of one of the halves that make
up a proper doctrine of analogy. That is to say, to
eliminate all differences between God and man--or to
eliminate all differences between God and anything
else--is to encroach upon illegitimacy. This is, of
course, to admit some sense of sameness between God
and man. I think that this cannot be avoided. Even
from the point of view of a Jewish or Christian ortho-
doxy, it would be very wrong to deny that there is at
least as much reality in God as there is in any creature. Although there are attempts at times to protect
the being of God by affirming that he is "altogether
other," such an extreme position steers directly into
a practical atheism.[67] It would be precisely this

---

66. W. G. de Burgh, Op. cit., PHILOSOPHY, VI (1931),
    p. 235.

67. In the DIALOGUES CONCERNING NATURAL RELIGION by
    David Hume, Demea is made to say, "The question
    is not concerning the being, but the nature of

<u>sort</u> of distance placed between God and man that would <u>make</u> totally unintelligible <u>any</u> theology.

In the attempted statement above--sympathetic to a meaningful doctrine of analogy at the lateral level of experience--it was declared that something of sameness and something of difference was essential to what is customarily included in the meaning of analogy. It is now further affirmed that this must hold at the "vertical" level with the result that between God and experience there must be some sameness along with the difference. It would appear that only if atheism is in fact the truth would it be possible to escape the recognition of <u>being</u> as, in some sense, inclusive of God and the world. There is simply no meaning left in human vocabularies that permits the absolute disjunction of God from the world and still hopes meaningfully to affirm that in some sense both participate in being.[68] Copleston explains,

> We have to use "human language," because we have no other; and human language is not properly fitted to deal adequately with what lies outside the sphere of our normal experience; we have to use human language "analogically"; and the question is whether such analogical language is to be admitted as significant. It seems to me that the logical positivists interpret "meaning" univocally; and I see no adequate reason for doing so.[69]

God. This I affirm, from the infirmities of human understanding, to be altogether incomprehensible and unknown to us." /Part II7 To this, Cleanthes later replies, "...how do you mystics, who maintain the absolute incomprehensibility of the Deity, differ from sceptics or atheists, who assert, that the first cause of all is unknown and unintelligible?" /Part IV7

68. There is an extant challenge--perhaps correctly attributed to Spinoza--that the church and the synagogue have <u>taught</u> the absolute difference between world-substance and God-substance, but cannot <u>think</u> the difference!

69. Frederick Copleston, <u>Op</u>. <u>cit</u>., p. 39.

It is the contention of this paper that there is in fact good reason to oppose the "univocal" reduction of meaning. It is this reduction that prepares for the charge above that "No qualitative difference can remain between the mineral, the vegetable, the animal, and man, other than such differences as can be detected descriptively and empirically." It is in the wake of this "univocal" reduction of meaning that classical recognitions of purpose, rationality, ethical norms, and the self (as independent of its reported experiences) have been denied as possessing transcendent significance and have been reduced to a description of the movements of the body.

To return, then, to the difficulty remarked by de Burgh, viz.,

> What we seem to need is an attribute possessed alike by God and man in widely differing measure, but without difference in kind. We cannot assert this either of goodness or of intelligence or of power.

Conformable to the tenor of this paper, there can be but one answer to this assumed difficulty. If the conclusion cannot be avoided that in some meaningful sense the being of God and the being of man possess a sameness, then, ipso facto, it may be affirmed that in the same meaningful sense the attributes of the being of God and the being of man possess a sameness. This, as we have seen, is not to deny differences: thus, we do not commit an illegitimate anthropomorphism; but, neither is sameness denied: thus, we do not sever identities that must be affirmed.

Acknowledgement has been made of tendencies to regard meaning as univocal and the existents of the world as qualitatively one. It would appear that it is precisely this assumption that so unfits one even to understand what a doctrine of analogy is attempting to say. Indeed, this dual assumption would virtually render meaningless a doctrine of analogy which depends upon a range of being--with its corresponding range of meaning--and which exhibits an entire spectrum of qualitative differences. The mood is reminiscent of the Bentham-Mill controversy over the quantification of pleasure and pain. There is something tempting about the simplification of a quantification reduction--even though it does appear to steer rather definitely away

from what human experience declares to be true; and
conversely, there is something more recognizable as
belonging to human experience in the suggestion of
Mill that there are qualitative differences in the
range of pleasures and pains--even though the concession does appear to demolish the hope of a scientific
formula.

If the spectrum of differences at the lateral level of human experience is viewed as exhibiting qualitative differences, any attempt to combine those acknowledged differences with the sameness that they also exhibit is to employ analogy. With this approach, the
classical recognitions of purpose, rationality, ethical norms, and the self, may be given a place in relation to experience that does not force these categories into a reduction to movements of bodies; if, however, this concession of qualitative difference is not
made, the resulting homogeneity of the totality of reality must severely inhibit the prospect of justifying
the use of such normative principles as have traditionally been viewed as necessarily distinct from that to
which their normative functions are applied.

The conjunction of value and existence. Preparation for that ultimate identification of the apex of
moral value and God is found in that of an everyday experience. It will hardly be disputed that in the normal use of value-predicates we intend the conjunction
of the specific value with some existent. Thus, we
speak quite naturally and quite unconsciously of the
rational order of things, of the beauty of the specific form, of the health of the body, of the moral worth
of the action. And it is precisely in this natural
conjoining of value with existents that we find the
strong and fruitful hint of both the fact and the meaning of the proposition being defended. The continuance
of the normal conjunctions of value and existence that
we daily make hints strongly of a natural affinity
that value and existence bear, and, conversely, this
persistent conjunction would be almost inevitably considered infinitely improbable if their conjunction
were no more than purely coincidental. If, indeed,
this conjunction of value with existence is determined
by the larger nature of reality--as Taylor holds--our
natural disposition to invest existence with value-
predicates significantly harmonizes with that very
fact. It provides (again) a sort of "observation

300

statement" harmonious with the claims of the hypothesis.

Value and existence: conjunction but not identity. Paradoxically, though on one hand one finds the most naturally assumed conjunction of value and existence, amounting to the suspicion that values are qualities inherent in particular existences, on the other hand, one cannot by deliberate analysis of particular existences find the value therein embedded or entailed. The former is what we mean by never finding value except as conjoined to fact; the latter is what we mean by not being able to argue straightaway from actuality to value. And by insisting upon these paradoxical positions as simultaneously true, the mind is lifted by the applied dialectic to the meaning of the allegation that a conjunction with existence is implied in all value-predication. It is precisely this enforced recognition of a conjunction that is not an identity that is the key to the relation of value to existence maintained by this paper. If we exclude the consideration of divine purpose for (say) a pebble, value is not immediately brought before the mind upon the appearance of this pebble.[70] In that sense, the value-existence relation is not mutually implicative. But, if one begins with a value, then some existent must be recognized as being the necessary condition for the meaningful use of valuation. But the value cannot be inferred from the existent even though it cannot be affirmed without some existent to which it may be said to belong.

---

70. Even the existent implies a value if theistic purpose is admitted. Working from the existential end of the relation, it would have to be an existent entirely devoid of any interest to anyone in order not to witness the recurrent conjunction of value. And if, in accordance with the theistic position, there is active purposive interest on the part of a controlling intelligence for the totality of existents, the value of the existent and the purpose of the existent are interwoven so inextricably as virtually to imply their identity and with that identity the further implication that the existent itself implies a value identical with its purpose as interpreted by the divine intention.

Without wishing at this point to defend the entire epistemology of Kant, it is nevertheless an aid
to understanding this our value-thesis by using his
phrases. Thus it is that the whole declared insight
of a dimension of reality that crowds in upon the narrower reductions of experience is illustrative of what
is here defended with respect to value. There is something about the values broadly identified with rational, esthetic, and moral categories that cannot be identified with the descriptive aspect of experience which
they are called upon to measure, to interpret, to validate. It is this going beyond the radically attempted
reductions of experience as a necessity for the preservation of meaningful experience that exhibits the native barrenness of a so-called pure or consistent empiricism.

The loose relation then between values and existents is understandable even as it need not be conceded in the sense that the relativist would claim. As
long as specific values are not entailed by existents
in the sense that specific properties of a triangle
are entailed by the conception of triangularity, it appears clear that these same values may be denied without denying the existent. Thus, it may be affirmed or
denied that a specific act is a moral act. It may be
affirmed or denied that Coleridge's waterfall was sub-
lime. Thus, uncertainty comes not from a limitless
freedom to affirm or deny values, but from an ignorance
of whether or not the subject in question does indeed
participate in the class of values denominated moral
or esthetic. With such limitations imposed upon our
ability to determine always and with accuracy what particulars are deserving of being identified with these
overarching value-categories, it is understandable that
values may be denied to specific existential situations
without contradiction. But the real question is whether such values may be reaffirmed without predicating
them of existents at all?

The ultimate conjunction. Although values, therefore, are capable of being dismissed on strictly empirical grounds, they are not thought to suffer the same
dismissal when a larger reference than that of the
strictly empirical is contemplated. Further, the
ceaseless preoccupation of man with value-claims of one
sort or another bids fair to indicate that this larger
reference is a valid part of experience and because

there is the quiet assumption that these same values
that constitute this larger reference can be made the
subject of significant agreement or disagreement, it
would appear to follow that we are involved with a
strictly objective situation. It is at the same time
and for such reasons as the emerging objectivity suggests that one can claim a transcendence for the value-
complex which has thus thrust itself before our attention by its many claims and our disposition to honor
them.

The ultimate conjunction of value and actuality
is in God. He becomes the presupposed repository of
normative value which, we have seen, must ground in
being. If then such is the case at the ultimate level, the conjunctions of value with existence at the
human level are reflections of the higher reality. By
the aid of the dialectic which we have employed
throughout the previous discussion, we have seen that
every appeal to normative consideration is necessarily
to rise above the experience to which the norms stand
as interpreters. As this 'rise' above experience applies at every level of the hierarchy except the apex
itself, it follows that the repository of every norm
is presupposed already, in principle, as being identified with the nature of this apex. Because, further,
the combined categories of the esthetic, the ethical,
and the rational are proportionately unintelligible if
this same apex is not personal, the fuller advent of
God as the ultimate presupposition of all value is
heralded as the ultimate concern of any philosophy
that takes value seriously.

OUTLINE OF BIBLIOGRAPHY

A. ALFRED EDWARD TAYLOR 1869-1945
B. BOOKS BY TAYLOR
C. ARTICLES BY TAYLOR
D. BOOKS REVIEWED BY TAYLOR
E. REVIEWS OF TAYLOR'S WRITINGS
F. OTHER WORKS REFERRED TO IN COURSE OF WRITING

BIBLIOGRAPHY

A. ALFRED EDWARD TAYLOR 1869-1945

Laird, J. "Prof. A. E. Taylor, F.B.A.," NATURE,
CLVII (February 16, 1946), 186-187.

Lerda, F. "Alfred Edward Taylor," ENCICLOPEDIA
FILOSOFICA. Roma: Istituto Per La
Collaborazione Culturale, 1957.

MacQuarrie, John. "Alfred Edward Taylor," THE
ENCYCLOPEDIA OF PHILOSOPHY, 1967,
VIII, 82-83.

Porteous, A. J. D. "A. E. Taylor (1869-1945),"
MIND, LV (April, 1946), 187-191.

Ross, W. D. "Alfred Edward Taylor 1869-1945,"
PROCEEDINGS OF THE BRITISH ACADEMY,
XXXI (1945), 407-424.

B. BOOKS BY TAYLOR

Taylor, Alfred Edward. ARISTOTLE. New York:
Dover Publications, Inc., 1955.

305

_____. ARISTOTLE ON HIS PREDECESSORS, BEING THE FIRST BOOK OF HIS METAPHYSICS. Translated with introduction and notes. Chicago: The Open Court Publishing Co., 1907.

_____. THE CHRISTIAN HOPE OF IMMORTALITY. New York: Macmillan, 1947.

_____. A COMMENTARY ON PLATO'S TIMAEUS. Oxford: Clarendon Press, 1928.

_____. DAVID HUME AND THE MIRACULOUS. Cambridge: University Press, 1927. /Reprinted in Philosophical Studies, 1934/.

_____. DOES GOD EXIST? London: Macmillan, 1945.

_____. ELEMENTS OF METAPHYSICS. London: Methuen & Co., 1903.

_____. EPICURUS. /PHILOSOPHIES ANCIENT AND MODERN/. London and New York: Archibald Constable & Co., and Dodge Publishing Co., 1911.

_____. THE FAITH OF A MORALIST. The Gifford Lectures, 1926 to 1928. Series I: The Theological Implications of Morality. Series II: Natural Theology and the Positive Religions. London: Macmillan & Co., 1930.

_____. editor. FORMAL LOGIC, by Augustus de Morgan. London: Open Court Co., 1926.

_____. THE LAWS OF PLATO. translated into English. London: J. M. Dent, 1934.

_____. THE MIND OF PLATO. (originally: PLATO). Ann Arbor, Michigan: University of Michigan Press, 1960.

_____. THE PARMENIDES OF PLATO, translated with introduction and appendixes. Oxford: Clarendon Press, 1934.

_____. PHILEBUS AND EPINOMIS, by Plato. Translated with introduction. Edited by Raymond Klibansky with the cooperation of Guido Calogero and A. C. Lloyd. London and New York: T. Nelson, 1956.

_____. PHILOSOPHICAL STUDIES. London: Macmillan & Co., 1934.

_____. PLATO. /PHILOSOPHIES ANCIENT AND MODERN/. London: Archibald Constable & Co., 1908. Also: New York: Dodge Publishing Co., 1909.

_____. PLATO: THE MAN AND HIS WORK. London: Methuen & Co., 1926; Third edition, revised and enlarged. London: Methuen & Co., 1929.

_____. PLATONISM AND ITS INFLUENCE. New York: Cooper Square Publishers, Inc., 1963.

_____. THE PROBLEM OF CONDUCT, A STUDY IN THE PHENOMENOLOGY OF ETHICS. London: Macmillan & Co., 1901.

_____. THE PROBLEM OF EVIL. London: Ernest Benn, 1929.

_____. SAINT THOMAS AQUINAS AS A PHILOSOPHER. /Aquinas Sexcentenary Lectures/. Oxford: Basil Blackwell, 1924. /Reprinted in PHILOSOPHICAL STUDIES, 1934/.

_____. SOCRATES. New York: Doubleday & Co., Inc., 1953.

_____. THOMAS HOBBES. /PHILOSOPHIES ANCIENT AND MODERN/. London: Archibald Constable & Co., 1908. Also: New York: Dodge Publishing Co., 1909.

_____. TIMAEUS AND CRITIAS, by Plato. Translated with introduction and notes. London: Methuen & Co., 1929.

_____. VARIA SOCRATICA. First Series. Oxford: James Parker & Co., 1911.

C. ARTICLES BY TAYLOR

Taylor, Alfred Edward. "Aeschines of Sphettus," PHILOSOPHICAL STUDIES. London: Macmillan and Co., Limited, 1934.

_____. "The Analysis of ΕΠΙΣΤΗΜΗ in Plato's Seventh Epistle," MIND, XXI (July, 1912), 347-370. /Reprinted in PHILOSOPHICAL STUDIES, 1934/.

_____. "Ancient and Medieval Philosophy." EUROPEAN CIVILIZATION. Edited by E. Eyre. London: Oxford University Press, 1934-1939.

_____. "Are History and Science Different Kinds of Knowledge?" MIND, XXXI (October, 1922), 451-466. /A Symposium by R. G. Collingwood, A. E. Taylor, and F. C. S. Schiller./

_____. "Back to Descartes," PHILOSOPHY, XVI (1941), 126-137.

_____. "The Belief in Immortality," THE FAITH AND THE WAR. Edited by F. J. Foakes-Jackson. London: Macmillan & Co., 1915.

_____. "Biographical," CONTEMPORARY BRITISH PHILOSOPHY. Second Series. Edited by J. H. Muirhead. London: George Allen & Unwin Ltd., 1925.

_____. "The Conception of Immortality in Spinoza's Ethics," MIND, V (April, 1896), 145-166.

_____. "Continuity." ENCYCLOPAEDIA OF RELIGION AND ETHICS, 1912, IV, 89-98.

_____. "The Decline and Fall of the State in REPUBLIC, VIII," MIND, XLVIII (January, 1939), 23-38.

_____. "Discussion of B. Bosanquet's paper, 'Recent Criticism of Green's Ethics,'" PROCEEDINGS OF THE ARISTOTE-LIAN SOCIETY, New Series. II (1901-1902), 62-66.

_____. "Doctor McTaggart on the Nature of Existence," MONIST, XXXIII (January, 1933), 139-159.

_____. "Dr. Whitehead's Philosophy of Religion," DUBLIN REVIEW, CLXXXI (July, 1927), 17-41.

_____. "Dreams and Sleep," ENCYCLOPAE-DIA OF RELIGION AND ETHICS, 1912, V, 28-32.

_____. "The ethical doctrine of Hobbes," PHILOSOPHY, XIII (1938), 406-424.

_____. "Forms and Numbers: a Study in Platonic Metaphysics (I)," MIND, XXXV (October, 1926), 419-440; (II), XXXVI (January, 1927), 12-33. /Reprinted in Philosophical Studies, 1934./

_____. "F. H. Bradley," MIND, XXXIV (January, 1925), 1-12.

_____. "Francis Bacon," PROCEEDINGS OF THE BRITISH ACADEMY, XII (1926), 273-294. /Reprinted in PHILOSOPHICAL STU-DIES, 1934/.

_____. "Francis Herbert Bradley 1846-1924," PROCEEDINGS OF THE BRITISH ACADEMY, XI (1924-1925), 458-468.

_____. "Freedom and Personality," PHILOSOPHY, XIV (1939), 259-280.

_____. "Freedom and Personality Again," PHILOSOPHY, XVII (1942), 26-37.

_____. "The Freedom of Man," CONTEMPO-
RARY BRITISH PHILOSOPHY. Second Series.
London: George Allen & Unwin Ltd.,
1925.

_____. "A further word on Spinoza,"
MIND, LV (April, 1946), 97-112.

_____. "Identity." ENCYCLOPAEDIA OF
RELIGION AND ETHICS, 1912, VII, 95-99.

_____. "Is Goodness a Quality?"
ARISTOTELIAN SOCIETY, Supplementary
Volume XI (1932), 146-168. /A Sympos-
ium with G. E. Moore and H. W. B.
Joseph. Reprinted in PHILOSOPHICAL
STUDIES, 1934/.

_____. "John Burnet 1863-1928." (Co-
authored with W. L. Lorimer). PROCEED-
INGS OF THE BRITISH ACADEMY, XIV
(1928), 445-470. Also: JOHN BURNET.
London: Humphrey Milford, 1930.

_____. "Knowing and Believing,"
PROCEEDINGS OF THE ARISTOTELIAN SOCIETY,
New Series, XXIX (1928-1929), 1-30.
/Reprinted in PHILOSOPHICAL STUDIES,
1934/.

_____. "Leibniz," ENCYCLOPEDIA AMERI-
CANA, 1908, XVII, 225-230.

_____. "The Metaphysical Problem, with
Special Reference to Its Bearing Upon
Ethics," INTERNATIONAL JOURNAL OF
ETHICS, X (April, 1900), 352-380.

_____. "Mind and Body in Recent Psy-
chology," MIND, XIII (October, 1904),
476-508.

_____. "Modern Philosophy." EUROPEAN
CIVILIZATION. Edited by E. Eyre.
London: Oxford University Press,
1934-1939.

_____. "MUNSTERBERG'S GRUNDZUGE DER PSYCHOLOGIE. Band i., Allgemeiner Teil. Die Prinzipien der Psychologie. Leipzig, 1900. Pp. vii, 565," MIND, XI (January, 1902), 227-246.

_____. "Note in reply to Mr. A. W. Benn," MIND, XII (October, 1903), 507-512.

_____. "A Note on Plato's Astronomy," THE CLASSICAL REVIEW, XLIX (May, 1935), 53-56.

_____. "Note on Plato's Republic, VI. 510 C 2-5," MIND, XLIII (January, 1934), 81-84.

_____. "Note on Plato's 'Vision of the ideas,'" MIND, XVIII (January, 1909), 118-124.

_____. "The Novels of Mark Rutherford," ESSAYS AND STUDIES BY MEMBERS OF THE ENGLISH ASSOCIATION, V (1914), 51-74.

_____. "On the Date of the Trial of Anaxagoras," THE CLASSICAL QUARTERLY, XI (1917), 81-87.

_____. "On the first part of Plato's PARMENIDES," MIND, XII (January, 1903), 1-20.

_____. "On the Interpretation of Plato's PARMENIDES (I)," MIND, V (July, 1896), 297-326; (II), V (October, 1896), 483-507; (III), VI (January, 1897), 9-39.

_____. "Parmenides, Zeno and Socrates," PROCEEDINGS OF THE ARISTOTELIAN SOCIETY, New Series, XVI, (1915-1916), 234-289. /Reprinted in PHILOSOPHICAL STUDIES, 1934/.

_____. "Philosophy," EVOLUTION IN THE LIGHT OF MODERN KNOWLEDGE. London: Blackie & Son, 1925. A collective work: No editor given. 429-476.

_____. "Philosophy," RECENT DEVELOPMENTS IN EUROPEAN THOUGHT. Edited by F. S. Marvin. Oxford: Humphrey Milford, 1920, 25-64.

_____. "The Philosophy of Proclus," PROCEEDINGS OF THE ARISTOTELIAN SOCIETY, XVIII (1917-1918), 600-635. /Reprinted in PHILOSOPHICAL STUDIES, 1934/.

_____. "The Place of Psychology in the Classification of the Sciences," THE PHILOSOPHICAL REVIEW, XV (July, 1906), 380-386.

_____. "Plato," ENCYCLOPAEDIA BRITANNICA, 1929, XVIII, 48-64. /copyright edition of 1948/.

_____. "Plato and the Authorship of the 'Epinomis.'" PROCEEDINGS OF THE BRITISH ACADEMY, XV (1929), 235-317.

_____. "Plato's Biography of Socrates," PROCEEDINGS OF THE BRITISH ACADEMY, VIII (1917-1918), 93-132.

_____. "The 'polytheism' of Plato: an apologia," MIND, XLVII (April, 1938), 180-199.

_____. "The Present-Day Relevance of Hume's Dialogues Concerning Natural Religion," ARISTOTELIAN SOCIETY, Supplementary Volume XVIII (1939), 179-205.

_____. "The Right and the Good," MIND, XLVIII (July, 1939); XLIX (April, 1940).

_____. "Science and Morality," PHILOSOPHY, XIV (1939), 24-45.

_____. "Socrates and the Myths," THE CLASSICAL QUARTERLY, XXVII (July, 1933).

_____. "Some features of Butler's ethics," MIND, XXXV (July, 1926), 273-300. /Reprinted in PHILOSOPHICAL STUDIES, 1934/.

_____. "Some Incoherencies in Spinozism (I)," MIND, XLVI (April, 1937), 137-158; (II), XLVI (July, 1937), 281-301.

_____. "Some Side Lights on Pragmatism," MCGILL UNIVERSITY MAGAZINE (April, 1904), 44-66.

_____. "Substance of Faith," SPECTATOR, CXXXXII (June 8, 1929), 888-889.

_____. "Theism," ENCYCLOPAEDIA OF RELIGION AND ETHICS, 1912, XII, 261-287.

_____. "Truth and consequences," MIND, XV (January, 1906), 81-93.

_____. "Truth and Practice," THE PHILOSOPHICAL REVIEW, XIV (May, 1905), 265-289.

_____. "Two notes on Plato," THE CLASSICAL REVIEW, XXXV (September, 1931), 119-121.

_____. "Two Pythagorean Philosophemes," THE CLASSICAL REVIEW, XL (November, 1926), 149-151.

_____. "The Vindication of Religion," ESSAYS CATHOLIC AND CRITICAL. Edited by E. G. Selwyn. London: Society for Promoting Christian Knowledge, 1926.

_____. "Why Pluralism?" PROCEEDINGS OF THE ARISTOTELIAN SOCIETY, New Series, IX (1908-1909), 201-216.

_____. "William George de Burgh," PROCEEDINGS OF THE BRITISH ACADEMY, XXIX (1943). Also: WILLIAM GEORGE DE BURGH, 1866-1943. London: Humphrey Milford, 1944.

D. BOOKS REVIEWED BY TAYLOR

Taylor, Alfred Edward. THE ARCHITECTURE OF THE INTELLIGIBLE UNIVERSE IN THE PHILOSOPHY OF PLOTINUS, by A. H. Armstrong. PHILOSOPHY, XVI (October, 1941), 426-427.

_____. ARISTOTELES' GEDANKE DER PHILOSOPHIE, K. Schilling-Wollny. THE CLASSICAL REVIEW, XLIII (September, 1929), 137-138.

_____. ARISTOTELES: GRUNDLEGUNG EINER GESCHICHTE SEINER ENTWICKLUNG, Werner Jaeger. MIND, XXXIII (April, 1924), 192-198.

_____. ARISTOTLE, by G. R. G. Mure. MIND, XLI (October, 1932), 501-505.

_____. ARISTOTLE, by W. D. Ross. MIND, XXXIII (July, 1924), 316-312.

_____. ARISTOTLE ON COMING-TO-BE AND PASSING-AWAY. A REVISED TEXT WITH INTRODUCTION AND COMMENTARY, by H. H. Joachim. MIND, XXXII (January, 1923), 67-79.

_____. ARISTOTLE'S METAPHYSICS. A REVISED TEXT WITH INTRODUCTION AND COMMENTARY, by W. D. Ross. 2 Vols. MIND, XXXIV (July, 1925), 351-361.

_____. ARISTOTLE'S PHYSICS, A REVISED TEXT WITH INTRODUCTION AND COMMENTARY, by W. D. Ross. MIND, XLV (July, 1936), 378-383.

_____. AUTOUR DE PLATON, ESSAIS DE CRITIQUE ET D'HISTOIRE, by A. Dies. THE CLASSICAL REVIEW, XLI (September, 1927), 132-133.

_____. THE BEYOND THAT IS WITHIN, by E. Boutroux. Translated by J. Nield. INTERNATIONAL JOURNAL OF ETHICS, XXIII (April, 1913), 354-357.

_____. BISHOP BUTLER, MORALIST AND DIVINE, by J. Norton, Jr. MIND, L (January, 1941), 83-85.

_____. COMMON-SENSE THEOLOGY, by C. E. M. Joad. THE HIBBERT JOURNAL, XXI (January, 1923), 396-398.

_____. THE CONCEPT OF NATURE, by A. N. Whitehead. MIND, XXX (January, 1921), 76-83.

_____. IL CONCETTO DEL TEMPO NEL SUOI RAPPORTI COI PROBLEMI DEL DIVENIRE E DELL' ESSERE NELLA FILOSOFIA DI PLATONE. SAGGIO SULLA TEORIA DELLE IDEE, by Adolfo Levi. MIND, XXX (April, 1921), 214-220.

_____. CREATIVE EVOLUTION, by H. Bergson. Translated by Arthur Mitchell. INTERNATIONAL JOURNAL OF ETHICS, XXII (July, 1912), 467-469.

_____. CREATIVE MORALITY, by L. A. Reid. MIND, XLVII (January, 1938), 61-73.

_____. A CRITICAL EXPOSITION OF THE PHILOSOPHY OF LEIBNIZ, by Bertrand Russell. INTERNATIONAL JOURNAL OF ETHICS, XI (July, 1901), 521-525.

_____. DIALOGUES ON METAPHYSICS AND ON RELIGION, by Nicolas Malebranche. Translated by Morris Ginsberg. THE HIBBERT JOURNAL, XXII (October, 1923), 200-205.

_____. EINFUHRUNG IN DIE ETHIK AUF GRUNDLAGE DER ERFAHRUNG, by G. Heymans. MIND, XXV (July, 1916), 375-399.

_____. EPICURUS: THE EXTANT REMAINS, WITH SHORT CRITICAL APPARATUS, TRANSLATION AND NOTES, by C. Bailey. MIND, XXXVI (April, 1927), 233-237.

_____. ESSAYS AND ADDRESSES ON THE PHILOSOPHY OF RELIGION, Second Series, by Baron F. von Hugel. THE HIBBERT JOURNAL, XXV (January, 1927), 374-377.

_____. ETERNAL LIFE: A STUDY OF ITS IMPLICATIONS AND APPLICATIONS, by Baron F. von Hugel. MIND, XXII (October, 1913), 574-579. Also: THE HIBBERT JOURNAL, XII (January, 1914), 452-463.

_____. GESCHICHTE DER GRIECHISCHEN ETHIK, by Max Wundt. Erster Band. DIE ENTSTEHUNG DER GRIECHISCHEN ETHIK. MIND, XVIII (April, 1909), 276-280.

_____. THE GREEK ATOMISTS AND EPICURUS, by C. Bailey. THE CLASSICAL REVIEW, XLIII (May, 1929), 68-70.

_____. THE GREEK PHILOSOPHERS, by A. W. Benn, 2nd Edition. MIND, XXV (April, 1916), 229-240.

_____. GREEK PHILOSOPHY BEFORE PLATO, by R. Scoon. THE CLASSICAL REVIEW, XLII (November, 1928), 180-181.

_____. GREEK POLITICAL THEORY: PLATO AND HIS PREDECESSORS, by E. Barker. MIND, XXVIII (July, 1919), 347-354.

_____. THE GROWTH OF PLATO'S IDEAL THEORY: AN ESSAY, by Sir. J. G. Frazer. MIND, XL (January, 1931), 102-105.

_____. HISTOIRE DE LA PHILOSOPHIE ATOMISTIQUE, par Leopold Mabilleau. MIND, V (October, 1896), 554-563.

_____. HISTORICAL STUDIES IN PHILOSO-PHY, by Emile Boutroux. Translation by F. Rothwell. INTERNATIONAL JOURNAL OF ETHICS, XXIII (July, 1913), 485-497.

_____. A HISTORY OF EUROPEAN THOUGHT IN THE NINETEENTH CENTURY, by J. T. Merz. Vol. IV. MIND, XXIV (July, 1915), 408-412.

_____. A HISTORY OF MODERN PHILOSOPHY, by H. Hoffding. Translated from the German by B. E. Meyer. Two Vols. INTERNATIONAL JOURNAL OF ETHICS, XI (April, 1901), 399-404.

_____. HOBBES, by J. Laird. PHILOSO-PHY, IX (July, 1934), 352-356.

_____. THE IDEA OF IMMORTALITY, by A. Seth Pringle-Pattison; MAN AND THE ATTAINMENT OF IMMORTALITY, by James Y. Simpson, Second Edition; A LIVING UNIVERSE, by L. P. Jacks. THE HIBBERT JOURNAL, XXII (April, 1924), 598-603.

_____. IDOLA THEATRI, A CRITICISM OF OXFORD THOUGHT AND THINKERS, by Henry Sturt. MIND, XVI (July, 1907), 424-430.

_____. IMMORTALITY, edited by Sir James Marchant. THE HIBBERT JOURNAL, XXIII (July, 1925), 754-756.

_____. THE INCARNATE LORD, by L. S. Thornton. PHILOSOPHY, V (April, 1930), 297-299.

_____. JOHANNES SCOTUS ERIGENA: A STUDY IN MEDIAEVAL PHILOSOPHY, by Henry Bett. PHILOSOPHY, I (April, 1926), 253-254.

_____. KNOWLEDGE AND TRUTH, AN EPIS-TEMOLOGICAL ESSAY, by L. A. Reid. MIND, XXXIII (January, 1924), 78-89.

_____. LECTURES ON THE ETHICS OF T. H. GREEN, MR. HERBERT SPENCER, AND J. MARTINEAU, by H. Sidgwick. THE HIBBERT JOURNAL, I (April, 1903), 595-599.

_____. LOGIC: PART III. THE LOGICAL FOUNDATIONS OF SCIENCE, by W. E. Johnson. THE HIBBERT JOURNAL, XXII (July, 1924), 820-825.

_____. MATTER AND MEMORY, by H. Bergson. Translation by N. M. Paul and W. S. Palmer. INTERNATIONAL JOURNAL OF ETHICS, XXII (October, 1911), 101-107.

_____. MEDIAEVAL AND RENAISSANCE STUDIES, edited by R. Hunt and R. Kilbansky. Vol. I, No. 2. PHILOSOPHY, XX (April, 1945), 78-79.

_____. MENS CREATRIX, by William Temple. MIND, XXVII (April, 1918), 208-234.

_____. THE METAPHYSICAL THEORY OF THE STATE, by L. T. Hobhouse. MIND, XXIX (January, 1920), 91-105.

_____. MYSTICISM, by E. Underhill. MIND, XXII (January, 1913), 122-130.

_____. LES MYTHES DE PLATON, by P. Frutiger. MIND, XXXIX (October, 1930), 492-496.

_____. NATURALISM AND AGNOSTICISM, by James Ward. MIND, IX (April, 1900), 244-258.

_____. OPERA HACTENUS INEDITA ROGERI BACONI. FASC. XIV. Liber de Sensu et Sensato: Summa de Sophismatibus et Distinctionibus. Nunc primum edidit Robert Steele. PHILOSOPHY, XII (July, 1937), 347-349.

318

_____. OPERA HACTENUS INEDITA ROGERI BACONI, XV. SUMMA GRAMATICA MAGISTRI ROGERI BACONI NECNON SUMULE DIALECTICES MAGISTRI ROGERI BACONI. Nunc primum edidit Robert Steele. PHILOSOPHY, XVI (October, 1941), 424-425.

_____. OUR DEBT TO GREECE AND ROME: ARISTOTELIANISM, by J. L. Stocks. THE CLASSICAL REVIEW, XL (February-March, 1926), 22-23.

_____. THE PATHWAY TO REALITY, by R. B. Haldane. THE HIBBERT JOURNAL, I (July, 1903), 823-825.

_____. THE PHILOSOPHICAL WORKS OF DESCARTES, translated by E. S. Haldane and G. R. T. Ross. In Two Volumes. Volume I. MIND, XX (October, 1911), 542-552.

_____. LA PHILOSOPHIE DE SAINT BONAVENTURE, by E. Gilson. MIND, XXXIV (January, 1925), 97-103.

_____. THE PHILOSOPHY AND PSYCHOLOGY OF PIETRO POMPONAZZI, by A. H. Douglas, edited by Charles Douglass and R. P. Hardie. INTERNATIONAL JOURNAL OF ETHICS, XXI (July, 1911), 494-498.

_____. PHILOSOPHY: ITS SCOPE AND RELATIONS, by Henry Sidgwick. INTERNATIONAL JOURNAL OF ETHICS, XIII (April, 1903), 377-385.

_____. THE PHILOSOPHY OF PLATO, by R. Demos. PHILOSOPHY, XIV (July, 1939), 350-356.

_____. THE PHILOSOPHY OF PLOTINUS, by W. R. Inge. MIND, XXVIII (April, 1919), 238-245.

_____. PLATO AND HIS CONTEMPORARIES, by G. C. Field. MIND, XXXIX (July, 1930), 367-371.

319

_____. PLATON, by Leon Robin. MIND, XLV (July, 1936), 373-378.

_____. PLATON: EIDOS, PAIDEIA, DIALOGOS, by P. Friedlander. THE CLASSICAL REVIEW, XLII (September, 1928), 146-147.

_____. PLATON. II. DIE PLATONISCHEN SCHRIFTEN, by Von P. Friedlander. THE CLASSICAL REVIEW, XLV (May, 1931), 64-68.

_____. PLATONICA, by H. Richards. MIND, XXI (April, 1912), 241-246.

_____. PLATONISCHE AUFSATZE, by Otto Apelt. MIND, XXII (July, 1913), 373-382.

_____. PLATONS VERHALTNIS ZUR MATHE-MATIK, by Seth Demel. THE CLASSICAL REVIEW, XLIV (February, 1930), 17-19.

_____. PLATO'S COSMOLOGY, by F. M. Cornford. THE CLASSICAL REVIEW, LI (December, 1937), 219-220.

_____. PLATO'S DOCTRINE OF IDEAS, by J. A. Stewart. MIND, XIX (January, 1910), 82-97.

_____. PLATO'S THEOLOGY, by F. Solmsen. MIND, LII (April, 1943), 178-182.

_____. A PLURALISTIC UNIVERSE, by William James. MIND, XVIII (October, 1909), 576-588.

_____. PROCLUS, THE ELEMENTS OF THEOLOGY. A Revised Text with Translation, Introduction and Commentary, by E. R. Dodds. PHILOSOPHY, IX (January, 1934), 108-110.

_____. PSYCHOLOGY ANCIENT AND MODERN, by G. S. Brett. THE CLASSICAL REVIEW, XLII (December, 1928), 226-227.

_____. THE REALM OF ENDS, OR PLURALISM AND THEISM, by J. Ward. MIND, XXI (July, 1912), 427-437.

_____. THE REALM OF TRUTH. BOOK THIRD OF "REALMS OF BEING," by George Santayana. PHILOSOPHY, XIII (April, 1938), 230-232.

_____. LA REAZIONE IDEALISTICA CONTRO LA SCIENZA, by Antonio Aliott. MIND, XXI (October, 1912), 536-546.

_____. RELATIVITY, THE SPECIAL AND THE GENERAL THEORY: A POPULAR EXPOSITION, by Albert Einstein, translated by R. W. Lawson. MIND, XXX (January, 1921), 76-83.

_____. REVALUATIONS: HISTORICAL AND IDEAL, by A. W. Benn. INTERNATIONAL JOURNAL OF ETHICS, XX (July, 1910), 482-484.

_____. SELECTED LETTERS, 1896-1924, by Baron F. von Hugel, edited, with a Memoir, by Bernard Holland. THE HIBBERT JOURNAL, XXV (July, 1927), 750-752.

_____. A SKETCH OF THE DEVELOPMENT OF PHILOSOPHIC THOUGHT FROM THALES TO KANT, by Ludwig Noire. INTERNATIONAL JOURNAL OF ETHICS, XII (April, 1902), 398-404.

_____. SOURCE-BOOK IN ANCIENT PHILOSOPHY, by C. M. Bakewell. MIND, XIX (April, 1910), 247-253.

_____. SPACE, TIME, AND GRAVITATION: AN OUTLINE OF THE GENERAL THEORY OF RELATIVITY, by A. S. Eddington. MIND, XXX (January, 1921), 76-83.

_____. STUDIES IN PHILOSOPHY AND PSYCHOLOGY, by G. F. Stout. PHILOSOPHY, VI (January, 1931), 117-119.

_____. A STUDY IN MORAL THEORY, by J. Laird. MIND, XXXV (October, 1926), 480-489.

_____. A STUDY IN PLATO, by W. F. R. Hardie. MIND, XLVI (April, 1937), 222-232.

_____. SULLE INTERPRETAZIONI IMMANENT-ISTICHE DELLA FILOSOFIA DI PLATONE, by Adolfo Levi. MIND, XXX (April, 1921), 214-220.

_____. THE SYMPOSIUM OF PLATO, by R. G. Bury. MIND, XIX (April, 1910), 242-247.

_____. THE THEORY OF MOTION IN PLATO'S LATER DIALOGUES, by J. B. Skemp. PHILOSOPHY, XVIII (April, 1943), 80-84.

_____. TIME AND FREE WILL: AN ESSAY ON THE IMMEDIATE DATA OF CONSCIOUSNESS, by H. Bergson. INTERNATIONAL JOURNAL OF ETHICS, XXI (April, 1911), 350-352.

_____. LA TRASCENDENZA, by G. Rensi. MIND, XXIII (July, 1914), 417-425.

_____. WITHIN OUR LIMITS, by Alice Gardner. INTERNATIONAL JOURNAL OF ETHICS, XXIV (April, 1914), 355-357.

_____. THE WORKS OF ARISTOTLE TRANSLA-TED INTO ENGLISH: DE COELO, DE GENERA-TIONE ET CORRUPTIONE, by J. L. Stocks. MIND, XXXII (January, 1923), 67-79.

_____. THE WORKS OF ARISTOTLE TRANSLA-TED INTO ENGLISH: METEOROLOGICA, by E. W. Webster. MIND, XXXIII (January, 1924), 95-97.

E. REVIEWS OF TAYLOR'S WRITINGS

Andrus, G. M. "Mind and Body in Recent Psycholo-gy." THE PHILOSOPHICAL REVIEW, XIV (March, 1905), 228-230.

Baillie, J. B. THE PROBLEM OF CONDUCT: A STUDY
        IN THE PHENOMENOLOGY OF ETHICS.
        INTERNATIONAL JOURNAL OF ETHICS, XII
        (January, 1902), 227-238.

Bart, P. J. PLATO, THE MAN AND HIS WORK. THE
        NEW SCHOLASTICISM, I (July, 1927),
        267-272.

Blanshard, Brand. THE FAITH OF A MORALIST. THE
        JOURNAL OF PHILOSOPHY, XXIX (March 3,
        1932), 129-137.

Blunt, Herbert W. VARIA SOCRATICA. MIND, XXI
        (July, 1912), 438-444.

Brett, G. S. VARIA SOCRATICA. THE PHILOSOPHICAL
        REVIEW, XXI (January, 1912), 94-97.

Broad, C. D. DOES GOD EXIST? MIND, LV (April,
        1946), 173-178.

Broad, C. D. THE FAITH OF A MORALIST. MIND, XL
        (July, 1931), 364-375.

Brown, S. M. "Hobbes: The Taylor Thesis,"
        PHILOSOPHICAL REVIEW, LXVIII (July,
        1959), 303-323.

Creighton, J. E. ELEMENTS OF METAPHYSICS. THE
        PHILOSOPHICAL REVIEW, XIV (January,
        1905), 57-64.

Cross, F. L. PHILOSOPHICAL STUDIES. CHURCH
        QUARTERLY REVIEW, CXX (April, 1935),
        104-108.

De Burgh, W. G. THE FAITH OF A MORALIST.
        PHILOSOPHY, VI (April, 1931), 229-236.

Evans, V. B. THE FAITH OF A MORALIST. INTER-
        NATIONAL JOURNAL OF ETHICS, XLI (April,
        1931), 351-353.

Field, G. C. A COMMENTARY ON PLATO'S TIMAEUS.
        MIND, XXXVIII (January, 1929), 84-94.

Field, G. C. PHILOSOPHICAL STUDIES. PHILOSOPHY,
X (April, 1935), 232-233.

Field, G. C. PLATO: THE MAN AND HIS WORK.
MIND, XXXVI (January, 1927), 87-98.

Field, G. C. SOCRATES. THE CLASSICAL REVIEW,
XLVII (May, 1933), 66-68.

Field, G. C. SOCRATES AND PLATO: A CRITICISM OF
A. E. TAYLOR'S 'VARIA SOCRATICA.'
Oxford: Parker & Co., 1913.

Finnegan, J. F. THE FAITH OF A MORALIST. THE
NEW SCHOLASTICISM, VI (July, 1932),
257-259.

Gibson, James. ELEMENTS OF METAPHYSICS. INTER-
NATIONAL JOURNAL OF ETHICS, XV
(January, 1905), 251-256.

Goodrich, W. J. VARIA SOCRATICA. THE CLASSICAL
REVIEW, XXV (December, 1911), 251-253.

Hallett, H. F. "Professor Taylor's 'A Further
Word on Spinoza,'" MIND, LV (July,
1946), 284-287.

Hammond, W. A. ARISTOTLE ON HIS PREDECESSORS:
BEING THE FIRST BOOK OF HIS METAPHYSICS,
translated, with introduction and notes.
THE PHILOSOPHICAL REVIEW, XVII (March,
1908), 223-226.

Hebb, C. A. "Mind and Nature." THE PHILOSOPHI-
CAL REVIEW, XII (January, 1903), 86-88.

Hicks, G. D. A COMMENTARY ON PLATO'S TIMAEUS.
THE HIBBERT JOURNAL, XXVII (October,
1928), 168-173.

Hicks, G. D. PHILOSOPHICAL STUDIES. THE HIBBERT
JOURNAL, XXXIII (January, 1935), 305-
310.

Inge, W. R. DOES GOD EXIST? THE HIBBERT JOURNAL,
XLIV (January, 1946), 177-179.

Keeling, S. V. DAVID HUME AND THE MIRACULOUS. PHILOSOPHY, III (October, 1928), 535-537.

Klausner, N. W. DOES GOD EXIST? THE JOURNAL OF RELIGION, XXVIII (January, 1948), 59-60.

Laird, John. PHILOSOPHICAL STUDIES. MIND, XLIV (April, 1935), 235-239.

Lamprecht, Sterling P. "Morality and Religion: A Critique of Professor A. E. Taylor's Gifford Lectures," INTERNATIONAL JOURNAL OF ETHICS, XLI (July, 1931), 493-506.

Lamprecht, Sterling P. PLATO: THE MAN AND HIS WORK. THE NEW YORK TRIBUNE, Books, III, No. 37 (May 29, 1927), 7.

Langley, G. H. WILLIAM GEORGE DE BURGH, 1866-1943. PHILOSOPHY, XX (November, 1945), 273-274.

Lefevre, A. THE PROBLEM OF CONDUCT: A STUDY IN THE PHENOMENOLOGY OF ETHICS. THE PHILOSOPHICAL REVIEW, XI (January, 1902), 56-69.

Leighton, J. A. ELEMENTS OF METAPHYSICS. THE JOURNAL OF PHILOSOPHY, PSYCHOLOGY AND SCIENTIFIC METHODS, II (April 13, 1905), 213-218.

Lindsay, J. "Critical Notes on Professor A. E. Taylor's Theism," BIBLIOTECA SACRA, LXXIX (October, 1922), 492-497.

Lodge, R. C. A COMMENTARY ON PLATO'S TIMAEUS and PLATO: TIMAEUS AND CRITIAS. THE PHILOSOPHICAL REVIEW, XXXVIII (September, 1929), 483-485.

Lodge, R. C. PLATO: THE MAN AND HIS WORK. INTERNATIONAL JOURNAL OF ETHICS, XXXVIII (January, 1928), 226-229.

McGuiness, J. I. DOES GOD EXIST? THE THOMIST:
A SPECULATIVE QUARTERLY REVIEW, X
(July, 1947), 379-381.

Mackenzie, J. S. ELEMENTS OF METAPHYSICS. MIND,
XIII (October, 1904), 555-564.

Mellone, S. H. THE PROBLEM OF CONDUCT: A STUDY
IN THE PHENOMENOLOGY OF ETHICS. THE
HIBBERT JOURNAL, I (January, 1903),
400-403.

More, Paul Elmer. PLATO: THE MAN AND HIS WORK.
THE SATURDAY REVIEW OF LITERATURE, III,
No. 51 (July 16, 1927), 976.

Morrow, G. R. PLATO: THE MAN AND HIS WORK. THE
PHILOSOPHICAL REVIEW, XXXVI (September,
1927), 488-493.

Muirhead, J. H. THE FAITH OF A MORALIST. THE
HIBBERT JOURNAL, XXIX (April, 1931),
553-559.

Oakley, H. D. SOCRATES. THE HIBBERT JOURNAL,
XXXI (January, 1933), 306-309.

Perry, R. B. "Prof. Taylor's Treatment of Space
and Time," MIND, XVI (April, 1907),
249-253.

Ross, W. D. ARISTOTLE ON HIS PREDECESSORS,
BEING THE FIRST BOOK OF HIS METAPHYSICS,
translated, with introduction and notes.
MIND, XVII (January, 1908), 110-113.

Ross, W. D. PLATO: THE MAN AND HIS WORK.
PHILOSOPHY, II (April, 1927), 239-240.

Ross, W. D. PLATONISM AND ITS INFLUENCE. MIND,
XXXV (January, 1926), 114.

Russell, L. J. FRANCIS BACON. PHILOSOPHY, II
(July, 1927), 396-397.

Schiller, F. C. S. "Empiricism and the Absolute," MIND, XIV (July, 1905), 348-370. /A critical review of A. E. Taylor's ELEMENTS OF METAPHYSICS/.

Sharpe, A. B. THE FAITH OF A MORALIST. DUBLIN REVIEW, CLXXXIX (October, 1931), 293-301.

Stewart, J. A. PLATO. MIND, XIX (January, 1910), 117-121.

Stocks, J. L. A COMMENTARY ON PLATO'S TIMAEUS and PLATO: TIMAEUS AND CRITIAS. THE CLASSICAL REVIEW, XLIII (December, 1929), 218-220.

Tarr, P. H. "Mind and Body in Recent Psychology." THE JOURNAL OF PHILOSOPHY, PSYCHOLOGY AND SCIENTIFIC METHODS, I (December 22, 1904), 718-720.

Turner, J. E. "Determinism and Moral Experience," INTERNATIONAL JOURNAL OF ETHICS, XXXVII (July, 1927), 419-430. /Review of "The Freedom of Man," CONTEMPORARY BRITISH PHILOSOPHY, Second Series, edited by J. H. Muirhead. New York: The Macmillan Company, 1925/.

Underhill, Evelyn. PLATO: THE MAN AND HIS WORK. THE SPECTATOR, CXXXVII (November 27, 1926), 971-972.

Waterlow, Sydney. EPICURUS. INTERNATIONAL JOURNAL OF ETHICS, XXII (January, 1912), 226-227.

Waterlow, Sydney. VARIA SOCRATICA. INTERNATIONAL JOURNAL OF ETHICS, XXIII (October, 1912), 101-103.

Wodehouse, H. "Freedom and Personality Again." PHILOSOPHY, XVII (April, 1942), 174-175.

F. OTHER WORKS REFERRED TO IN COURSE OF WRITING

Aristotle. THE BASIC WORKS OF ARISTOTLE.
METAPHYSICS, Book IV. Edited with an
Introduction by Richard McKeon. New
York: Random House, 1941.

Atkinson, R. F. "'Ought' and 'Is,'" PHILOSOPHY,
XXXIII (January, 1958). /A discussion
with A. C. Montefiore/.

Ayer, Alfred Jules. LANGUAGE, TRUTH AND LOGIC.
New York: Dover Publications, Inc.
(N.D.) /First edition published in
1936; second edition, in 1946/.

Bechner, Morton. "Teleology," THE ENCYCLOPEDIA
OF PHILOSOPHY, VIII. Edited by Paul
Edwards. New York: The Macmillan
Company and The Free Press, 1967.

Black, Max. "The Gap Between 'Is' and 'Should,'"
THE PHILOSOPHICAL REVIEW, LXXIII
(April, 1964).

Bowman, Archibald Allan. A SACRAMENTAL UNIVERSE.
Princeton, New Jersey: Princeton
University Press, 1939.

Brightman, Edgar S. A PHILOSOPHY OF RELIGION.
New York: Prentice-Hall, Inc., 1940.

Burtt, Edwin A. TYPES OF RELIGIOUS PHILOSOPHY.
Revised Edition. New York: Harper and
Row, Publishers, 1951.

Copleston, Frederick. CONTEMPORARY PHILOSOPHY.
Westminster, Maryland: The Newman
Press, 1956.

_____. A HISTORY OF PHILOSOPHY, Volume
II. Mediaeval Philosophy, Part I.
Augustine to Bonaventure. New York:
Doubleday & Company, 1962.

Descartes, Rene. MEDITATIONS ON FIRST PHILOSOPHY.
New York: Dover Publications, Inc.,
1955.

Feigl, Herbert. "Logical Empiricism," TWENTIETH CENTURY PHILOSOPHY. Edited by Dagobert D. Runes. New York: Philosophical Library, 1943.

Flew, Antony. "On Not Deriving 'Ought' From 'Is,'" ANALYSIS, 25, No. 2 (December, 1964).

_____. "On the Interpretation of Hume," PHILOSOPHY, XXXVIII (April, 1963).

Flint, Robert. AGNOSTICISM. New York: Charles Scribner's Sons, 1903.

Frankena, William K. ETHICS. Englewood Cliffs, New Jersey: Prentice-Hall, Inc., 1963.

_____. "Value and Valuation," THE ENCYCLOPEDIA OF PHILOSOPHY, VIII. Edited by Paul Edwards. New York: The Macmillan Company and The Free Press, 1967.

Hall, Roland. "Monism and Pluralism," THE ENCYCLOPEDIA OF PHILOSOPHY, V. Edited by Paul Edwards. New York: The Macmillan Company and The Free Press, 1967.

Hanley, Kenneth. "Zimmerman's 'Is-Is': A Schizophrenic Monism," MIND, LXXIII (July, 1964).

Hare, R. M. "Descriptivism," PROCEEDINGS OF THE BRITISH ACADEMY, XLIX (1963).

_____. "'Ought' and "Is,'" PHILOSOPHY, XXXIII (January, 1958).

Hick, John. "The Problem of Evil," THE ENCYCLOPEDIA OF PHILOSOPHY, III. Edited by Paul Edwards. New York: The Macmillan Company and The Free Press, 1967.

Hudson, W. D. "Hume on Is and Ought," THE PHILOSOPHICAL QUARTERLY, 14 (July, 1964).

_____. "The 'Is-Ought' Controversy,"
ANALYSIS, 25, No. 6 (June, 1965).

Hume, David. DIALOGUES CONCERNING NATURAL RELI-
GION. Indianapolis, Indiana: Bobbs-
Merrill Publishing Company,(N.D.).

_____. A TREATISE OF HUMAN NATURE.
Edited by L. A. Selby-Bigge. Oxford:
The Clarendon Press, 1888.

Hunter, Geoffrey. "Hume on Is and Ought," PHILO-
SOPHY, XXXVII (April, 1962).

Jobe, Evan K. "On Deriving 'Ought' From 'Is,'"
ANALYSIS, 25, No. 5 (April, 1965).

Kant, Immanuel. CRITIQUE OF PURE REASON. Translated by Norman Kemp Smith. New York:
St. Martin's Press, 1965.

_____. FOUNDATIONS OF THE METAPHYSICS
OF MORALS. Translated with an Intro-
duction by Lewis White Beck. New York:
The Liberal Arts Press, 1959.

_____. "On the Radical Evil of Human
Nature," CRITIQUE OF PRACTICAL REASON
AND OTHER WORKS ON THE THEORY OF ETHICS.
Translated by T. K. Abbott. London:
Longmans, Green and Company, 1923.

Lewis, Douglas. "'Good' and Naturalistic Definitions," ANALYSIS, 24, No. 3 (January,
1964).

Mavrodes, George I. "'Is' and 'Ought,'" ANALYSIS,
25, No. 2 (December, 1964).

McClellan, James E. and B. Paul Komisar. "On
Deriving 'Ought' From 'Is,'" ANALYSIS,
25, No. 2 (December, 1964).

McTaggart, John McTaggart Ellis. THE NATURE OF
EXISTENCE. Cambridge: The University
Press, 1927.

Mill, John Stuart. MILL'S ETHICAL WRITINGS. Edited with an Introduction by J. B. Schneewind. New York: Collier Books, 1965.

Montague, Roger. "'Is' to 'Ought,'" ANALYSIS, 26, No. 3 (January, 1966).

Montefiore, A. C. "'Ought' and 'Is,'" PHILOSOPHY, XXXIII (January, 1958). /A discussion with R. F. Atkinson/.

Mure, G. R. G. RETREAT FROM TRUTH. Oxford: Basil Blackwell, 1958.

Orr, James. THE CHRISTIAN VIEW OF GOD AND THE WORLD. The Kerr Lectures for 1890-91. Grand Rapids, Michigan: Eerdmans Publishing Company, 1948.

Phillips, D. Z. "The Possibilities of Moral Advice," ANALYSIS, 25, No. 2 (December, 1964).

_____ and H. O. Mounce. "On Morality's Having a Point," PHILOSOPHY, XL (October, 1965).

Plato. THE COLLECTED DIALOGUES OF PLATO. Edited by E. Hamilton and H. Cairns. Bollingen Series LXXI. New York: Bollingen Foundation, 1961.

Price, Richard. REVIEW OF THE PRINCIPAL QUESTIONS IN MORALS. Edited by D. D. Raphael. Oxford: The Clarendon Press, 1974.

Ross, William David. THE RIGHT AND THE GOOD. Oxford: The Clarendon Press, 1930.

Russell, Bertrand. A HISTORY OF WESTERN PHILOSOPHY. New York: Simon and Schuster, 1945.

Searle, John R. "How to Derive 'Ought' From 'Is,'" THE PHILOSOPHICAL REVIEW, LXXIII (January, 1964).

Shaw, P. D.   "Ought and Can," ANALYSIS, 25, No. 6
        (June, 1965).

Smith, Huston.   THE RELIGIONS OF MAN.   New York:
        Harper & Row, Publishers, 1958.

Stace, W. T.   A CRITICAL HISTORY OF GREEK PHILOSO-
        PHY.   London: Macmillan and Company
        Ltd, 1962.

Stout, G. F.   MIND AND MATTER.   London: Cambridge
        University Press, 1931.

Thompson, James and Judith.   "How Not to Derive
        'Ought' From 'Is,'" THE PHILOSOPHICAL
        REVIEW, LXXIII (October, 1964).

Weedon, William S.   "Being," DICTIONARY OF PHILO-
        SOPHY.   Edited by Dagobert D. Runes.
        Totowa, New Jersey: Littlefield, Adams
        & Company, 1966.

Wheelwright, Philip.   THE WAY OF PHILOSOPHY.
        Revised Edition.   New York: The Odyssey
        Press, 1954.

Whitehead, Alfred North.   "Mathematics as an Ele-
        ment in the History of Thought," THE
        WORLD OF MATHEMATICS.   Edited by James
        R. Newman.   New York: Simon & Schus-
        ter, 1956.

Windelband, Wilhelm.   A HISTORY OF PHILOSOPHY.
        New York: Dover Publications, 1958.

Zimmerman, M.   "The 'Is-Ought':   An Unnecessary
        Dualism," MIND, LXXI (January, 1962).

SUBJECT INDEX

Formalism
  statement according to Kant, 35-39
Free agent
  nothing contradictory in the notion, 134
Freedom
  empirical, 141f.; metaphysical, 141f.; of the will:
  fundamental for morality, 146; freedom of the will:
  its strategic conjunction with rationality, 145
'Function'
  argument from '<u>function</u>' to an environment supporting hope for immortality, detailed in Chapter 7,
  172f.

God
  as Absolute, equation necessary if ontological argument is to hold for 'the God of religion,' 208;
  eventual conclusion to which each of the several
  chapters point, 197f.; finite god hypothesis rejected, 109f., 111f.; existence indicated by the mind's
  awareness of its own ultimate presuppositions, 197;
  existence necessary to the retention of all value-
  norms, 172; presupposed by the meaningfulness of
  moral evil, 108; ultimate presupposition of all
  value, 303
The Good
  form of "the master light of all our seeing," 91;
  idea of (according to Plato), 55, 237; idea of, possesses a teleological aspect, 88, 130; necessary
  condition of moral worth, 274, 278
The good will
  (Kant), 274
Green Prize
  won by Taylor at Oxford ("On the Reciprocal Relations
  Between Ethics and Metaphysics"), 1899, 7

Hinduism
  95
History
  impossible unless conceived in teleological terms,
  86, 87

Idealism
  at Oxford, 5; finds world uniquely suited to intellectual analysis, 227
Ideals
  as universals, 281; have existential status, 74, 75,
  81; otherwise would be perfectly vacuous, 82; their
  aim: to concretize human values, 282

The Ideas
   (of Plato), supreme principles of intelligibility,
   290
Identity
   as introduced by memory, requires that a self be
   posited, 189; its personal aspect appeals to memory
   as an essential condition, 187; personal, 184-185;
   personal, denied by Hume, 187 (critique by Taylor),
   187-190; personal, dynamic view, 186; personal,
   "essentially psychical," 185; personal, for Hume,
   memory creates the illusion of personal identity,
   189-190; personal, interpreted as "formal," 186
'Identity theory'
   (of mind-body), inimical to both freedom and teleology, 223
Immortality
   argument for, rests on two assumptions, 172; argument from 'function,' 172f., 179; Butler's critique
   of arguments against, 182; desirability must be
   judged by its quality, 171; doctrine of, summarized,
   190-195; 'intimations' of, 173-179; logical value of
   the argument, 180; never an option attended by man's
   indifference, 168; not argued by appeal to the soul's
   simplicity, 169; nor by appeal to spiritualism, 169;
   not strictly demonstrable, 179
Imperative
   the categorical, 38; the hypothetical, 38
Impressions
   Hume's ultimate plank of empiricism, 239
Indetermination
   meaning and defense of, 151-155
Induction
   problem of (Feigl), 245; Russell's "independent
   logical principle," 164
Infinite
   implied by any finitude, 257
Inorganic
   interconnects with the organic realm, 217
Ionian science
   inadvertently paved way for atheism, 199
Interaction
   dualistic position with respect to mind and body,
   182f.
Interest
   goal of ethical action, 90
Irrationality
   privation and mere negation of the rational, 181

Moral acts
'functions' demanding a transcendent environment,
173
Moral evil
several differentiating aspects, 123-130; that which
"<u>absolutely</u> ought not to be," 132
Moral freedom
143; defined, 144; not an illusion, 143; of choice
(Kant), 135; relation to motive, 144, 146-147; relation to rationality, 144
Moral imperative
a 'function' of the hope for immortality, 173f.
The moral 'ought'
introductory of human free will, 132; an autonomous
responsibility, 133; touchstone of religion, 104f.
Moral standards
imply a divine person, 131
Moral value
classical views of, Chapter II, 21ff.; dialectic of,
253; difficulties of standardization, 12; eventually
leads to true thought related to right action, 257;
its relation to evil, Chapter V, 107ff.; its relation to existence, Chapter III, 57ff.; its relation
to freedom, Chapter VI, 141ff.; its relation to God,
Chapter VIII, 197ff.; its relation to immortality,
Chapter VII, 167ff.; its relation to time, Chapter
IV, 83ff.; norm and mandate for persons, 280, 283
Morality
'antinomy of,' (Bradley), 136; "eternal and immutable," proponents of, 142; has meaning independent of
its war against evil even as science has meaning independent of the correction of error, 137, 139; it
is <u>the</u> <u>subject</u>, the true <u>self</u>, that is defiled, 130;
moral sense is virtually ubiquitous, 124; polluting
quality of the moral experience, 128-129; "...we
must think of it as an adventure which begins at one
end with nature, and ends at the other end with
supernature," 63, 78f.
Motives
"a reasonable incentive," 153; never a sufficient
cause, 134

Nationalism
properly embraced, a 'function' of the hope for immortality, 174f.
Natural law
77, 104

'Naturalistic fallacy'
  a variant, 258-259, 266, 279
Nature
  the problem of getting 'outside' of nature or experience, 229f.
Neo-Platonism
  here, "Greek philosophy succeeds in being fully
  theistic," 201
Nihilism
  the issue of radical empirical reduction, 239

Obligation
  fundamental in any ethical inquiry, 33f.; tests
  Utilitarianism, 27
'Observation-statements'
  292, 300-301
'The one and the many'
  242
Ontological argument
  defended, 204-207; secured in part by our knowledge
  of "experience as saturated with its own transcendent ground," 203
Ontology
  implied by epistemology, 241-242

Pan-mathematism of Leibniz
  rejected by Taylor as incompatible with history,
  73, note
Pantheism
  its element of truth, 113
Parallelism
  in psychology, rejected, 183f.
Personality
  of man,--a rational being, 156f.
Phenomenology
  247
Philosophy
  high and proper goals, 63; its ultimate unity impossible to avoid, 288
Pluralism
  instability of, 242
Possibility
  limited only by what is formally contradictory, 181
Pragmatism
  substitute for philosophy, 251
Predication
  'critical' vs. 'descriptive' (Frankena), 58

Presuppositionalism
   A. E. Taylor's, 144; in use, 275f.; contribution to
   epistemology, its use illustrated in Kant's terminology, 214; illustrated in knowledge of the self, 224
PRINCIPIA MATHEMATICA
   an end in itself? 255
Prudentialism
   in ethics (Butler), 35
Punishment
   "indispensable to sound ethics," 126; retributivist
   position (footnote), 127-128
Purpose
   216f., 219ff.; in nature, according to Aristotle,
   220; related to moral value, 254; purposive behavior
   makes use of the causal laws of physics, 220

Rationales
   the eternal norms, 33
Rationality
   bears clearest testimony to universality and necessity, 142; cannot be 'naturalized' under pain of losing its critical function, 283; its essential freedom, 145; its possibility of a personal hypostatization, 285; necessary condition of rational worth,
   274; part of the essential nature of things, 181;
   perfectly univocal, 285; performs a natural itinerary of the human spirit to God, 290ff.; progression
   from free thought to free will, 155f.; proper predicate of the universe: the 'faith' of the scientist,
   168; relation to moral freedom, 144; tampering destroys hope of truth and validity, 145; ubiquity, 284
Realist-nominalist controversy
   281
Reality
   wherever encountered, is meaningful through rational
   penetration, 291
Reason
   alleged limitations, 238
Reductionism
   mind to body, rejected, 183
Relativity
   in value-theory, 270ff., 275f.
Religion
   fulfilling condition of moral aspiration, 97-98, 120
Revelation
   may validly offer a fruitful hypothesis to be confirmed by its general coherence-value, 9

Rule-deontology
   44

Sacrifice
   'function' of the hope for immortality, 174
Science
   assumptions, 210-215; not the whole of knowledge,
   209; nothing to say one way or another about God's
   existence, 208; revelatory of an objective world,
   167; scientific investigator is encouraged by a
   faith that reality has no opaque or impenetrable aspects, but will yield in principle to rational
   advances, 291f.
Secondary qualities
   remark on their alleged 'ontological status,' 77-78
Self
   capable of free, spontaneous acts, 134; (in Kant),
   that which is always subject, 223; knowledge of, 224;
   mechanical view of, criticized, 85, 87; moral dis-
   ability strikes the self--the true center of personality, 130; no a priori need to admit its ultimate
   dissolution, 181-182; not a part of 'nature,' 230;
   teleological concept, 181; unique modality of being,
   230-231
Spiritualism
   169f.
Subjective
   in the interpretation of experience it is the 'subjective' (or self) that interprets the objective,
   250
Synthetic-a priori
   (Kant), suggestive of a general principle that all
   knowledge involves universals in relation to particulars, 73

Taylor, Alfred Edward
   academic appointments, 1; autobiographical sketch,
   4-7; chronology of major events, 19-20; comments on
   Ayer's 'emotivism,' 49-55; comments on Kant's 'formalism,' 39-47; comments on Mill's 'utilitarianism,'
   29-35; education, 1; postulational field in his epistemology, 10-11; theistic presuppositionalism (outline), 9-11
Teleological argument
   215ff., 217f.

Teleology
   confirmed by a sort of <u>reductio</u> <u>ad</u> <u>absurdum</u>, 227;
   supported uniquely by <u>mind</u>, 218
Temporality
   awareness of temporality "is already to transcend
   the form," 88
Theism
   challenged by restrictions imposed by reason's alleged limitations, 201; defined, 200; historical endorsement, 200f.; presupposition of a rationalized
   ethics, 9, 103
'Thing-in-itself'
   240
Time
   and the ever-vanishing 'now,' 88; as mere succession,
   92; "characteristic form of the life of moral endeavour," 83, 92, 254; relation to eternity, 93; successive moments united by conative disposition, 93;
   transcended at the moment we are aware of temporality, 92
Transcendence
   how affirmed, 238, 240
Truth
   transcends methods of laboratory experiment, 209

Universals
   (for Taylor), "embodied <u>in rebus</u>," 67; without which
   particulars are meaningless, 215
Universe
   believed supportive of intelligibility and moral
   purpose, 103; if truly reasonable, it must not be at
   hopeless variance with the moral order, 168
Unmoved mover
   (Aristotle), 135
UTILITARIANISM
   99; according to Mill, 22-28; an optimistic writing,
   27; severely tested on the basis of its ability to
   answer the question of moral obligation, 25f., 104;
   "superficial falsification of moral experience," 129

Value
   "accidental" character denied, 68f.; cannot be validated upon the basis of experience, 172; distinguished from existence, 58, 65; its eventual implication leads to God, 257; objective,--an implication
   of the attitude of even the anti-religious man of
   science, 167; universal norm, 58; virtually indefinable, 57; without a dependence upon existents, 64f.,

NAME INDEX

Adamson, Robert, 142
Aquinas, St. Thomas, 2, 68, 177
Aristotle, 117, 135, 162, 186, 195, 214, 222, 240, 243
Atkinson, R.F., 261
Augustine (Aurelius Augustus), 107, 133, 257, 290, 291
Ayer, Alfred Jules, 47-49, 50, 52, 256, 253

Beckner, Morton, 86-87
Bentham, Jeremy, 84, 299
Berkeley, George, 162, 163
Black, Max, 261, 262, 263, 264, 265
Blake, William, 95
Blanshard, Brand, 8-9, 257
Boethius (Anicius Manlius Severinus), 95
Bosanquet, Bernard, 1, 142
Bowman, Archibald Allan, 231
Bradley, Francis Herbert, 5, 142, 204
Braithwaite, Richard Revan, 269
Brightman, Edgar S., 98
Broad, Charlie Dunbar, 271f.
Burtt, Edwin A., 235
Butler, Joseph, 142, 182

Caird, Edward, 142
Caird, John, 142
Clarke, Samuel, 118, 142
Copleston, Frederick, 137, 138, 216, 245, 247, 248,
    249, 253, 292, 294, 295, 298
Cudworth, Ralph, 118, 142

de Burgh, W. G., 236, 237, 272f., 297, 299
Descartes, Rene, 91, 117, 184, 223, 224, 240, 257, 294

Feigl, Herbert, 244, 245, 251, 252
Fite, Warner, 237
Flint, Robert, 253
Frankena, William K., 35, 37, 40, 57, 58

347

Gaunilo, 204, 205
Green, Thomas Hill, 5, 92, 142
Guzzo, Augusto, 55

Hall, Ronald, 242, 243, 244
Hanley, Kenneth, 268
Hare, R. M., 261, 269
Hegel, Georg Wilhelm Friedrich, 117, 204
Heraclitus, 240
Hick, John, 107
Hume, David, 117, 118, 158, 186, 187, 190, 195, 201,
    204, 219, 224, 239, 253, 259, 260, 297
Hunter, Geoffrey, 260
Hutcheson, Francis, 178
Huxley, Aldous, 32

Inge, William Ralph, 248

Jacobi, Friedrich Heinrich, 197, 202
James, William, 244

Kant, Immanuel, 36-39, 60, 61, 100, 101, 104, 105,
    117, 125, 126, 135, 143, 158, 159, 176, 177, 178,
    188, 192, 201, 203, 212, 213, 214, 215, 223, 232,
    238, 239, 240, 241, 247, 273, 274, 295, 302

Lamprecht, Sterling, 79, 81
Leibniz, Gottfried Wilhelm, 73, 79, 117

Mach, Ernst, 5
Mavrodes, George I., 260
McTaggart, John McTaggart Ellis, 92
Mill, John Stuart, 22-29, 178, 299, 300
Mounce, H. O., 270
Muirhead, J. H., 256
Mure, G. R. G., 248, 252-253, 278f., 280

Nettleship, Lewis, 142

Orr, James, 197

Paley, William, 217
Parmenides, 240
Paul (St. Paul, the Apostle), 15
Phillips, D. Z., 264, 270
Plato, 91, 117-119, 142, 200, 216, 238, 240, 257, 290,
    291, 295
Price, Richard, 118, 151